T0333586

ESOTERIC EGYPT

"An important investigation into the deep prehistory of ancient Egypt and the lost roots of ancient Egyptian spiritual wisdom."

GRAHAM HANCOCK, AUTHOR OF
FINGERPRINTS OF THE GODS

"In his last book, *Esoteric Egypt,* the late John Gordon delves deeply into the origin of ancient Egyptian beliefs and explains the mystery of their symbolism about Man and the Cosmos. It was in Egypt that man first recognized his two dimensions: physical and spiritual. While the body dies, the spirit joins the heavenly beings awaiting resurrection."

AHMED OSMAN, AUTHOR OF
THE LOST CITY OF EXODUS AND *MOSES AND AKHENATEN*

ESOTERIC EGYPT

THE
SACRED SCIENCE
OF THE
LAND OF KHEM

J. S. GORDON

Bear & Company
Rochester, Vermont • Toronto, Canada

Bear & Company
One Park Street
Rochester, Vermont 05767
www.BearandCompanyBooks.com

Bear & Company is a division of Inner Traditions International

Library of Congress Cataloging-in-Publication Data
Gordon, J. S. (John S.), 1946– author.
  [Khemmea]
 Esoteric Egypt : the sacred science of the land of Khem / J. S. Gordon.
    pages cm
  "Originally published in the United Kingdom in 2001 by Orpheus Publishing House under the title Khemmea : The Sacred Wisdom Tradition of Ancient Egypt"—Title page verso.
  Summary: "A study of the 100,000-year-old spiritual science of ancient Egypt"—Provided by publisher.
  Includes bibliographical references and index.
  ISBN 978-1-59143-196-1 (pbk.) — ISBN 978-1-59143-777-2 (e-book)
 1. Mythology, Egyptian. 2. Mysteries, Religious—Egypt. 3. Astronomy, Egyptian. I. Title.
 BL2443.G67 2015
 932—dc23
                                                                    2014029063

Printed and bound in the United States by P. A. Hutchison

10 9 8 7 6 5 4 3 2 1

Text design by Debbie Glogover and layout by Priscilla Baker
This book was typeset in Garamond Premier Pro with Gill Sans, Futura, and Avante Garde used as display typefaces

CONTENTS

Acknowledgments   vii

Introduction   1

PART ONE
CELESTIAL AND
METAPHYSICAL BACKGROUND

ONE	The Spheres of Creation	16
TWO	The Astronomical and Astrological Dimensions of Creation	37
THREE	The Multi-Sevenfold Mill of the Gods	62

PART TWO
THE SUBTLE
NATURE OF EXISTENCE

FOUR	Kosmic Genesis—The Origin and Nature of the Gods	94
FIVE	Sidereal Genesis—The Origin and Nature of Man	130
SIX	Man, the Multiple Being	158

PART THREE
EGYPT'S HISTORICAL BACKGROUND

SEVEN	The River Nile and Its Symbolism	190
EIGHT	The Ancient Colonization of Egypt	218
NINE	The Spread and Decline of Ancient Mystic Culture	244

PART FOUR
ANCIENT EGYPTIAN CIVILIZATION AND CULTURE

TEN	Egypt's Sacred Art, Architecture, and Statuary	272
ELEVEN	The Ritualized Magic of Egypt	305
TWELVE	The Mystery Tradition and the Process of Initiation	337
EPILOGUE	The Future of the Sacred Mystery Tradition	366

APPENDICES

A	The Geometrical Correspondence to the Cycle of Involution and Evolution	371
B	Polar Misconceptions	374
C	The Funeral Positions of Orion-Osiris	378
D	The Primary Celtic Festivals	381
E	The Slaughter of Mankind	383
F	Correlations between the Ancient Egyptian and Tibetan Mystic Systems	385
	Notes	387
	Bibliography	395
	Index	398

ACKNOWLEDGMENTS

My thanks must first of all go to those people who bought my first book on the esoteric side of ancient Egyptian culture and were kind enough to indicate that it had opened up for them a completely different and unsuspected perspective on the subject. That they struggled hard initially but followed all the way through, determined to understand the nature of that completely different perspective, is a credit to their tenacity and the sincerity of their interest in the subject itself. Without such a positive reaction, the incentive to go ahead with a sequel—although this is more of an extension than a sequel—probably would not have been quite so strong. I hope, therefore, that they will find this new work just as rewarding.

For part of the reference background to the book I am indebted to both the British Library and also the library of the Theosophical Society in England. For that on horological issues, I must thank David Thompson of the Horological Department of the British Museum, who answered my extremely puzzling questions (as to clock mechanisms possibly paralleling the workings of the universe) with great courtesy and otherwise pointed me toward a number of agreeably clear reference books of which I was completely unaware.

On Masonic issues, Matthew Scanlan proved a veritable fount of knowledge in response to historically related questions, which then led me in all sorts of other intriguing directions, while Clare Pover, at very short notice, found me several very elusive examples of the three-legged cross in the Isle of Man. Thanks also to Marie Tharp for the use of part of an explanatory map of the Middle East.

For a great many laughs along the way and also for their help while in Egypt, my grateful thanks are due to Robert Bauval and Simon Cox. Further thanks are due to Robert for his helpful comments on the manuscript while in the editing stage, plus the use of a couple of important photographs.

Finally, most grateful thanks are due to Stuart Littlejohn for his line drawings of ancient Egyptian statuary.

INTRODUCTION

This sequel to my last book on Egypt, *Land of the Fallen Star Gods,* has been written—like its predecessor—largely in response to the still active, overfascinated furor surrounding the Pyramids and Sphinx at Giza, which has been to the detriment of understanding ancient Egypt as a whole. The combination of commercially driven media hype, conspiracy theories, psychic voyeurism, and all sorts of inadequately argued New Age speculations, all focused on Giza, has reached a point of near farce. Were some of it not so hilarious in its extent and improbability, it would be desperately sad to witness. Much, however, has occurred as a result of pure reaction to the myopic literalism of those last few generations of Egyptologists who have woefully misrepresented and belittled the metaphors and allegories of Egyptian mysticism as no more than products of mere superstition on the part of the supposedly unevolved minds of ancient humankind, notwithstanding their proven all-around astronomical, engineering, artistic, and architectural genius.

The three main arguments currently centered on Giza revolve around: (a) the actual age of the Sphinx and Pyramids; (b) the originally intended function of the Pyramids; and (c) whether there is a concealed chamber—a Hall of Records—either in the Great Pyramid or under the Sphinx (or both) containing either secret (perhaps Atlantean) writings or even ancient magical artifacts or scientific technology. The former are of bona fide scholarly and scientific interest. However, the world's media, in fastening on to the third (and rather ancillary) issue in their usual unobjective manner, have merely primed the pump of superficial public voyeurism. While perhaps providing them with a lucrative return on the original journalistic and televisual investment, this has simultaneously distracted interest from much more interesting issues. Sadly, the immediate and first casualty or loser in all this—as in war—has been the pursuit of truth, and intelligent objectivity along with it. This book is thus in part aimed at puncturing some of the hype and trying to return intelligently based public debate to the wider subject of what ancient Egypt and its mystic culture were actually all about when viewed against a wider perspective than that offered merely at Giza.

Questioning the Orthodox Approach

With that in mind, a part of this book has been oriented toward looking at the various assumptions made by both Egyptologists and scientists to support their various theories concerning the age of Egyptian architecture and statuary, the length of Egyptian history, and the wholly erroneous supposition that the original Egyptian culture was fundamentally based upon a mixture of superstitious animism, star worship, and morbid fascination with (and fear of) death itself. It was not. As we shall see, the very structure of modern orthodox thought about ancient Egypt looks highly unsound when subjected to close examination. In fact, the presently adopted scholarly technique of trying to shore up Egyptian (theoretical) history by propping it against the even more shaky history of the Hebrew Old Testament is somewhat akin to two drunks trying to remain upright by feverishly clutching at each other, more and more tenaciously yet ever more desperately and precariously. Correspondingly, the current methodology of modern science in trying to find the keys to ancient culture and civilization generally, almost entirely through the use of technological support, is like the same two inebriates, having lost their car keys in the gutter, going and searching for them under the street lamp twenty yards away "because that is where the light is."

In *Land of the Fallen Star Gods* I sought to bring into the field of discussion (concerning Egypt's cultural origins) a variety of geological, paleontological, and linguistic factors (as well as various other ancient traditions), which indicated very strongly that the original civilization of Egypt must have been many tens of thousands of years old, and also that its cultural influence must have extended much farther geographically than currently believed to be the case. In this book, I have added several more suggestions and supporting references in the same line. Similarly, in *Land of the Fallen Star Gods* I tried to open up not only the subject and rationale of sympathetic magic and its use by the Ancients, but also the esoteric methodology of their hierarchical system of gods and goddesses and their associations with particular temples along the Nile. These subjects too are extended and explained in greater detail in this present book, in a manner that I hope will appeal to both the lay mind and that of the open-minded scientist and scholar as well.

However, bearing in mind the extent of criticism I have levied on the views of scientists and scholars in both this book and *Land of the Fallen Star Gods,* I should perhaps make the point clear from the outset that I am as fundamentally "pro" both science and scholarship as I am "anti" both scientism and scholasticism—the self-propagating beliefs that you have to be academically or scientifically qualified in a particular field before you can understand it properly, and thus that only what the academically qualified or scientifically experienced believe to be possible or true is possible or true.

Orthodox Dogma

As the great physicist Prince Louis de Broglie wrote in the early years of the twentieth century, "History shows that the advances of science have always been frustrated by the tyrannical influences of certain preconceived notions that were turned into unassailable dogmas. For that reason, every scientist should periodically make a profound reexamination of his basic principles."[1] Sadly, this admonition rarely seems to be taken up.

Both scientists and scholars tend to live and work in a self-made, semi-autonomous psychological environment, which too frequently comes to be seen as an end in itself, rather than as a mere means to an end for the benefit of society at large. Thus, sadly, the pure love of truth for its own sake, which characterized the Renaissance and the founding of the Royal Society—and most of the subsequent research in science and scholarship up until the early part of the twentieth century—is these days somewhat rarely found. The reason for that lies in three factors: technological dependence (notwithstanding its evident deficiencies) resulting from intellectual laziness and fear or ignorance; dependence on politically and commercially sponsored research funding; and the ruthless threat of job loss for those in academia and scientific circles who seriously query the status quo. In the face of these, is it any real wonder that any truly serious questioning of current orthodoxy finds itself mainly in the hands and minds of disparate groups of New Age researchers, unrestricted by such overpowering inhibitions?

Willful Scholarly Myopia

The situation—as far as ancient Egypt is concerned—has been made far worse by the most recent generations of scholarly and scientific specialists who, in their localized research, appear to brush aside the fact of Egyptian mysticism as almost irrelevant, on the basis that mummy corpses and sociological artifacts are more interesting and will tell us all (of any real importance) that we need to know about this ancient culture. However, this altogether perverse attitude—geared to the usual scholarly preoccupation with wanting to know more and more about less and less—merely drops the incentive for much-needed research concerning Egyptian mystic and occult belief systems into the hands of a range of ill-prepared and not always very objectively minded types, many pre-armed with their own often only half-baked modern mystic agendas, thereby bringing the whole subject into quite unnecessary disrepute. It should be added in parallel to this, however, that the ever-more-definitive scholarly or scientific approach of the specialist also very quickly tends to run out of context and thus lose the plot altogether. Hence, for example, we now find a bizarre situation in which the widespread ancient use of the sacred blue lotus plant as a *metaphor* for the psychospiritual evolution of consciousness is apparently viewed in some Egyptological quarters as merely indicative of ancient Egyptian preoccupation with narcotics and sexual self-gratification!*

The New Age Approach

Rather unfortunately, anything that generally flies in the face of scholarly or scientific orthodoxy is these days immediately branded as a "loony New Age idea" by the Establishment, irrespective of how intelligently its case is argued from an unorthodox viewpoint. This is nothing more than prejudice arising out of sheer intellectual arrogance or laziness. However, there is no denying the fact that this same problem operates at the other end of the spectrum of consciousness as well, for many New Agers are only too willing to indiscriminately pick up and absorb, more or less wholesale, almost any half-baked conceptual ideas with which they find themselves psychologically in sympathy (for a variety of reasons) or which they feel "ought to be true," without even considering the available alternatives. In such cases, objectivity flies rapidly out the window, leaving logic and reason stranded, and one is accordingly left feeling immediate sympathy with the predictable reaction of mainstream scholarship and science. However, even those who have tried to find a reasonable and reasoned middle way have found themselves facing the unforgiving ire of the orthodox Establishment.

The Populist Approach

Since *Land of the Fallen Star Gods* was first published, there have been several books written and television films produced on the subject of both Atlantis and ancient Egypt. Some of these—notably by the journalistically trained and high-profile author Graham Hancock—have sought to enlarge upon the idea of human culture and civilization being far, far more ancient and widespread than our modern archaeologists and anthropologists would have us believe. Others (by members of the scholarly Establishment) have quite deliberately set out—using attempted character assassination—to undermine public interest in the pursuit of such ideas.

Many of those on the "pro" side (like Graham Hancock) have unfortunately made the cardinal error of limiting their angles of approach almost entirely to the association of ancient architecture with speculative history, or to archaeoastronomy, without any very much wider frame of supporting reference. Rather optimistically trusting that scientists and scholars or academics would admit their fundamental sincerity and objectivity, they have

*Which is surely a case of trying to graft modern Western sociological problems onto ancient history in a manner that has no sound justification, bearing in mind that our present era has little conception of the paramount social importance of ancient religiosity.

tried to fight many of their battles on the same marshy ground that orthodox archaeology has itself been tramping for well over one hundred years. However, they are at a distinct disadvantage by virtue of not yet having evolved the politically and intellectually webbed feet with which orthodox scholarship and science now unself-consciously pad across the quicksands of heterodox "evidence," while equally unself-consciously using the latter to try to trap the unwary New Age researcher. The shameless willingness of the orthodox scholarly and scientific Establishment to gang up on the academically unqualified who dare to venture onto their learned patches is really very instructive. Objectivity very quickly seems to become a rather scarce commodity in such cases.

Having otherwise criticized commercially driven media hype and frenzy, there is no doubt that there is now (much more than even five years ago) a much greater—although still largely superficial—public awareness and general debate about the originally spiritual nature of places like Giza, Borobudur, Tiahuanaco, and so on, previously treated as mere tourist curiosities. The archaeological community has also been forced to come out more into the open, not only to address more effectively the issues of ancient religion and mystic belief, but also to expose its own currently limited (because largely speculative and dismissive) understanding of these issues. Its greatest fight, however, has been and will continue to be a rearguard action to stave off the accelerating stream of heterodox evidence that human civilization and culture is far, far older than it is itself willing to admit. For when the weight of evidence eventually becomes too great—as it undoubtedly will within the next two generations or so—much of accepted ancient history (and much that passes for associated science too) will almost certainly have to be substantially rewritten.

Modern Refutations of Mainstream Scientific Theory

One very recent move in this direction involves Robert Temple's book *The Crystal Sun,* in which he shows with great erudition that optical technology and the associated mathematics were so well known to the Ancients that telescopes, binoculars, and spectacles can now be shown—by retranslated ancient manuscripts—to have been around for at least the last 4,500 years. He also shows in the latter chapters of the same book the extent of sophisticated mathematical knowledge possessed by the ancient Egyptians, which enabled them to perceive fractional universal constants and other universal principles such as the Golden Mean and then to apply them widely and practically in their architecture and civil engineering practices. But the Ancients certainly did not need a highly industrialized society to achieve such things, even though many of our modern commentators, imbued with the misconception that mass industrialization and high culture go hand in hand, seem unable to grasp the fact.

In *Land of the Fallen Star Gods* I pointed out that Darwin's rather simplistic theory of evolution (from apes) by natural selection was too full of holes to be universally accepted*—particularly in relation to man, where ancient tradition in all historically known cultures took a fundamentally different viewpoint, based upon its own clearly defined logic, which we shall consider at further length within this book. I also dwelt on the willful myopia of anthropologists and paleontologists who, though faced with the firmest evidence of *Homo sapiens* being at the very least 1.5 million years old, still continue to hang on like grim death to the established orthodoxy that the figure is only about 120,000 years and that human urban civilization is only some 12,000 years old. We are therefore being asked—even on their terms *and* with a completely straight face— to believe that, notwithstanding having a creative intelligence and physique *exactly* similar to our own, ancient humankind hung around *for over 100,000 years* before developing a halfway civilized preference for urban civilization and coherent forms of culture.†

In their books *Forbidden Archeology* and *The Hidden History of the Human Race* (the condensed edition of *Forbidden Archeology*), Michael Cremo and Richard Thompson have otherwise already driven several even longer nails into the coffin of current archaeological theory by showing why and how *Homo sapiens* must in fact have been around *at least ten million years ago*. Their scholarly documentation of many cultural artifacts and even of building works found in fossil beds and geologically deep sedimentary layers— some even tens of millions of years old—has so far remained quietly but completely unchallenged by mainstream archaeology. Yet the ramifications of these findings are truly volcanic in terms of their potential effect on the foundations of accepted prehistory. These same authors have taken the somewhat charitable view that both scholarship and science instinctively operate an unconscious filtering process in which new ideas that support or appear to advance their own existing (orthodox) theories are allowed to pass through the intellectual mesh, while all others are caught, automatically rejected, and then quietly but firmly "lost." This author takes a rather more narrow-eyed view of such nefarious behavior, although firmly rejecting generally paranoid conspiracy theories involving deliberately subversive government or other institutional intervention in

---

*Rather interestingly, Darwin (*On the Origin of the Species,* 484–89) was himself of the opinion that all our modern animals were actually derived from four or five prototypal creatures (of some unspecified type), which existed prior to even the Silurian era. But he produced no satisfactory suggestions as to why (and thus how) such prototypes should have come into existence in the first place.

†The usual scientific rejoinder to this criticism is that the Ice Age would have prevented such a development. But, given humankind's proven ingenuity under the most hazardous and meteorologically trying circumstances on Earth in our own era, this just does not begin to add up. In addition, the last Ice Age produced a by no means universal glaciation across the northern hemisphere and so there were plenty of places where highly sophisticated cultures might have existed without the need for an attendant *industrial* civilization per se.

the process.* In any case, this book intends to throw down the gauntlet of challenge to mainstream orthodoxy on a rather wider front.

The Approach to Writing about Ancient Egypt

A few people—while having self-admittedly enjoyed reading *Land of the Fallen Star Gods*—have criticized me for writing a book with such a broad sweep and with no immediately obvious or specifically central focal point, such as employed by Bauval and Hancock (in their *Keeper of Genesis* and other writings). I have to say in response, however, that this was quite deliberate and it operates again in this present work. But I should perhaps explain. It would undoubtedly have been a great deal easier (and probably more profitable) to concentrate on, say, the Masonic and initiatory associations of Giza and then write a further series of books on similar specific issues. My personal feeling was, however, that this would detract from virtually all possibility of conveying any true sense that ancient Egypt's culture was united from the outset in one great system of conceptual thought (still unperceived by Egyptologists) by its many sequentially logical threads. That this approach perhaps makes the book rather more complex and thus also more difficult to follow for some people is an accompanying fact I have to accept and live with.

However, I have rather more faith in the intelligence and staying power of most of my readers than obviously do some critics. I also unapologetically draw comfort from the reported views of many past commentators who, when asked about aspects of Egyptian religion, replied that because the associated religio-mystic attitudes were so all-pervasive, no one aspect of its culture could really be separated either intellectually or factually from another.

In addition to all these other issues, there lies the problem of interpreting ancient cultures accurately, *on their own terms*—something that the general run of archaeologists seems somewhat ill-equipped to do because of the range of conditioning modern prejudices that they bring along with them.† Perhaps the greatest difficulty in either understanding or explaining ancient Egyptian (or other) mystical-metaphysical thought lies in its abstract nature and in its use of allegory, metaphor, and sacred name variations to depict both macrocosmic and microcosmic events or circumstances in relation to their divine,

---

*One of the greatest problems in advancing objective discussion in recent years on so-called New Age ideas (all actually based on very ancient concepts) has been the proliferation of conspiracy theory authors and their anxiety-inducing, rabble-rousing literature. It is entirely due to their sort of paranoid mentality that the Salem witch hunt and the Spanish Inquisition occurred in recent history. I personally have found the CUCU (cock-up and cover-up) theory much more easily confirmed and generally applicable.

†And also because they willfully refuse to take a positive interest in the astronomical background, which is so fundamental to ancient Egyptian culture. In fact, current orthodoxy has it that Egyptian astronomy and astrology were entirely derived from Chaldea in the third millennium BCE—ignoring the fact that specific stars and their mystic associations are mentioned in the early Old Kingdom texts.

spiritual, or psychic causes. Yet research over many years in several ancient and modern systems of thought leads one to believe that there could have been no other unequivocally safe and truly satisfactory method of expression.

The process of psychospiritual castration, by which the esoteric metaphors represented by the ancient gods became intellectual eunuchs in modern thought, actually commenced quite early on in the Christian era, when evangelists were first involved in trying to convert the locals in northern Europe from their age-old pagan cultures. Charles Squire, in his book *Celtic Myths and Legends,* describes how the process began in relation to the gods of Ireland, when he says: "Therefore a fresh school of euhemerists arose to prove that the gods were never even saints but merely worldly men who had once lived and ruled in Erin. Learned monks worked hard to construct a history of Ireland from the Flood downwards. . . . Having once worked the gods, first into universal history and then into the history of Ireland, it was an easy matter to supply them with dates of birth and death, local habitations and places of burial."[2] And he adds rather pithily: "It is only fair, however, to these early euhemerists to say that they have their modern disciples."[3] One might add that these modern disciples (the doyens of academia) have been involved for most of the twentieth century and at present in trying to emasculate ancient Middle Eastern, Indo-European, and Native American spiritual cultures in exactly the same way—and also by presenting mystic texts as mere gibberish.

In fact, the real problem here lies with our modern linear-rational way of thinking, derived from the intellectually brilliant technique of Aristotelian thought, which was itself, from the outset, so appallingly deficient in spiritual reason or insight. The modern intellectual approach (at least in the Anglo-Saxon West) has likewise tried to avoid abstract (and particularly metaphysical) thought in general and has thus encouraged a refusal to believe that the *apparently* irrational or supraphysical could have any real existence. Consequently, orthodox science and scholarship—which also have their provenance in Aristotle via both Roger Bacon and the reaction of scholars against merely degenerate forms of Dark Age mysticism—now tend to live on a self-supporting diet of wholly materialistic theories that bear little relation to the various worlds of subjective experience and perception. Hence it is, perhaps, that we find the tendency of modern historians (of various orthodox persuasions) trying to wring even more than the very marrow out of the dry bones of the Old Testament as supposed folk memory-history with later mystic additions, rather than the mixture of sacred metaphor and allegory it clearly was and is, from start to finish.

Defective Attitudes in the Field of Archaeoastronomy

The very same sort of problem is to be found even in the case of those rather more open-minded scholars and scientists who are positively interested in the field of archaeoastronomy as a means of determining the true extent of ancient stellar knowledge. The vast majority of these researchers start with the unjustified (and unjustifiable) assumption that the ancient myths centered on heavenly bodies were purely allegorical ways of describing observed stellar and planetary movements over given periods of time or even of depicting unusual or even cataclysmic events in Nature. They give no consideration to the possibility that the mystic aspect might have come first, or that the Ancients might have regarded such celestial activity as the mere *effects* of ever-active noumenal principles of kosmic intelligence, operative behind the scenes. So, in trying to rationalize the origins of myth in terms of purely materialistic modern-day logic, these moderns too have thus completely missed the basic plot of what the Ancients were really about.

The Naturally Chaotic Substratum of the Universe

Fortunately for us, however, modern psychology and quantum science have been able to demonstrate very effectively that the background to everything that both the logical mind and the universe appear to create *is* irrational, and that this—although all-potential in itself—*is* the natural, chaotic state of the subliminal reality underlying transient physical existence. Consequently, we may now say (in concert with the Ancients) that it is the self-consciously applied principle of intelligence (in both the macrocosm and microcosm) that orders mind-knowledge and matter into objective existence, but that it (perhaps paradoxically) can only temporarily contain it. Although relatively few scientists as yet openly acknowledge the fact (even as a possibility), intelligence and mind can quite easily be shown as two completely different and unrelated principles in Nature, irrespective of the fact that they can be made to work together. Mind and its associate, memory, possess no inherently self-driven sense of purposeful order, for they are like the components of a machine, each of which produces its own natural function in the right sequence *only* when put together in the correct order by an intelligence that foresees their potential when in combination. Unfortunately, due to our inadequate education and incredibly sloppy modern belief systems, we have come to the wholly unsupported conclusion that mind and intelligence are the same thing. This has resulted—among a raft of other things—in the absurdly materialistic proposition of some scientists that the mind and the brain, or thought and perception, are also synonymous.*

---

*Which is roughly equivalent to suggesting that a car designer plus the driver and his vehicle actually comprise a single entity.

The Ancient Approach to Our Human Thought Process

The Ancients were concerned to show—in their systems of thought—how the whole dynamic process of intelligence and mind actually works in the kosmos in both a macrocosmic and microcosmic sense, as well as in both the non-material and the material states of being. Consequently they used a system of interactive visual metaphors and allegories, each of which—like a component in a machine—could be arranged in such a way as to express or depict variations, plus the dynamic structure and sequence of a *potential* perception arising out of some sort of experience.

In order for this to work properly, however, every stage of Creation and subsequent evolution had to have a symbolically representative form, the application of which varied only according to its orientation or its embellishment. Thus, in the ancient Egyptian culture, a god figure sitting down, or with a headdress on, meant something quite distinctively different from the same god-figure standing up or appearing bareheaded. The direction of potential movement—facing either left or right—respectively signified an objective or a subjective focus. The specific numbers of component parts of a statue or of a god-figure's dress all had a very distinctive significance in relation to states of consciousness or being. And so on, in every field imaginable.

To our modern way of thinking this might all seem unnecessarily complex. However, to the Ancients it had a further crucial significance. To them, the universe was a living Being comprising an infinitude of different hierarchies of Life—each expressing one or other aspect or facet of the Universal Mind. Thoughts were themselves psychospiritual or psychoelemental entities with their own very self-evident patterns of instinctual behavior. Consequently, to think, say, or artistically depict something unavoidably involved the summoning into a cycle of existence of one or more of these hierarchies of being. However, to have had these entities permanently and dynamically active in one's personal and social environment, once called "on-stage," would have been unacceptable. And so the ancient Egyptians retained their near presence at all times, but under firm psychological control—that control being inherent in the peculiarly static (and intentionally distorted) nature of their illustrative temple art.

To the rational mind of today, this might well seem like nothing more than superstitious nonsense, but the rationale behind it is absolutely and unquestionably logical. We ourselves use exactly the same principles today in a thoroughly materialistic manner in our visual advertising and marketing techniques. However, as the quality of elemental thought evoked by the latter in our own minds is of a generally very low caliber, so the general quality of human mentality has diminished accordingly. Imagery is extremely powerful in its capacity to evoke either superficial or deep feelings, thereby prompting us to thoughts inclined toward either selfish or unselfish action. The Ancients fully recognized this and thus ensured that all imagery in their society had a spiritual background or bias, so that the subliminal effects upon the general populace would always be of the highest possible quality.* Thus it was—as so many foreign observers noted—that Egypt *was* religion (incarnate). And it is for this reason that one needs to understand the ancient Egyptian psyche and Egypt's culture *as a whole and on its own terms.* To that aim this book is dedicated.

The Format of This Book

The present book is written in four parts. The first part commences from the universal to the particular by introducing us to our subject via the sidereal and metaphysical dynamics and structure of our home universe within the context of the greater kosmos—as seen by the ancient Egyptians, Greeks, Celts, and several other traditions, all being mere variations on the same grand central concept.

The second part starts with a chapter describing the origin and nature of the gods as seen by the Ancients, and another concerning the many and varied ancient traditions about Man himself as an essentially divine being, born from the substance of the stars into a semidivine body form and thereby "falling" into a vast cycle of kosmic reincarnation, of which his time on our planet is but a small part. A further chapter provides additional detail in a more personally and definitively human sense.

The third part of the book starts with a combined geographical and esoteric bird's eye view of the River Nile and its all-embracing importance to the Egyptians. It also takes a broad look at some of the associated traditions concerning the fabled Atlantis and then considers the question of the original (apparently semi-Caucasian) races, which actually seem—about a hundred thousand years ago—to have populated greater Egypt, then a huge island, which incorporated the Horn of Africa at a time when the Mediterranean was still connected to the Atlantic Ocean over what is now the Sahara Desert. It otherwise looks beyond Egypt at the concept of there having possibly been (under twenty thousand years ago) a worldwide civilization dominated by a common religio-mystic culture, epitomized in the Sacred Mysteries of Egypt itself. Having considered this, the book looks at the various historical reasons for Egypt's eventual internal decline as a result of spiritual corruption, quite apart from international politics, warfare, and foreign invasion.

The fourth part of the book specifically looks at various aspects of ancient Egyptian civilization and culture that made it so apparently unique. This takes into account rather

---

*However, the peculiar nature of Egyptian temple art was deliberately intended to ensure that the deities therein depicted were not merely idolized. The gods of Egypt were called *neteru*—a name from which our English word *nature* is derived. The gods were not only intelligently organized principles in Nature; they also individually represented particular aspects or stages of the outward (involutionary) process of Creation itself. However, the ancient Egyptians were always clear in their minds that Man himself came from a yet higher realm of being. Worship, per se, was thus not (at least originally) on the menu.

more detailed consideration of the esoteric and occult backgrounds (and their logic) of the formal architectural and artistic appearances with which we have become so familiar today. Without understanding these, it is utterly impossible to understand the ancient Egyptians themselves. This part ends with an epilogue, which considers the practical relevance of what ancient Egypt perhaps symbolizes for the future in a modern world civilization, the social fabric of which is quite evidently crumbling around us—while the various national and international Establishments frantically try to shore up its internal structures with increasingly less-than-visionary, short-term politico-economic, technological, and sociological solutions, which pay no attention to the structure and dynamic of spiritual reality behind it all.

Following the main body of the book is a section of six appendices, which cover some specific topics in greater detail. Appendix A, "The Geometrical Correspondence to the Cycle of Involution and Evolution," helps to explain the natural sequence of evolutionary progression referred to throughout the book. Appendix B, "Polar Misconceptions," clarifies the distinction between the Earth's magnetic and gravitational poles and their relation to a fundamental concept of ancient metaphysical thought. Appendix C, "The Funeral Positions of Orion-Osiris," points to the idea that both Osiris-Orion and the spiritual soul principle are involved in a twenty-threefold cycle of astronomical influence or activity, and appendix D, "The Primary Celtic Festivals," links their ancient timing with the *celestial* equinoxes and solstices associated with the Great Year. Appendix E, "The Slaughter of Mankind," explains that this myth involving the great god Ra actually has to do with the foundation of the solar world scheme, while appendix F presents "Correlations between the Ancient Egyptian and Tibetan Mystic Systems."

On Literary References and Argued Theories

It is usual in books of this sort—particularly where proposing radical new theories—to support one's concepts with a stream of supporting literary references from other, previous authors in the same genre. This is all very well, up to a point. However, when the structure of modern orthodoxy becomes as inflexible and narrow as it has in the Egyptology of the late twentieth and early twenty-first centuries, much of the most recent material has to be openly disregarded or positively cast aside in order to get at the original idea buried well beneath the morass of scholarly and scientific prejudice. The same is true in relation to current views of a historical nature in reference to the Egyptian Old Kingdom and predynastic periods, where much of the modern orthodoxy is based upon pure speculation and assumption, much of it again founded on prejudice.

With that in mind, the approach I have adopted generally in this book involves a deliberate drawing together of modern science and rational common sense, plus some suggested explanations of ancient myths and metaphysical concepts from a variety of Mystery culture sources all around the world. From the coordination of these, argued in as sympathetically lucid and graphic a manner as possible, I have tried to present a picture of the ancient viewpoint in a modern context. Contrary to modern scholarship, I have also adopted the stance that, notwithstanding the well-attested existence of increasingly widespread, often blind superstition among the more materialistically minded general populace of the intermediate and later dynastic periods (post 2250 BCE), the earlier priesthoods of ancient Egypt (and elsewhere throughout the ancient world) were more than intelligent enough to distinguish between symbolic fact and mythic fiction.

Literary References

On the issue of supporting references, I have made quite extensive use of quotes from the works of Sir E. Wallace Budge as well as Sir Walter Scott's translation of the *Hermetica* of Hermes Trismegistus. Many current Egyptologists find it fashionable to believe that Budge's ideas were misguided—probably because he took a definite interest in the meanings of ancient Middle Eastern mystic thought (unlike the somewhat Calvinistically narrow-minded Sir Flinders Petrie). But this, peculiarly, has resulted in the weirdly irrational assumption by some present-day Egyptologists that Budge's knowledge about Egypt was odd and must itself have lacked depth. However, his interdisciplinary range of knowledge concerning Egypt and the ancient cultures of Mesopotamia, Assyria, and Persia was pretty well unrivaled in the twentieth century—even if his actual interpretations of local esotericism were usually well wide of the mark. In addition, many of his books are still being widely reprinted and are thus easily available for reference by readers among the lay public.

In the case of the *Hermetica,* many scholars write this off merely as the work of neo-Platonic writers in the first and second centuries CE—following blindly in the verbal tracks of the Renaissance philologist-scholar Isaac Casaubon. However, had Casaubon had a rather wider experience and understanding of ancient oriental thought and also paid slightly less attention to the writing style but rather more to what the work actually says, he would perhaps have recognized that its historical origins must have been far, far more ancient. His approach is somewhat akin to that of a future scholar of the late third millennium CE saying that the New Testament must actually have been written in the seventeenth century, by virtue of his only having a King James Bible and the works of William Shakespeare to refer to for linguistic comparison.

To complete a quartet of authors regarded as unacceptable in some quarters, I have otherwise touched on certain theosophical ideas from the works of H. P. Blavatsky and A. A. Bailey. Despite the quite uncalled-for (and thoroughly unobjective) vilification they and their concepts have received at the hands and pens of journalists, scholars, and scientists, it becomes increasingly evident from studying the ancient systems of thought of the Middle and Far East (as well as of Greece, Scandinavia, Britain, and the Americas) on their own terms, and at source, that these two authors were merely the faithful modern recorders of a metaphysical and mystical lineage that was held and understood *worldwide* in prehistoric times, long before our modern attempts at recorded history were even first considered. However, the correlations mentioned in this book must be allowed to speak for themselves.

Finally, I should perhaps also mention that my use throughout the book of the word *kosmic,* instead of and in addition to the modern *cosmic,* is quite deliberate and based upon the ancient perception of the universe having both phenomenal and noumenal dimensions, rather than just the former. The word *cosmic* really only applies to the *objectively* visible universe. Hence it is that the greater kosmos could be described or depicted by the Ancients (in metaphysical terms) as possessing or comprising its own higher sequence of (to us entirely subjective, or noumenal) states of being,* which, although lying beyond the realms of sidereal existence and the furthest range of human perception or imagination, still necessarily conform with Universal Law in terms of its structure and dynamics. Hence also the frequently made distinctions in this book between *Man* and mere *man.*[†]

---

*Hence the words of the Vedic Krisna in the *Bhagavad Gita:* "With but a fraction of myself I invest the universe. Yet I myself remain (apart)."

†Esoteric philosophy places considerable emphasis on the distinction between *Man* and *(hu)man. Man* is an evolving "god" from a yet higher dimension, which projects a mere aspect of itself down into the lower world to enable each incarnation as a human being. The spiritual Man remains ever in situ, while the projected fragment becomes the lesser "spark" of intelligence buried within the nature of the objective human individual.

PART ONE

CELESTIAL
AND
METAPHYSICAL
BACKGROUND

ONE

THE SPHERES OF CREATION

The Kosmos then has been made immortal by the Father Who is eternal. The Father took that part of matter which was subject to His will and made it into a body and gave it bulk and fashioned it into a sphere. . . . Moreover, the Father implanted in this sphere the qualities of all kinds of living creatures and shut them up in it, as in a cave. . . . And He enveloped the whole body with a wrapping of immortality that the matter might not seek to break away from the composite structure of the universe and so resolve into its primal disorder. . . . [But] the bodies of the celestial gods keep without change that order which has been assigned to them by the Father at the beginning; and that order is preserved unbroken by the reinstatement of each of them in its former place. But the reinstatement of terrestrial bodies is brought about by the dissolution of their composition; and through this dissolution they are reinstated by absorption into the bodies which are indissoluble, that is, immortal. When this takes place, consciousness ceases, but life is not destroyed.

HERMETICA

Although this fact is usually overlooked, the Ancients saw our local universe, enclosing the Milky Way galaxy, as being a gigantic kosmic sphere, the genesis of which had been initiated by the directed thought of an imponderable Logos* and the creation of which had been organized by a hugely evolved and powerful hierarchy of kosmic intelligences acting as his Demiurge. This hierarchy was literally the Masonic and Hermetic "Great Architect of the Universe." But what about the latter's own creations—the many groups of stars, the

---

Logos is a Greek word meaning "light," in the sense of the Divine Intelligence whose radiant consciousness noumenally illuminates a field of kosmic or sidereal existence. But there were greater and lesser Logoi in the metaphysical systems of the Ancients, their hierarchies being responsible for whole galaxies and constellations, as well as stars and planets.

constellations—which make up the sidereal structure and fabric of this little, local universe in the wilds of space? Where did they fit in and what part did they play in the great kosmic ideation currently being played out? And how, in passing, does modern big bang theory fit into all this—if at all?

First of all, we need to bear in mind the ancient tradition that the stars and their solar systems were quite literally the vehicles and homes of hierarchical groups of intelligent divine principles—that is, kosmic gods—of some or other evolutionary standing, each with their own part to play in the great unfolding universal drama. As Plato tells us: "When each of the stars necessary for the constitution of Time had obtained a motion adapted to its condition, and their bodies bound or encompassed by living chains had become Beings possessing Life, and had learned their prescribed duty, they pursued their course [in space]."[1]

The implications of this profound statement by one of the world's greatest ever philosophers are: that every single star and constellation had indeed a specific purpose to fulfill within the organism of our local universe; that each such purpose or function was guided and controlled by Intelligence; that, before being able to participate, each solar deity had to evolve for itself a sidereal body form out of the organic substance of the universe—hence the living chains (of sidereal light). The selfsame views were, however, commonly held by the wisest men of all the ancient religions and philosophies, as we can see from the many and varied writings and oral traditions passed down to us from antiquity, from all over the world. We shall take a look at some of these in later chapters.

The second main point to remember is that with the universe being thus seen as an (eternal) organism, conjured into manifest existence by a great extra-cosmic Thought, every speck of substance within it had to be regarded as a holographic aspect of that Thought. Thus, the nature of every *organized* sidereal body, plus its location and movement, logically—according to the Ancients—had to have due meaning and significance, plus a corresponding (astrological) influence. Similarly, the movement of either major or minor streams of energy-substance anywhere within the universe (for whatever reason) had inevitably and unavoidably to result from some transmission or dissemination of the spectrum of Divine Knowledge or Purpose—hence the old Hermetic axiom that "energy follows thought."*

---

*It follows quite plainly from this that our modern big bang theory appears to be complete nonsense. Founded fundamentally on the "red shift" principle, it has already been effectively disproved by the fact that some galaxies are moving closer (hence blue shift), when theoretically they *all* ought to be moving apart. Few astrophysicists yet, it would seem, take into consideration the possibility that galaxies might themselves be elliptically orbiting around other greater galaxies or cosmic centers of force (like our own Earth around its Sun) and thus intermittently getting closer to each other before drifting apart again hence the red shift. In addition, the farther scientists are able to look into the depths of space using increasingly sophisticated modern technology, the more they puzzlingly find the same sort of stellar density as in our part of the universe. When mainstream research science drops its materialistic mind-set and intellectual arrogance, it might actually learn an extra thing or two from the ancient approach to this subject.

Arising from these same principles came the fundamental perception that astrological influences, although subtle, necessarily had to be very real and definitive, while also possessing a spectrum of potential that affected different forms (and people) in different ways. For the same reasons, there was a general understanding—born from a perception of the associated principles of sympathetic magic—that sensitivity to a particular quality of astrological influence automatically created an anchorage for it in the individual (or group) consciousness, upon the foundation of which a web of living light then built itself. In this manner the Ancients believed that destiny was formed and that the self-spiritualized consciousness of Man could literally transform his own (subtle) body form progressively into a vehicle of increasingly spiritualized light, from the inside outward.

Man as the Fons Et Origo of the Universe

Another primary but common tradition that has come down from ancient times is that, although the universe itself is an illusion—a merely temporary phenomenon of ideation taking place within the unfathomable Mind-consciousness of a great (but unknowable) Logos—Man is both the alpha and omega of the whole process. Thus, in one sense, everything in Creation aspires to become Man. Hence it is that some of the ancient religions put forward the idea that the universe was actually created *for* man. In truth this might be so; but we are here talking of the macrocosmic divine Man, a far cry from the minute fraction of his consciousness that invests itself in the pitifully small mind of the individual human being, itself a merely partial and transitory projection of localized Divine Purpose. Yet it is the fragmented passage of (divine) Man into and through this metaphysical *and* physical universe that seems to have occupied the concerns and the finest minds of ancient philosophy. And they saw this same passage as taking place within the field and through the agency of the stars. But what did this actually involve?

In attempting to answer that, we have to take into consideration several other main issues that preoccupied the Ancients. The first concerned the very nature of our own home universe; the second, the nature of each solar deity; the third concerned cycles of astronomical time; the fourth concerned issues of (re)incarnation and of eventual liberation from the Wheel of Rebirth. However, all of these were very closely related and even interlinked; for although there is no such thing as time itself per se—it being a merely conditioned effect in the perceiving consciousness of the observer—the hierarchically organized cycles of emanation into (and subsequent withdrawal from) the theater of Life were considered to be very real, for they formed the practical sequences of the overall Divine Plan in action.

The Nature of Our Local Universe

As we can see from fig. 1.1, our local universe—the Milky Way—is aurically surrounded by two spheres of influence, of which astronomers are aware but concerning the real nature of which they know virtually nothing. While these peripheral auras might appear to be merely gatherings of interstellar dust that reflect light from space, the fact that they are spherically regular in shape confirms that they are the manifestation of some or other sort of field of influence, having something of an electro-magnetic nature to them.* Now the Ancients took the view that such spherical fields of influence were actually souls, common to *all* organically organized forms in universal Nature (such as our solar system), and were not effects but *causes*—in this particular case, generated by a Kosmic Mind.

The essence of the ancient idea was that—notwithstanding the apparent presence of interstellar dust around them—these fields demiurgically ensouled otherwise invisible

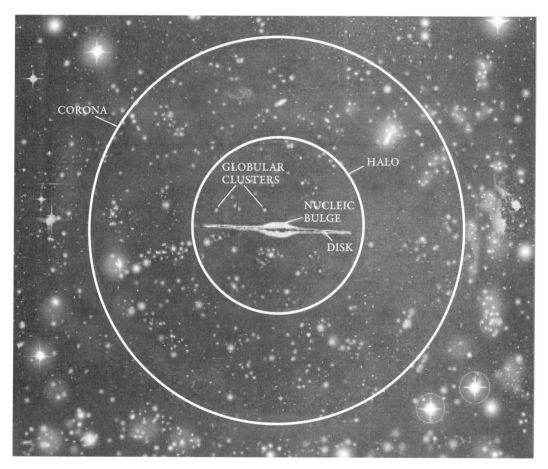

FIGURE 1.1. OUR GALAXY AND ITS AURIC SHEATHS

---

*From their research into dark matter and the nature of what holds galaxies together, astrophysicists have concluded that such containers must exist, thereby ensuring that the enclosed dark matter is not flung off into space through galactic rotational velocity.

heaven worlds, populated by innumerable hierarchies of divine and semidivine beings, some of which were destined to fall into generation *within* the objective sidereal systems to be found below—that is, at the center, within the actual plane of the galaxy. We find this same idea expressed early on in the biblical Book of Genesis, where the Demiurge (i.e., the Elohim) separated the waters (of space) above from the waters (of space) below, through the creation of a firmament, which then became a heaven-world in its own right. In the Hindu tradition, we have the primordial figure of Siva Nataraja, the great ascetic, who danced upon the waters (again of space) and thereby generated the (spherical) field of Creation. Plato follows exactly the same idea in his statement that the first principle of Creation by Nous is that of privation[2]—that is, the Mind of the unseen and unknowable Logos isolates within space a spherical field of intended self-expression, again contained by a heavenly firmament. To the Ancients, however, there was a progressive series of such firmaments, all concentrically contained within each other, all together comprising a sequential ladder of consciousness leading from the highest state of being to the lowest, and thereby comprising a radical unity of existence as between the kosmically noumenal and the terrestrially phenomenal.

The Concentric Function and the Septenary Principle

The Ancients went a stage or two further than this in their general concept, however, for they clearly saw the movement of the various concentrically organized spheres as being dynamically geared to each other. Interestingly, we find this rather obliquely described in the Egyptian gnostic *Hermetica* as follows:

> There is a body which encloses all things. You must conceive the shape of that body as circular [i.e., spherical], for such is the shape of the [home] universe. . . . And you must understand that below [i.e., within] the circle [sphere] of this body are placed the thirty-six decans, between the circle of the universe and that of the Zodiac, separating one circle [i.e., sphere] from the other. . . . They retard the all-enclosing body—for that body would otherwise move with extreme velocity if it were left to itself; but they [also] urge on the seven other circles [i.e., spheres] because these circles move with a slower movement than the circle [i.e., the outer sphere] of the [home] universe. And subject to the Decans is the constellation called the [Little] Bear, which is centrally situated with regard to the Zodiac. The Bear is composed of seven stars and has overhead another [Greater] Bear to match it. The function of the [Little] Bear resembles that of the axle of a wheel; it never sets nor rises, but abides in one place, revolving about a fixed point and making the zodiacal circle revolve.[3]

Now this text clearly describes an inner and outer sphere of being, driven by an operationally living gear or bearing mechanism of the thirty-six decans, each of the latter being an abstract god figure representing ten degrees of arc in a circle, or sphere. While the actual function might perhaps sound obscure, what seems to be described—as shown in fig. 1.2—involves the constant meshed circulation between them of six, equally sized lesser spheres, rotating around a seventh of exactly equal size.

Each of the six intervening spheres, as it were, "contains" sixty degrees of arc (i.e., six decans), and as each rotates on its own axis, so the six together roll forward, thereby bringing to bear the full 360-degree rotation of both the innermost and outermost spheres—*but at different speeds.** What we therefore have is seven spheres (and states) of Being within a

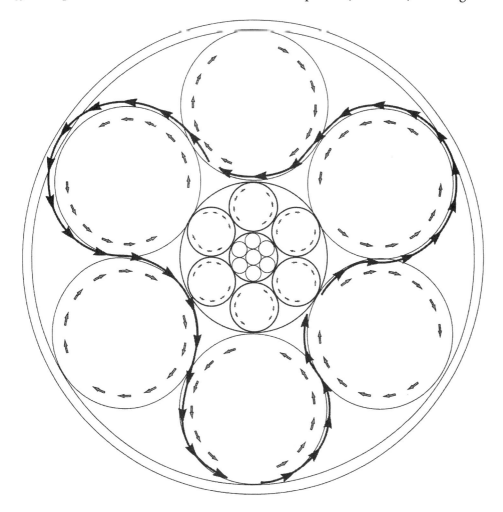

FIGURE 1.2. THE INTERLOCKING SAROS CYCLES OF THE DECANS

---

*This appears to be the origin of the Chaldeo-Babylonian saros system of astronomical and mathematical measurement/calculation, in which the *saros* is a period of 223 synodic months (approximately 6,585.3211 days, or 18 years and 11⅓ days) that can be used to predict eclipses of the Sun and Moon.

parent octave sphere. It is otherwise interesting to note that the ancient Egyptian system had the decans—each having ten days dedicated to it—being led around the heavens by Sirius and Orion.[4] As we shall see in chapter 3, this apparently minor piece of information has immediate and far-reaching implications as regards the relationship of Sirius to our own solar system and thus to Earth itself.

Kosmic Polarity

These six intermediate spheres containing the decanates were otherwise seen as the expression of a great duality, itself arising from the principle of polarity. The fundamental nature of Universal Being has always traditionally been regarded as comprising the three principles of Life, Consciousness, and Creative Instinct (or Omnipresence, Omniscience, and Omnipotence), and this same triplicity was seen as becoming dual in operational function within the greater soul-sphere—hence the appearance of the six intermediate spheres containing the decans. However, the innermost sphere was seen as both being a microcosm of the macrocosmic outer sphere and also as regulating and coordinating the function of the two triplicities, thereby having an intermediate or mediating function. It was therefore regarded as the *fourth* in the series of the lesser seven spheres. This is important because it serves to show how the fourth state was regarded as being a reflection (or double) of the overshadowing parent soul-sphere and also why it was described as a secondary heaven world, itself containing seven lesser powers or centers of divine force.

These same principles—being seen as universal in application—were thus also to be found in relation to each galaxy, local universe, or individual solar system and planet. However, the Ancients distinguished between these various spheres and the associated states of both duration and consciousness by the simple use of the zero to designate the relative power or extent of the soul-sphere in question, for reasons to be explained in the next few pages. Thus in their system of septenary thought, the following sequence arose (following the Hermetic principle of working inward from the universal to the particular):

1.	1,000,000	-	the divine state*
2.	100,000	-	the semidivine state (represented in hieroglyphics by the frog)
3.	10,000	-	the pure spiritual state
4.	1,000	-	the state of spiritual soul being (of the lesser—i.e., fallen—gods)
5.	100	-	the psychological state
6.	10	-	the psycho-elemental state
7.	0	-	the physically objective state

*It is consequently not altogether surprising when, in the ancient Egyptian tradition, we come across the solar barque of the great god Ra (an esoteric metaphor for a great cycle of existence) being called "the boat of millions of years," for Ra *contained* the whole of existence and phenomenal manifestation within his own nature. It was to this supremely elevated state that the Egyptians ultimately aspired via the Mysteries.

In support of this concept of the synonymous relationship between the soul and the sphere of individualized existence, we find elsewhere in the *Hermetica:* "For the Decad, my son, is the number by which soul is generated. Life and Light are a Unit; and the number One is the source of the Decad. It is reasonable then that the Unit contains in itself the Decad."[5]

In order to relate the subsequent and sequentially practical modus operandi of this concept more clearly, we ought perhaps to commence our more detailed considerations by taking a brief look at the associated ancient Greek myth, which is somewhat simpler to understand than some, even though saying precisely the same thing using both metaphor and allegory. In that myth then we find the supreme Titan god Ouranos (i.e., Aura-Nous, the sphere of kosmic ideation) ensouling a portion of space (Gaea)* by enfolding it within his mighty embrace and forcing it to conceive first of all the three Cyclopes and the three Hundred-Handed Giants.[6] This, however, is an esoteric allegory representing the primordial principle of dual triplicity within the as yet generalized field of kosmic manifestation. Within it the Cyclopes symbolize the one-eyed Soul principle—divine, spiritual, and terrestrial—while the Giants correspondingly symbolize the principle of associated evolutionary ambition.† However, because these six were depicted as malformed—i.e., lacking true kosmic consciousness—the Ouranos principle is shown hurling them down into the depths of Tartarus—material existence itself, the lower pole of the Gaea sphere of existence.[7]

The Birth of the Lesser Titans

Ouranos is next shown as forcing Gaea to conceive six further pairs of Titan gods, all living powers but having no fixed shape—an esoteric metaphor for the formation of six kosmic states of Being and their associated (dual) hierarchies of kosmic consciousness. The youngest of the six—represented by Kronos and his sister-wife Rhea—themselves produce three pairs of lesser gods, three male and three female. Kronos is then shown cutting off his father's generative faculty (symbolized by his phallus) and thus himself assuming supreme power and responsibility for the great cycle of kosmic duration. The phallus of Ouranos, however, falls into the ocean of matter within the local universe, where its combined blood

---

*The altogether simplistic modern interpretations of Ouranos as Sky and Gaea as Earth are as erroneous as those associated with Geb and Nut in the ancient Egyptian tradition. However, the Greek pair symbolized kosmic principles whereas the Egyptian pair symbolized the corresponding solar principles.

†The Cyclopes represented the female aspect of this duo, while the Hundred-Handed Giants—depicted as vast treelike creatures with tentacle-like branches growing outward in every direction, symbolizing their acquisitively creative nature—represented the corresponding male aspect. This seemingly comprised three types of creative "spark," the motive strength of which (in concert) was huge. Zeus (symbolic of the highest aspect of the Kosmic Mind) later casts his own deformed son Hephaestus down into Tartarus—in the midst of the Underworld—where he sets up his forge, in which the Cyclopes and Hundred-Handed Giants work with him to produce those forms requested by the higher gods.

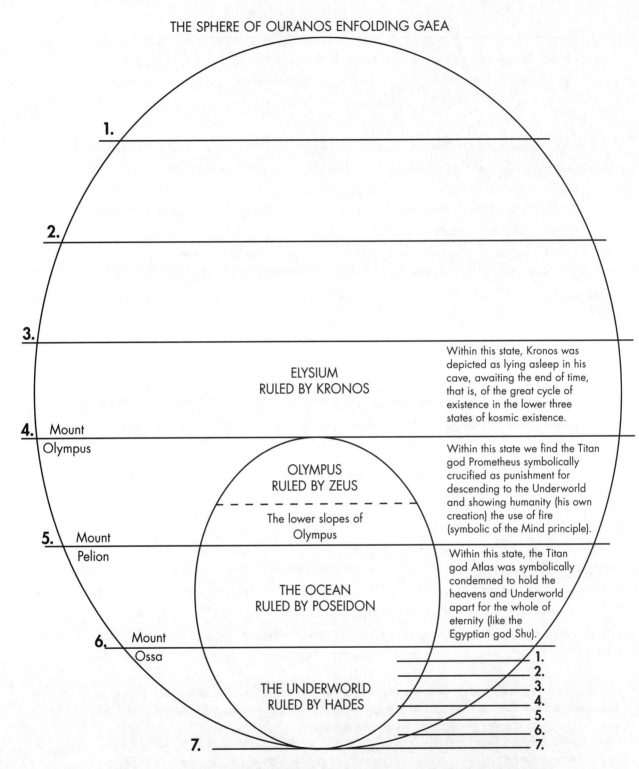

THE SPHERE OF OURANOS ENFOLDING GAEA

1.

2.

3.

ELYSIUM
RULED BY KRONOS

Within this state, Kronos was depicted as lying asleep in his cave, awaiting the end of time, that is, of the great cycle of existence in the lower three states of kosmic existence.

4. Mount Olympus

OLYMPUS
RULED BY ZEUS

The lower slopes of Olympus

Within this state we find the Titan god Prometheus symbolically crucified as punishment for descending to the Underworld and showing humanity (his own creation) the use of fire (symbolic of the Mind principle).

5. Mount Pelion

THE OCEAN
RULED BY POSEIDON

Within this state, the Titan god Atlas was symbolically condemned to hold the heavens and Underworld apart for the whole of eternity (like the Egyptian god Shu).

6. Mount Ossa

THE UNDERWORLD
RULED BY HADES

1.
2.
3.
4.
5.
6.
7.

7.

FIGURE 1.3. THE ANCIENT GREEK VIEW OF THE SEVENFOLD KOSMIC WORLD

Note: The god nature is regarded by the Ancients as essentially tenfold because the ladder of Creation and subsequent evolution comprised the octave of the Underworld plus the next two higher kosmic states through which the "divine spark" had to pass en route to returning to the highest aspect of Kosmic Mind—from which it had originally been emanated.

FIGURE 1.4. THE ROMAN JUPITER
(PICTURED) WAS CLOSELY IDENTIFIED
WITH THE GREEK ZEUS, GOD OF THE SKY.
(Photo by Andrew Bossi)

and semen dissolve and, in so doing, infect everything with its life and creative instinct.* However, the youngest of Kronos's own children—Zeus—is subsequently depicted as dethroning his cruel and overbearing father (a reflection of Ouranos) by uniting with the Cyclopes and the Hundred-Handed Giants to overcome him and the other Titans. Thereafter, Zeus and his two brothers Poseidon and Hades apportion the rulership of *manifest* existence—the Sky, the Oceans, and the Underworld—between themselves.[8]

The Meaning of the Myth

The essence of the overall concept is that the Titans represent the seven kosmic *states* within the sphere of our local universe, the Cyclopes and Giants being the least evolved aspects,

---

*In the myth, the surface of the ocean foamed in response and from it then arose the goddess Aphrodite, symbolizing not only the principle of attraction associated with the procreative instinct, but also the beauty of form itself.

while Kronos—although the youngest—becomes the fourth in the series and thus dominates all the rest. His own creative power is then emanated into the lower three kosmic states—symbolized as three lesser pairs (or polarities) of male and female Titan gods who have to unite their force with that of the lowest (the Cyclopes and Giants) before an overall kosmic equilibrium is reached. Then and only then does it become possible for the process of *objective* Creation and the appearance of semidivine Man and mortal mankind to take place.

This latter phenomenon is itself allegorically represented for us in the story of Prometheus, who represents the personally oriented Kosmic Mind principle that actually creates mankind within the Underworld, in his own image (i.e., from his own imagination), and then gives man the principle of self-consciousness, symbolically represented as fire. Zeus—representing the highest aspect of the Kosmic Mind—is furious and so creates Pandora, whom he gives in marriage to Epimetheus, Prometheus's slower-witted brother, representing the concrete or merely instinctively organizational aspect of the Mind principle. Prometheus, however, possesses a box in which he has managed to contain all the spirits of potential karmic misery in the lower world, which Epimetheus and Pandora are told not to open under any circumstances. But the inquisitive Pandora cannot restrain her curiosity and so, in opening the box, allows these malicious spirits to fly out and thereafter eternally plague mankind—as Zeus had intended.[9]

The Nature of the Ancient Underworld

Because mythologists in general have nearly always started their interpretations from the anthropomorphic base of purely human experience, they have generally managed to serially misunderstand how the Ancients themselves viewed the Underworld, resulting in a view that it had to be *below* the state of daily human waking existence. This is completely false, because the Ancients started off with the view that Man was essentially of a divine (i.e., kosmic) nature and that everything below *that* state then constituted the Underworld. Thus Man and man were two quite different aspects of the same principle. However, as we can see from the apportionment of the lowest three kosmic planes to Zeus, Poseidon, and Hades, it was the lowest of these (that governed by Hades) that truly comprised the Underworld—i.e., our home universe—which was itself also both dual and sevenfold in nature. The duality was subjective—comprising in Nature what we today call spiritual and material consciousness—and also objective—being expressed in both solar (or sidereal) and terrestrial (or planetary) terms, each of these pairs being found in a multitude of ever-changing combinations. Thus changing astronomical positions led to a variety of astrological aspects having a direct bearing upon the associated faculties of consciousness.

Now, remembering that these god figures were themselves regarded as symbolically representative of living universal principles of a certain order or quality, we can perhaps understand (by comparison) the parallel metaphysical concept that the originating Logos of any particular sidereal system actually exists *outside* it and merely projects cyclically operative aspects (or reflections) of itself *within* it. Consequently the various stars and planets in our own system were regarded as mere vehicles of superior extra-cosmic influences endeavoring to express themselves in mathematical sequence and order within the field of objective manifestation. So, on that basis, let us now take a look at what the Ancients regarded as operative in the constitution of each individual solar system and its surrounding sidereal relationships.

The Constitution of a Star-Sun

To begin with, then, scholars over the centuries have very successfully managed to serially misunderstand the nature of the Sun (itself a star) as the Ancients saw it; for to the Ancients the physical Sun was but a secondary Sun. The true Sun, according to them—the home of the local Demiurge—was a crystal sphere *containing* our whole solar system,* which discriminatingly absorbs within itself the invisible yet ambient light of the stars surrounding it in space and refracts it inward. Now, this crystal sphere contained, in their view, an invisible outer aether—a literal ring of (cold) fire—which bears a very striking resemblance to the invisibly electrified outermost atmosphere (the ionosphere) surrounding our Earth.†

As Robert Temple tells us in his book *The Crystal Sun,* Philolaus the Pythagorean (a noted writer on this same subject) was reported by a number of early commentators (in Greek and Roman times) as holding that the Sun was triple. For example, he quotes Achilles Tatius (circa third century CE) as writing: "Philolaus says that the Sun receives its fiery and radiant nature from above, from the aetherial fire, and transmits the beams to us through certain pores, so that according to him the Sun is triple, one Sun being the aetherial fire, the second that which is transmitted from it to the glassy thing under it which is called Sun and the third that which is transmitted fom the Sun in this sense to us."[10] Some modern commentators have taken the view from this that the crystal Sun and its aether refer to the surface of the physical Sun and that the Ancients considered there to be a glassy counterpart beneath this, that is, at the very core of the Sun. But this is manifestly *not* what the Pythagoreans were talking about.‡

---

*Hence the violent reaction of the Egyptian priesthood to Akhenaten's worship of the merely physical Sun, the Aten, for it was regarded as merely a vehicle of the god Shu, whereas the celestial crystal sphere was made in the beginning by the creator-god Ptah.

†The electromagnetic field surrounding our planet at a distance of thirty-some miles above its surface. However, the Ancients saw *every* sidereal sphere as being ringed by a similar ring of fire (or divine flame).

‡The distinction between the solar soul-sphere and the physical Sun was clearly understood by the Egyptians, as we can see from the Theban Recension of the Book of the Dead, where we find: "Thou Ra shinest from the horizon of heaven and Aten is adored when he resteth upon this mountain to give life to the two lands."

It is interesting to note from this quotation of Philolaus that the Ancients were aware of the porous nature of the solar surface, when modern scientific theory would suggest that such a perception would have been impossible without the sort of sophisticated equipment scientists themselves use. However, we find the same perception as a feature incorporated into the Mayan legend of the birth of the fifth solar cycle. Here, to begin with, the kosmic gods are depicted as being uncertain as to who among them would take on the role of the next Sun, as the job involved a necessary self-immolation. Eventually two gods put themselves forward, one (Nanahuazin) remaining at the edge of the sacred fire, burning slowly, while the other (Tecciztecatl)—a lowlier god *with a "pock-marked face"*—jumped courageously straight into the central flame. Then once these two (aspects of the Demiurge) had thus committed themselves, the great solar deity Quetzalcoatl (the feathered serpent) manifested himself in order to further the evolution of Man.[11]

The Pythagorean concept itself appears to have been learned either from the Egyptians during Pythagoras's twenty-two-year sojourn as a student at the sacred college of Heliopolis, or during an equivalent stay of his in Babylonia. But the Mayan tradition, told in its style of mythic allegory, says fundamentally the same thing, and it also indicates that, at some time or another, this highly advanced knowledge was held by cultures in common right across the world. From it was derived the universally held soul principle, which applied to all kosmic, sidereal, and terrestrial organisms. And, because knowledge was held to be (necessarily) cyclical in operation in Nature, it automatically followed that astrology, as a science, was fundamental to any possibly clear understanding of the rationale behind the whole kosmic process.

Astronomical Time and the (Spiritual) Evolutionary Impulse

We suggested a little earlier that time itself does not actually exist, although duration does*—the latter being founded upon the principle of cycles of activity generated, as the Ancients saw it, by the sequential response of hierarchies of divine and spiritual entities (solar gods and demigods and their own subhierarchies of angelic and elemental beings) to the Mind emanations of an overshadowing (kosmic) Intelligence. Thus it was seen in the ancient system that celestial genesis had first to involve an inward or downward movement, like a plant putting down roots or a fetus growing from a tiny seed within an ovum.

---

*In practical terms, time per se does not exist. The sense of it is merely a conditioned effect resulting from repetitive phenomenal experience by the five senses. Duration does exist, however, and it is subject to cycles of activity and rest, which are fundamentally of a dualistic nature. The idea that at the speed of light time ceases to exist is thus correct, insofar as light is that unitary universal medium that comprises the all-embracing consciousness of the gods. Hence, in that state, duality of existence in and out of form ceases to be, as does also any potentially associated sense of time. But far faster than light is the speed of the Mind principle itself.

Returning to the mainstream of our theme, however, there is a further implicit but highly important duality in the Pythagorean concept as reported. It is that certain of the celestial influences (i.e., the spiritual ones) reach our planet direct from the crystal Sun of our own solar system, while others are merely reflected back to it from the physical Sun, after first having been tinged or conditioned by its fallen nature. This itself bears a close resemblance to the Greek myth (allegory, rather) just mentioned, inasmuch as the stories told describe a remarkably constant (but nevertheless colorfully varied) to-ing and fro-ing of activities and influences as between the *meta*physical Olympus and Underworld.

Symbolic Influence of the God Ra

A point that arises out of what has been said in the last few paragraphs is that in order to prevent unnecessary conflict from arising in the movement of celestial bodies and the constant transmission and reception of kosmic and solar energies, a necessity arises in Nature for a routine regularity of basic rhythm in its overall operations. Hence this constant and rhythmic in-and-out motion became synonymous with the breath; and so, in the Egyptian system, the cyclic flow of Life within the solar environment became the barque of Ra, or the breath of Ra, the latter being symbolized by a god holding an ankh toward the mouth of a pharaoh, for example. The implicit message, however, was that the particular deity or divine principle was imparting its specific spiritual (and thus Life-bearing) influence, almost inevitably of an accompanying astrological nature.

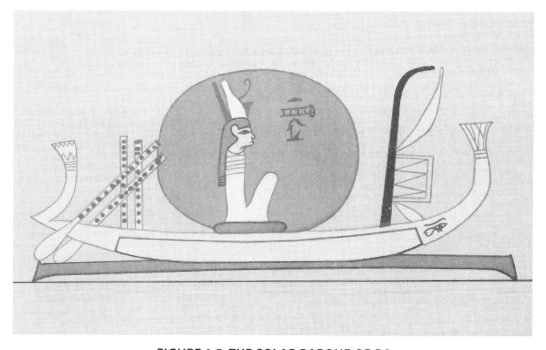

FIGURE 1.5. THE SOLAR BARQUE OF RA

The True Nature of Ancient Astrology

Regrettably, most Egyptologists are self-determinedly even less interested in understanding the basic nature of astrology than they are with understanding astronomy—a somewhat extraordinary standpoint when it is so widely known that ancient Egyptian culture was actually founded upon these and other related metaphysical issues. However, the purpose and nature of astrology as seen by the Ancients appears to have been markedly different from that understood and practiced by our modern savants.* As far as the Ancients were concerned, this particular science related to a better understanding of and necessary conformity with the Will and Purpose of Deity. It had little if anything to do—*as a primary consideration*—with the purely personal destiny and character of the individual. Notwithstanding this, individuals would undoubtedly have been astrologically assessed upon entering the Mystery Schools in order to see how they fit in with the pattern of sidereal Nature and how best therefore they could be absorbed into a society concerned with the highest possible expression and further development of the divine and spiritual natures of humankind.

The Cycles of Time Affecting Our Earth

Now our galaxy is a very large place and our solar system within our local home universe is located, according to astronomers, in the outer reaches of one of the spiral arms of the Milky Way. Consequently, as the distance from the center to the periphery is currently calculated as something on the order of thirty light-years, the great kosmic energies issuing centripetally from the galactic periphery and then returning centrifugally from the center through the medium of the intervening stars theoretically take a considerable time to accomplish their circuit. This in-and-back cycle is of the greatest importance. In our own tiny solar system (the galaxy's microcosmic equivalent) it takes about twenty-two years—hence the mathematical importance of pi (π), representing a multiple cycle divided by the number seven, which itself conditions the material nature of our solar existence, for reasons to be explained later on. Hence also the reason for the solar sunspot activity, which always affects our highly charged ionosphere (and life on Earth itself) so dramatically every eleven years, in the recurrent twenty-two-year cycle.

To view this cyclical efflux merely as a passage of energy, however, would have been inconceivable to the Ancients. To them it represented the transfer of literally living

---

*Modern astrology, sadly, bears very little resemblance to that of the Ancients in either scope or context. Whereas our modern astrologers seem to take the view that we are *governed* by the stars and planets, the Ancients saw them as rather providing very powerful, psychospiritual *conditioning* influences, which the "divine spark" or inner Man was nevertheless progressively able to bring under his power (automatically, at will), once he had learned how to achieve perfect mastery over his own merely human nature.

knowledge back and forth between the demiurgic soul nature of the galactic firmament and its fallen fellow hierarchies of being. Thus the centripetal fall of lesser "sparks" from the peripheral heavenly flame to the center was a constant one, while the centrifugal return, from the center to the periphery, necessarily involved a constant process of liberation as a result of the conglomerate realization achieved by the Deity (Logos) behind the whole process. Hence the whole sequence involved an incessantly sequential cycle of (re)incarnation and release until the whole of the great Purpose originally inseminated into the demiurgic consciousness had run its gamut. Consequently, the *self-conscious* god nature could only emerge during the latter part of the cycle, driving the return from the fall, through its own self-generated liberation; and it was in this liberation that groups of lesser "divine sparks" themselves emerged within a planetary environment *as man* for the first time. However, as we shall see, the odds stacked against their emergent individualization and gradually increasing spiritual liberation were huge, as to some extent described in the Book of the Dead.

The Complexity of Individuality

Let us otherwise remember that *all* entities in (universal) Nature were seen as unified *groups* comprising myriad subgroups of lesser beings, which then themselves gave rise to further myriads of even lesser subgroups. The human organism and its localized sense of self is a perfect example of this very principle. Hence, in the local universe of the Ancients, we find all sorts of major and minor hierarchies of gods, angels, and elementals, as well as correspondingly more highly or lesser evolved types of "divine sparks" or spirits—all part of one greater god-being, but also simultaneously members of distinct groups, each possessing a spectrum of instinctual consciousness of its own.

The expression "divine spark"—found in both the Egyptian and the Hindu metaphysical traditions, as the *akh* and *jiva,* respectively—frequently causes problems of interpretation for scholars because the "spark"—synonymous with the Pythagorean *monas* (itself derived from the Sanskrit *manas*)—is a metaphysical no-thing and thus *appears* to be a complete spiritual abstraction. However, in a scientific age where we are used to ideas such as electromagnetic and even telepathic transmissions of energy, information, and thought over great distances, without any apparently accompanying form or "vehicle" other than a "wave," this should not present any real problem. To the Ancients, the "divine spark" and its lesser counterpart the "spark" in the heart of man (also found in lesser degree in the animal, plant, and mineral kingdoms, so the tradition had it) were the Mind-transmitted expressions of the Will of God. Hence it was that the "fall from Grace" (i.e., from the local "heaven world," or World Soul) was always that of a *metaphorically* alienated hierarchy of mind-born divine beings, which subsequently had to fight its way back to its divine "home," its faculty of consciousness necessarily dominating all planes of local matter en route.

The "fallen divine spark" was specifically associated by the Ancients with Man, while the soul principle was just as specifically associated by them with the angelic or *deva* hierarchies. When the two were united, their combined intelligence was that of a fully self-conscious god. When temporarily separated by the processes of Creation, however, each tended instinctively to pursue its own nature, thereby creating an incessant conflict between them as the angel strove to maintain the status quo while Man strove to overturn it, so as to initiate a new system in better conformity with the "new" Divine Plan and Purpose. This particular duality of being within the consciousness of the parent Logos is of paramount importance to our understanding of how the whole ancient metaphysical system of thought actually worked, and it consequently needs to be kept constantly in mind.

As far as the ancient Egyptians were concerned, the fully individualized god-Man was a (reintegrated) being of light. However, the groups of lesser "divine sparks" forming part of his lower nature had evolved through passing primordially en masse from the solar periphery to its center, there to be clothed in material forms (i.e., atomic matter), before progressively entering the various kingdoms of Nature en route to taking on a human form and an associated consciousness—in the words of the Hermetic tradition, "first as a stone, then as a plant, then as a beast, and finally as man." This, however, is not in sympathy with modern Darwinian theory, which sees man and his mind-consciousness as really no more than the objectively physical human being, a mere arrangement of cells. It might instead be said, contrary to this, that the *essence* of what ancient philosophy saw as making and identifying man is actually the noumenally based impulse to intelligently cooperative creative originality (hence change). Thus to the Ancients it is *this* very principle—via the soul's agency—that both produced the world of morphogenesis and also drove the engine of evolution in Universal Nature, producing in transit the cycle of conception, birth, and death of *forms*.

The Esoteric Metaphor of the Two Pillars and Their Astronomical Counterparts

In the Egyptian tradition, it is suggested, the distinction between the two fundamental hierarchies of Life—angel and Man (the *neteru* and the *akhu*)*—was symbolically depicted in the form of the Djed (or Tet) Pillar (see fig. 1.6), respectively in its upright position and then leaning at an angle. The upright position represented the status quo and the Great Law as manifested in the Will-to-Be of the Demiurge. The leaning position then

---

*Please refer to chapter 5 for an elaborated discussion of *neteru* (angels or *devas*) and *akhu* (Man).

FIGURE 1.6. THE RAISING OF THE DJED PILLAR
(from a relief in the Temple of Osiris at Abydos)

Note: Rather interestingly, given the evident phonetic associations of the temples of both Ankhor Wat and Ankhor Tum in Cambodia with Egypt, we also find there the annual Festival of Tet, which is traditionally associated with the advent of the Khmers. Now Tet is another way (as confirmed by Egyptologists) of writing Djed, while the Khmers are themselves none other than the Kumaras—the eternal god-youths whom we find in the Vedic tradition. According to the Vedic tradition, it is these same Kumaras who descend to the planetary spheres as kosmic avatars, in order to stimulate and further the evolutionary progress of the kingdoms of Nature. They themselves appear to be of equivalent status to the Buddhas, the Indo-Tibetan equivalent of the Egyptian Ptah.

correspondingly symbolized the movement away from the status quo, involving the *apparently* aberrational evolutionary instinct (the Will-to-Know) leading to kosmic liberation—which Man represented. Thus Man was in some traditions metaphorically described as a rebel angel.

However, this same subjective movement away from the upright and true had its objective expression in sidereal terms as well: as the various star systems cycled around the galactic nucleus (in their constantly thwarted scheme of self-liberation), they were forced to do so at an angle to the galactic equator, or celestial horizon, thereby generating semi-independent celestial poles.* Thus it was that smaller star systems rotated in orbit in this way around giant parent stars in lesser cycles, while the giant stars progressed in

---

*The associated principle is the same as that involving an athlete running around an elliptical or oblong track, needing to lean inward and forward to maintain economy of momentum on bends while returning to an upright position on the straights.

the same fashion around the galactic nucleus. However, the intelligent sense of order and self-discipline, which is needed to achieve and sustain this constant organic weaving without accident, clearly had to be of an all-pervasive kosmic nature. Nobody in their right mind could seriously believe that this perpetual process—widely described as "the dance of the gods"—was a mere matter of prolonged chance. Yet this, quite self-evidently, is the unavoidable corollary of the purely materialistic view of Creation.*

As far as the Ancients were concerned, it followed quite logically from their other ideas that, if there were indeed a progressive sequence of relationship and intercommunication between the planet and the solar heaven world of the demiurgic hierarchy (Elohim), there had to be a corresponding kosmic counterpart within the greater sphere of our home universe as well. Consequently, by knowing which star systems represented each sequential kosmic step and by also knowing the cyclic proximities of each such system to our own, they felt that it should (theoretically at least) prove possible for enlightened humankind to liberate itself, by its own efforts, and thus eventually climb back up the "ladder," in progressive order, to its point of divine origin. But this could only be achieved by a gradual process of spiritually oriented renunciation (within the individual's innermost field of self-awareness), in which personal fascination and self-association with the *local* (planetary or solar) environment was progressively given up. However, that is the essence of *all* ancient sacred teaching and it is perhaps most obviously known to us today in the Buddhist and Hindu doctrines concerning liberation from the Wheel of Rebirth.

The Problem of Kosmic Self-Orientation

Returning to the issue of the progressive sequence of the kosmic fall and liberation within our home universe, it becomes clear that, according to the ancient mode of thought, each star system and planetary system had to combine this same duality simultaneously. Hence involvement in matter and liberation from it had to coexist in harness. But this itself—while forming the very foundation of Creation—presented a problem of very real potential conflict for Man's modus operandi, between those entities falling and those unconsciously but instinctively trying to liberate themselves—that is, unless he could gain inside knowledge as to how this delicately balanced system worked and so learn to work intelligently within it, thus avoiding the otherwise inevitable pitfalls arising out of dualis-

---

*Our astrophysicists are still unable to work out why it should be that some galaxies gather together in space in great social cluster, while between these great gatherings lie vast empty areas, devoid of stellar life, although clearly full of something inexplicably else. But this dark matter of astrophysics which accounts for over 90 percent of the mass of the universe and which also somehow provides the substructure of the galaxies, thereby maintaining their coherence, is itself none other than the Egyptian *ka* (ether) of universal space, within which the background microwave radiation noise is the generalized sound of Universal Life itself.

tic self-association.* So, within the framework of our own neighborhood universe, the first problem to be solved involved answering the question "Where do *we* stand (in sidereal and planetary terms) in this equation?"

Although astronomers as yet have no real recognition as to our solar system belonging to any specific star group, the Ancients seemed fairly certain that we are actually part of the Pleiades. In fact, various mythic allegories (those of the Greeks particularly) point to our Sun probably being what is referred to as "the missing Pleiad."† As the Pleiades also form a small part of the constellation of Taurus, it is not altogether surprising to find that the concealed Deity of our immediately local system was extensively associated (in so many ancient religions and mystic cultures) with the Bull of Heaven and the corresponding characteristics of generative potency of the mundane animal form. We shall see more of the Pleiades in the next two chapters, but in the meantime, let us pause briefly to consider the somewhat radical concept of the constellation of Taurus perhaps itself playing the part of our parental home universe.

Has Orthodoxy Missed the Plot?

It is by now a well-established fact among social anthropologists and archaeologists that the bull or ox played a very central role in ancient mystic traditions all around the world. To the anthropologist this importance has been assumed to arise from the bull, buffalo, ox, and so on being the main beast of burden and main source of meat diet and leather clothing. To the archaeologist, it seems probably also to have derived from association with Taurus being one of the most important constellations in the zodiac and to the Age of Taurus (between about 2200 and 4400 BCE) being (supposedly) the period of origin of human civilization in the Middle East. However, both these views are based upon largely speculative assumption, neither having taken into consideration the possibility that the

---

*Quite clearly, such knowledge was of the highest importance and—if it were to be used sensibly and to maximum effect for the common benefit of all—it had to be properly organized and maintained. It also had to be treated with due reverence and respect. However, because humankind itself consisted of a constantly varied motley of evolutionary intelligence—the majority of which could not yet even begin to conceive of the overall kosmic process in their own objective consciousness—the process itself had to be described and knowledge of it circulated in the form of esoteric metaphor and allegory, under the aegis of the Mystery Schools and the carefully organized initiatory process they operated and directed. The reason for this is that the unified intelligence within the soul nature of man *can* recognize the inner or esoteric meaning by an instantaneous act of sympathetic resonance, which evokes its own latent memory and so stirs it into producing response. However, because such knowledge produces power, it has to be protected from selfish misuse and abuse by the even less evolved (elemental) nature in man. However, we shall deal with this in greater detail in part 3.

†The Pleiades were the daughters of the Titan god Atlas, himself condemned by his nephew Zeus to permanently hold up the heavens on his shoulders—an image exactly paralleled by those of the Babylonian Merodach and the Egyptian Shu, both being the gods of light in their respective traditions. However, it seems fairly evident from various traditions that the Ancients saw our lost Pleiad as being in orbit around Alcyone, the central and brightest star in the Pleiades nebula. But more on this in chapter 2.

mystic tradition might have had a much more profound and far more ancient origin.

There are several clues to the alternative scenario we have just suggested. First of all, the root word *tau* in Taurus is to be found in several very ancient mystic traditions. In ancient China, the Tau or Tao meant "the way"—that is, the natural or spiritual way in which Life in Universal Nature organized itself through the yin-yang process of interactive duality.* In ancient Assyria and Persia, the name became Al Thaur (hence our word *altar,* meaning the place of sacred fire)[12] and Tora, from which we appear to derive our Old Celtic word *tor,* meaning "a sacred hill." The Polynesian peoples referred to the Pleiades as Tau-ono (or Tau-anu),[13] while the ancient Egyptians incorporated the same root phonetic into Taui, the duality of upper and lower worlds, plus Ta'Urt, the name given to their hippopotamus goddess, the concubine of the kosmic Set and World Mother of our local universe—hence also the bearer of the gods.[14]

Second, in all the ancient zodiacs that have remained sufficiently intact for modern examination, Taurus always began the solar year.[15] Third, an associated tradition had it that the human race was itself created at a time when the Sun rose in Taurus—although which Sun this was is not altogether clear. However, we shall examine some of these ideas and traditions in greater detail in later chapters, in the meantime endeavoring to keep an open mind on the issue.

Now, all that we have looked at so far has a definite logic to it, even if possibly repugnant in certain respects to some scientists and scholars. But we next face the major problem of trying to establish a conceptual image (corresponding with that of the Ancients) as to (a) quite how our own solar system was seen as moving in relation to the remainder of the constellation of Taurus, (b) how Taurus itself related to the issue of the fallen "divine sparks," and (c) how the latter related to the atom of our local universe in the first place. This will inevitably prove difficult, particularly if to begin with we do not have a reasonably clear image in our own minds of the geography of our home universe. What we shall therefore do is break the imagery down into sections, so that the general principles related to each can be understood before we try to ally it to the sequentially next section.

To begin with then, in the next chapter we shall look at the way in which our Earth and Sun, and the Sun and solar system, actually appear to move as one body in space, within the galaxy, relative to other stars and constellations. We shall then consider the various ancient traditions concerning the changing positions of certain of the constellations relative to our own system. Our main points of reference in all this will be the circumpolar stars, from within which the Ancients believed that Man was born into the system; the zodiac; the constellation of Taurus; and the Pleiades nebula.

---

*In ancient Egypt, Taui meant the duality of Upper and Lower Egypt. However, this was itself merely a metaphor for the worlds of Spirit and Matter, as was the yin-yang symbol of the Taoists of China. Clearly then, Taui and Tao had the same origin.

TWO

THE ASTRONOMICAL AND ASTROLOGICAL DIMENSIONS OF CREATION

Destiny generates the beginnings of things; Necessity compels the results to follow. And in the train of Destiny and Necessity goes Order—that is, the interweaving of events and their arrangement in temporal succession. There is nothing that is not arranged in order; it is by order above all else that the kosmos itself is borne upon its course; nay the kosmos consists solely of order.

HERMETICA

In the last chapter, we saw how the fundamental basis of ancient perception of the divine nature focused on and revolved around the spheroidal soul-body principle within which all formative Creation was regarded as taking place. In this chapter, we shall take a look at the extension of this same principle in connection with the structure of our local universe, paying particular attention to the associated cycles.

The Cycle of The Great Year

As outlined in *Land of the Fallen Star Gods,* ancient myths depicting the various adventures of the gods appear fundamentally based upon the movement of the individual stars and constellations relative to each other. However, the associated changes of location in the night sky clearly appear to have been seen as due to the relative cyclic movement of our own planet and solar system within our home constellation, the Pleiades. This change of position was seen primarily relative to the celestial pole and ecliptic pole, for it involved a vast elliptical cycle around them taking some 25,920 Earth years to complete. This particular cycle, which is what was referred to as "the Great Year of the Pleiades,"[1] or simply "the Great Year," was considered by all the Ancients to be of immense importance; we need to understand it properly if we are to fully understand the ancient Egyptian mystic system. However, bearing in mind that few people have any real conception of our local stellar environment, and that even mainstream science holds on to a number of self-conflicting astronomical ideas, let us have a closer look at the mechanics and dynamics of this particular cycle in relation to our own Earth and its Sun, in rather more graphic terms.

The Earth–Sun Cycle

In order to clarify the principles and associated effects involved in our solar system's progression around the zodiac during the cycle of what was known to the Ancients as the Great Year, we need to consider it (from their viewpoint) in parallel with the much better understood modern correspondence involving our own planet's angled orbital path around the Sun during each Earth year. While usually described as an angled ellipse, the actual figure described by this orbit, as shown in fig. 2.1, is actually a helical figure of eight.

As otherwise shown in fig. 2.2, the orbital movement also takes place within the inter-

FIGURE 2.1. THE SUN'S MOVING TRACK OVER THE COURSE OF A YEAR

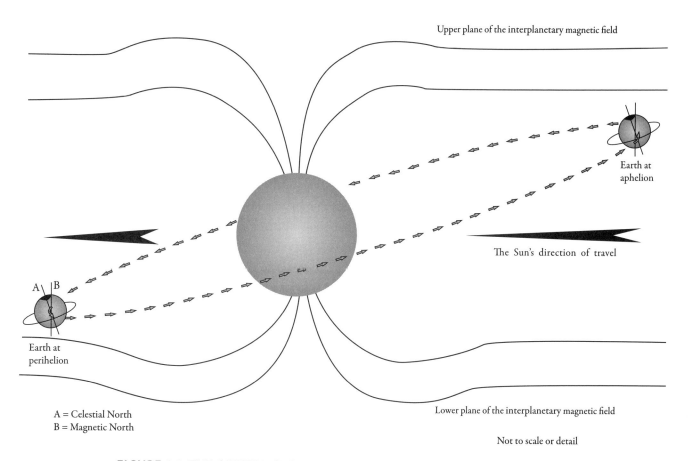

Upper plane of the interplanetary magnetic field

Earth at
aphelion

The Sun's direction of travel

A = Celestial North
B = Magnetic North

Earth at
perihelion

Lower plane of the interplanetary magnetic field

Not to scale or detail

FIGURE 2.2. THE ORBITAL CYCLE OF THE EARTH'S SOLAR YEAR

planetary magnetic field—the electric field phenomenally generated by the Sun.* This, like an electric cable, is positive at its core, or center, while being electrically negative on the outer sides. Consequently, there seems to be a strong likelihood that while the Earth's forward movement in space is actually generated by the slipstream effect of the Sun's own forward motion, the angled orbital path of the planet is generated by a combination of this and the repulsion of the Earth's own magnetic poles to the positive and negative potentials of the interplanetary magnetic field.

As we can see from fig. 2.2, the celestial or true North Pole of the Earth is set vertically to the plane of its own axial orbit around the Sun, whereas the magnetic North Pole of the Earth is (and remains eternally) vertical to the plane of the solar equator. There is consequently an angle separating these two poles—currently 23.5 degrees, though it varies, apparently by just under 2.5 degrees—which twentieth-century science believes to be due to a (rather inadequately explained and ratified) wobble in the Earth's axis. However,

---

*As the Egyptians would have seen it, however, this emanation from the physical Sun is merely a response to the noumenal influences and accompanying energies emanating centripetally from the solar firmament. From this viewpoint, the interplanetary magnetic field is like an umbilical cord permanently connecting the two.

it is the principle of the angled orbital path that is of immediate interest to us, because it appears to be universal in application and itself gives rise to the way in which we perceive other celestial phenomena, such as the twelve constellations of the zodiac, the changing circumpolar stars, and the associated Great Year.

The Spheres Surrounding Us

To begin with, we need to remember that the Ancients saw our tiny Earth globe as being contained by (and revolving orbitally within) a concentric series of progressively more vast spheres of Being, between each of which the principle of the decanate gearing operated in both macrocosm and microcosm. The associated sequence—logically a sevenfold one—seems to have been as follows:

1. The galactic corona—the Oversoul* of our local universe
2. The galactic halo—within which the galaxy itself axially rotates
3. The sphere of the fixed stars—within which the zodiac rotates
4. The sphere of the constellation Taurus—which orbits axially within the movement of the zodiac
5. The sphere of the Pleiades group—which orbits axially within the constellation of Taurus, quite possibly around the constellation of Orion, which lies midway between Taurus and Gemini†
6. The sphere of our solar system—which orbits around the central star of the Pleiades
7. The sphere surrounding planet Earth—which, with our planet inside it, orbits around our Sun

Now because the polar orientations of the various spheres thus surrounding us differ somewhat and also because of our extremely limited visual perspective from the surface of this planet, our own perceptions of the dynamic relationship between them very easily become disoriented. With that in mind, it is probably simpler for us to work visually outward, through the above sequence, as follows.

Mainstream modern science, with its rather restricted and as yet wholly materialistic

---

*According to the Ancients, each soul is itself but an expression of a hierarchically greater and more knowledgeable soul, which, in turn, is itself a cellular expression of something far greater still that nevertheless embodies the same principle. In other words, each soul entity is but a partial emanation or projection of a far greater and more powerful parent soul, an all-soul or "Oversoul" as the Greek philosopher Plotinus (204–270 CE) put it.

Thus the Oversoul of the Earth is itself a cell derived from the yet greater Oversoul of our solar system. The Oversoul of our solar system is in turn a cell derived from the vastly greater Oversoul that contains the stellar nebula within which our solar system exists, and so on.

†It may well be that this suspected movement of the Pleiades over the body of Taurus and axially around Orion was what lay behind the ritual sport of bull-leaping in ancient Crete and also the myth that the figure of Orion chases the Pleiades, despite never quite catching up with them.

view of the universe, believes that the 25,920-year cycle is due to another mere wobble of the Earth's axis, the reason for which it puts down merely to the influences of the Moon and Sun and the motions of the other planets respectively. This answer—based upon accumulative mathematical formulas—is unsatisfactorily full of anomalies, however. The Ancients, on the other hand, seem to have believed that the Great Year cycle was actually due to our own Sun's angled orbital cycle around a parent star—apparently, Alcyone, the central and brightest star in the Pleiades nebula. The essence of the idea was that as Alcyone and the Pleiades orbited at great speed around the constellation of Taurus, within the plane of the zodiac, so our Sun (like our Earth in relation to it) orbited *at lesser speed* around Alcyone, at an angle to Alcyone's own forward path.

Within the inner part of the solar system, however, the Earth travels far more slowly. So, relative to the Sun's and Alcyone's greater orbital speeds (although moving in the same anticlockwise direction), Earth *appears* to travel backward (clockwise) through the zodiac as our line of sight moves sequentially through it. This apparent retrogression is called the "precession of the equinoxes"* and it is based upon a complete visual illusion—one that would become immediately apparent if seen from a few miles up above the Pole. The further proof of this suggestion lies in the fact that, notwithstanding this apparent clockwise movement of the Earth relative to the zodiac, the change in the Pole Star—as also seen from Earth—follows an anticlockwise sequence. It is just not physically possible to travel in two completely opposing directions at the same time. Therefore, the visual phenomenon has to be based upon a misinterpretation, irrespective of whether scientific sleight-of-hand is able mathematically to suggest the contrary.

This slower orbital movement of our Earth, relative to that of the Sun,† otherwise appears to be the cause of our Earth year being 365.25 days long rather than just 360 days, to coincide with the 360 degrees of the circle. The extra 5.25 days (one seventy-second part of 360) clearly represented the extra time needed by the Earth to return to the same position (relative to the Sun) at which it commenced the year. These five epagomenal days thus became representative of terrestrial Creation and were accordingly dedicated to those gods—Horus (the Elder), Osiris, Isis, Nephthys, and Set—particularly associated with life on Earth.

---

*This same apparently retrogressive movement was itself symbolically depicted by the ancient Egyptians (long before the Greek astronomer Hipparchus recognized it in the second century BCE) in the form of the god Kheper-Ra, the kosmic scarab beetle. This flying beetle gathers together a spherically organized ball of dung (representing the refuse of space) and, having laid its eggs in it, then proceeds to roll it around on the ground by walking backward and propelling the ball along with its hind legs.

†Thus the diagram at fig. 2.3 (page 42) also shows us the reason for the importance universally ascribed to the spring equinox on Earth. At this time in its cycle around the Sun, the Earth is actually at its closest point to Alcyone, hence this position between the polar duality of the two Suns also doubtless gave rise not only to the Ancients' use of it as the primary astronomical reference point, but also to the phenomenon of our planetary Nature's own most potent season of regrowth each year.

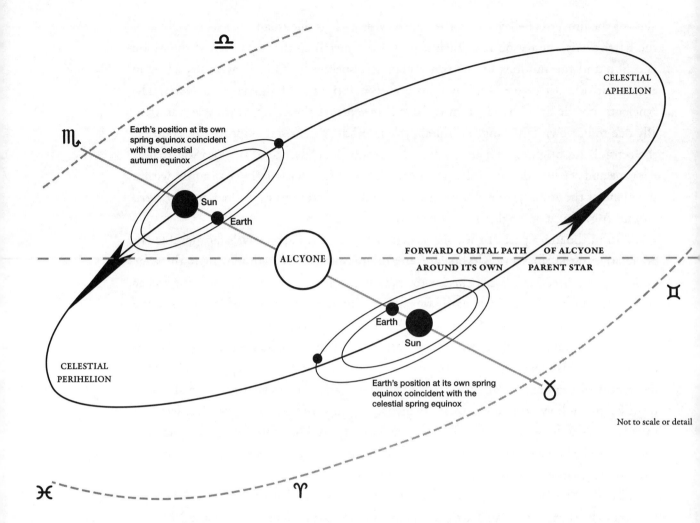

FIGURE 2.3. THE ASTROLOGICAL SIGNIFICANCE OF EARTH'S SPRING EQUINOX

Note: At the spring equinox every year, our planet lies sandwiched between Alcyone and our own Sun, thus receiving the maximum force of their dualistic (i.e., spiritual and material) influence.

Celtic Correspondences

Rather interestingly, this simultaneous anticlockwise movement of the Sun and apparently clockwise movement of the Earth was self-evidently symbolized by the Celts at the annual (Taurean) May festival of Beltane. At this festival, the Maypole was erected (an obvious parallel to the raising of the Djed Pillar in Egypt) and boys and girls danced around it while holding on to ribbons or streamers (representing rays of celestial light), which were fixed to the top of the pole, where some sort of significant object was placed to symbolize the celestial Pole Star itself. During the dance, the boys proceeded anticlockwise, thereby representing the male solar principle, while the girls proceeded clockwise, thereby representing the female Earth principle. The in-and-out pattern of the dance then caused the interweaving of the ribbons more and more closely around the Maypole itself, until all fused at the center.

The Egyptian Duat

The effect of our Sun's angled elliptical path around Alcyone, as shown in fig. 2.3, results in the celestial equivalent of aphelion and perihelion, plus the associated summer and winter (celestial) solstices. At these two solstitial points, at either end of the Great Year, the celestial Pole Stars immediately above the Earth are then Polaris and Vega respectively, these stars however being found within the next surrounding sphere of celestial Being—that is, that enfolding the constellation of Taurus as a whole. Before we proceed any further, however, we should perhaps expand slightly on the last statement, to ensure that the background principles are clearly understood.

The Ancients took the view that every organized physical body in the kosmos owed its very origin and existence to the parent soul-sphere that eternally preexisted it, aurically surrounded it, and eternally survived it. In the microcosm of animal and human existence, this soul-sphere was itself derived from the World Soul–sphere surrounding our own planet. In the macrocosm, it comprised the heavenly firmament surrounding each solar system, constellation, galaxy, and so on, and was referred to in the Egyptian tradition as the horizon, or *akhet*—the home of the divine spirits animating the system as a whole with their very being and consciousness. With this in mind, the Ancients saw the axial and orbital revolution of each sidereal body as actually that of the soul-sphere, the turning of each physically objective body within it being merely a secondary motion induced by it.

Now, as each minor soul-sphere then rotated axially and orbited elliptically (with others) within the greater soul-sphere of which it formed part—just as all the planetary schemes do within our solar system—so it joined in the development and maintenance of a complex, concentric system of geared cyclical influences. These progressive, cyclical influences then became the basis of the *local* astrological system. However, by virtue of association through sympathetic magic, the lesser sphere of being had partial access to the influences within the greater sphere of Being within which its own parent soul-sphere moved. Consequently, this higher sphere of astrological influence was deemed to have an inductive, *evolutionary* effect upon certain hierarchies of lesser lives within the lesser soul-sphere. In this way, the various kingdoms of Nature living within the soul-sphere of our planet were seen as responding automatically to planetary influences circulating within the sphere of our solar system.

Man, however, was seen as having not one soul, like the animals, but two—if not three—all again concentrically arranged, even if unknown to himself, in a manner that we shall endeavor to describe in greater detail in later chapters. By virtue of having a more subtle soul-body comprising matter of the solar firmament, which had fallen into the merely planetary environment, man was seen as being subconsciously (and eventually consciously) able to respond to extra-solar (i.e., zodiacal) influences via a living chain of sympathetic resonance between his higher (spiritual) soul nature on the one hand and his lower terrestrial soul nature (the Egyptian Ba) on the other—the latter then supplying his physical waking consciousness and the various elemental aspects of its organic being with its own vitality and instinctual sense.

The concentric arrangement of soul-spheres in the greater sidereal environment of our local universe was seemingly seen somewhat as shown in fig. 2.4. Unfortunately, due to the sheer limitations of scale and the vast relative distances in space between sidereal bodies, it is just not possible to give anything here other than the faintest idea of what might be involved.

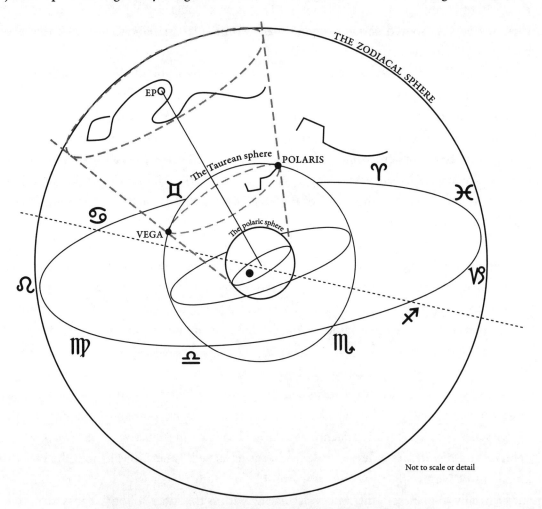

Not to scale or detail

FIGURE 2.4. THE SUGGESTED ANCIENT WORLDVIEW OF THE CONCENTRIC SOUL-SPHERES OF OUR LOCAL UNIVERSE

Note: By virtue of sheer size and relative distance apart in space, it is just not possible to give in this illustration anything other than a faint indication of the real arrangement between the various spheres and their associated constellations. The illustration is thus itself highly distorted. It is also otherwise unable to depict the range of movement of each sphere within its own superior "parent sphere."

However, the illustration aims to highlight two features in particular. First, certain constellations that we have come to regard as being part of our own immediate sidereal soul-sphere actually appear—by inference from ancient tradition—to belong to others. Second, through the movement of each soul-sphere in space within its parent soul-sphere, the relative angle of each major and minor orbital path progressively increases. Consequently, higher and lower sidereal (elliptical) paths *appear* to cross over cyclically at angles relative to each other, in a manner that must vary quite dramatically over long periods of time, as seen from our viewpoint on Earth.

This same latter principle, taken in relation to the ecliptic cycle of our own solar system around Alcyone during the 25,920-year Great Year, also defines the Egyptian Duat, involving the celestial descent of the solar deity Ra into the so-called Underworld. Not unnaturally, it is then this particular cycle and its major and minor relationships that appear to have been of primary interest to the Ancients, for the following reasons.

The Duat itself (see fig. 2.5) had seven primary divisions or planes of being, and consequently the cyclical movement down through these and then back up to the plane of the heaven world took twelve progressions to complete. These twelve progressions—depicted by reference to the twelve zodiacal constellations seen rising obliquely on Earth's eastern horizon—were also known (in terms of sympathetic magic) as the "twelve hours of the night," a concept we shall consider in greater detail in a later chapter. The important thing to remember about the twelvefold cycle, however, is that the zodiacal signs are largely reference points. It was the actual stages of the cycle itself that were of prime concern because of the sequentially progressive seasonal influences associated with each of them.

The Great Year likewise had twelve celestial months, each of 2,160 years (plus four celestial seasons of just under 6,500 years), the principle being exactly the same as for our similarly angled and orbital Earth year of 365.25 days. Within this we have the parallel of twelve months and four seasons, although our altogether haphazard modern system

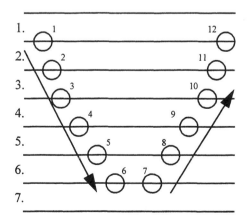

FIGURE 2.5. THE DUAT

attributes an arbitrary variety of days to each month. The Egyptian Earth year also had twelve months (and three seasons),* with each month being thirty days, making a total of 360 days, with the remaining five days being dedicated, as we have just heard, to the five gods specifically associated with human existence on Earth.

The Pole of the Ecliptic

Now, directly affecting our home universe there is a further and yet greater operative cycle than the Great Year, extending to nearly eight-two thousand years, which was also clearly known to the Ancients. Our present astronomical science has itself recognized this cycle, although but one half of it—believing it to be only just under forty-one thousand years—and has called it "the obliquity of the ecliptic." As the correspondences might well seem obscure, let us consider the following suggested explanation.

If we take a point locationally at the center of the great solar cycle of 25,920 years and we then describe a line through it, vertical to the plane of our Sun's orbital path around Alcyone, that line appears to pass through a point among the circumpolar stars, a little way behind the serpent's head of Draco (see again fig. 2.4), where, seemingly, no star exists. This then is called the ecliptic pole. Rather curiously perhaps, it is this same point that—as Robert Bauval has pointed out—is the true pole around which our larger local universe appears to revolve, for while the Pole Star keeps changing, this draconic point only shifts very slowly. But, we may well ask, how exactly does this whole sidereal operation function?

What happens as seen from Earth is that there *appears* to be a slight wobble of just under 2.5 degrees in the position of the ecliptic pole (relative to a fixed observation point on Earth) over a period of just under forty-one thousand years. But this must logically be followed by an equivalent movement away from the pole *on its other side*. Thus the true overall variation is actually just under 5 degrees, with the result that this pole visually returns to its original position after nearly eight-two thousand years. However, this supposed wobble is itself purely the result of another visual illusion, again derived from the fact that our astronomical perceptions are still largely Earth-centric and do not take into consideration the axial movement of the various concentric spheres of our local universe—or, consequently, of the different rotational speeds of those constellations specifically associated with them. On this latter point, there appears to be a clear indication that the constellation of Draco (as is also quite definitely the case with Ursa Major) actually belongs to the next sphere *beyond* that one containing Ursa Minor and Lyra at its northern periphery, as again shown in fig. 2.4.

*The threefold nature of the seasons in Egypt was undoubtedly due to their association with the threefold nature of Deity. (See Budge, "Translation of the *Papyrus of Nesi Amsu*.")

The Circumpolar Constellations in Ancient Metaphor

This latter suggestion seems to be confirmed from a variety of other angles. First of all, Draco was always, in other traditions, associated with the Dragon (hence its name), which is visually not unlike the crocodile. Second, although Egyptologists generally regard Draco as being represented by the hippopotamus goddess Ta'Urt, it is the crocodile god Sebek who has to climb on her back (see fig. 2.6) in order to reach and bite off the leg of the otherwise invisible Heavenly Bull—the leg being commonly acknowledged as referring to Ursa Major. Now Sebek is not even shown in the Dendera zodiac (see fig. 2.7, page 48), and the fact that Ta'Urt is clearly displayed there holding Ursa Minor (the Jackal of Set) *at the celestial pole* makes it quite clear that she cannot be symbolic of Draco, whose astronomical position is quite different. It is thus Sebek who represents Draco, while Ta'Urt is herself merely the permanently pregnant concubine of (the kosmic) Set. As bearer of the gods, she thus represents the demiurgic sphere or heavenly firmament of our immediate (Taurean) system.

FIGURE 2.6. SEBEK ON THE BACK OF TA'URT

In the corresponding Babylonian tradition, Enkidu—the male consort of Tiamat, the dragon goddess of space—tears out the right thigh (Maskheti,* i.e., Ursa Major) of the Bull of Heaven and flings it in the face of the goddess Ishtar who appears on the walls of Uruk.[2] Now Ishtar and Ursa Minor appear to be synonymous, while Uruk seems to be derived from Ur-*akh,* meaning the peripheral heaven world (i.e., the demiurgic firmament), home of the primordial divine spirits of *our* own (Pleiadic) system. Ursa Minor—as the axle of our local World Wheel—was itself seen in other myths as being towed around in circles by the seven oxen of Ursa Major,[3] whose orbit within the greater sphere is, however,

---

*The name Maskheti appears to be derived from the compound root words *meskh,* meaning "to unite" (hence our English word *mesh*), and *ti,* a widely found ancient word meaning the "heaven world." Thus Ursa Major appears to have been seen as representing the driving mechanism between the higher and lower heaven worlds.

**FIGURE 2.7. THE DENDERA ZODIAC WITH TA'URT HOLDING
URSA MINOR AT THE CELESTIAL POLE**

of very considerable extent and also set at a markedly different angle to the plane of the celestial equator. As Ursa Major could not be sensibly regarded as towing Ursa Minor around if contained within the same celestial sphere of existence, it follows that it must (according to the Ancients, at least) belong to the next wider sphere of Being—that is, that of the zodiacal ocean.

In the ancient Hindu tradition, we correspondingly find the story of the celestial sage Aurva (or Aur-Ba), who, persuaded by his friends to beget children, does so by producing from his thigh (symbolic of Ursa Major) an all-devouring divine flame in the shape of a horse's head (symbolic of Ursa Minor). However, in order to save his own part of Creation from imminent destruction, the great god Brahma has to place this horse's head at Badava-Mukha—the mouth of the ocean[6] (i.e., the zodiacal ocean surrounding our Taurean sphere)—at which point we find the star Polaris in the constellaton of Ursa Minor.

The True Cycle of Obliquity of the Ecliptic Pole

It would seem that the time it takes for Alcyone to complete a complete orbital cycle around Taurus, relative to the pole of the ecliptic in Draco—and thus for the ecliptic pole to wander to its full distance away and then back again—is in fact marginally under 81,500 years. Rather interestingly, this figure coincides pretty well exactly with that arrived at by simply multiplying the cycle of the Great Year (25,920 years) by π. That in turn suggests that here also lies the reason for π being the primary (mathematical) reference point for all cycles affecting all sidereal bodies (both stars and planets) within our home universe as a whole. But fig. 2.8 provides us with a geometrical explanation

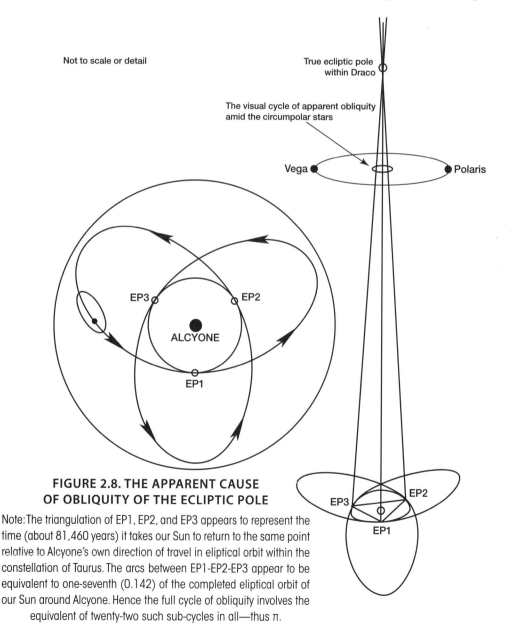

FIGURE 2.8. THE APPARENT CAUSE OF OBLIQUITY OF THE ECLIPTIC POLE

Note: The triangulation of EP1, EP2, and EP3 appears to represent the time (about 81,460 years) it takes our Sun to return to the same point relative to Alcyone's own direction of travel in eliptical orbit within the constellation of Taurus. The arcs between EP1-EP2-EP3 appear to be equivalent to one-seventh (0.142) of the completed eliptical orbit of our Sun around Alcyone. Hence the full cycle of obliquity involves the equivalent of twenty-two such sub-cycles in all—thus π.

FIGURE 2.9. THE "THREE LEGS OF MAN," SYMBOL OF THE ISLE OF MAN

for this, while at the same time perhaps otherwise serving to supply the rationale for the three-legged cross—the (Celtic) symbol of the Isle of Man, just off the northwest coast of England.

What is depicted in fig. 2.8 involves our solar system orbiting three and one-seventh times around Alcyone, during just over three Great Year cycles, at the end of which the ecliptic pole visually returns to its original position. The letters EP1, EP2, and EP3 thus signify the three apparently varying positions from which the ecliptic pole is seen by us during the cycle of obliquity. It would otherwise appear that, during this cycle, the ecliptic pole and the celestial pole might very well visually coincide—something orthodox astronomical opinion would currently regard as altogether impossible. It also seems not unlikely that this overall cycle of obliquity and the consequently changing sidereal view of Orion from Earth lay behind the ancient Egyptian depiction (in the temple of Dendera) of the twenty-three funeral positions of Osiris.*

Now rather interestingly to be found in the Greek tradition is the story of Alkyoneus, who was a giant and leader of the Earthborn who were described as trying to invade the very home of the gods. In their efforts, two of the Earthborn giants—sons of Aloios (i.e., El-Eos)—piled Mount Pelion on top of Mount Ossa in order to cross over to Olympus.[4] Thus Ossa symbolically represents the seventh and lowest kosmic state, Pelion the sixth, and Olympus the fifth (as shown in fig. 1.3). Piling the sixth on top of the seventh was meant to indicate that the lowest kosmic world was able to extend its consciousness beyond both its own state and the next one above it. However, by virtue of the fact that Ossa is a merely corrupted version of Ursa and Pelion, similarly of

---

*This is a great curiosity. Twenty-three is a prime number that fits into no known astronomical cycle. Interestingly, however, we sometimes find (see appendix C) the dancing figure of Siva Nataraja, in the Hindu tradition, surrounded by an aura of twenty-three flames, while holding an originating twenty-fourth in his left hand, *within* the aura (Dowson, *A Classical Dictionary of Hindu Mythology,* 32). As the concept of a heavenly circle of flame (the crystal sphere) was common to many ancient mystic cultures, can this be regarded as mere coincidence?

Bel-Aeon* (i.e., the celestial sphere containing Draco), the myth is clearly intended to describe the parallel fact that Draco actually lies one celestial stage beyond that within which we find Ursa Minor, with Ursa Major orbiting around and just above the latter.

Ancient Egyptian Symbolism of the Poles

There has, over many decades, been much heated discussion on the issue of the true extent of ancient Egyptian knowledge of astronomy. Orthodox Egyptology (with its curiously complete absence of interest in archaeoastronomy) prefers to see such knowledge as having been imported from Chaldea during the second half of the third millennium BCE. However, this view flies in the face of the fact that all sorts of astronomical references (particularly concerning the circumpolar stars) have been found in the very earliest known sacred texts in Egypt and that all the Nile temples were very precisely oriented toward the heliacal rise of specific stars. In addition, Egyptologists—because of their head-in-the-sand attitudes toward sacred allegory and metaphor—tend to miss all sorts of other pointers to far older traditions.

As an example of these, the two images shown in fig. 2.10 on page 52 ostensibly depict the god Horus on a hunting expedition, spearing crocodiles and hippopotami from his boat. That is generally how they are interpreted by Egyptologists, to show the Egyptian love of the hunt. However, nobody in their right mind would dream of trying to kill either of these thoroughly ferocious and unpredictable wild animals in this way, or they would very quickly pay for their stupidity with their life. In fact, there can be no doubt whatsoever that the pictures are purely symbolic. The one showing Horus spearing the crocodile would appear to be representative of the pole of the ecliptic,[†] whereas that showing Horus spearing the hippopotamus would correspondingly be symbolic of the celestial pole.

---

*The name Bel appears to have been derived from Ba-El (the lesser celestial soul heaven of the demiurgic Elohim), which became the absurdly demonic Baal of the Old Testament. Paranoid Christian theologians have managed to distort this even further in their eternal search for various aspects of Satan, a name itself derived from the Sanskrit *shaitan,* meaning an elemental being, predominantly associated with the Hindu god Agni. From the name Bel there originates the story of Belle and the Dragon—hence the story of St. George slaying the beast and rescuing the fair maiden—which has even managed to pass down through English history into the name given to an English public house, namely "The Bell and Dragon." All of these, however, have a common astro-mystic origin in the sacred allegories attributed to the nature and movement of the circumpolar constellations. According to the *Hermetica,* quoted more extensively on this topic in chapter 4, Aeon "is the power of God. . . . The kosmos is encompassed by the Aeon. The Aeon imposes order on matter, putting immortality and duration into matter."

†It may well be that the European Renaissance image of St. George (a.k.a. St. Michael) slaying the dragon by spearing it through the neck or head with his lance is a straight copy of this.

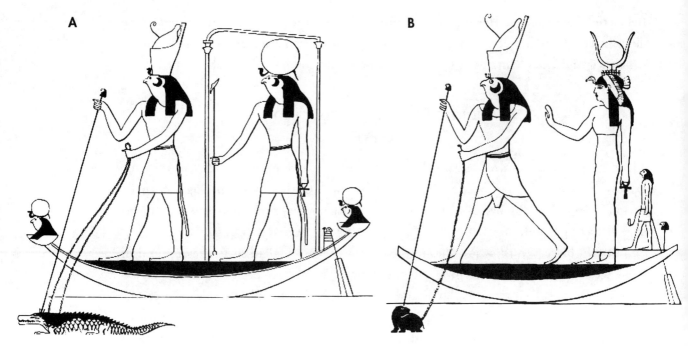

FIGURE 2.10. (A) HORUS SPEARING THE CROCODILE, SYMBOLIC OF THE POLE OF THE ECLIPTIC, AND (B) HORUS SPEARING THE HIPPOPOTAMUS, SYMBOLIC OF THE CELESTIAL POLE

The Great Fall and Return via the Poles

We turn finally in this chapter to the functional relevance, in the ancient traditions, of the poles to the sequence of the great involutionary "fall from Grace" and the subsequent evolutionary cycle of redemption of those divine beings involved in the whole process. In considering this question it needs to be remembered how the Ancients believed that in the great downward spiral cycle of the kosmic Life wave, many different hierarchies of Being appeared out of their own latent soul state and, by joining with it, gave rise to the unfoldment of one great semicoordinated mass of unified Being. The critical points in the overall cycle were seen by reference to the position of our solar system during the Great Year, relative to the plane of the Milky Way and the location of our Taurean system within the zodiac, these being roughly as shown in fig. 2.3. In the many mythic allegories and metaphors available to us today, it would appear that the overall downward sequence was seen somewhat as follows.

First of all, those lesser god-souls, emanating and thus falling from the heavenly firmament of the zodiacal sphere, seem first to have appeared at the ecliptic pole and then to have descended into the plane of the Milky Way by, as it were, slithering down the body of Draco at that point in cyclical time when its tail was seen as dangling in the river of light. Thereafter, these god-souls (represented in the mass in the Egyptian tradition as the body of Osiris cast into the Nile in a coffin) circulated around within the plane of the

Milky Way until they came into contact with that point at which the plane of zodiacal constellations actually crossed its path at an angle. At this vortex point, they were then swept downward into the next lower plane of existence, this seemingly occurring close to the constellation of Leo; for as the philosopher Macrobius claimed:

> So long as the souls heading downwards still remain in Cancer, they are considered in the company of the gods, since in that position they have not yet left the Milky Way. But when in their descent they have reached Leo, they enter upon the first stages of their further condition. . . . The soul descending from the place where the zodiac and the Milky Way intersect, is protracted in its downward course from a sphere—which is the only divine form—into a cone . . . [i.e., a vortex].[5]

Bearing in mind this quotation from Macrobius, it is interesting to note that the same tradition from which he drew his knowledge seems also to have associated the constellation of Crater (the bowl of Dionysus/Bacchus), situated just between Leo and Cancer, with the fall, for it was here that the descending god-souls were described as becoming infected with Lethe, the sleep of forgetfulness (of their divine origins). To this we might add the observation that Cancer is astrologically the sign in which the noumenally dual energies of Gemini were seen as becoming phenomenally semiseparated twin souls.

This latter duality was traditionally regarded as generating the process of man's own final, objective manifestation. In addition, astrologers even today associate the next house, ruled by the constellation of Leo, with childbirth and children. The ancient Egyptians correspondingly saw their festival of Zep Tepi (the time of the "great return of the gods")—which took place during the Age of Leo—as indicative of this same by now inherent dualism, in the symbolic form of the god Ak'r, the two-headed sphinx. Consequently, the final sequence of objective kosmic manifestation did not occur until the involutionary (i.e., downward) cycle was relatively close to the point of moving from Leo to Virgo and thus entering the Duat.

In another corresponding Greek tradition, this same duality seems to have been depicted in the form of the divine mother-daughter relationship of Demeter and Persephone. The latter—representing the lower (astro-terrestrial) soul principle—was dragged down into the Underworld where, as Hades' wife, she was given the alternative name Kore; it appears to have been some of her offspring—thereby known as the Korebantes (or Corybantes)—who then became the wild, elemental followers of the god Dionysus-Bacchus. Her Babylonian counterpart, Ishtar, representing the Divine Soul principle, when following her daughter down into Hades to demand her return, was depicted as having to divest herself, in sequence, of seven parts of her clothing, symbolic of the seven states of *solar* being comprising the *kosmic* Underworld.

Celestial Snakes and Ladders

As one can very quickly see from an astronomical map of our local sidereal environment, Draco is by no means the only constellation depicted as a serpent or associated with serpents (or dragons). It is also highly doubtful that Draco was seen as the only serpent-like constellation in which some sort of progressive fall of higher beings into lower states occurred. Thus, bearing in mind that the angled orbital pathways described by various solar and planetary schemes were seen as celestial ladders, up which the god-soul could pass back into higher states of being, it seems not unlikely that our modern children's game of snakes and ladders was actually derived from this most ancient of mystic traditions.

Now, bearing in mind that what we have seen so far involves a cyclic fall of lesser god-souls first into the Milky Way and then downward into the zodiacal plane of existence, there inevitably came a point where the downward involutionary cycle was seen as coming to a halt and then to reverse, by virtue of sequential organization leading to evolution-oriented development. While the zodiac as a whole was undoubtedly seen as intimately involved in this great kosmic sequence of progressive differentiation, our primary concern must of course lie with the Taurean sphere of being within which our own home system is seemingly to be found. Nevertheless, it is also quite clear from various ancient traditions

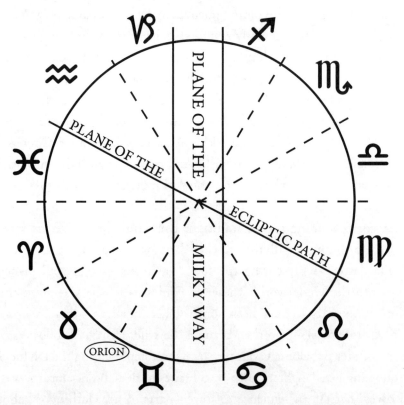

FIGURE 2.11. THERE WAS A MYSTIC OR METAPHYSICAL INTERRELATIONSHIP BETWEEN TAURUS AND THE IMMEDIATELY ADJACENT CONSTELLATIONS OF ARIES AND ORION.

around the world that there was some sort of mystic or metaphysical interrelationship between Taurus and the immediately adjacent constellations of Aries and Orion, which *jointly* gave rise to the phenomenon and sequence of evolutionary development, in which humankind's experience obviously plays a part. Before we consider this, however, let us take a brief look at Aries, the zodiacal constellation that precedes Taurus.

The Role of the Constellation of Aries

Aries precedes Taurus in the anticlockwise zodiacal sequence and it has traditionally been regarded as actually commencing the zodiacal round of the Great Year. However, there is good reason for this and it explains why the designation could in no way have been considered arbitrary. The essence of the idea seems to have derived from the directional orientation of our planet relative to the difference between the curvature of orbit of our solar system around Alcyone, on the one hand, and that of Alcyone around its own parent star, on the other. Hence the first degree of the sign of Aries was to be found located (see fig. 2.3) at that point just preceding the *celestial* spring equinox (at which time our Sun rises in Taurus) when Alcyone looks past our solar system directly toward its own parent star.* Hence at this point in the 25,920-year cycle, our solar system would have been deemed to stand in exact alignment between our Sun's own parent star (Alcyone) and the latter's own even greater orbital focus—although precisely which giant star this may have been, we can only speculate. Consequently, due to the resistance provided by Alcyone's position in astrological opposition, a direct stream of immensely potent celestial energy would have been seen as temporarily linking our system with the even greater cosmic influence at that time.

It is perhaps because of this cyclical linkage that in front of the outer pylon of so many of the major Egyptian temples—Thebes providing particularly good examples—we find the avenue of approach to the temple flanked on either side by dozens of inward-facing giant ram or sphinx statues on large pedestal bases. It would consequently appear that Aries the Ram did indeed govern the initial approach to the greater Mysteries. However, it was within the sphere of astrological influence of Taurus (and within the temple confines) that the truly first stage of the local fall was logically seen to take place.

The Role of the Sphere of Taurus

Taurus has always been associated by astrologers not only with wealth and power, but also with an associated, almost majestic stability. The macrocosmic metaphysical background to this, however, seems to lie in the fact that the glyph of Taurus also represented the principle of *containment,* in reality involving the incarceration of divine beings (*akhu*) with

---

*Thus astrologers who follow the sidereal or moving zodiac—as in Vedic astrology—as opposed to the tropical zodiac are mistaking the merely terrestrial spring equinox as the astrological determinant.

a potentially huge organic power of their own—hence making them symbolic of wealth and majesty. This same potential, however, was regarded as not yet developed in the main mass of humanity (due to ignorance) and it consequently lacked the faculty of *divine* self-consciousness. Consequently, so it would seem, the process of aggregation and preliminary definition of a divine self-awareness was seen as the evolutionary product of experience within the Taurean realm, before the cycle passed onward to Gemini and the greater duality of kosmic consciousness associated with the latter.

This concept is perhaps more readily understood if we draw an association here between the seven solar states of the Underworld—the lowest kosmic plane—as shown in fig. 2.12. Here we can see some of the clearly underlying symbolisms within the involutionary/evolutionary cycle of the zodiac. For example, the glyph of Aries represents not only the ram's head, but also the vortex within which the descending "divine sparks" fall into the lower world scheme from a higher kosmic dimension. This then evolves in the next downward stage, in Taurus, into the primordial soul principle, which actually *contains* the falling sparks. In Gemini, the generic soul principle evolved in Taurus develops an internal duality, which thereafter, in the Cancerian fourth stage, evolves into two lesser soul types. At the very bottom of the overall cycle, where the involutionary and evolutionary sequences meet and part, we then find Libra, representing the point of balance or equilibrium.* And so on via the ascending cycle.

The Constellation of Orion

Between Taurus and Gemini, however, lies the apparently non-zodiacal constellation of Orion, the Egyptian god-name of which—Sah(u)—clearly indicates that it was nevertheless seen as the expression of the unfolding god-Man principle (i.e., the spiritual soul) in the greater solar environment of our local universe, hence populated by superior gods who could fall no farther. These beings—seen as suspended in time and space pending the long delayed moment of their own upward liberation—were nevertheless deemed (passively and by sympathetic association) to influence the process of evolutionary development taking place within the Underworld sphere of existence, itself comprising in toto, as we have already seen (fig. 1.3), the lowest of the seven kosmic planes of Being. The very same principle was then to be found in microcosm within the subjective consciousness of the individual human being at the very heart of the Taurean sphere, within the constellation of the Pleiades. The latter, located within the neck or throat of the Taurean Bull of the Heavens, seems to have been seen as an environment in which the divine spark itself underwent a developmental transition between the heart and head consciousness of the Taurean Logos.

---

*For this reason, so it would appear, mankind on Earth was regarded as both the lowest manifest expression of Divinity and the pivotal fulcrum on which the balanced cycles of involution and evolution rested.

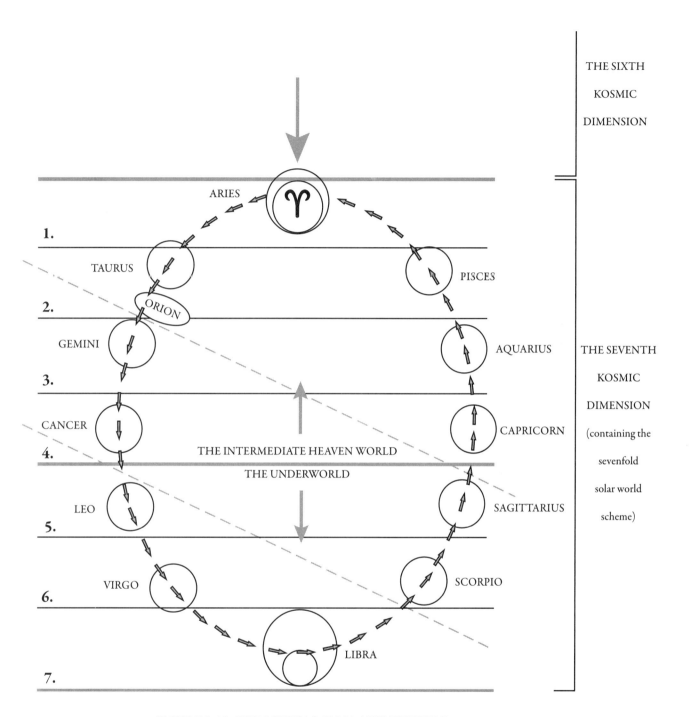

THE SIXTH
KOSMIC
DIMENSION

THE SEVENTH
KOSMIC
DIMENSION
(containing the
sevenfold
solar world
scheme)

ARIES

1.

TAURUS

PISCES

ORION

2.

GEMINI

AQUARIUS

3.

CANCER

CAPRICORN

4.

THE INTERMEDIATE HEAVEN WORLD

THE UNDERWORLD

LEO

SAGITTARIUS

5.

VIRGO

SCORPIO

6.

LIBRA

7.

FIGURE 2.12. THE ASTROLOGICAL UNDERWORLD

Note: The completion of the downward (involutionary) cycle in the Underworld from Leo to Libra represented the reincarnation of the various unfulfilled aspects of the solar god-man's own lower self-expression, left over from the previous incarnation. This was itself paralleled in purely human terms by the tradition that the individual only "came of age" at the age of twenty-one, after completing three periods of seven years, only thereafter being ready to resume his properly evolutionary spiritual journey. Here we also see why it was that the zodiacal sign of Cancer (symbolizing the mediating fourth state—that of the Kosmic Ka, or "Double") was regarded by the Ancients as the "Gate of (Spiritual) Death," while Capricorn was correspondingly regarded as the "Gate of (Spiritual) Life."

A further inference of the relationship between Taurus and Orion seems to be inherent in our modern (rather travestied and cruel) Iberian tradition of the bullfight, where the bull, egged on by the matador, passes close by him sequentially on either side while he himself remains more or less in the same position, merely turning to face the animal. If this association is correct, it would suggest that the Ancients actually perceived the sphere of Taurus elliptically orbiting the constellation of Orion. It may well be that the sport of bull-leaping practiced in ancient Crete also had the same origin, as previously mentioned.

An Astrological Question Mark

Before we move on, it might be worthwhile pausing here a moment in order to clear up a point of potential confusion. In fig. 2.12, Taurus is shown as being directly connected with the second (semidivine) of the seven solar states,* and as we have already heard, our own solar system is supposedly located *within* the constellation of Taurus. Yet the twelvefold zodiacal progression is shown as specifically related to each of the sevenfold states in very distinct succession. Now, if the Ancients believed that each zodiacal constellation had a specific function in the progressive involutionary/evolutionary unfoldment of a greater Divine Purpose, how could they simultaneously believe that, while still located within Taurus in the early stages of the overall cycle, humankind on our tiny Earth could still be astrologically influenced by all the other zodiacal constellations? How could the Life in one state be influenced by the Life in a completely different state at the other end of the solar spectrum?

The answer to this perfectly reasonable question lies in the Ancients' belief in the power of sympathetic association as a matter of incontrovertible fact, in conjunction with the idea that everything in the universe contained within itself a partial reflection of everything else. In other words, there was a sevenfold/twelvefold cycle *within* the field of the Taurean sphere of being, which was itself a microcosm of the zodiac. And, in fact, the same principle held good for every single constellation. Thus, because there was but one great, overriding Kosmic Purpose, the life cycle of which was passing constantly through the field of the zodiac, all shared simultaneously (even if differently) in its unified consciousness. It might also be worth mentioning that, while we think of these seven great states of solar Being as far apart, to the hugely greater perception of an Intelligence already evolved far beyond the somewhat pitiful human state, they would appear not only close together, but also physically and interactively integrated. Perceptual consciousness is a very relative faculty with no ultimately impermeable book-ends to contain it.

---

*The ancient Assyrians had Taurus as the second month of their year and called it A-aru.

The Ancient View of Consciousness

It is also worth noting in passing that, while the principles of Life and Consciousness were ever seen as in perpetual circulation, they were also perceived as complementary, in the sense of moving in opposite directions—something that we find again surfacing in astrological terms. To the Ancients, the Life cycle of the Logos (the Demiurge) moved anticlockwise and was accompanied by the singular Awareness (*not* Consciousness) of the associated hierarchies of gods and demigods involved in steering it and inflexibly maintaining its course in line with Divine Purpose. However, the dualistic principle of Consciousness—the subjective uncertainty or doubt of the greater Logos behind the scenes being objectively expressed by man in his sense of individualized identity—was seen as following a simultaneously *clockwise* direction of travel and was also essentially centrifugal in Nature—hence self-centered.

These two accompanying universal principles were clearly perceived by the Ancients as having a macrocosmic sidereal expression; for, as we have already seen in the case of modern science's false impression of the Great Year, the greater and lesser kosmic bodies all orbit in an anticlockwise direction. Man's self-centered and ignorantly Earth-centric view, on the other hand, perceives the very opposite, notwithstanding the fact that the heliocentric theory is now generally accepted. Not surprisingly, we find the general principle in all mystical systems of thought that when the immediately greater reality is experientially perceived, doubt vanishes and dualistic Consciousness per se is itself replaced by an all-embracing Awareness based upon certainty and resulting in unhesitatingly clear forward movement.

It would appear not illogical, however, that in the wider round of universal existence, even this must eventually be replaced by a yet greater doubt—which underlies the paradoxical proposition that one's field of ignorance grows exponentially with one's increasing wisdom. Hence the ancient proposition of the ancient philosopher that there were such things as fallen gods in the first place and that the very universe is itself an illusion arising out of the great "Doubt" of the One Unmanifest Deity behind it all.*

The Connection with the Ancient Mystery Schools and General Human Evolution

The reason for mentioning all this is that it underlies the ancient view that it was the perception of the interactive nature between Consciousness and Awareness that enabled man to evolve through his own self-motivation. Hence it was that the orientation of the Mystery

---

*It follows quite logically that if the omniverse exists within the limitless field of the Universal Mind of the Unknowable Logos (the Father) and if the Aeons are themselves the expression of that Mind, then our universe and every single form within it—whether macrocosmic or microcosmic—are themselves merely Ideas.

Schools—wherever in the world they were to be found—was directed toward focusing the individual's perceptual intelligence and sense of discriminating reason *inward* to his subjective nature. It was also specifically with the intent of demonstrating the distinction between Consciousness and Awareness that the Sufi and Zen schools, for example, concentrated their students' attention on the nature of paradox. Unsurprisingly, therefore, evolution itself was seen in predominantly subjective (i.e., psychospiritual) terms, resulting in the faculty of inner perception only subsequently becoming manifest in the physical nature and appearance.*

While this might seem almost Darwinistic in its general application, the Ancients took the view—as we shall see in more detail in later chapters—that man, although physically and temperamentally an apparent hybrid between the animal and god natures, was a quite distinctively different something else. In the words again of the *Hermetica:*

> For man is a being of divine nature; he is comparable not to the other living creatures upon Earth, but to the gods in heaven. Nay, if we are to speak the truth without fear, he who is indeed a man is even above the gods of heaven, or at any rate he equals them in power. None of the gods of heaven will ever quit heaven and pass its boundary and come down to Earth; but man ascends even to heaven and measures it. And what is more than all besides, he mounts to heaven without quitting the Earth. To so vast a distance can he put forth his power. We must not shrink then from saying that a man on Earth is a mortal god and that a god in heaven is an immortal man.[6]

The Connection Between Evolution and Spiritual Liberation

Returning to our main theme after this digression, it is perhaps helpful—when trying to get inside the general mind-set of the Ancients—to think of our Taurean home environment as merely a localized and temporary sphere of incarceration within the greater field of the zodiac. In that sense, the Taurean firmament—dominated by the circumpolar Ursa constellations—can be seen as but the *ba* (the astral soul) of a far greater scheme of kosmic Being. However, because the circumpolar stars were perceived by the Ancients as the first major rung on the sevenfold upper ladder of truly kosmic existence, it became the natural ambition and intent of the spiritually self-aware initiate in the Mystery School to attain to that high state by leaving behind the world of human existence—at least in terms of direct personal involvement in it.

Having apparently been hitherto dragged around in incessant cycles of reincarnate

---

*Hence the idea that the consciousness of each generation of humankind down the ages itself gives rise to genetic mutations in subsequent generations. Thus the biblical "sins of the fathers being visited upon their children's children unto the nth generation."

human existence within the planetary environment of the lower world scheme, it is perhaps not altogether surprising that we find in ourselves a sympathetic psychological response to the concept of liberation from the Wheel of Rebirth, as found in the Hindu and Buddhist traditions. However, the Ancients took the view that such an attitude on its own was entirely selfish and did not properly represent the true motivation of the god nature, which was actually one of self-abnegation and concern for all lesser creatures.

This idea is not merely one based upon the compassionate ideals of any particular religion, however. It clearly derived from the perception that the true god nature involved a continuing but altogether impersonal responsibility for promoting and steering the evolutionary development of a higher perceptual awareness in *all* the lesser kingdoms of Nature. Thus we also find in the Egyptian Pyramid Texts (if interpreted correctly) the idea that the self-made god (derived from the nature of the initiate) became responsible for seeing to the natural perfection even of the material expression of Divine Purpose in the lower world order—something unfortunately misrepresented by scholars as mere self-indulgence on his part upon reaching the heaven world.

Both of these (involutionary and evolutionary) functions were thus seen as complementary within the greater scheme of things, so that the metamorphosis of the lesser soul and spark in Nature into man and the subsequent spiritual development of the consciousness of man the human being into that of Man the demigod could take place. However, we shall deal with these issues in greater detail in chapters 4 and 5. Having in this chapter looked at the various individual parts and astronomical mechanisms that make up the organism of our local universe, we shall in the next chapter take a closer look at how they all appear to work together—although again, *as seen by the Ancients.* Because they deal with the interactive, metaphysical relationships between consciousness and different states of Being in a macrocosmic and microcosmic sense, some parts of the next chapter may prove rather complex for some readers. However, for the explanations they provide, they should prove to be well worth the struggle.

THREE

THE MULTI-SEVENFOLD
MILL OF THE GODS

*The forces which work in all events that befall men collectively come from
the Decans. . . . And besides this, my son, you must know that there is yet
another sort of work which the Decans do; they sow upon the Earth the seed of
certain forces, some salutary and others most pernicious, which the many call
"daemons." . . . Moreover, there are other stars also which travel in heaven
and obey the Decans, namely the so-called "Liturgi" . . . commanded by the
Decans (they) are borne along floating in the aether, filling all the region of
that element . . . and they help to maintain the order of the universe, putting
forth a force that is their own, but is subject to the force put forth by the six and
thirty Decans.*

HERMETICA

While we described in faint outline, in chapter 2, the ancient idea of a progressive fall from
Grace of various hierarchies of Being from one sphere of existence down into a lesser one—
followed by their subsequent return—we have not so far explained the detailed modus operandi of this overall (cyclic) process, except as a functional product of the yin-yang principle.
Indeed, it might seem almost impossible to do so. However, the Ancients took the view that
the sparks that thus fell were caught and contained within spherically organized soul-bodies,
the latter themselves being arranged in graded hierarchies of celestial being, having specific
family relationships with different planets and stars, or star groups.*

---

*Notwithstanding this, the Ancients well understood the principle of nonlocality—the fact that the Mind prin-
ciple is unrestrained by either time or space and can (if trained) thus project itself instantaneously from one
state of soul existence to another. This is something we moderns are only just beginning to reappreciate in the
fields of quantum science and psychology.

The consequent potpourri might seem to us altogether incoherent and mentally unmanageable. Nevertheless, the Ancients believed that the cyclical appearance and disappearance of these serried hierarchies of living beings varied in accordance with specific, astronomically observable changes of relationship as between the constellations, stars, and planets. It thus became possible to formulate a universe-wide science combining both astronomy and astrology, which rationally coordinated these organically and hierarchically arranged life cycles as between the immediate and wider sidereal environment. And it is this principle of sympathetic celestial association that we shall look at more closely in this chapter, in correspondence with the sevenfold principle, which the Ancients regarded as providing the very structure of Universal Creation in both the subjective and objective worlds of Being.

Threefold Being and the Sevenfold System of Planes of Consciousness

In the ancient metaphysical system of thought, the Creator-Deity (i.e., the Demiurge) comprised a unified hierarchy of Being, invested by its parental Unknowable Logos with a triplicity of fundamental aspects, or universal principles—Life, Consciousness, and the Creative Instinct, also known as the Will-to-Be, the Will-to-Know, and the Will-to-Create. This triple essence of the Creator-Deity became manifest as a Duality within the sphere of Creation, which then gave rise to the sevenfold principle, which applied to cycles, states of Being, and their associated hierarchies.

To the Ancients, the omniverse was an expression of Divine Law and that Law operated through consistently repetitive patterns, cycles, and systems, each of different magnitude but all inevitably having the same mathematical basis. However, greater and lesser cycles, systems, and patterns were able to interweave with each other in harmonious sequence to produce the ordered universe only because they were guided by the intelligent Will of the demiurgic hierarchies of gods of each associated kosmic or sidereal system.

Now while each demiurgic hierarchy—the Great Architect of the (local) Universe—was seen as doing the planning and guiding, it was not involved in the actual building processes that produced the many manifest forms in Universal Nature. Instead, it was regarded as continuously emanating (yin-yang fashion, throughout the cycle of its activity) two aspects of itself, thereby giving rise to the principle of a persistent Duality (and polarity) in Creation—"Creation" really being somewhat of a misnomer. These two aspects—being of its own nature—were themselves triple, each aspect of each triplicity being a lesser god hierarchy in its own right and thus self-manifesting as a noumenal sphere (*and state*) of Being. However, gathered together in a state of perfect balance within the parent demiurgic sphere of existence, stasis would have supervened and further Creation been arrested

FIGURE 3.1. THE "MILL OF THE GODS"

Note: This relief shows the kosmic Set (symbolizing the principle of kosmic individuality) and Horus (symbolizing the principle of self-consciousness) jointly involved in rotating the augur of creative Kosmic Desire (of the demiurgic Logos, symbolized by Kheper-Ra) and thereby inseminating the Will-to-Be within the *ka* of space (symbolized by the open arms at the bottom of the cartouche), which rests upon the upper handle of the augur.

had not each of these six lesser god natures contributed one aspect of its being to a seventh, hitherto unmanifest, sphere of equal size, rotating between and touching them all in perfect regularity, as with the decans.*

---

*By way of direct correspondence, we find in the Nordic Creation epic, the Kalevala (as quoted by de Santillana and von Dechend, *Hamlet's Mill,* 97), the virgin goddess Ilmater (i.e., the Great Mother Goddess), daughter of the Aether, descending to the surface of the great waters of space (like the Spirit of the Elohim moving upon the waters in Genesis)—that is, to the uppermost periphery of the lowest of the seven kosmic planes of Being. Here she remains for seven hundred years (i.e., seven great cycles) until Ukko (i.e., *akhu*), the Nordic Father-God, sends a bird (not unlike the Egyptian Bennu phoenix bird) to her. The bird builds its nest between her knees and lays in it seven eggs, from which there then emerges the objective (sevenfold) world state—that is, of our home universe.

The Crucial Fourth State and the Principle of the Double

As we saw in chapter 1, the youngest of the lesser god spheres—having been formed by the interactive cyclic motion of the other six—effectively became the intervening principle that both separated and connected the two triple dualities. Consequently, this intervening sphere and state acted as a passively reflective double (or *ka*) of the parent octave.* Thus we arrive at the image in fig. 3.2, which depicts seven planes or states of being and consciousness contained within that of the Demiurge of whatever system may be under consideration, whether kosmic, sidereal, or planetary.[†]

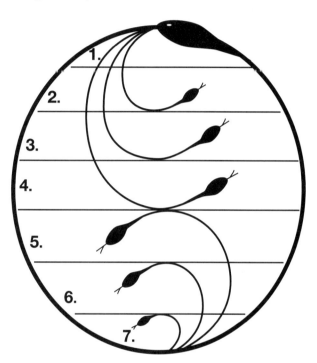

FIGURE 3.2. SEVEN PLANES OR STATES OF BEING AND CONSCIOUSNESS CONTAINED WITHIN THAT OF THE DEMIURGE OF THE SYSTEM— WHETHER KOSMIC, SIDEREAL, OR PLANETARY

Although described here, for merely illustrative purposes, in a purely two-dimensional or linear manner, these various states and substates of being and consciousness all eventually became intermingled and interassociated (metaphorically as divine or semidivine beings in the various mystic cultures) according to their varying degrees of subtlety. The

---

*Because the *ka* is a universally recurring principle, it is to be found at the heart of every seventh or lowest state (or substate) within a septenary system of being or consciousness, acting as the agent of distribution of energies within each such system. In the human, *ka* is the etheric double (essentially an unorganized substratum of universal substance that relies entirely upon *ba,* the astral soul, for its organization, stimulation, and direction), while the world *ka* is a universal fluid medium/agent (i.e., the ether). (A more detailed discussion and explanation of *ba* and *ka* can be found in chapter 6.)

†The image of a higher three states of being imposing themselves upon a lower four states of material existence is fundamental to the design and shape of the Egyptian pyramid. Hence also the Aztec Chicomoztoc—the Cavern of the Seven Chambers of Creation.

FIGURE 3.3. *KA* SYMBOLIZED BY OPEN UPSTRETCHED ARMS

fourth state (the *ka*)—the being that expresses the principle of light—then became the secondary source of illuminated self-expression *within* the sphere of being.

A final point to be borne in mind is that the Ancients saw the principle of duality as expressing itself in forms of Spirit and Matter, knowledge and ignorance, intuitive perception and instinct, or light and darkness. Hence that which descended from the positive pole of the demiurgic sphere represented the former, while that which ascended from the negative pole represented the latter. Thus, while the sevenfold principle underlay the whole structure of Creation, whether in the macrocosm or the microcosm, the intervening fourth state (the *ka*) was regarded as representing the intermediate vehicle of higher perceptual consciousness *and* the central area of expression of all psychosensory faculties. Consequently, that which descended from this intermediate state into the lower three first took the form of individualized mind-knowledge within the fifth state and then desire for its expression in the sixth. The seventh and lowest state (the physical Underworld) then became the *objective* field of that expression in conjunction with the influence produced by the negative pole of the demiurgic nature. It consequently became a septenary entity in its own right—a nevertheless somewhat distorted microcosm of the Macrocosm. By ancient tradition, exactly the same principle is then found on Earth and in incarnate mankind—as we shall see later.

Now it might appear to some readers that all this looks far too mechanistic to be properly associated with the expression of Divine Purpose in the universe. However, the Ancients were very certain in their application of the "As below, so above" principle that, the universe being a living organism, *everything* within it, *without exception,* had to be subject to exactly the same laws. The very same principles of circulation would thus have been applied by them throughout the greater and lesser soul-spheres of the local system, thereby showing the concentrically organized universe to be a gigantic commutator of Life, Consciousness, and Creative Instinct in eternally cyclic activity.

In astronomical terms, this same cyclically operative sequence of insemination and liberation of different hierarchies of Life must have been considered as continuous throughout the mass of visible and invisible galaxies, nebulae, and individual solar systems, in accord with the intelligent will of the guiding demiurgic hierarchies of each such system. However, our concern lies with our own home universe within the field of the Milky Way galaxy, insofar as it can be seen to relate to Man. Consequently, we shall restrict ourselves to considering the interrelated sequence that the Ancients evidently saw as taking place within the spheres of influence of the zodiac, the constellation of Taurus, and the Pleiades.

The Life Wave Cycle

One of the main expressions of this septenary principle in the ancient Egyptian system was the Duat, formed by the undulating movement of the divine Life wave (the "barque of millions of years" of the god Ra), down through seven states of existence and then returning through them back to its point of origin. However, the Egyptians saw the sevenfold principle as absolutely fundamental to the whole sequence of the great kosmic fall of the gods (and of man) and their subsequent restoration to the state of heavenly Grace through the medium of our astronomically organized home universe. So that is what we shall now take a closer look at, although first briefly considering the operational nature of the astrological decans previously mentioned in chapter 1.

FIGURE 3.4. RA'S "BARQUE OF MILLIONS OF YEARS"

The Multi-
Sevenfold
Mill of the Gods

The Operating Gear Mechanism of the Decans

In the first chapter, we saw how both the concentric and septenary principles operated as a result of the gearing function of the decans.* However, it should become obvious from considering fig. 1.2 that at certain points—even in a purely mechanical sense—some sort of magnetic traction would occur between two adjacent spheres of Being in temporary contact with each other, particularly when seen as divinely electrified rings of fire. Thus this same divine activity—the metaphorical "war in heaven"—was seen as giving rise to the appearance of sparks emanating from the peripheral flame of the heavenly firmament; and, following an old established electrical principle, it was ever the greater electrical potential that attracted the greater charge, in Nature's attempt to maintain an overall equilibrium. Consequently, the less powerful soul-sphere cyclically absorbed some of the Life energy of the adjacent, more powerful soul-sphere, and this transfer was deemed to take place—as it does in our electrical science—at the poles.

It is here then, one might suggest, that we see the decans of the outer sphere sowing the divine seeds of their karmic nature (i.e., the daemons or divine spirits, the Egyptian *akhu*) into the lesser spheres of existence that they encircle. But this same fall was regarded as progressive—first into the plane of the galaxy (the Milky Way, also known as the Pilgrims' Way), then downward into the plane of the zodiac and then yet further on into our own home area of the local universe, within the constellation of Taurus. As far as the Ancients were concerned, this same downward transfer or fall of kosmic and sidereal Life energies (i.e., of the *akhu*) from the zodiacal sphere took place at the magnetic pole of our local universe—which we saw earlier as being directly associated with the constellation of Draco.

The Fixity of the Stars

In the ancient Egyptian Mystery Tradition we come across the constantly repeated idea that the successful initiate of the higher orders—having fully recovered the memory of his divine nature, which had been lost in the fall and thereafter, having left behind his merely human nature—became a fixed star in the heavens, there to remain and revolve in celestial splendor for the remainder of eternity, ensuring the continuity of Divine Purpose. In addition, medieval astrologers talked about the (zodiacal) ring of fixed stars. But what are these traditions trying to convey to us?

---

*The continuing movement within the lesser sphere of existence occurs as a result of simple harmonic motion. However, the driving force—like that of the coiled spring within a clock mechanism—is (according to the ancient metaphysical system of thought) that of the Mind principle. That is to say, the Mind—by its concentration or relaxation, either autonomically or as a result of applied will-force—acts exactly like a coiled spring. Thus, in the view of the Ancients, it was the principle of focused mental attentiveness that enfolded the soul principle within its auric embrace and so induced it, at will and by compression, to disgorge its store of knowledge—that is, to conceive. Thus the Mind itself does not create. It merely initiates, sustains, organizes, discriminates—and terminates the cycle of Creation, merely by enfolding the Soul and applying selective pressure upon it.

In chapter 1 we questioned the idea that all stars always stay eternally and exactly fixed in the same place relative to each other, even though many may remain fixed in relation to the axially and orbitally revolving sidereal sphere of which they form a part. Thus, at certain cyclic points it might well appear to us from our own constantly changing visual vantage point in space that some constellations periodically approach and separate—although often over vast periods of time. The ancient tradition of this happening in relation to Ursa Major and Ursa Minor is perhaps the best known. In at least one such tradition (the Arabic), our local universe was regarded as the "mill of the gods," with Ursa Major as the driving mechanism and Ursa Minor as the axle.[1]

Ta'Urt and Sebek-Draco—the Circumpolar Deities

As described in chapter 2, the heavenly atomic periphery, or World Soul-body of our Taurean home universe, was symbolically represented in Egypt by the ever pregnant hippopotamus goddess Ta'Urt, the concubine of the kosmic Set,* while the associated Kosmic Mind principle enfolding it was depicted in the form of the crocodile god Sebek (symbolized by the giant constellation of Draco) climbing upon her back. As we have already also seen, this symbolically depicts the fact that Draco appears to belong to a greater (although concentrically sequential) sphere of kosmic Being than our own.

FIGURE 3.5. IN THE DENDERA ZODIAC THE FIGURE OF THE JACKAL OF SET EXTENDS OUTWARD FROM THE WEDGE-SHAPED PLUG HELD BY TA'URT.

---

*In telling of the Phoenician Creation myth, the historian Damascius used the name Tauthe to signify Chaos—which is precisely the subjective nature of the Demiurge (and of the Set principle) as otherwise depicted by the Egyptians. However, Ta'Urt was the wayward concubine of the *kosmic* Set, who—like the biblical Seth—was regarded by the Egyptians as a benevolent deity.

In the Dendera zodiac we otherwise see extending outward from the wedge-shaped plug held by Ta'Urt the figure of the Jackal of Set, which represents (in physical terms) the constellation of Ursa Minor. As we also saw earlier, the Ancients viewed Ursa Minor as true North (as far as we on Earth are concerned), this therefore being upright when considered in either physical or metaphysical terms. It was consequently seen as representing the home of the greater kosmic gods of the immediate system, who directed and managed the affairs of our local kosmic atom within the wider universe*—as implied by the fact that the Jackal of Set is rigidly fixed in situ on a nautical sextant, rather like a weather vane on a church steeple, registering (via its associated outward-looking consciousness) the direction of every passing breeze.

Esoteric Implications of Certain Constellations

Having looked in fairly general terms at our local universe, let us now consider some of the individual constellations in rather more detail, from the viewpoint of the metaphorical and allegorical associations attached to them by ancient tradition. In addition to Draco, Ursa Minor, and Ursa Major, we shall also consider Orion, Sirius, the Pleiades, and the Hyades, for all of these appear to have been seen as involved in one colossal and sequentially interkosmic relationship.

The Constellation of Draco

To one side of the northern arc of the celestial atom, we come across the ecliptic pole, the cosmic equivalent of our planet's magnetic pole, the latter being, we shall recall, represented in one sense by the leaning Djed Pillar. Surrounding this apparently starless point in the heavens lies the semicoiled constellation of Draco (which was symbolized in ancient times by the dragon, or winged serpent, as well as by the cosmic crocodile), with its head (currently) pointing away from Ursa Minor and its body and tail extending toward it at an angle (see fig. 2.4). However, as we saw earlier, the Dragon's body seemingly rotates on a different axis to the circumpolar constellations of Ursa Minor and Lyra, and thus, during part of the greater cycle, it could well be that part of it hangs down the side of the celestial atom in such a manner that the end of its tail would appear to dip into the plane of either the Milky Way or the solar horizon.

---

*As Richard Hinckley Allen tells us in his book *Star Names* (456), in relation to the religious focus placed on Ursa Major by the peculiar mystic sect known as the Mandeans or Nasoreans—respectively derived from the Egyptian god Mntw and the word Nasr (meaning "follower of the sacred serpent")—"the sky is an ocean of water, pure and clear but of more than adamantine solidity, upon which the stars and planets sail." However, this is merely yet another variant on the crystal sphere/firmament of our home universe. The Nasoreans appear to have been the same as, or closely related to, the Essenes—who were among other things known as Nasars. From this appears to have been derived the idea that the biblical Jesus was a Nazarene.

There are a variety of ancient traditions concerning this largest and slowest-moving of the circumpolar constellations. In the ancient Persian it was known as Azdeha (the man-eating serpent)*[2] from which the fearsomely warlike Babylonian goddess Ishtar, the Egyptian Isis (as As't), and the Indo-Persian Ahura Mazda seem to have derived their names, the prefix *az* itself being synonymous with the Sanskrit root word *as,* meaning "the state of primordial Being into which the higher kosmic Impulse falls." As Az in the Zoroastrian tradition, it rather appropriately appears to have become associated with kosmic greed or lust, enveloped in a blazing fire, a characteristic conveyed upon Ahriman (the demonic Tempter) by the Demiurge, Zurvan.[3]

Although these days generally regarded as having sixteen stars, the main astronomical images of Draco in antiquity may perhaps have involved a rather longer form of constellation than that now known to us, at a time when it was apparently seen as enfolding both Ursa Minor and Ursa Major within its coils. Surrounding and enfolding Draco itself was also supposed to exist the visually imperceptible form of the Egyptian goddess Net (sometimes translated as Necht or Neith), the wife of the greatest god of all, Amen-Ra, and mother of both the *kosmic* Horus gods and the *neteru* gods,[4] the latter seemingly having derived their name from her. Of the various stars in this constellation, the brightest was Alpha Draconis (known to us as Thuban). It was called by the ancient Akkadians of Chaldea Tir-an-na—the Life of Heaven—and also Dayan Sidi or Dayan Shisha.†[5] This star, the third from last in the dragon's tail, was cyclically visible by both day and night from the foot of the Descending Passage in the Great Pyramid and seems to have been the Pole Star at the *celestial* equivalent of the spring equinox on Earth.

The Constellation of Ursa Minor

Known to the people of Finland as Taehti (the Star at the Top of the Heavenly Mountain) and to the Egyptians as the Jackal of Set, Ursa Minor became the Throne of Thor to the Danish Vikings.‡ To the ancient Arabs, however, it was Al Rakabah[6]—a name seemingly derived from the multiple Egyptian Ra-*ka-ba,* meaning the combination of the kosmic

---

*The idea being that divine Man was the expression of the Kosmic Mind of the Unknowable Logos of the greater system. Thus Draco, in capturing and assimilating a portion of this, also "ate" Man. Rather interestingly, the Mayans of Central America seem to have had precisely the same idea for naming this constellation as the ancient Egyptians, for their crocodile god was Cipactli. However, after detaching the common local suffix *tli* and allowing for Anglo-Saxon pronunciation of the rest, Cipac phonetically mutates without hesitation into Sebek. This would appear to be something more than just mere coincidence.

†*Dayan* is the anglicized version of the Sanskrit *dhyan*(a), meaning "meditative" or "meditating," while Tir-an-na is strikingly similar to the Celtic heaven world of Tir-nan-oc.

‡Which surely—by virtue of the Polynesians having given their Pacific island home the selfsame name (as Tahiti)—must surely confirm beyond doubt the worldwide extent, in ancient times, of a common, astronomically based mystic-metaphysical culture. In addition, the name (as also with Thor) might itself be regarded as merely a localized form of Ta'Urt.

universal Life principle, the ethereal kosmic double, and the kosmic Oversoul, that which contains the world of sevenfold terrestrial being. The brightest star in Ursa Minor—our present Pole Star—is Polaris, which was commonly regarded as the celestial pivot or the center of the world axle of our local universe, which thus became the turning handle of the "mill of the gods"—with mankind as the "wheat" to be threshed and ground within the mill by the process of incarnatory experience in order to release the divine flour that lay naturally within it. The same handle became in Egypt the *apuat* tool used to open the mouth of Osiris, whereas in Greece it seemingly mutated into the sidereally metaphorical sickle, which Kronos used to cut off the phallus of his Titan father, Ouranos.

FIGURE 3.6. THE *APUAT* TOOL USED TO OPEN THE MOUTH OF OSIRIS

This constellation (or otherwise Vega at the other end of the Great Year cycle) was also known to the Assyrians as seven celestial maidens, "weavers" of sidereal light,[7] who lured passing kosmic beings into the webs of delight they spun out of it, in a manner not altogether dissimilar to the Greek myth of the Sirens who tried to lure Jason and the forty-nine other Argonauts onto an offshore reef.*

The Constellation of Ursa Major

The third major circumpolar constellation is Ursa Major, referred to by the Ancients as both the leg of the Heavenly Bull and also the Heavenly Hearse. The former of these names clearly associates it with the constellation of Taurus, which has ever been depicted by astrologers as minus a rear leg; the leg should have been located in the immediate vicinity of the constellation of Orion, for Taurus itself (at least currently) faces backward, toward Aries. However, it is the odd names and other associations that are of more immediate interest, because the ancient Egyptians showed the Heavenly Bull itself (minus a leg) firmly attached by an iron-linked chain to the hand of Ta'Urt. The consequent implication is that Ta'Urt (i.e., the World Soul-sphere of our Taurean home universe) *excludes* the missing leg, while the energy of the extra-cosmic Bull (i.e., the Taurean Logos) pulls the whole local system along in space.

The missing leg of the Bull of the Heavens seems to have been associated in the Greek tradition with the fact that the Celestial Bull (a form of Zeus) was depicted as swimming in the Great Sea (bounded by the zodiac); thus the hind leg was submerged. But as the

FIGURE 3.7. THE HEAVENLY BULL (MINUS A LEG) FIRMLY ATTACHED BY A CHAIN TO THE HAND OF TA'URT

*In the Greek myth, the Argonauts—who sailed in search of the Golden Fleece—were so called after their ship, the *Argo*. However, this looks to be another clear corruption of the word *akhu*—which thereby demonstrates another self-evident correlation with the Egyptian tradition, from which it was probably borrowed in the first place. The Greek story has the Argonauts endeavoring to sail safely between the two obstacles of Scylla and Charybdis, monster nymphs who respectively inhabited an adjacent cave (with glassy smooth sides) and a whirlpool, and who made a habit of eating passing cattle (McLeish, *Children of the Gods,* 62 et seq). However, these two images are actually but a symbolic combination of the local World Soul-body and the vortex entrance to it. The Sirens were themselves the children of the local river god Akhelos—a name that is probably derived from Ak-Hel-os or Akh-El-os.

hind leg provided the main source of locomotive power, so it seems to have been associated in the Egyptian tradition with Hp(i), the great god of the hugely powerful river and sea currents. And as the Bull's leg and Ursa Major were supposedly synonymous, so Ursa Major and Hp(i) appear to have been seen as directly associated.

Ta'Urt's own name also meant "maker of coffins"—that is, the undertaker.[8] Consequently the separated leg of the extra-cosmic Bull of Heaven (bitten off by Sebek, her partner) traditionally turned into a hearse containing the "bodies" of likewise *extra-cosmic* Beings. These divine spirits, or higher "divine sparks" (known to the Egyptians as *akhu*), were thus seen as having fallen from the field of Mind-consciousness of an altogether imponderable, overshadowing extra-cosmic Intelligence, yet having remained intact within the form of this vast and widely ranging orbital constellation. Hence the seven stars of Ursa Major were known in the ancient Indian cosmology as the Seven Rishis or All-Knowing Sages.

Now the "hearse" of Ursa Major cyclically travels in orbit around Ursa Minor—and thus also the present celestial North Pole—but its orbit was seemingly known in ancient times to be of a much freer nature than our modern astronomers appear aware. Hence—over many thousands of years—it was apparently seen (from Earth at least) to pass cyclically downward in the night sky, into and through the constellations of Orion and Taurus. It seems to have been this same apparent movement that gave rise to other ancient allegorical myths and also ritualized sacred memorials. Perhaps the most obvious of these involved the slaying of the Bull within the rites of the Mithraic cult. Another perhaps lies in connection with the origin of the sport of bullfighting in Spain—involving the Bull's leg turning into a sword and, held in the hand of Orion (acting as the matador), being plunged vertically downward between the shoulder blades of the constellation of Taurus, right through the center of the Pleiades. If indeed the Pleiades is our own home constellation, the esoteric implications of this would be dramatic, to say the least, because at least one tradition (the Hindu) had it that these two star groups were maritally associated.

The Mutual Revolutions of Ursa Major and Ursa Minor

In the late Celtic folk traditions of southwestern England we find the orbital movements of the two Ursa constellations around each other being symbolically represented in the "dance of the hobby horses." One variation of the tradition has but one hobby horse carried by a single man while accompanied by six other dancers (thereby all together representing the seven stars of Ursa Major),* while another involves two hobby horses, the dance

---

*In the Celtic tradition, Ursa Major seems to have been especially associated with debts—hence karma. In both this and the parallel tradition of the Drawing of the Plough (around the town/village), money was collected—or an unpleasant forfeit became payable, somewhat in the vein of the modern trick-or-treat practiced by children on All Hallows Night (Hutton, *Stations of the Sun,* 127).

FIGURE 3.8. MITHRAS AND THE BULL

According to Yuri Stoyanov, in *The Other God* (78), "The secret rites of the Mithraic Mysteries were celebrated in subterranean shrines, the 'mithraea,' which were supposed to mirror the cave in which Mithra Tauroctonus (the bull-sacrificer) was believed to have performed the central act of Mithraic ideology—the capture and murder of the primordial Bull of Heaven. The Mithraic temple was conceived as a 'world cave,' a symbol of the cosmos and among the cult reliefs adorning its walls the scene of the bull sacrifice, the 'tauroctonia,' was usually placed on the rear wall of the sanctuary and on the front of the altar."

of each around the town being quite separate from that of the other, far apart for some of the time, but quite close together during the rest,[9] just as occurs in the movements of the Great Bear and the Little Bear in the heavens, during their greater cycle. The actual expression *hobby horse* appears to have been derived from fairly ancient sources. *Hobby* seems to be a colloquial adaptation from the hugely powerful Egyptian Nile god Hp(i), while the common horse itself appears to be derived from Urs(a)—particularly the horse's head by which Ursa Minor was also often represented.

The Constellation of Orion

Probably derived from either Aur-Aeon or Ur-Aeon, Orion was known to the Hebrews as Gibbor, and to the ancient Syrians and Arabs as Gabbara and Algebra,[10] which—quite apart from the obvious mathematical association—seem to be localized versions of the Egyptian Geb-Ra, father of Osiris and Horus the Elder. As well as being associated with the tradition of Mithra(s) and the Bull* and that of the Egyptian alter ego of Osiris-Horus striding across the heavens, there are a number of other allegorical myths surrounding the figure of Orion in the night sky. One Greek myth, for example, associated Orion with the great hunter Actaeon (a name clearly derived, at least in part, from the Egyptian, i.e., as *akhet*-Aeon)† who saw the goddess Artemis bathing and was in revenge magically transformed into a stag whose own dogs—driven by her angry magic—then tore him to pieces,[11] just as the body of Osiris was cut into pieces by his brother Set. However, the esoteric idea within both allegories involves the originally unified consciousness of the *akhet*-Aeon being divided into separate creative hierarchies of gods and then dispersed.

Orion and the Giza Connection

On a home front, the world is by now very familiar with Robert Bauval's intuitive perception that the three pyramids at Giza are themselves representative of the three stars of Orion's Belt. What is not commonly understood, however, is the ancient metaphysical background of this association, which could perhaps be explained, relatively briefly, as follows.

First of all, the stellar figure of Orion—just like Ursa Major and Ursa Minor—is importantly composed of *seven* stars, laid out in the very distinct combination 2:3:2. This same combination seems to have represented to the Ancients: (a) the duality (within the lowest kosmic register) of the divine and semidivine states; (b) the triplicity of the lower (spiritual) heaven world; and (c) the duality of the Underworld. Just as importantly, the overall figure is split more or less in half by the celestial equator. This, however, viewed from our planet during its changing position amidst the hugely greater solar cycle, appears to move up and down, relative to Orion's Belt, which it currently runs straight through. More specifically, it at present runs through the gap between the smallest star (symbolized by the Menkaura pyramid at Giza) and the middle star (symbolized by the Khafra

---

*The Roman Mithraic tradition was derived originally from the demiurgic and hermaphroditic Mazdean god of light, Mithra, an Indo-Persian deity whose name and function may well have been synonymous with the combined Mut and (Amen) Ra, the mother-father god aspects of the presiding Egyptian trinity at Luxor-Karnak. Mithra—also connected with the ritual death of the Celestial Bull in the Iranian tradition—otherwise appears somewhat comparable to Indra in the Vedic system.

†The Egyptian word *akh(e)t* means "horizon"—not in the sense that we would use the term, but rather to denote the Divine Soul–body of the fallen (higher) gods, which was itself the emanative cause of time, or cyclic duration (Aeon). Thus *akhet*-Aeon (or Aur-Aeon), the hunter, symbolized the investigative consciousness of the higher fallen gods, who thus—through spiritual curiosity—fell further into segregated generation.

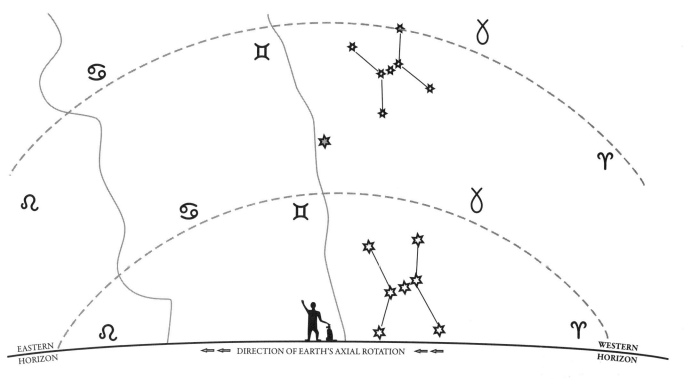

FIGURE 3.9. THE RISE AND FALL OF ORION DURING THE GREAT YEAR

Note: The lower zodiacal arc and constellation of Orion "standing" on the horizon represent the zenith of the Great Year—the celestial winter solstice. Correspondingly, the higher arc represents the celestial summer solstice, at the other end of the Great Year cycle. This is where we stand today.

pyramid). Now, as the celestial equator itself represented the "iron plate" considered to separate the lower celestial heaven world and the Underworld (the figure of Orion in turn representing the fallen kosmic Osiris), its cyclically changing location relative to the belt of three stars would have had great esoteric significance.*

Rather interestingly, it was the second and middle star in the Belt that was traditionally regarded by the Ancients as the repository of the sacred fire—that of the Promethean Mind principle. This star is also the fourth and central one in the overall figure and is thus, metaphysically, representative of the heart of the seven states of kosmic being that Orion represented. The influence of this fourth, mediating principle would thus have been regarded as working in both directions, separating and uniting the triple heaven world and the triple Underworld, thereby also acting as the engine driving the whole sevenfold scheme of solar being. Of even greater importance is the clearly held ancient view that the whole process of Creation involved the insemination of the Mind principle into Matter in

---

*The essence of the conceptual association seems to have been that the position of the celestial equator above or below the three stars defined whether the associated spiritual principles were manifesting generally in the Underworld—thus providing a cycle of opportunity for mankind's further spiritual development in the mass— or whether they had been temporarily withdrawn from action.

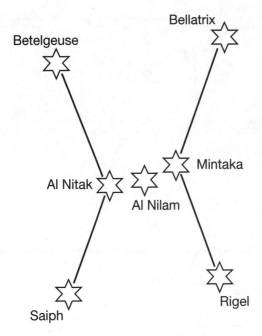

FIGURE 3.10. THE SEVEN STARS OF ORION, SHOWING THE 2:3:2 FORMATION,* WITH THE THREE CENTRAL STARS FORMING THE BELT

conjunction with Divine Purpose,[†] thereby leading to the evolution of a discriminating, hierarchically organized sense of intelligence and a consequent individualization of faculty and character—in man, the lesser god.

The Cyclical Inversion of Orion

In trying to undermine and ridicule Robert Bauval's idea that the Giza pyramids were intended by their builders to be initiatory temples representative of the three stars of Orion's Belt, much has been made by critics of the fact that there is an inversion of the two relative to each other. The argument against seems to stand on this sole fact. However, if one takes into consideration the angled path of our solar system in its orbit around its own parent star during the Great Year, as already described, it would naturally follow that the figure of Orion must cyclically become inverted from our viewpoint on Earth.

The reason for this is shown diagrammatically in fig. 3.11. In addition and by way of sympathetic confirmation, the fact that the Great Nebula of Orion is representative of the

---

*This configuration may well be behind the enigmatic statement in the Pyramid Texts (paragraph 2156, utterance 694) to the effect that: "The king is a bull . . . a trio in the sky and a pair on Earth." This would appear to define the separation of the three stars of Orion's Belt and the two lower stars, supposedly in the knees of the celestial figure. While the two highest stars, in the shoulders of the figure, appear to have been representative of the divine and semidivine states, the lower five represented the five kosmic planes of being and their associated elements. Now at least one ancient tradition had it that the celestial figure of Orion in the night sky was actually *inverted*, symbolic of his headlong fall from the state of heavenly (i.e., kosmic) Grace.

†It has been otherwise suggested that the three stars of Orion's Belt could perhaps have provided the metaphorical basis for the Christian tradition of the Three Wise Men, or Three Kings who supposedly appeared in Bethlehem—led from the East by a great star (Rigel?)—at the birth of Jesus. But this is pure conjecture.

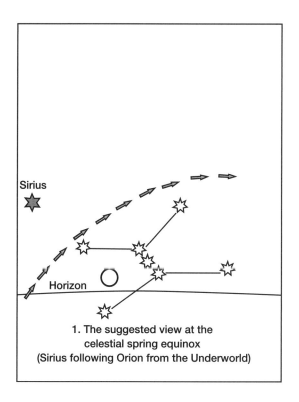

1. The suggested view at the
celestial spring equinox
(Sirius following Orion from the Underworld)

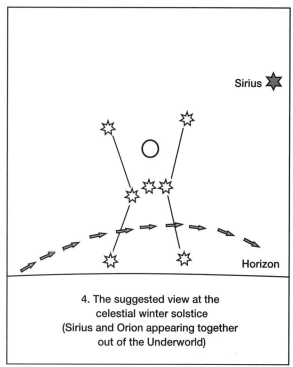

4. The suggested view at the
celestial winter solstice
(Sirius and Orion appearing together
out of the Underworld)

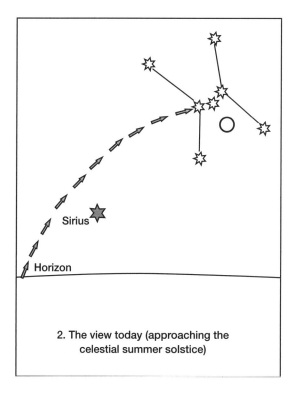

2. The view today (approaching the
celestial summer solstice)

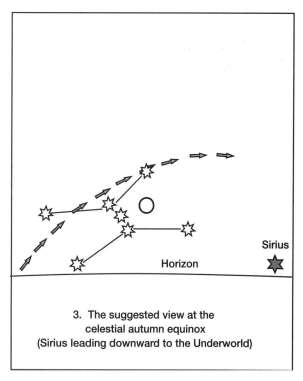

3. The suggested view at the
celestial autumn equinox
(Sirius leading downward to the Underworld)

FIGURE 3.11. THE CYCLICALLY CHANGING VIEWS OF ORION
Note: The circle among the constellation of stars represents the Orion Nebula.

heart of the constellation and that this is currently located in its lower part itself suggests that the figure might *at present* be upside down. Hence at the other end of the Great Year from that at which we currently stand—synonymous with the Egyptian festival of Zep Tepi—it would stand upright and the Belt would then directly conform with the layout and alignment of the three Giza pyramids.

The Jackal Metaphor

The "hounds of Actaeon" were the stars of the constellations Canis Major and Canis Minor (the greater and lesser Dog Stars), headed by Sirius and Procyon respectively, whose parts in the overall allegorical sequence are further enshrined in the Egyptian mystic tradition. Here their metaphysical counterparts became Anubis and Apuat, the two jackal-headed figures who, to the Egyptians, were the Openers of the Ways (of the south and north respectively) on the heavenly homeward path. In order to understand their part in the overall drama, however, we need to bear in mind (yet again) that the ancient view of existence was threefold—kosmic, sidereal, and terrestrial (or human). Thus of the three

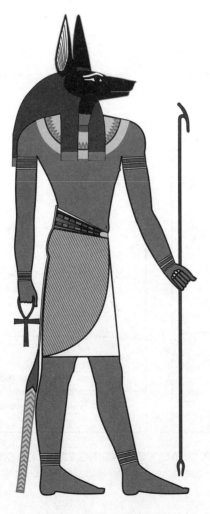

FIGURE 3.12. JACKAL OF SET
(Illustration by Jeff Dahl)

jackal figures in the Egyptian god scheme, Anubis was related to the solar Underworld, Apuat to the intermediate spiritual world, and the Jackal of Set to the divine world of the demiurgic state.*

By virtue of the actual animal's instinctual behavior, the jackal became a living metaphor for the ever-searching sense of discriminating curiosity and natural intelligence. It was regarded as a duality in each of the three (kosmic, sidereal, and terrestrial) states. In relation to man, the Anubis figure signified the instinctively active sense of sympathetic relationships found in the heart, while its psychospiritual correspondence, the Apuat, lay in man's higher subjective intelligence and the Will-to-Know concerning abstract causality. The astronomically corresponding *sidereal* duality seems to have involved the stars Sirius and Procyon, both closely connected with the zodiacal progression of our solar system around the ecliptic path and thus crossing the plane of the Milky Way. The astronomically corresponding *kosmic* duality involved the Jackal of Set (i.e., the constellation of Ursa Minor) in both a higher and a lower register. That is to say, the Ancients saw Ursa Minor as fulfilling a dual role as discriminating intermediary between the demiurgic consciousness of our own home universe and the greater field of altogether imponderable kosmic Consciousness that eternally surrounds it in space.

The Role of Sirius

The cycle and influence of the blue giant star Sirius was regarded by the Ancients—the Egyptians particularly—as of immense importance. Sirius's orbital cycle—as seen from Earth—amounted to 1,461 years, and it was the one star in the sky clearly *not* affected by precession. That alone clearly indicated that its cycle had to be very closely linked to the cycle of our solar system's own orbital path in space—a fact that has led some researchers to believe that Sirius is the parent star around which our own solar system orbitally cycles and others to believe that Sirius and Isis were one and the same. However, this does not accord with the way in which Sirius seems to have been fitted into either Egyptian or Hindu myth at least.

The heliacal rising of Sirius on the eastern horizon each year was roughly coincident with the rising of the Nile's floodwaters. It accordingly became synonymous with the cycle of rebirth and regeneration of Nature on our planet—in Egypt at least. The tradition revolved around the fact that Sirius and Orion were absent from the night sky for some seventy days during the year, evidently by virtue of the differential speed of movement of the earth's axial and orbital rotations on the one hand and that of the zodiacal sphere on the other, putting it out of sight behind the Sun's coronal photosphere. Consequently, tradition had it that during this time it had disappeared into the Underworld. As the

---

*It seems to be as a corresponding parallel to this same concept that we find in the Greek tradition the metaphorical figure of Cerberus, the three-headed hound, guarding the entrance to the Underworld.

pharaoh was synonymous in magical terms with Osiris, the funerary rites of each deceased pharaoh also took seventy days (i.e., 7 x 10) to complete before *he* was regarded as being fully reborn in the heaven world. The actual funeral of his mummified corpse then took place on the seventy-first day and the coronation of the new pharaoh on the seventy-second day,[12] mirroring the full rising of both Orion and Sirius on the eastern horizon.

However, Sirius seems to have fulfilled a much wider astronomically and mystically coordinated role in Egypt, corresponding with that of Anubis, the son of Set and Nephthys and dedicated servant and helpmate of Isis. In the latter part, Anubis—as the jackal-headed god of the Underworld—took on the responsibility of actually finding the various severed parts of the dismembered body of Osiris, so that Isis could reconstitute them. The astronomical associations of this myth may perhaps not be quite so immediately obvious, even though there is a curiously exact synchronicity in the fact that four Earth years (in days) is exactly equal to the number of years of the Sirian (or Sothic) cycle (i.e., 365.25 x 4 = 1,461).*

The essence of the idea, however, seems to have been that Sirius was the permanent companion of our Pleiadic system, within which our solar system exists (clearly as one of seven such stars). Consequently, as the Pleiadic system seemingly orbits around the figure of Orion-Osiris, so Sirius-Anubis would appear to have been seen as involved in a permanent series of cyclic forays, going off into the depths of space and coming back with information and celestial material comprising the psychospiritual equivalent of the missing Osirian body material, which it then presumably deposited within the auric field of the stellar giant. In that respect, it is interesting that Anubis-Sirius was seen as going off to find the *fourteen* body parts of the dismembered Osiris, because 14 = 2 x 7, which can surely be no mere coincidence, as it implies the sum of two sevenfold planes of celestial existence, within the greater Underworld scheme.†

It appears from this and other associated mythic traditions that—just as our own Sun seemingly revolves around Alcyone in the Pleiades—so the Pleiades might as a whole revolve around Sirius. However, whether this is actually a normal *orbital* cycle is still not clear. As our primary orientation on Earth is naturally toward our own Sun appearing on

---

*A further exact synchronicity involves the fact that the sum of the four base sides of the Great Pyramid totals 1,461 sacred cubits. According to Gosse (*Civilization of the Ancient Egyptians,* 118), the commencement of the last confirmed Sothic cycle took place on July 21, 139 CE, ending in July 1600. Interestingly, the Sothic cycle seems to correspond with the Earth's own weather cycles, which seem to produce climatic extremes (involving prolonged "cold snaps" several years in length) every 700 to 750 years.

†As we saw in chapter one, the ancient Egyptian tradition had Sirius and Orion leading the decans around the heavens. That—taken in conjunction with their position relative to the circumpolar stars—indicates that Sirius and Orion were viewed by them as orbiting around the equator of the sphere of our local (Taurean) universe, following a celestial path that must itself be slightly at an angle to that of the zodiac. That in turn implies that the orbital path of Alcyone is set at an angle to the Sirian equator.

the eastern horizon, along with other rising constellations and stars, we actually fail to look in any other direction. Consequently, as Alcyone lies in the opposite direction to the rising Sun, we fail to even consider the possibility of it having an associated role. Fig. 2.3 illustrates the reasoning behind this idea and at the same time provides us with an implicit indication as to why and how it might be that Sirius is cyclically blocked from our view by our own Sun.

The Titan God Atlas and His Family

Before we go any further, we need to factor into the equation of our understanding the god Atlas—the Greek counterpart of the Egyptian god Shu—because both these two were metaphors for the principle of *divine* (not physical) light, which held up the heavens of our localized home universe. In Atlas's case, this job was a penance set by Zeus (himself symbolic of the highest aspect of the Kosmic Mind principle) for Atlas having helped Kronos in his struggle against Zeus and his brothers for control of the local universe.[13] Atlas—the name being derived from Ad-Lhas—actually means a hierarchy of "primordial divine (i.e., kosmic) spirits." The metaphorical "separation of the Earth from the Sky" or the "holding up the heavens on his shoulders" actually refers to the power of this hierarchy of Divine Intelligences being specifically associated with and responsible for the sixth kosmic plane of existence, which otherwise separated the multi-aspectual Kosmic Mind principle (Sky) from the kosmic physical lower Underworld state (Earth).

Now Shu's goddess counterpart was Tefnut (whose daughter Nut—the sky goddess—was Tefnut's own mutation purely within the solar system), while that of Atlas was his twin sister, the Titan goddess Pleione. This same god and goddess pairing thus appears to have symbolically represented the actual state or plane of kosmic existence between the Olympian Sky, or Heaven, and the Underworld, the latter comprising our Taurean sphere of existence—that is, the sevenfold kosmic physical plane of being (see fig. 2.12). Furthermore, there appears to have been astronomical associations between Tefnut-Pleione and Ursa Minor on the one hand and betwen Atlas-Shu and Ursa Major on the other. Now Atlas (through various wives) was described in the esoteric tradition as having produced *ten* nymph-daughters, in two different groups, each living separately on Mount Nyasa, along with the Hesperides (their half-sisters) and the four Fates.[14] Both the groups of the five Hyades and the seven Pleiades form local astronomical nebulae within the greater constellation of Taurus. However, the third group of sisters—the three Hesperides—seems to have had no clearly obvious astronomical attribution at all.

The Hesperides

The Hesperides had been given the job of looking after a magic apple tree from which were produced golden apples, given by Gaea to the goddess Hera, wife of Zeus, as a wedding gift at the time of her marriage to him. This magic tree was a Tree of Life, like those found in other ancient mystic cultures. But the garden in which the tree of the golden apples was to be found was guarded by a giant serpent—seemingly an esoteric metaphor for Draco—which lay coiled among its branches.[15] Now, although it may not be immediately clear to most readers why it should be so, this tree represents the unfoldment of Nature within the sevenfold Taurean sphere as a whole. The fact that the three Hesperides were responsible for guarding the fruit hanging from the branches of this tree (golden apples probably being an esoteric metaphor for Mind-knowledge) indicates that they perhaps represented three divine (perhaps abstract) principles associated with the nature or process of spiritual evolution within the Taurean system.

Turning next to the Hyades and Pleiades, we find that, unlike the Hesperides, these two groups were described in the myth as "surrounding their father Atlas in their grief"— that is, at his enforced eternal labor. However, this same visual image of their surrounding him could itself well be an esoteric metaphor for some form of orbital or concentric arrangement.

The Hyades

This local nebula traditionally comprised the children of Atlas and Aethra,[16] the latter representing (as Aether) pure spiritual existence *within* the local system, whereas Atlas's wife Pleione seems to have been the female counterpart of Bel-Aeon—that is, that which *contained* the system. The Hyades then—supposedly seven in number originally—when rising astronomically in conjunction with the Sun, were regarded as rain bringers. However, quite apart from their meteorological associations, this appears to be an esoteric metaphor related to the fact that rain brings with it that inherently nourishing principle in Creation that initiates rebirth and growth. From that perspective, rain would then appear to be synonymous with fresh influxes of revitalizing soul groups, descending from the higher planes of existence into the local system.

It also seems quite possible—as the Ancients occasionally used the metaphor of the sacred serpent with heads at both ends of its body—that the five Hyades were otherwise seen as an expression of the lower (i.e., five-headed) end of the draconic impulse. If so, there would be an obvious association between them and the five-headed serpent god Vasuki (in the Hindu tradition) whose body was used by the *devas* and *asuras* (angels and fallen angels) to stir the Ocean around Mount Mandera. The Chinese even knew the Hyades as the "Announcers of Invasion on the Border"![17]

According to the ancient Greek tradition, the infant demigod Dionysus (representing one group of fallen "divine sparks")—son of Zeus through an illicit liaison with the mortal Semele—was left in the charge of the Hyades (disguised as a ram) by Hermes, god of the solar Mind principle, with the instruction to bring him up to manhood, out

of reach of the goddess Hera, who wanted to have him destroyed, just as she did with Herakles, another illicit son of Zeus.* However, as Hera—like the Egyptian Het-Heru—symbolically represented the principle of spiritual soul consciousness that endeavors to contain the "divine spark" by fragmented isolation and so produce in it a differentiation of conscious perception, the allegory surely stands clear.

The Pleiades

So much has been said both metaphorically and allegorically about the Pleiades by every conceivable mystically or poetically oriented cultural group in human society around the world, throughout history, that it is very difficult to pick out a clear central factor common to them all. It is equally difficult to overstate the importance in which they were generally held by all civilizations and cultures throughout the ancient world.[10] The ancient Hindus regarded them together as the great flame of the god Agni (symbolic of the demiurgic Mind principle), within which countless sparks could be seen glittering brightly.[†] The ancient Egyptians regarded them as having a specific association with the primordial, self-created goddess Net (or Neith),[19] but even more specifically with her solar counterpart, Hathor—for there were *seven* Hathors. The ancient Arabs (and others too) believed that they stood at the center of the universe and represented the seat of immortality itself.[20] In all traditions the Pleiades seem to have been clearly (although indirectly) associated with the sevenfold constellation of Orion, while the timings of their risings, culminations, and so on appear to have closely matched the four main Celtic festivals.

Bearing in mind how well the Pleiades were generally regarded by different cultures worldwide, it comes as something of a shock to find that some ancient astrologers regarded them as a portent of blindness,[‡] while their forty days' annual disappearance by day (i.e., being invisible in sunlight) was regarded as of generally bad significance for mankind as a whole.[21] However, the ancient Indian astrological view was that the seven maidens of the Pleiades were married to the seven rishis of Ursa Major, while the Chinese referred to them as Maou[22]—which may have a connection with the Great Cat of the Egyptians,

---

*Shortly after his birth, Dionysus was incinerated by the Titans at the instructions of the goddess Hera. However, his body was almost immediately reconstituted by his grandmother, the Titaness Rhea, wife of Kronos, and it was then sewn up in the Thigh of Zeus (a.k.a. Ursa Major), from which he was later reborn a second time (Graves, *Greek Myths*, 44; McLeish, *Children of the Gods*, 38). The essence of the underlying idea here is that the Dionysian hierarchy of demigods were never intended to fall any further than the second, or semidivine, solar plane.

†It also seems possible that the Celtic Druids saw an association between them and the mistletoe that grew on the sacred oak or apple tree. If so, the ritual cutting of the mistletoe with a golden sickle would undoubtedly correspond with the cycle of Ursa Major.

‡Doubtless by association with ignorance through falling into Matter.

called Ra-Maou. It was the latter that was depicted as the aspect of the god Atum-Ra that cut off the head of the great five-headed kosmic serpent that had enfolded him in its many coils. As the Hindus also otherwise pictured the Pleiades as a short-handled razor,[23] this too seems to produce a sympathetically cross-cultural fit.*

The Lost Pleiad

Of all the traditions governing the Pleiades, however, it is the Greek myth of the lost Pleiad that seems to bring us closest to home. As we have just seen, the Pleiades were also very closely connected indeed with the seven rishis of Ursa Major, the latter itself being just as closely connected with Ursa Minor. So what exactly might the connecting principle be?

As the two lowest states or planes in any sevenfold scheme were regarded by the Ancients as related to purely objective existence, when we find that the youngest of the Pleiades (Merope) was described in the Greek myth as marrying a demi-mortal, our ears should prick up, for Merope is clearly a metaphor for the lowest substate of the fourth solar state. They should do so even further when we find that her husband was none other than Sisyphus—son of Aeolus, god of the Wind, who farmed a fine herd of cattle on the equally metaphorical Isthmus of Corinth. Upon discovering that his cattle were being progressively stolen by Autolycus, a son of Hermes (who had been given the power to render temporarily invisible the objects of his thefts), Sisyphus engraved his own initials on the undersides of their hooves and then followed the tracks, thereby discovering that they had been hidden in a cave. He, in revenge, seduced Autolycus's daughter Anticleia, who later bore him a son—the famed Odysseus.†[24]

Notwithstanding being a demigod himself and having also sired a demigod, Sisyphus later made the cardinal error of betraying one of Zeus's infidelities to his goddess wife Hera. As a consequence, Sisyphus was condemned to eternal punishment in Hades, this punishment being commuted, however, by the three Judges of the Dead,‡ to that famous task of incessantly having to push a great boulder up to the top of a hill, only to have it roll back down to the bottom every time he had just about reached the summit with it. His

---

*The Pleiades were known to the Hindus by their Sanskrit name Krittika—itself derived from the root word *krt,* meaning "to cut"—hence probably the origin of the English word itself, as also with Maou and the English word *mow*—i.e., the "mowing" of grass.

†The metaphorical use of symbolic cattle is found throughout both Egyptian and Greek myth. This particular Greek myth involves an allegory in which divine (i.e., kosmic) *souls* are being led downward into the (also metaphorical) cave of the local demiurgic World Soul. Autolycus (*auto-lycos*) is himself representative of the instinctively repeating thief mentality of the World Soul, constantly trying to add to its repertoire of kosmic faculty, while Anticleia (*ante-cleia*) appears to represent the World Soul itself, from which emerges the semi-"divine spark," or god-Man. Odysseus represents semidivine Man himself.

‡The three Judges of the Dead (appointed by Zeus) were specifically associated with the three lowest states of existence within the sevenfold kosmic or sidereal system. Existence in these three Underworld states was seen as death by comparison with the heavenly state in which the divine spirits and gods lived.

**FIGURE 3.13.
SISYPHUS**

goddess wife Merope, so the same tradition had it, was so ashamed at her husband having been committed to this form of celestial hard labor that she disappeared, never to be seen again[25]—hence being the missing Pleiad.

The Suggested Interpretation of the Myth

There seems little doubt that the overall interpretation of all these interrelated myths involves the Pleiades representing the seven aspects or *sub*states of the fourth solar principle and plane, the least evolved of which becomes involved with the triple lower world system (hence the involvement of the three Judges of the Dead) in which our own solar demigods (representing spiritual humankind itself) are to be found. The Isthmus of Corinth clearly appears to be the narrow strip separating being and consciousness (depicted in the myth as land) that divides the triple lower world from the triple higher world, while the boulder that Sisyphus constantly pushes uphill only to have it roll back down again is an allegory related to the demiurgically inspired movement of our own solar system up and down the ecliptic path (within the lower solar states) over the 25,920-year cycle of the Great Year. Merope, the lost Pleiad, becomes subsumed within the latter process because she is herself the very soul of our solar system—the seventh

Hathor. Odysseus, the demigod son of Sisyphus and Merope, meanwhile is symbolic of none other than the constantly reincarnating Spiritual Ego of Man himself*—wandering far and wide within the solar system, trying to get back home to his own kingdom of Ithaka—a name that defines its own meaning by also incorporating the root word *ak(h)*.

Coordinating the Mystic Scheme

When one begins to coordinate the initially bewildering variety of kosmic metaphors and allegories found in the Egyptian, Greek, Indian, and other mythologies, it becomes increasingly clear that they were intended to depict definite mystic *sequences*. And, as all the myths are tied to individual stars and constellations, it is also evident that they were intended to correspond with the sequences of particular star movements, as seen from Earth over (undoubtedly) very extended cycles. However, it is only when the metaphysical and mystical associations are synchronously allied to specific stars and star groups that the whole takes on real meaning—and very dramatic meaning at that. With this in mind, let us take another and quite briefly summarized look at the central series of astronomical progressions around which all the component myths appear to have been built, where specifically associated with the sevenfold principle.

The Sevenfold Constellations

As already explained at some length, the Ancients paid immense significance to the number seven in all aspects of life, perhaps nowhere more so than in relation to the circumpolar and lower celestial constellations with seven stars, or associated combinations, of which (in descending stellar order from the northern celestial pole) there were six—Draco, Ursa Major, Ursa Minor, the Hyades, the Pleiades, and Orion.† However, the way in which these were sequentially organized was equally important. That sequence seems to have been as shown in fig. 3.14, Ursa Major and Ursa Minor guarding the *evolutionary* aspect of the divine and semidivine planes respectively. Draco, however, being concerned with the *involutionary* principle associated with the primordial fall from Grace, and also having sixteen stars, extends its sidereal body-form downward not only through the fourteen substates of the divine and semidivine planes of existence but also into the corresponding

---

*The name Odysseus appears to be derived from Adi-Zeus. *Ad* or *adi* is another Sanskrit root word meaning "primordial," as in Adi-ti, the primordial heaven world. Odysseus, regarded as "the most cunning of all men," is actually representative of the ever-active capacity for adaptation to circumstance of the "divine spark" in Man.
†The supposition that the Pleiades were regarded as related to the fourth state of solar existence would make of them the expression of the double of the incarnating Logos of the Taurean system. Hence the seven stars of the Pleiades would represent, in one sense, the seven doubles of the overall god, our solar system merely providing one of these.

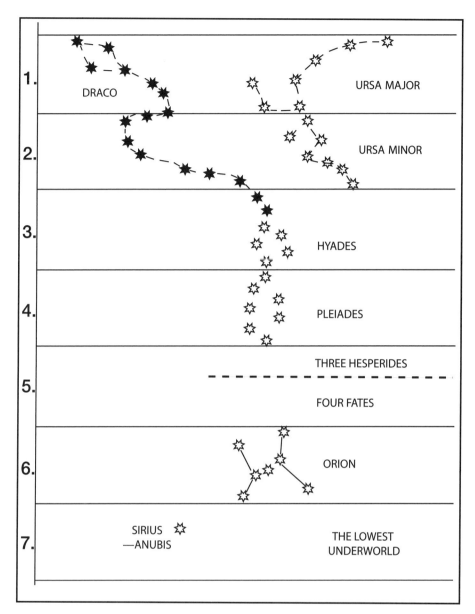

FIGURE 3.14. THE SEVENFOLD CONSTELLATIONS AND THE SEVENTH KOSMIC STATE

first two substates of the third plane* (the latter being synonymous with both the Hindu *atma* and the Greek *aether* principles). Two of the seven substates of the third plane having thus been, as it were, absorbed by Draco, the remaining five substates appear to have been ceded to the five Hyades—logically the daughters of Aethra.

---

*Rather interestingly, this leaves below Draco a total of thirty-three substates, which could perhaps have a Masonic significance (via the Ancient and Accepted Rite). Of additional interest is the indication that the time of the *celestial* spring equinox coincides with the period during which Thuban (Alpha Draconis) becomes our cyclical Pole Star, as seen from Earth. Even further confirming the correspondences, it is from this same location in the serpent's body that its young emerge at birth.

Now because it is exceptionally difficult to draw very many detailed inferences or straightforward supporting interpretations from the Egyptian texts to confirm this proposition, it might again be useful to provide an input here from a different culture. Sir James Frazer in his *Folklore of the Old Testament* describes the tradition—almost certainly derived from either Babylonia or Egypt—that: "The holes in the sky [i.e., in the heavenly firmament] by which the upper waters escaped [i.e., into the local universe] were made by God when he removed stars out of the constellation of the Pleiades; and in order to stop this torrent of rain, God had afterwards to bung up the two holes with a couple of stars borrowed from the constellation of the [Little] Bear."[26] Now bearing in mind that the Hyades by tradition originally had seven stars like their sisters the Pleiades, yet were subsequently shown as having only five, it seems not unlikely that this is an error and that the removed stars were actually from the Hyades, which were themselves known as the rain bringers, as we saw earlier on.

When we consider this diagram (fig. 3.14) specifically in relation to the myth of the death of Osiris-Orion at the hands of Set and his forty-two accomplices, the fourteen pieces of the jigsaw immediately fall into place. In that respect, the seventh and lowest solar state represents purely physical or terrestrial existence; the sixth solar state then represents Lower Egypt, while the fifth solar state represents Middle Egypt. The idea that the Set principle scatters the fourteen dismembered pieces around Lower and Middle Egypt is itself symbolic of the process of incarnation of the Osirian nature in the lower Underworld scheme. Here Isis represents the lowest state in its maternal entirety—the *ba* of the overall lower scheme.

Thus, with Sirius-Anubis as her dedicated servant, she puts together thirteen of the fourteen pieces (or substates) of the fifth and sixth solar states (the psychological and the psychic, respectively) and then unites them with herself. This then induces a proportion of the *higher* aspect of Osiris-Orion (in the fourth solar state, that of the kosmic *ka*) to be drawn down—as the missing fourteenth part of his *lower* body form—into psychic alignment and union with her nature. In this manner, the three lowest solar states are united and—with the spiritual infusion from the fourth solar state—the self-conscious entity, known to us as the human being and to the Egyptians as Horus the Younger, is then conceived and born within the veil of Isis. However, to the ancient Egyptians, this same process and sequence of events had to have its kosmic correspondence within the celestial field of the stars.

Et Sequitur

If these summations are anything like correct, what we are then left with should involve the Hyades and Pleiades apparently fulfilling a function within the local, sevenfold system of our local universe somewhat akin to that of the conjoined *atma-buddhi* principles in the

Hindu tradition. In other words, the Ancients would have seen them as providing an auric spiritual bridge between the circumpolar stars and the lower trinity of solar states in both an involutionary and evolutionary sense. From the Egyptian viewpoint, they bear a striking resemblance to the combined function of Isis and her sister Nephthys, so frequently shown as standing together immediately behind or to either side of Osiris. As Osiris is synonymous with Orion, the Egyptian name—Sah—of the latter being synonymous with the Spiritual Soul principle, these various linkages seem to coincide quite efficaciously. That becomes even more the case if we link the fifth state with Set and the Ego principle. But let us proceed a little further in the same speculative vein.

The seven stars of the Pleiades here appear to be representative of the seven substates or powers of the fourth solar state (the *ka*), from which the subsidiary cycles of (re)incarnation take place within the three lowest solar states. Interestingly, the Pleiades were closely associated in the Hindu culture with the festival of Diwali (as also the Festival of Lamps at Sais in Egypt). The essence of the rather beautiful associated symbolism during Diwali in India—when tiny candles are set loose on floating saucers in the river to drift away with the current—is that the candle flame represented an aspect of Man, the "divine spark," being taken by the desire (the river current) of his parent Logos to fulfill its destiny in an incarnation somewhere far away in the local universe. In the purely human sense, the lesser "divine spark" that is traditionally to be found in the human heart—which represents the principle of self-consciousness—does precisely the same during its cycle of temporary separation from its own spiritual source.

The fact that the youngest of the Pleiades goes missing after marrying a demi-mortal

FIGURE 3.15. ISIS AND NEPHTHYS STANDING TOGETHER BEHIND OSIRIS

who is condemned to a penance clearly associated with the Duat cycles of our own solar system during the Great Year then indicates that it is indeed our solar system, which—as we otherwise know—constantly cycles down into the lower Underworld and back again. Orion, on the other hand, seems to have represented the seven substates of the sixth kosmic planes in toto. Hence what happened in and around Orion was seen as the objective representation or expression of kosmic Purpose. The Hyades and Pleiades together represented the compound subjective nature of this great Being, in both an involutionary and evolutionary sense. The Pleiades thus acted as a bridge of consciousness in the field of Divine Awareness, while the missing Pleiad—our solar system—had a particularly important part to play by virtue of being seen as the representative expression of the lowest substate of the kosmic *ka* of our sidereal system.

Conclusions

Now all this metaphorical and allegorical complexity might well sound utterly bizarre to many readers. However, it is merely the corollary of the extremely ancient hylozoistic idea that the universe is an *organism* with its own hierarchical systems of organized intelligence and that there is not and never has been such a thing as truly inert or inorganic matter. Thus, from this viewpoint, Universal Matter would provide an infinite spectrum of potential states of evolutionary being in which even base matter has its own heaven world and its own genesis, its potential interaction with the next higher octave of being only occurring once it has attained that degree of general stability that enables it to provide more interactively complex forms to act as experiential vehicles through which more highly evolved hierarchies of life would be capable of expressing themselves. Somewhat inevitably, therefore, the Ancients took the view that the sidereal bodies themselves became the very expressions of all these associated principles and the interactive vehicles of their manifestation.

With that general outline in mind, we can now proceed to the next chapter, in which we shall examine in more detail the ancient Egyptian tradition (and others) concerning the appearance of the various hierarchies of god-principles within our home universe. Then, after that, we shall concern ourselves with the ancient view as to how Man himself first appeared on the scene in both a celestial and a terrestrial sense.

PART TWO

THE
SUBTLE NATURE
OF
EXISTENCE

FOUR

KOSMIC GENESIS

THE ORIGIN AND
NATURE OF THE GODS

The Egyptians had two ideas about the origins of life. The first was that it emerged in God out of the primeval waters; the other was that the vital essence—Heka—was brought hither from a distant magical source. The latter was the "Isle of Fire," the place of everlasting light beyond the limits of the world, where the gods were born and revived and whence they were sent into the world. The phoenix is the chief messenger from this inaccessible land of divinity. . . . So the phoenix came from the far away world of eternal life . . . to land at last in Heliopolis, the symbolic centre of the earth.

The rising of the mound [of Tum] and the appearance of the phoenix are not consecutive events but parallel statements, two aspects of the same supreme moment.

ROBERT THOMAS RUNDLE CLARK,
MYTH AND SYMBOL IN ANCIENT EGYPT

The peoples of the ancient world all seem to have shared much of the same conceptual imagery when addressing the subject of Creation itself. Commencing with the idea that the universe is a living organism, containing an infinite spectrum of Intelligence and capacity for self-expression, they saw the Universal Life Principle (Ra in Egypt and Polynesia) as underlying all possible existence.* They also saw every stage of the process of Creation as comprising the outer workings of a great Mind, functioning through the demiurgic

---

*This is the essence of the Greek doctrine known as hylozoism—the idea that there is no such thing as *ultimately* inorganic matter. Thus every atom of substance possesses the principle of Life in its own right, no matter how inert or ethereal it might appear to mere human perception. This is also the essence of Pantheism (the modern Pan-entheism)—the idea that God is present in everything, in every part and aspect of Universal Nature. Relativity theory has otherwise already confirmed that all matter is actually composed of a spectrum of different densities of light energy in different rates of motion. But, so far, this has not been seen in a *qualitative* sense.

agency of a hierarchically organized series of progressively less evolved (albeit still spiritual) Intelligence. The latter gave rise, in turn, to progressively and correspondingly denser states of material existence in a universally repetitive, concentrically organized, sevenfold sequence—hence the Hermetic axiom "As above, so below."

Each stage or substage of the outward progress of Creation (involution) had its own creative hierarchy—to which they gave the name and characteristic attributes of a particular god—and its own supporting hierarchical vehicle, or form—to which they gave the name and attributes of a goddess. In Man's nature, however, all of these principles, stages, and states of Creation were regarded as integrated and sequentially united, even though only *partially* developed and functionally coordinated. Man was thus himself a god—"in potentia."

All the ancient stories of Creation shared the same fundamental idea that, even when or where there is no *objective* universe, there is still an eternal state of essential Being—the primeval waters (i.e., of infinite space) according to the Egyptians, Hindus, Babylonians, and many others all around the world. Into this noumenal essence the originating creative impulse of the Unknown Supreme Divinity was cyclically inseminated and so initiated the process of genesis. This eternal, divinely homogeneous "root" state (to which all eventually returned at the end of a cycle of experience) was known by a variety of names. To the Greeks it was Chaos; in Brahmanic India it was Mulaprakriti; to the Egyptians, Nu-Nun. But it essentially comprised the diffused and as yet unorganized (although all-potential) universal soul state behind all future subjective (noumenal) and objective (phenomenal) existence, which emerged, ex nihilo, from the divine state as dualistic Being once fully activated by Divine Desire for self-expression.

The Logos and the Demiurge

First of all, then, all the great ancient traditions drew a firm distinction between, on the one hand, the Unknowable Supreme God, or paramount Logos (the Father), who initiated the process of Creation by emitting—*within the field of his consciousness*—a great Idea and accompanying Desire for its expression, and, on the other, the kosmic Demiurgos—the unified hierarchy of gods who were responsible for the manifestation of Creation itself. Thus the latter—the divine stewards of logoic memory—were called the Great Architect of the Universe, the Creator-Logos *on behalf of* the Supreme Urgos within whose consciousness that great Thought-Creation would take place. They were thus responsible for providing a vehicle of mind-thought for each logoic Idea,* in exactly the same way that

---

*Which is why the Ancients regarded the gods as (ethereal) heads, as evidenced in two other selections from Scott's translation of *Hermetica* (339): "As to the celestial gods, it is admitted by all men that they are manifestly generated from the purest part of matter and that their actual forms are heads, as it were, and heads alone in place of bodily frames." And again: "The kosmos is a sphere, that is to say, a head; and so all things that are united to the cerebral membrane of this head, the membrane in which the soul is chiefly seated—are immortal."

Kosmic Genesis—
The Origin and
Nature of the Gods

95

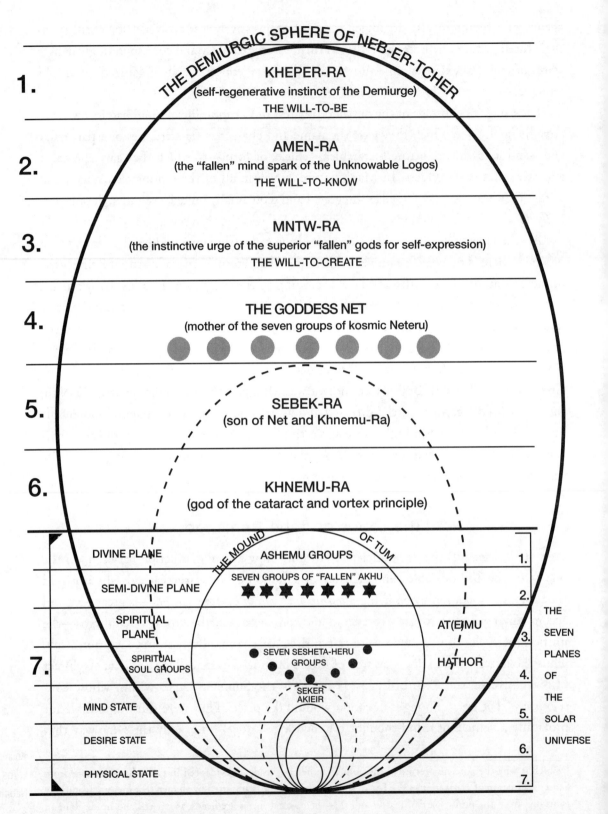

FIGURE 4.1. THE SEVENFOLD SOLAR SCHEME WITHIN THE SEVENFOLD KOSMIC SCHEME

our own memory of past experience provides a "test bed" for each new speculative idea we conceive. But their vehicle was the living kosmos itself. As Hermes Trismegistus puts it in the *Hermetica* (thereby confirming Egyptian monotheism):

> Now this whole kosmos—which is a great god and an image of Him Who is greater and is united with him and maintains its order in accordance with the Father's Will—is one mass of Life; and there is not anything in the kosmos, nor has been through all time from the first foundation of the universe, neither in the whole nor among the several things contained in it, that is not alive. There is not and has never been and never will be in the kosmos anything that is dead.[1]

There is no point in our trying to consider this idea in its totality, as it is utterly beyond conceptualization. However, we can consider it in relation to our own local universe—our galaxy, the Milky Way—and it seems not unlikely, from the form their esoteric metaphor and allegory took, that the Ancients took precisely the same view. Thus the approach we shall follow here in parallel is that the Great Architect of the Universe refers to the demiurgic god-hierarchy responsible for the creation and maintenance of *our* galaxy within the great ocean of Being that surrounds it—still in response to the Mind-impulse originating from the Supreme and Unknowable Divinity of whom we can, as stated, have no faint conceptualization but who, for all we know, is responsible for all the galaxies in the omniverse.

So, within this area of the completely homogeneous, primordial state of divine Chaos, or ocean of Being, and prior to the emission of the great Impulse, this very same hierarchy of Creator-Gods (i.e., the Demiurgos) was regarded as remaining in a purely subjective state—as do our own mind-memories when not in active use. However, upon responding to the great Impulse, these great Intelligences then gathered themselves together and unitedly formed out of their own nature a literally individualized sphere of Divine Being within which a genesis of Divine Ideation could take place. While still in the homogeneous state of Chaos, constantly moved by the autonomic motion of the Life current within the ocean of Being (Nu), the consciousness of this same divine hierarchy was regarded as having followed a serpentine, wavelike existence, like the peaceful rolling motion of the ocean. However, once inseminated with the urge to Creation, part of the serpentine form separated itself from the rest of the mass and altered shape to become spherical (hence A-Nu),* this being depicted by the Ancients as the kosmic serpent biting its own tail.† These gods

---

Anu, the word for the soul principle, derived from A-Nu, thus literally means "that (soul form) that is self-created from the energies of Universal Chaos."

†An image found in both the Hindu Brahmanic tradition and also that of the Gnostics, who derived their concepts from the Egyptians. In the European tradition we see it in the form of the Norse dragon Jormungand, whose serpentine body surrounds Midgard.

FIGURE 4.2. SERPENTINE CIRCLES

were thus the *kosmic* Elohim, the Ah-hi or Aeons, the demiurgic harbingers of duration itself.

The World of Divine Being

We find the Aeons defined thus in the *Hermetica:*

> The Aeon is the power of God; and the work of the Aeon is the Kosmos, which never came into being but is ever coming into being by the action of the Aeon. And so, the kosmos will never be destroyed for the Aeon is indestructible. Nor will anything in the kosmos perish; for the kosmos is encompassed by the Aeon. The Aeon imposes order on matter, putting immortality and duration into matter . . . the kosmos is then dependent on the Aeon as the Aeon is dependent on God. The Aeon's source of Being is God and that of the kosmos is the Aeon.[2]

The idea inherent in this was that the aeonic serpent represented an instinctive knowledge, derived from past cycles of experience; yet—as with the human being—this knowledge remained latent within the autonomic movement of Universal Consciousness until required to express itself in conjunction with a new Idea-Impulse emanating from the Supreme Divinity. Hence it was that, once activated, the old knowledge (the demiurgic principle) reconstituted itself as a self-contained sphere of consciousness *in conjunction with* the new creative Impulse, which "fell" into it. This spherically peripheral state is the Egyptian Amenti, an agglutinative word, which, when broken down into its component parts, is to be translated as the "secret (or concealed) heaven world."* It is here then that the process of duality is set in motion and Genesis accordingly initiated within its auric embrace. However, the seeds of discord are simultaneously sown because of the new impulse to reorganize the status quo having to battle against the instinctive reaction of the old, tried, and tested system of thought, which is naturally against change. This is the source of the biblical idea of the War in Heaven, as a result of which certain subhierarchies of gods, representing the new Impulse, fell from Grace and thus became destined to create spheroidal subworlds of being out of their own nature.

The Soul Principle (The Anu)

We moderns tend to assume that Creation is an outward or centrifugal or even linear process. However, we fail to take into consideration that this phase is but partial and has to be preceded by a foundational *inward* genesis, having a subjective nature to it. But the Ancients *did* realize this and consequently incorporated it into their metaphysical concepts. The fact that we fail to do so is very probably the cause of our usually being unable (or unwilling) to understand what the Ancients were talking about in their mystical ways, so putting their concepts down to mere superstition. In fact, *all* the ancient traditions viewed both the demiurgic Creation and its Deity—whether in the Macrocosm or the microcosm—as being spherical or circular in shape, each such entified "atom" of individualized knowledge being complete in itself as a soul—this thereby being a general principle in Universal Nature. Thus in the outer periphery of each such soul-body there existed the ultimate heaven world of its unified being and latent consciousness.

To the Ancients, therefore, this peripheral world contained the god nature inherent in *every* soul entity, each being a holographic microcosm of its parent god-soul. However, within the auric embrace of each soul's spheroidal body form, the very process of its own self-genesis was seen as having, en route, encapsulated a whole mass of the less evolved and chaotic matter of local space. Consequently, it was from and within this encapsulated mass (which subsequently became the *ka*) that the primordial process

---

*In fact, the prefix *a* in front of any name—such as with A-Tum or A-Men—like the Latin (with its Sanskrit origins) implies "away from" or "detached from." *Men, min,* or *man,* as a prefix, always signified the Mind principle, as in Minos and Menes, while *ti* was a very common ancient word (also found in China and the Americas) meaning "heaven world." Thus A-men-ti really meant "detached (or derived) from the Mind-heaven," where the great initiating Thought and Purpose of the initiating Divinity—that is, the Logos—was deemed to originate; hence this was the true point of origin of the "divine sparks," the agents of the new Divine Purpose—that is, "the Word." Hence also in the Old Testament Book of Genesis (1:6) we find: "And God [Elohim] said 'Let there be a firmament in the midst of the waters and let it divide the waters [of space above] from the waters [of space below]' . . . and God [Elohim] called the firmament 'Heaven.'"

of formative Creation had to take place.* Because (according to the ancient traditions) the nature of Universal Nature is to unswervingly follow suit with the Divine Will (as impressed upon it by the Aeon), all the captured mass of chaotic Life—once subjected to the dynamic motion of renewed logoic Thought—also began to separate into spherically organized soul beings in a vast hierarchically organized spectrum of Life, which contained its own infinite spectra of still as yet potential consciousnesses. The least evolved of these then would ultimately become the atoms of our modern science, only *some* of which, however, would be infused with the spark of Divine Purpose *and thus themselves harbor the creative instinct.*

The Sequence of Subjective and Cosmic Creation

As we have just seen, there could be but one law in the universe of consciousness of the initiating Logos. Thus the demiurgic soul hierarchy of our local universe, encased in its own Ring-Pass-Not[†] heaven world, and consequently forced into bringing about the Creation process *within* its own auric sphere of reference, had no option but to follow the very same process of self-emanation as its parent Logos. But the same living matter it had already contained within its auric embrace subsequently also changed shape and structure in conformity with the general "follow-my-leader" instinct in Universal Nature. The whole of it thus became atomic in shape and molecular in its form of consciousness—a completely homogeneous, ethereally *spiritual* state, which the Hindu metaphysical tradition calls *svabhavat.*

However, the next inward part of the creative cycle generated within this a polarized duality of Spirit and Matter (the Hindu *purusha* and *prakriti*), which itself arose out of the principle of the (demiurgic) Creator-God having three aspects. In the various main ancient traditions, this trinity was known as follows.

BABYLONIAN	GREEK	EGYPTIAN	INDIAN (HINDU)	CHRISTIAN
Anu	Ouranos	Amen-Ra	Siva	Father
Ea	Gaea	Mut	Visnu	Son
Bel	Eros	Khonsu	Brahma	Holy Spirit

---

*This auric enfoldment of primeval matter at the dawn of Creation appears to be referred to in the Book of the Dead (Saite Rescension, quoted by Budge, *Gods of the Egyptians,* vol. 2, 99) where the candidate for initiation is made to say: "I am Osiris who shut in his father Seb together with his mother Nut on the day of the great slaughter"—a clearly metaphorical reference (with associated modern misinterpretation). Wallace Budge otherwise makes the point that this same statement is itself very similar to that describing the action of Kronos upon his father Ouranos in the Greek myth.

†Ring-Pass-Not is the peripheral field surrounding a celestial body, otherwise known as an Oversoul.

Of these, the "Father" aspect of the Demiurge was regarded as remaining in its heaven world* (again, in both the Macrocosm and the microcosm), while the other two polarized aspects were projected, yin-yang fashion, down into the mass of pure, homogeneous soul substance, thereby conditioning it and causing its differentiation into Spirit and Matter. These centripetal vortex trajectories then united at the center of the demiurgic sphere to form the plane of a secondary, dualistic heaven-world—the Elysium of the Greeks and the Mount Mandera of the Hindus. To the ancient Egyptians, however, it was the mound of Tum, and to the Babylonians, the body of Tiamat, which the god Marduk had split in half and then rejoined. At the center of this nucleus then were to be found the foundational "fires" out of which were created all primordial (though still as yet ethereal) forms—that is, the sidereally spiritual soul-body forms of the "fallen" gods themselves.

The Sequence of Objective Creation

Now this inward metaphysical sequence of Creation (of our own home universe) was itself clearly regarded as that which resulted in the formation of the plane of our galaxy, the Milky Way. The nucleus of god-sparks that fell from the upper pole of the primordial heaven world thus found themselves trapped in the very midst of a mass of dualistically polarized kosmic substance from which they perforce had to make their escape. However, the ancient tradition had it that they could only do so by reuniting Spirit and Matter in harmonious combination around their own divine nature, thereby themselves becoming fully individualized as a self-conscious and semi-independent hierarchy of gods, in a manner not yet achieved even by the parent demiurgic hierarchy. Thus it was that they became "star-beings," each naturally also containing its very own solar universe—a spheroidal microcosm of the macrocosmic parent Demiurge (the Aeon)—at the center of which was its own further "fallen" aspect, an objective Sun.†

Interestingly, this imagery is itself entirely consistent with the conceptions of modern science, which now accepts the microcosmic Sun of our own solar system as the furnace in which all *atomically organized* matter is generated by nuclear fusion out of a plasmic state—comprising particles in a totally free and chaotic state—and is then centrifugally emanated outward into the solar system (there to circulate and gain experience).

---

*Hence Siva was known in the Hindu tradition as both Mahadeva and also the Great Ascetic, for it is the Siva-Ouranos principle that ever *contains* the world of manifest being within itself as the Aeonic Soul. Hence Plato's dictum that the eternally first stage of Creation—that of privation, or isolation—pertains to both Macrocosm and microcosm alike.

†As we saw in chapter 1, the Ancients drew a very clear distinction between the "real" Sun (which aurically contained the whole solar system) and the merely physical Sun. Hence it was *the former* that was regarded as containing the true Deity.

The *Benben* Bird

Referring back to the quotations at the beginning of the chapter, we can also now see that the Egyptian phoenix (Bennu or *benben* bird)* is itself symbolic of the fiery falling Mind-sparks of Divine Purpose, while the "Isle of Fire" from which it brings the flame (which will ultimately consume it) is an intermediate heaven-world surrounding the demiurgic "mound of Tum." This imagery is clearly paralleled in the Old Testament Book of Genesis in the symbolic fall of Lucifer and his angels, the living vortex of helically centripetal motion within the spiritual worlds being described in the text as "light lightning." Herodotus tells us something of this tradition of the Egyptian phoenix in the autobiographical book of his own travel experiences in the Middle East, known to us as *The Histories:*

> They [the priests of Heliopolis] tell a story about this bird which I personally find incredible; the Phoenix is said to come from Arabia carrying the dead parent-bird encased in myrrh. It proceeds to the Temple of the Sun [at Heliopolis/Anu] and there buries the body. In order to do this, they say it first forms a ball as big as it can carry, then hollowing out the ball it inserts its dead parent, subsequently covering the aperture with fresh myrrh.[3]

FIGURE 4.3. THE EGYPTIAN PHOENIX (*BENBEN* OR BENNU BIRD)

---

*The name *benben* appears to derive from the Egyptian word for "seed." Thus the repetition of the word signifies a cyclical process of self-reproduction, which itself demonstrates that the ancient Egyptians believed in the principle of reincarnation.

This might seem as incredible to us as to Herodotus. But if we recognize the "dead parent-bird" as an esoteric metaphor for the karma of the previous universe or solar scheme (or for that of the reincarnating human soul)—myrrh having traditionally been symbolic of tragic sorrow—the whole story immediately begins to make sense. The *local* universe (the spheroidal Anu representing the soul-body self-generated by the Kheper-Ra principle at the center of the greater universe) must itself—as all else in Nature—causally (re)condition everything contained by it with the imprint of those experiential effects produced in its last incarnation. This it must achieve before it can proceed to make its full, objective appearance in the new one. The fact that there are two phoenixes, the live one remaining outside the Anu or soul-sphere, is also highly instructive, as the latter indicates the overshadowing new Divine Purpose (the "fresh myrrh" perhaps representing the equivalent of the Hindu *dharma,* meaning "higher purpose") of the incarnation now just set in motion. In the purely human sense, the dead phoenix bird might well be regarded as related to the latent *kundalini** energies at the base of the spine, whereas the living phoenix fire would correspondingly have been related to the spiritual energies hovering in the vicinity of the crown center, above the head.

The Universal Sevenfold Principle

As already suggested, in the ancient system of thought, the idea that the Creator-Deity was a Unity of Being (i.e., the Demiurge) invested with a triple nature by its unknowable "client" Logos, was of paramount importance. The essence of this idea is fundamental to Christian theology even today, although somewhat confused in interpretation. In the Egyptian system, the trinity of Amen-Ra, Mut, and Khonsu represented: (1) the intelligently animating Divine Purpose and Will-to-Be; (2) the associated Divine Memory, incorporating All-Knowledge and also the associated Sense of One-Life Relationship; and (3) the Creative Instinct. They were all to be found in the heavenly state of Amenti, which was omnipresent in the sense of being the nature of *all* soul beings. However, the trinity itself gave rise to the sevenfold principle,[†] which was regarded as underlying all fully *objective* existence and which we therefore need to understand rather more clearly in conjunction with what we have already said concerning the "fall."

The fundamental nature of the sevenfold principle is that the Amenti triad—during

---

Kundalini is the sacred psychospiritual fire of Creation itself, which traditionally resides within the spinal column.

[†]We saw a little earlier from fig. 1.2 that the number of equal-sized spheres able simultaneously to touch another sphere of the same size in the same plane is six. Within the greater three-dimensional sphere it becomes twelve—synonymous with the Pythagorean dodecahedron. Hence we have here another reason for the number seven possessing such great numerological significance as far as the Ancients were concerned.

FIGURE 4.4. WINGED FIGURES OF ISIS AND NEPHTHYS WITH SYMBOLS OF AMEN-RA, MUT, AND KHONSU

the process of Creation—becomes dualistically polarized, positive-negative—hence six-fold. The two poles of the sphere of Creation then—as we have already seen—centripetally emanate these two complementary triple influences, yin-yang fashion, toward a central point of balance between them, which they themselves enfold. This then is the harmonizing fourth principle, which, with the two triads, makes up the sevenfold nature of Creation, within the unifying parent octave—the surrounding sphere of Being, often depicted as a "soul boat." Because of its combined dual status, the central, fourth state is regarded as a partial *reflection* of the nature of the sphere of Creation—hence it is here that we find the fallen gods and it is from here that *objective* Creation is itself initiated, in the Underworld of Matter. However, this too follows a centripetally inward and downward sequence in which the yin-yang influences of the first stage turn back upon themselves and then constantly cycle back and forth, thereby generating the reincarnation process. It is because of this that the fifth state or division in the septenary sequence was regarded as being that of the *second* fall from Grace, as we shall see in greater detail later on.

By way of an aside to this, the present Astronomer Royal, Sir Martin Rees, admits of the number 0.007 in his book *Just Six Numbers: The Deep Forces That Shape the Universe*: "What is so remarkable is that no carbon-based biosphere could exist if this number had been 0.006 or 0.008 rather than 0.007."[4] Although the coefficient mentioned here is one thousand times less than the full number seven, if we take into consideration the fact that the Ancients saw Creation (the fall into matter) as centripetally triple in function, that is, from spirit to soul to matter (or from the kosmic to the sidereal to the terrestrial), and we then apply the coefficient 10^{-3}, we arrive exactly at 0.007— in other words, carbon-based (i.e., terrestrial) matter, which is, effectively, crystallized

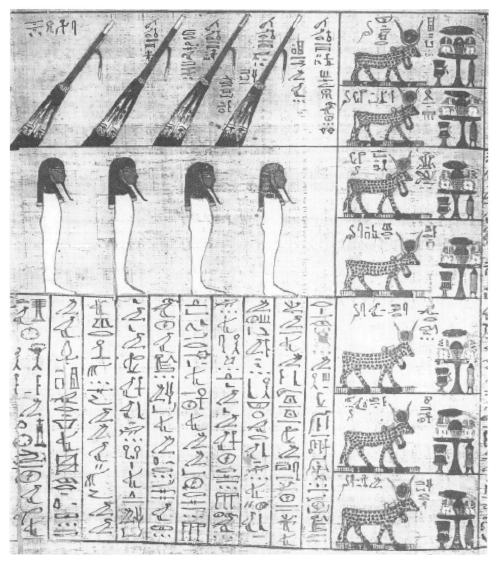

FIGURE 4.5. THE SEVEN CELESTIAL COWS
(representing the matter and function of the seven solar planes)

light, or fire.* Thus, in a very real sense, *everything* that exists is wholly composed of various qualities of light, not just the organic lives of science on our tiny planet.

---

*Bearing in mind that carbon and light are thus synonymous—differing only in state as do ice and water—it is perhaps not surprising that the Ancients saw the principle of light creating ethereal structures in space (hence the sidereal web spun by the goddess Net, or Neith) just as carbon does in the objective world of organic terrestrial existence. Hence also the fact that the god Heru-Behutet (the principle of spiritual consciousness and perception) dominated his environment by the use of light. We should also remember that the Ancients used the number 1,000 to signify the possessions of a god, as opposed to the 100 of the soul and the 10 of man. (See, for example, the Pyramid Texts I.1939 or 1956–8, utterances 667 and 667D.)

The Seven Aspects of the Great God Ra

The demiurgic hierarchy of Ra, responsible for creating our home universe, thus organized itself as seven primary hierarchies of *kosmic* Being, as follows, all within One Being.* These same principles then became universally common to all the star systems within it, each of which correspondingly comprised seven solar states (or planes) of being and consciousness, each with its own septenary systems and subsystems. This concept, however, has to be regarded as involving a dynamic *sequence* of unfoldment.

1. Kheper-Ra—the principle of self-regeneration (as soul) and Universal Memory
2. Amen-Ra—the principle of intelligent universal being and creative purpose
3. Mntw-Ra—the principle of intelligently ordered cyclic activity
4. Net (the kosmic form of Hathor)—the plane of intelligently ordered Universal Consciousness (the universal double)
5. Sebek-Ra—the Kosmic Mind principle
6. Khnemu-Ra—the principle of sentient kosmic (astral) existence
7. Atum-Ra—the principle of existence in objective kosmic form

It is worth noting, at this point, that the Egyptians commonly used the cow as the universally applicable symbol of material existence on *all* planes of being, hence the depiction of the seven cows of Ra, as shown in fig. 4.5, ruled by the unseen Bull of Heaven, the originating (logoic) Creative Impulse itself. The seven cows are thus themselves representative of the seven qualities of *substance,* the two highest planes being those of the Demiurge and the returning Divine Purpose (i.e., the kosmically fallen hierarchy of the highest "divine sparks")—hence the symbolism of the steering rudders (of the soul boat) at upper left. The lower five of the great cosmic septenate of Ra's aspects then otherwise represent the five universal elements of objective Creation[†]—aether, fire, air, water, and earth, in that order. But let us now take a rather closer look at each of the seven aspects of the god Ra, first of all dealing with the name Ra itself.

---

*According to Budge's *Gods of the Egyptians* (vol. 1, 267), "The seven-headed serpent of the Gnostic system has his prototype in the great [Egyptian] serpent Nau, which was called 'the bull of the gods' and has seven serpents on seven necks." In the Pistis Sophia, we otherwise find Jesus depicting the outer darkness as a great serpent with its tail in its mouth and otherwise comprising twelve halls of varying experience and form.

†Which is why the Egyptians depicted the stars of the sky as five-pointed. The five elements of our world, however, are said to be merely the objective expressions of the universal elements in their pure, primordial state. Thus, for example, the element of earth is the expression of the principle of coherence and relationship, whereas that of water is the expression of the principle of dynamism and fluidity.

Derivation and Use of the God-Name Ra

The symbol of the god Ra is the disk of the Sun encircled by the serpent Khut. Somewhat bemusingly, the most modern Egyptological delight seems to have involved a wholesale distortion of the name Ra, now in some quarters spelled "Re" and ludicrously pronounced "Ray." This is far worse than the previously extended "Raah," neither, however, paying more than lip service to the fact that the actual pronunciation should involve a short out-breath with the "a" gutturally muted, as in both the Sanskrit and the Arabic.* The origin of the name seems obscure but looks to have been associated with the royal serpent of Egypt—the cobra—by virtue of the fact that the tongue, when made ready to pronounce "Ra," is poised at the roof of the mouth, just like an upright cobra, ready to strike. The ancient Egyptians paid great attention to such details, particularly as Ra was associated with the Breath of Life itself and the magical properties of the breath played such a vitally important part in their system of thought.

This same importance was universal in ancient times. The most sacred name of the One God—the Ever-Unknowable Deity—was Iao (or Iaho), seemingly derived from the three phases of the breathing process: inhalation, assimilation, exhalation. From this name were derived many others, including the dualistic Hebrew Jah-veh. But the original root appears to have been Sanskrit and it gave rise to both yog(a) and Jaggenath, the god of the Vedic Mysteries. It also appears in the Zoroastrian fire religion as Ahura-Mazda (via Iao-Hura, which probably became Iao-Sura and then A-Sura) as well as in the Hebrew Book of Creation, the Sepher-Jezira (probably derived from Suf-Ra-Iao-Sura). The ancient word for Divine Breath (Suf-Ra) eventually mutated into the Arabic *ciphra,* a number with a meaning attached to it, thereby agreeing with the equally ancient idea that the emanation of God is as number.

The God Neb-er-tcher

Although Kheper-Ra was regarded as the "father of the gods and the Creator of all things in Heaven and on Earth," having self-created himself out of the chaotic essence of the universe, he was very specifically regarded as a mere aspect of the god Neb-er-tcher. It is thus that Neb-er-tcher is made to say, in the sacred writings: "I am he who evolved himself under the form of the god Kheper-Ra. I, the evolver of evolutions, evolved myself, after a multitude of evolutions and developments which came forth from my mouth. . . . By the strength of my will I laid the foundations (of things) in the form of the god Shu [the god of light] and I created for them every attribute which they have."[5]

The "evolutions and developments which came forth from my mouth" (by an act of Divine Will, according to the tradition) would further suggest that Neb-er-tcher is perhaps

---

*In Egyptian hieroglyphics, the letter "r" is depicted as a crouching lion, or a lens/vesica.

himself the (local) Logos, for it is "the Word"—the bearer of Divine Purpose—that traditionally emanated from the "mouth of God." As Neb-er-tcher was himself described as "Lord of the Universe," all this seems to be clearly confirmed.

The God Kheper-Ra

Symbolically represented by the scarab beetle, Kheper-Ra* is the organizing, self-creative principle in Universal Nature. In that sense, he represents the self-regenerative aspect of the demiurgic hierarchy—the Elu or Elohim who generate the World Soul of our local universe out of their own Being. But he is also symbolic of the soul principle generally, in man or otherwise, for all soul entities are likewise demiurgic in nature. Like the scarab beetle then, the Demiurge emerges fully regenerate from the dark and (it would seem)

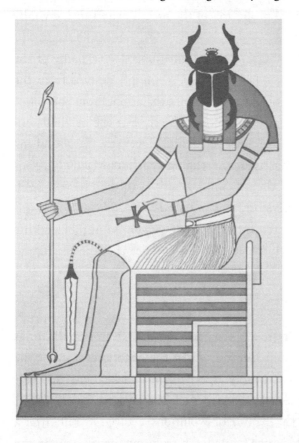

FIGURE 4.6. KHEPER-RA

---

*We might add in passing that the name Kheper-Ra is phonetically very close to Geb-Ra (the kabbalistic *Geburah*) and the god Geb—the god of the Earth—was of course symbolized by the amphibious goose (or swan in certain other traditions), which laid its eggs on a nest built just above the waterline of the river. Kheper also otherwise appears to be synonymous with the Babylonian Kabir, depicted as a gigantic winged bull with a human head—as can be seen from a massive example in the main gallery of the British Museum, in London. The Kabiri(m) were themselves the Creator-Gods of Babylonia and therefore synonymous with the demiurgic Elohim of the Hebrews, of which there were seven classes. In the Hindu system, yet another alter ego appears in the form of Kubera, the god of kosmic Earth and wealth, who lives on Mount Mandera. In the kabbalistic system, it is Keter, the supreme Sephiroth.

chaotically massed matter of space, its first instinct being to accumulate part of space for itself, thus fashioning it into a spherical ball in which it lays its own "seeds." In the macrocosmic sense, this ethereal sphere (of our local universe, enclosing the future Milky Way) is then rolled around the heavens, just as the scarab beetle rolls his dung ball around the ground—always backward, using his hind legs to propel it along.

Khepera* was otherwise essentially a symbol of cosmic duality. As Budge tells us: "But there was a primeval matter out of which heaven was made, and also a (primeval) matter out of which the earth [i.e., the objective universe] was made, and hence Kheperà . . . is said in Chapter *xvii* (line 116) of the Book of the Dead to possess a body which is formed of both classes of matter."[6] In that respect, the first creation of Kheper-Ra was the Eye of Nu (i.e., the kosmic *sah*), while a second Eye (the kosmic *ba*) was subsequently created that had only some of the powers of the first one but which was given dominance over the whole Earth—after which the creation of the soul hierarchies of plants, reptiles, and insects took place.[†7]

The God Amen-Ra

As already indicated, the name A-men means not only "invisibly concealed" but also "detached from the Mind." As Ra was the Universal Life principle, the combination as Amen-Ra seems to have meant a formless "Mind-born Breath," which is, perhaps paradoxically, omnipresent and thus omniscient, as well as omnipotent. Interestingly, as Budge points out, Amen-Ra was never in any way shown as associated with the god Osiris, yet he was the creator of "the food of the gods"—otherwise known as Ma'at—which here must mean Universal Knowledge, as well as inviolable Divine Purpose and Truth. Bearing in mind that the Sanskrit principle of *mahat* is also generally taken as meaning the activity of the Universal Mind, there can be no doubt whatsoever that the two cultures (Egyptian and Hindu) shared the same fundamental metaphysical principles, as can also be clearly shown by a variety of other shared expressions, where only the associated spelling has changed through cross-cultural interpolation.

The primary temple of Amen-Ra was at Karnak[‡] on the north side of Thebes (modern Luxor). However, the temple dedication also incorporated lesser (or rather, ancillary) aspects attributed to both Mut and Khonsu, the other members of the celestial triad, and

---

*We find this same god at Giza in the form of the Sphinx—as the multi-purpose Ra-Temu-Khepera-Heru-khuti. As Heru-khuti (Horus in the Horizon) represents the principle of self-consciousness in the demiurgic nature, the god here denotes the principle of a secondary self-genesis—that of the initiate in the Mysteries who must re-create himself by a self-motivated process of *spiritual* individualization.

†As in the Creation sequence described in the first few verses of the biblical Book of Genesis, what is here being described involves the "germs" of these same groups within the various kingdoms of nature, the latter however being seen as astral soul prototypes.

‡Almost certainly derived from Ka-Nak, meaning the ethereal double of the great kosmic serpent Nak.

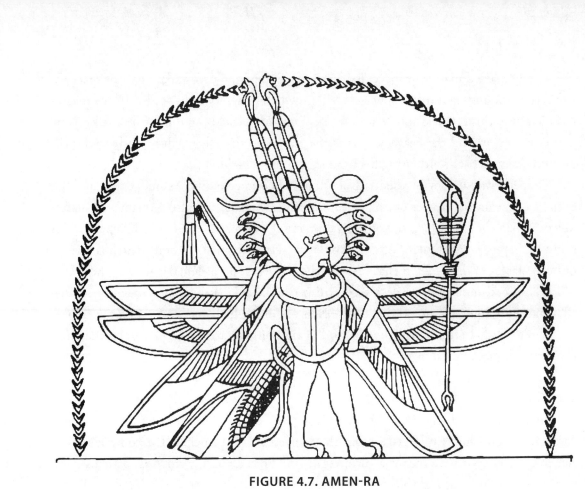

FIGURE 4.7. AMEN-RA

it is only in conjunction with these that Amen-Ra can be properly understood. As to some extent already seen, Amen-Ra (as a universal principle in Nature) represents the reorganizing Intelligence par excellence behind the noumenal universe.

As the functional aspect of the Demiurge, Amen-Ra is the direct agent of the Unmanifest Logos, whose creative impulse he is. Thus in the curious picture of him here (fig. 4.7) he is depicted essentially as a jack-of-all-(divine)-trades, because he represents in himself the new Divine Purpose and Will extending to all potential parts of Creation. Mut and Khonsu then respectively represent the corresponding and associate principles of Spiritual Knowledge/Wisdom and Creative Intelligence. Of these three, (very logically) the dualistic, hawk-headed Khonsu principle—the messenger*—is alone depicted as bound up in funeral bandaging, metaphorically representing incarceration (i.e., entombment) in Matter. The other two aspects remain free.

This triad is otherwise particularly associated with the spiritually evolving aspect of the human kingdom in Nature, the *neferu,* for it also represents the *vehicle* of the tri-

---

*Not only was the hawk-headed Khonsu the god of all growth, he was also represented as having complete command over all the elements in Nature (Budge, *Gods of the Egyptians,* vol. 2, 37).

ple "divine spark," which fell into generation as the Creative Word of the Unknowable Logos. It is thus fundamentally an expression of the other branch of the consciousness of the Logos—that of the *neteru,* the *devas,* or angels. These, as the direct offspring of the Demiurge, have no sense of choice; they are only able to regenerate and maintain the status quo in Nature and to provide all the associated knowledge. It is because of this specific association with Man and the associated process of involution/evolution that we find the triad of Amen-Ra, Mut, and Khonsu based at Thebes, which was also, importantly, the city of the fifth nome or district of Egypt. The importance of this is directly associated with the corresponding fifth division of the Duat, for it is from here—as we shall later see—that *objective* Creation originates.

The God Mntw-Ra

Mntw-Ra then—who also has a temple dedicated to him at Karnak—is synonymous with the outwardly active Kosmic Breath, the conveyor of Life. He corresponds with the Sino-Tibetan Fohat, the primordial divine energy of the Logos that circumgyrates through space, causing its ceaseless cyclic motion.* It is the kosmic version of the vital solar aether, the pulsating, ever volatile, hypertenuous essence of space, comprising both its energy and its foundation of potentially material existence. It was known to the North American Indians as Manitou, the Great White Spirit—the closeness of the names Manitou and Mntw leading one to query the geographic extent of Egyptian (or Atlantean) mystic influence in very ancient times. We find the very same name also in the Sanskrit words *mantram (mnt[w]-ram)*—a repetitive word or sentence used in prayer or meditation—and *mandala*—the turning and thus cyclic wheel of Fate incorporating abstract or mundane pictures (intended to be magically invocative). The latter is derived from *mntw-lha,* the *lha* being a common and geographically very widespread ancient name for the demiurgic gods known to the Semitic peoples of the Middle East as Elu or Elohim and to the Muslim as Allah(u). Both of these—the mantram and the mandala—are of course used in sympathetic magic to create phenomenal effects either in the consciousness of the individual uttering the mantram or in the psychospiritual environment and welfare of the person/people using the mandala.

The *mntw* principle was also that which caused the spiral-cyclic movement of sidereal

---

*Fo is actually an ancient Tibetan or Chinese onomatopoeic word, signifying the expelled outbreath (of the Creative Logos). Interestingly, the horned viper in Egypt was known as Fu, a name also often used in the name of the pharaoh. The Egyptian word *mntw* (possibly derived from *man-tau*) and its meaning also have their direct correspondences in the Sanskrit word *mnti,* for the *"mnti* cup" is that in which Brahma is said to be stirred up by the goddess Vach, the representative of the Word of God. The Sanskrit root word *mnt*—meaning "to swing or twist," like a drill or bore—is also found in the same role in the Nordic myth as Mundilfoeri, the unknowable god or kosmic force that moves the "handle" of the orb of heaven, i.e., of our local universe (de Santillana and von Dechend, *Hamlet's Mill,* 139).

matter of our local universe, thereby resulting in the angled orbital movement of our galaxy, the Milky Way, and all the stars and planets within it. It is found in the Hindu tradition in a variety of forms, perhaps the best known of which is that of Mount Mandera, the celestial mountain around which the cosmic serpent god Vasuki coils himself (seven times) and which is "turned" back and forth by the *suras* and *asuras* to churn the great ocean of Matter, thereby bringing to the surface fourteen kosmic gifts.* However, in the next stage, the actual accumulation of sidereal substance, resulting in the formation of the stars, became the body processes of the goddess Hathor, in the form of the mass of stars, which themselves formed the celestial curds of her cosmic milk. Hence the next temple northward—at Dendera—was dedicated to Hathor.

The Goddess Net/Neith

Net was the one and only Egyptian goddess regarded as self-born. Of her it appears to have been said: "I am everything which hath been and which is and which shall be, and there hath never been any who hath uncovered (or revealed) my veil."[8] And again: "She it was who gave birth to the Sun, who made the germ of gods and men, the mother of Ra who raised up Tem in primeval time; who existed when nothing else had being and who created that which exists after she had come into Being."[9] Elsewhere described as "the great

FIGURE 4.8. NET/NEITH, MOTHER AND WIFE OF AMEN-RA, THE FATHER OF ALL THE GODS

*Evidently akin to the fourteen scattered parts of the body of Osiris, itself a metaphorical reference to fourteen substates of matter.

Cow, the great lady who fashioned the company of the gods, the mother of Ra who gave birth to Horus,"[10] she was, in fact, mother and wife of Amen-Ra, the father of all the gods.

From all these various quotations and other descriptions it becomes fairly self-evident that Net (also known under other, different aspects as Ra't and Apt'uat[11]) was in fact the primordial *kosmic* progenitor and counterpart of Hathor. From the earliest predynastic times she was seen as closely identified with the great primeval waters of kosmic space, although not in a chaotic sense, for she was otherwise depicted as the goddess of weaving, one of whose responsibilities was to clothe the dead.[12] This latter metaphor, however, actually means that her role (as a principle in Nature) was that of a weaver of primordial *light*, which thereby evolved into an invisible web or net (named after her). This then became the chassis upon which the objective universe was subsequently formed.* For that reason, her pictorial accoutrements often included a bow and two arrows, the latter symbolizing shafts of light. At Sais in the Delta—the main temple associated with her—there was accordingly held each year the great Festival of the Lamps, the equivalent of the Hindu festival of Diwali.

In line with the general scheme associated with all Egyptian gods and goddesses, Net—as a universal principle—was to be found within the solar Underworld as well as the kosmic Overworld. But, in relation to the former, she immediately became associated with other lesser gods and goddesses, thereby giving rise to a complexity of *aspects,* or dynamic subprinciples. Because of these combinations, considerable confusion has arisen in the minds of Egyptologists, who tend to see them as indicative of the generally chaotic approach of the ancient Egyptian mystic mind. This, however, is completely wide of the mark. The Egyptians had a very clear and sophisticated understanding of the meanings behind their visual and verbal metaphors and the sacred allegories connected with the associated myths.

By way of example, one part of the sacred tradition had Net united with Khnemu-Ra, thereby giving birth to the crocodile god, Sebek-Ra. This denotes a clearly *kosmic* function associated with the consciousness of the Demiurge of our local universe. She was also very closely identified (in terms of both name and function) with the sky goddess Nut, wife of the Earth god Geb. This denotes a *solar* function, associated with the framework of the sidereal universe. Her association with Hathor derives from the fact that both were seen as giving birth to the Horus principle—Net in the greater kosmic (i.e., divine) dimension and Hathor in the solar (i.e., spiritual) dimension. The fact that Isis also was seen as giving birth to Horus, and thereby taking precedence over the other two in Egyptian public

---

*This symbolism is found in other mystical cultures, in exactly the same way. In the Babylonian Creation myth, the god Merodach used a great net to trap Tiamat, the goddess of kosmic Chaos. In the Indian tradition the great god Indra—like Shu, god of the principle of light—used a net to trap his enemies, representing the chaotic matter of space, in order to enable the work of Creation to begin.

The Origin and
Nature of the Gods

113

popularity, appears almost certainly to derive from the fact that the marital tribulations of Isis and the difficulties of conceiving her son—Horus the Younger—were regarded as coming closest to the purely human experience.

The God Ptah

Although sometimes known as the Disk of Heaven, Ptah was not otherwise directly associated with the multi-aspectual god Ra. In fact, his characteristics are quite different from those of almost every other god, although there are some distinctly parallel resemblances with the god Shu. However, he plays an absolutely crucial role in the way in which the metaphysical world of the Egyptians came about and he therefore needs to be mentioned at this sequential point. As previously indicated, Ptah, the Great Artificer, appears (both phonetically and functionally) to be synonymous with the Indo-Tibetan (Dhyani) Buddha

FIGURE 4.9. THE GOD PTAH AND HIS GODDESS CONSORT SEKHET

principle—there being, however, a variety of Buddhas and associated Buddha vestures/ethereal body types.* In the Egyptian culture—or at least as much as is known of it—the same degree of complexity does not exist, although the god Khnum (regarded as Ptah's co-working partner in the Creation process) was undoubtedly an aspect of the same being's nature. Additionally, both Horus and Tehuti were regarded as forming an intrinsic part of his nature, that is to say as externally oriented aspects of his creative Intelligence.

However, the self-created Ptah[†] was regarded as a part of the noumenal Godhead itself, "who came into being in the earliest time[‡] . . . [and] hath established Ma'at throughout the two lands."[13] Thus part of his role in the Creation process seems to have been that of bringing about living associations between the divine principles of the kosmic gods and the merely solar forms created by Khnum, the deva-related aspect of the Demiurge. He was accordingly also regarded as the patron of all craftsmen and is considered among Masons even today as the Great Architect of the Universe.

Rather curiously perhaps, given that Atum was regarded as the father of the Heliopolitan Ennead (set of nine) gods, they were all regarded as subsumed within the nature of Ptah, who was himself known as the Lord of Darkness or Lord of the Dark Sun. A further clue to his true nature and role in the overall pantheon is to be found in the Book of the Dead, where he is said to have covered the sky with crystal[§][14] in addition, else-where, to having fashioned a huge metal plate supporting the heaven world and separating it from the Underworld.[15]

All of these clearly point to his role as the Creative Logos overshadowing the conscious-ness of the solar Demiurge. Perhaps most tellingly, he was also closely identified with the hawk-headed god Sokar, or Seker, who presided over the fifth division in the solar world and was thus responsible for the revolving Wheel of Rebirth of the human kingdom—an issue to which we shall return in a later chapter. This seems to imply that Ptah was perhaps associated with the *kosmic* fifth division or plane—which would make him a direct agent of the creative Kosmic Mind. Thus, in this role, Ptah (as Ptah-Nu and Ptah-Hpi) would have been responsible for creating and vitalizing (by ensoulment) the archetypal Heaven and Earth, while the distinctively sevenfold Khnemu—as the correspondingly sevenfold

---

*These are the Nirmanakaya, Dharmakaya, and Samboghakaya. In this tradition, these Dhyani Buddhas are the exponents of a Kosmic Consciousness, which contains and informs the solar scheme. Their Consciousness thus generates the three lowest kosmic states.

†Probably in the same creative connection, Ptah was regarded as the presiding god of Memphis, which was itself the administrative capital city of Lower Egypt, as well as being, apparently, the geographic expression of the Egyptian national sacral chakra. However, in the temple there it was his *double*—rather than Ptah himself—to which aspirational tribute was paid.

‡Ptah was depicted as immaculately conceived and subsequently born from an egg emanating from the mouth of the great kosmic serpent Kneph, who himself represented Divine Wisdom (Hall, *The Secret Teachings of All Ages,* 60)—which makes of Ptah a direct symbol of the avataric Kristos principle.

§The crystal sphere being the auric firmament which comprises the outer World Soul of our solar system.

local Demiurge—held the associated responsibility for generating the multitudinous hier-archies of forms with which to fill them.*

The Lower Triad of Kosmic Creation

The three primary gods of the kosmic Underworld were Sebek-Ra, Khnemu-Ra, and Atum-Ra. However, they have really to be understood as the three related aspects of the *objective* World Soul of kosmic Matter, the lower half of that greater duality described a little earlier. Remembering that the "mound of Tum" arose above the waters within the kosmic continuum, in conjunction with the descent of the fiery *benben* bird, it seems fairly clear that the vortex thus created was directly analogous to the cataract,† the River Nile imagery playing a highly important role in the workings of the overall concept. Thus the conjoined principles of kosmic earth and kosmic water were fundamental to the existence of the objective world, that combination being depicted in the form of the ever-pregnant hippopotamus goddess Ta'Urt. As a consequence, it was metaphorically upon her back that the Sebek (crocodile or dragon) principle was able to lie in wait for its prey, which roamed the element of kosmic air.

The God Sebek-Ra

Sebek-Ra (offspring of the union of the goddess Net with the god Khnemu-Ra)‡ was the kosmic crocodile god that appears to have enjoyed a particular relationship with the cir-cumpolar constellation of Draco, the Dragon. The animal metaphor ascribed to this kos-mic principle seems to have been derived from the behavior of the crocodile, which lies in wait for its prey, just below the surface of the river, and then, when it comes close, leaps forward and grasps it in its jaws, thereafter dragging it under and tearing it into bits to consume it. This, however, is very similar to the way in which the (lower) Mind works in relation to those *spiritual* perceptions we call "inspirations," or "intuitions." In the higher context, the Kosmic Mind reaches out and drags down an aspect of the knowledge of the fallen gods from within the fourth kosmic state—that aspect of it which must be sacri-ficed for the evolutionary sake of the lower realms of kosmic Creation. This same sacrifice is thus effectively Man himself—the *divine* Man, who is the Son of the Unknowable God.

---

*Hence the goat-headed Khnum became the (unfortunately erroneous) focus of Knights Templar worship as the G.A.O.T.U. (Great Architect of the Universe) himself—an error which the Freemasons appear to have corrected.
†The six cataracts of the Nile had great mystical and metaphysical significance.
‡This is surely a clear confirmation of the previously suggested sequential allocation of Net as the *neter* expression of the kosmic fourth state, Sebek-Ra as that of the kosmic fifth state, and Knemu-Ra as that of the kosmic sixth state. That then logically leaves Atum-Ra as the expression of the seventh and lowest kosmic state, which emerged from amid the surrounding waters associated with Sebek-Ra and Khnemu-Ra—and also the hippopotamus goddess Ta'Urt, Sebek-Ra's constant companion.

**FIGURE 4.10. SEBEK-RA,
CROCODILE GOD**

Thus the One Son of God—the Logos *within* the cycle of objective Creation—becomes the (hierarchically diffuse) Many.

The pulling down of the divine influence into the field of human existence was of course one of the tasks of the temple priests, on behalf of the populace. Consequently, in the Israelite tradition (borrowed from the Egyptian) the priest became a Zedekite or Zadokite, while the Lord of the World who performed the same task on behalf of our planetary Life as a whole was known as Melchizedek—possibly derived from the quasi-kabbalistic

Malkuth-Sebek.* As Budge tells us: "From the cviiith chapter of the Book of the Dead, we learn that Sebek . . . assisted Horus [the principle of self-consciousness] to be reborn daily. . . . He opened the doors of heaven to the deceased."[16]

The God Khnemu-Ra

Khnemu was the goat-headed god[†] of the First Cataract of the River Nile (hence the peculiar depiction of his laterally wavy horns), which lay between Elephantine and Philae. Thus Khnemu-Ra may be logically considered as his kosmic counterpart. He was specifically regarded as having a sevenfold nature and was depicted as fashioning the world (and man) "on a potter's wheel"—an obvious metaphor for the cyclic turning of the local, material universe—in conjunction with the god Ptah. However, the indications are that the Ptah principle was responsible for inseminating the consciousness of the various hierarchies of Nature into the seven planes of solar *form* built by Khnemu.[‡] The latter was thus spe-

FIGURE 4.11. KHNEMU-RA

---

*It is also possible that the name is derived from the Egyptian Setekh (as Sebek was regarded as closely associated with the kosmic Set) and is probably derived from the agglutinative Set-*akh*. The functions of the two are, however, not entirely dissimilar. One should note that the hippopotamus goddess Ta'Urt—regarded as the concubine of Set (not his wife)—was constantly to be found in union with the god Sebek. So this triumvirate is of fundamental importance to any metaphysical understanding of the fall.

†Although he is commonly regarded as a ram-headed god by Egyptologists, the features are actually ambiguous. It is otherwise as well to remember that the *u* suffix on any Egyptian name connotes a collective plurality. Thus the god himself was Khnem or Khnum, while the Khnemu were the angelic hierarchies whose instinctive task appears to have been the creation of (soul) body forms to act as the vehicles for those other Intelligences designated as having to incarnate in the objective world.

‡Rather interestingly, the primary female consort of the god Khnum was the goddess Sati. She was depicted as a seed thrower and was connected with the star Sirius—an issue on which we touched in earlier chapters dealing with astronomical and astrological issues. Sati's sister was the goddess Anquet, who, as Budge confirms, bore a mystic relationship to her, very similar to that expressed between the goddesses Nephthys and Isis (Budge, *Gods of the Egyptians*, vol. 2, 55–58 [quoting from the Book of the Dead, ch. xvii]).

cifically associated with the angelic or deva hierarchies emanating from the Demiurgos, the Great Architect of the Universe. In that respect it is interesting to note that Ptah is regarded by the modern fraternity of Freemasons as being directly representative of the G.A.O.T.U., while the rites of the Knights Templar seem to have involved his co-creative partner god the goat-headed Khnemu—hence, perhaps, the name Ba-Fo-Met. The five points of his features—the two horns, two ears, and beard—then became the downward-pointing pentacle of the Hermeticist.

In his role as this aspect of the Demiurge, Khnemu-Ra—in the form of the cataract—separated the waters above from the waters below. But it was amid the waters below that the god Atum-Ra, the god of the objective sidereal universe (i.e., of our galaxy), first appeared.

The God Atum-Ra

There are to be found a number of apparently varied traditions concerning the god (A)Tum. Within the Heliopolitan tradition we find Nu-Nun—the god of the great waters (of space)—taking on the undulating form of Nehebkau, the great serpent of many coils (also possessing five heads, symbolic of the five universal elements) and enmeshing (A)Tum within his coils. It is then within these latter—the wave undulations of primordial matter—that the great god Ra (as Atum) lies in a state of quiescent potential. However, as the logoic impulse (symbolized in fig. 4.12 by the presence of Kheper-Ra, the Becoming One) reaches this hierarchy, it begins to wake, and in so doing was depicted as evolving into the ovoid or auric form of the manifesting World Soul, which thus individualizes itself into existence ex nihilo. An extended form of the same tradition had Atum thereafter evolving himself into the great Cat Ra-Ma' and cutting off the head of the serpent, as a result of which the great World Tree (symbolized by the Persea) sprang into existence.[17]

The god Atum was most graphically depicted as the mound that arose (of its own accord) above the serpentine waters of kosmic space to meet the descending *benben* phoenix bird. It is thus clearly an esoteric metaphor for the instinctive response of primeval matter within the field of Chaos to provide a vehicle for the materialized expression

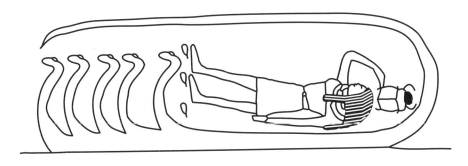

FIGURE 4.12. RA AS ATUM, THE "MOUND," WITH KHEPER-RA

of Divine Purpose. This god is thus directly associated with the omphalos, which—as Aum-phalos—is a metaphor for the creative instinct inherent in the matter ensouled by the *neteru,* thereby later (understandably) becoming regarded as a phallic symbol.* As a direct result, the later tradition has Atum-Ra creating the gods Tefnut and Shu by an act of (apparent) masturbation, although "the act of congress with myself" was perhaps not quite so unsubtly intended by the original authors. As the phallus of Tum and his *ka* are one and the same, the fact that Shu and Tefnut are emanated "into the embrace of his *ka*" (obviously from an external source, or higher state of being), thereby creating the principle of polarity within it, it makes little sense if seen from a purely sexual viewpoint.

Atum's alter ego (a source of confusion to many) was the god Tem or Temu—sometimes At(e)mu—evidently an alter ego of the Sanskrit *atma,* the divine emanation of Spirit, which directly related Atum to Hathor, the latter being Atum's consort. It was the combination of Atum and Hathor that gave birth to the brother and sister god-principles Tefnut and Shu, who, according to one version of tradition, thereafter conceived the gods Nut and Geb—the *objective* duality of Spirit and Matter.

Hathor, the Cosmic Cow Goddess

Hathor, daughter of Nut, was the goddess wife of At(e)mu, the latter being—as we have just seen—synonymous with the Hindu metaphysicist's principle of *atma,* meaning "pure Spirit"—the emanated "Breath" of Divinity. The name Hathor—although derived from Het-Her(u), the "house of Horus" (Her(u) signifying a hierarchy of beings expressing the function of self-consciousness)—was in symbolic terms associated with the cosmic cow goddess whose milk is the ambrosia upon which the gods themselves fed. In the wider sense, therefore, Hathor was actually a metaphor for a secondary and thus limited *solar* form of Universal Consciousness, that is, the Hindu *buddhi,* for it is here, in this state, that the divine hyperactivity of Mntw comes to rest—or rather, to a state of controlled, semi-independent cyclic activity known as Amen-tet. The Sino-Tibetan Fohat (the volatile vehicle of the demiurgic Life expressed in the nature of Mntw-Ra) becomes *Hat*-hor, the spiritual vehicle of semi-independent divine liberation, which the Egyptologist Brugsch

---

*Hence we may also say that the rising of the mound of Tum is synonymous with the *lingam,* which (held sacred to the god Siva) is directly associated with the Sanskrit *linga sarira*—which is itself a portion of the (magical) astral light of nineteenth-century kabbalism and is thus form-generative. In that sense, the *lingam* represents the *ka* (aura or etheric double) enclosed by the *ba,* while Neheb-kau has otherwise been translated as meaning "provider of life energies" (Budge, *Gods of the Egyptians,* vol. 1, 62). The same principle gave rise to the term *omphalos,* from which the word *phallus* is derived. Thus it is that we find in the Greek tradition that the objects of veneration in the Dionysian Mysteries were the vine and the phallus. That in turn gave rise to a metaphorical association between the young man Emphalos and Dionysus himself—quite erroneously (and ludicrously) treated as signifying a homosexual relationship with the god.

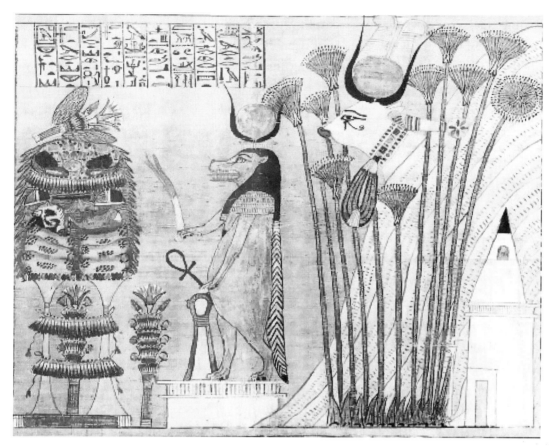

FIGURE 4.13. HATHOR, THE COSMIC COW GODDESS, WALKING OUT FROM THE FUNERAL MOUNTAIN

translated as "mother of the light." Budge also tells us that "as the 'lady of the Holy Land,' i.e., the Underworld, . . . she appears [see fig. 4.13] in the form of a cow walking out from the funeral mountain."[18]

The rationale behind all of this is an interesting one and its metaphysical logic needs to be clearly understood. Simply stated, it means as follows. The "divine sparks" (the offspring of Kosmic Mind and Desire) initially emanate ex nihilo as a single, homogeneously fiery mass, propelled downward into the field of demiurgic Being (the body of Tum) by the inherent energy of the Mntw-Ra principle. But they have no independence of each other, for they are all still as One. However, as they fall into the body of local kosmic consciousness of the Demiurge, or World Soul, it in its totality becomes their temporary home, which (metaphorically) is also a mortuary. From this environment, some fall yet further into the chaotic mass of Matter, which the Atum principle has ensouled, hence the Greek myth of Ouranos enfolding Gaea in his embrace and forcing his sexual attentions upon her, as we also saw earlier.

Now the creative energies that the Demiurge has thus absorbed are emanated by it within a mass of semi-individualized, spheroidal bodies of living light created out of its own nature, these latter being metaphorically represented as coffins. It is then these that were paradoxically called Het-Her(u)—meaning "house of spiritual consciousness," which only later in the succeeding evolutionary sequence came to signify "liberation."* But, while this great cosmic interlude lasts, these "sidereal bubbles" take on a massed semi-independence, which generates between them an abstract geometrical pattern of relationship, producing a vast web (or net) of light†—the ethereal chassis upon which the *objective* form of the demiurgic Creation itself is to be built. It is this same pattern that thus becomes the expressed or *outer* form of the originating Divine Purpose. In the cosmic dimension, the stars themselves thus come into being, each a "divine spark" at the center of its own localized celestial sphere of Being, which in turn contains its own myriad subhierarchies of lesser beings—the self-created progeny of each such "god."

It is this principle of liberation into a *cosmically* semi-independent spiritual vehicle that underlies the very name Her(u)—the hierarchy of Horus. From it the Greeks derived their word *hero*—the one who succeeds in his psychospiritual endeavors. Their mythical character Herakles (our anglicized Hercules) was himself an esoteric metaphor for the fallen "divine spark" in Man, which has to fight its own way back to self-conscious divinity by undergoing many worldly experiences, plus twelve (zodiacal) labors—but more of that later on.

In a purely material sense, Net and Hathor then represent the wider cosmic container of what our modern astrophysicists are pleased to call the "dark matter" of sidereal space, which holds together in thrall all the many galaxies and constellations of stars.‡ Thus the cowlike Hathor (logically depicted as the consort of (A)Temu)§ was clearly depicted as a generally passive and benevolent spiritual principle, symbolically depicted as the goddess figure who provides the deceased with food and drink under her sacred sycamore

---

*As there were actually *seven* Hathors, we may suggest with some reasonable degree of certainty that there were seven associated groups of Heru and of fallen "divine sparks," which in toto constituted the nature of the god Shu. This includes the Shemsu-Heru.

†This web of light was depicted by the ancient Egyptians as a great net that existed in the Underworld but came under the aegis of Tehuti, the god of the organizing Mind and Memory principles. Thus the layout or form of the net depicted as put and held together by the goddess Net/Neith (a direct associate of Hathor)—was the result of karmic memory from a previous cosmic cycle.

‡It is important to remember, however, that while Hathor symbolized the purely localized principle of *Universal* Consciousness (i.e., the Sanskrit *buddhi*), Horus represented an individualized *self*-consciousness. Although Hathor was regarded as an aspect of the goddesses Net and Isis—both of whom were described as giving birth to the Horus principle—she has to be seen as such in a much more general sense. Like Isis, she was also directly associated with the star Sirius, which was known as "the second Sun in heaven" (Budge, *Gods of the Egyptians,* vol. 1, 435).

§Hence we find an immediate association with the Nordic mystic tradition in which the celestial cow goddess is Audumlah—a clear corruption of Atum-Lha, whose son is Bur—who in turn marries Besla (Bes-Lha), a female from the tribe of giants. The name Bur gives rise in turn to Boreas, via association with the Greco-Babylonian Eos—the deity of the light of dawn and dusk (Graves, *Greek Myths,* 57).

tree or date palm—yet another metaphor for the regenerative nature of the spiritual state, which enables the reincarnating Ego to return, thoroughly refreshed and renewed, to the Underworld in another round of human incarnation. Not surprisingly, Hathor was regarded as one of the most generally popular of the Egyptian goddesses.

In apparent contradiction of this, however, we find Hathor taking part, with the goddess Sekhet (wife of Ptah), in the mass destruction of Mankind, at the behest of Ra, who becomes thoroughly irritated at Man's lack of respect for him. However, this is yet another esoteric allegory (see appendix E for details and interpretation)—this time paradoxically dealing with the sequence by which essentially *kosmic* Man was seen by the Egyptian philosophers and metaphysicists as being born into a *solar* existence. Thus destruction was in fact a metaphor for transition, or metamorphosis.

The God Tehuti (Thoth)

Tehuti is often regarded by Egyptologists as the self-begotten Egyptian Demiurge, but this is actually not so.* While he certainly symbolizes the Universal Mind and Memory of the Demiurge, and he was described as "both the heart and the tongue of Ra,"[19] he has to be seen as only expressing a part of its nature. The key to this lies in the fact that he *appears* to be a lunar god. But the Moon in esoteric terms means the *reflection* of the noumenal solar deity. Tehuti is thus not the Demiurge but rather its subsidiary agent, lower down the septenary scale. Curiously, however, he was regarded as having powers greater than either Osiris or Ra himself.†

As a principle, Tehuti really needs to be understood by relating him to his consort Ma'at, the goddess of Truth (of whom more in just a moment), and to the sacred heron/ ibis, which hatched the *lesser* world egg on the Isle of Flames at Hermopolis Magna (Khemennu).[20] This city was famous in Egyptian mythology as the place containing the high ground on which Ra rested when he arose for the first time. Here in the temple of Ab'tit there existed the House of the Net (a web of light fashioned by the goddess Neith), which, although under the guardianship of Tehuti, was owned by Ra and used in his perpetual war against the lesser *neteru* of the Underworld. Here also Tehuti was the leader of the *pauat* of four pairs of gods: Nu and Nut, Hehu and Hehut, Kek and Keket, and Kerh and Kerhet.‡[21]

---

*One tradition had it that he was born of the union of Horus the Elder with the kosmic Set (Griffiths, *The Conflict of Horus and Seth,* 82). He was otherwise certainly regarded as an aspect of the intelligence of the god Ptah.

†Probably because Ra only represents the dynamic cycle of Life within the sphere of Creation, while Tehuti represents the memory aspect of the great Kosmic Mind that gave rise to its appearance in the first place.

‡These were the frog-headed deities, symbolic of the ever-fertile creative principle that generates "strings" of lesser soul-bodies.

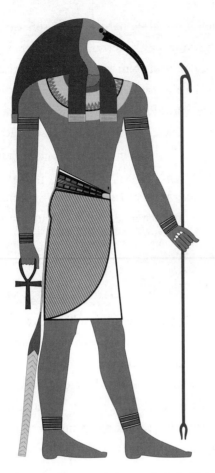

FIGURE 4.14. TEHUTI (THOTH)
AS THE SACRED HERON
(Illustration by Jeff Dahl)

Under the form of the god Aah-Tehuti, Tehuti is depicted "as a mummy, standing upon the symbol of Ma'at and holding in his hands the emblem of life, stability, sovereignty and dominion . . . also with the side lock of youth upon his head."[22] But as Budge comments: "The head has two faces, intended presumably to represent the periods of the waxing and waning of the moon."[23] In fact, the two faces are themselves representative of the dual Mind principle—that which looks up to the spiritual world and that which also looks down into the Underworld. It is like the Roman god Janus, who looked forward into the future and backward to the past. Other aspects of the Tehuti principle are to be found in the form of the sacred heron* and the baboon. The former was called the messenger of Tehuti. The latter was symbolically regarded as skilled in the field of arithmetic and the measurement of time, thereby indicating that it was representative of the analytical and organizational aspects of the Mind principle.

---

*The sacred heron otherwise represented that aspect of the Mind principle that contains and impresses itself upon the demiurgic soul principle. The esoteric metaphor involves the fact that, when hunting for food, the heron wades through shallow water, and carefully selecting its favorite prey—the smaller water snakes or eels—it pounces with its long beak and then swallows them whole. As the serpent form and the soul were synonymous, the eel or water snake thus became synonymous with each *idea* selected by the Mind.

The God Shu and His Consort Tefnut

These particular deities, although referred to in the ancient texts as "lion gods," were nearly always represented in human form—Shu particularly. Shu was best known for the one, two, or four feathers of Ma'at stuck in his headband. Like his Greek counterpart, Atlas, Shu represented the principle of light. However, while Shu symbolized the energetic aspect of that (universal) principle—incorporating the corresponding phenomena of levity, dryness, and evaporation within the plane of physically objective experience—Tefnut represented its material counterpart—the phenomena of moistness, condensation, and the equivalent of gravity. Both, however, were seen as united within one soul principle and must therefore be regarded as together representing the principle of a dual polarity within the field of vitality.

While Shu was described as being the very soul of the god Khnemu and having otherwise been primordially emanated from the eyes of his father Ra-Tem(u), he was otherwise seen as having power over serpents and as manifesting the strength of the creator-god

FIGURE 4.15. SHU WITH FEATHER OF MA'AT IN HIS HEADBAND

Ptah.[24] In that sense, he not only held up the four pillars of the heavens but also provided the very ladder (of light) that enabled the initiate to climb heavenward. But "light" here means that principle in all the *subjective* planes or states of Nature, rather than merely the physically objective.

Light, or illumination, has been known since time immemorial in human society as synonymous with perceptual intelligence, a principle that is nevertheless very different from that of the Mind per se. Whereas the Mind—represented by Tehuti—orders the actual format and sequence of expression of Divine Purpose (and thus immediately constrains and artificially limits it), the Intelligence sees immediately and directly through the mere representation to the *essence* within. As seen from below, the Intelligence rises ineffably through the mass of the mind-forms, unimpeded by them. In the sense of perception alone, the Intelligence does not need the Mind, for it merely observes the inner reality. However, when used in application with the Mind, its force guides the latter's expression in much closer conformity with the Divine Will—hence the common symbolic use of the sacred ostrich feather by both Shu and Ma'at.

The Goddess Ma'at

Always depicted symbolically with the sacred feather of light pointing vertically upward from her headband, Ma'at was representative of straightness, truth, and justice. In the sense also that the light world of the intermediate heaven (of Net), looking down upon the solar Underworld, was itself the expression of a directing kosmic Purpose, it might be said that Ma'at represented the universal principle of perceptive Intelligence itself, as Divine Law. As the single feather is merely the fragment of the wing, this attribution is quite logical. The Egyptians were not concerned about mere appearances. They actually wanted to see the representation of symbolic *function*.

Now the name Ma'at is clearly synonymous with the word *mahat* in Sanskrit, the latter being commonly translated these days as the Universal Mind—*mah* meaning "great" and *hat* actually meaning the *vehicle* of dynamic Intelligence, rather than Mind per se. These two words, *Mind* and *Intelligence,* are commonly used synonymously, but as we have just seen, they in fact mean quite different things, for Mind is a derived function, whereas Intelligence is a natural faculty. The Mind functions well or poorly according to the quality and control of the Intelligence that "drives" it. It was because of this that Ma'at was regarded as the female consort of Tehuti. He represented the Omniscient Universal Mind principle, but Ma'at acted as its directional agent. Thus in a hymn to Ra we find "the god Thoth and the goddess Ma'at have written down thy daily course for thee every day . . . may I see Horus acting as steersman (in the boat of Ra) with Thoth and Ma'at, one on each side of him."[25] As Horus represented the principle of psychospiritual

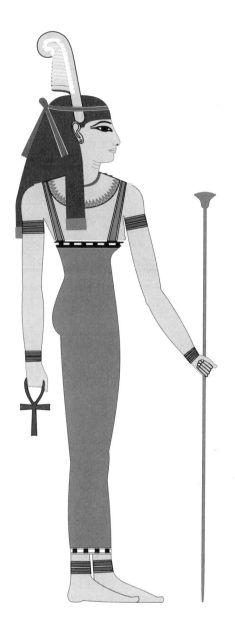

FIGURE 4.16. MA'AT, WITH THE SACRED FEATHER OF LIGHT
(Illustration by Jeff Dahl)

self-consciousness, we can see precisely what is intended by this navigational triumvirate.

It is true that, in a practical day-to-day sense, the Egyptians saw Ma'at as the personification of truthfulness, ordered existence, and moral law in their society, but this represents only the outer face of the much wider and deeper meaning. Bearing in mind that Amen-Ra was said to "rest upon Ma'at" while Ra was said to "live by Ma'at" and that Osiris "carries along the Earth in his train by Ma'at in his name of Seker,"[26] we can see that the principle for which Ma'at stood was wholly fundamental to the proper and ordered existence of our local universe as a whole.

Ma'at was described as sitting in Maati, her Hall of Judgment, accompanied by forty-two Assessors—paralleling the forty-two nomes or districts of Upper and Lower Egypt, as also the forty-two substates of the six solar planes below the divine plane in the sevenfold scheme of things. These Assessors were depicted as asking searching questions of those passing through the Hall of Maati, to confirm whether they were pure enough of heart to progress on to the higher, divine state beyond. However, even after satisfying all these criteria, the individual was not allowed to pass out of the Hall until he had also first satisfied the goddess Mau-Taui, who is herself defined as an alter ego of Tehuti.[27]

The Goddess Seshat/Sesheta

Daughter of Nut, sister of Osiris, and mother of Heru-neb, Seshat (although usually treated by Egyptologists as only a minor figure in the overall pantheon) was the vitally important goddess of the sevenfold principle, who was closely involved with the god Tehuti in the unfolding of the Universal Memory to produce the inherently sevenfold structure of *all* forms in Universal Nature. It is thus that she was regarded as the goddess not only of con-

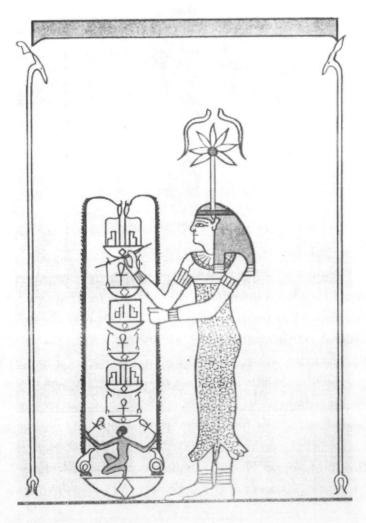

FIGURE 4.17. SESHAT/ SESHETA, WITH A SEVEN-FOLD FLOWER

Apart from the sevenfold flower upon her head, seven states of being are incorporated within the peculiar tiered arrangement in front of Seshat, the second, fourth, and sixth of these tiers being the same but progressively smaller in size. These three all enclose the ankh, symbolizing the (passive) principle of the animating Breath of Life. Man—i.e., the human being—is to be found at the seventh and lowest level of the arrangement, hanging from two serrated counting poles (representing time), which are themselves being steadied by the human figure holding them in place. Seshat, meanwhile, is holding what appears to be a writing stylus, strategically positioned between the first and second tiers (symbolic of the divine and semidivine states in the sevenfold system).

struction but also, perhaps curiously, of literature. As the whole of the noumenal and phenomenal universe was regarded by the Egyptians as sevenfold in actuality—as also Man himself—she (like Ma'at) was absolutely fundamental to the structure of ordered existence. In relation to the constructional side, the Egyptologist Margaret Murray confirms to us that "one of her chief functions was to take part in the founding of temples and, down to the latest times, the 'stretching of the cord' for measuring the size of a new temple was performed by the pharaoh and Seshat"[28]—or presumably by one or more of the temple priestesses of her cult.

In relation to the sevenfold nature of Man—something which we shall look at a little more closely in the next chapter—we find in the Book of the Dead the initiate or deceased being made to say: "I have my place of peace in Annu, wherein is my house [i.e., the *ba*]; it was built for me by the goddess Sesheta and the god Khnemu set it up for me upon its walls."[29] In this sense the Sesheta principle is shown as inherent in the nature of the (astral) soul-body—hence the appearance of the seven main *thesu* (chakras) in the *ka* (etheric double). She is otherwise shown, as Budge tells us, "as a kind of 'recording angel, not so much of the deeds committed by man, but of their names."[30]

At that point we shall conclude this preliminary introduction to the greater gods of Egypt. What we have dealt with so far, however, covers only the broad general principles active in Creation (as the Egyptians saw it). In the next two chapters we shall take a much closer look at the appearance of Man himself plus those lesser gods associated with him and purely *solar* existence, within the lowest of the seven kosmic planes of being.

FIVE

SIDEREAL GENESIS

THE ORIGIN AND NATURE OF MAN

And Man, having learned to know the being of the Divine Administrators and received a share of their nature, he willed to break through the bounding circle of their orbits; and he looked down through the structure of the heavens, having broken through the sphere and showed to downward-tending Nature the beautiful form of God. And Nature, seeing the beauty of the form of God, smiled with insatiate love of Man, showing the reflection of that most beautiful form in the water and its shadow on the earth. And he [Man] seeing this form, a form like to his own, in earth and water, loved it and willed to dwell there. And the deed followed close on the design and he took up his abode in matter devoid of reason.

HERMETICA

As far as the Ancients were concerned, Man was a multidimensional being whose innermost nature was divine.* While the associated complexity is perhaps a puzzle to lay students of ancient Egyptian culture, it is even more so for formally trained modern Egyptologists who sadly have little true knowledge of, or sympathy with, the mystic and metaphysical side of the mind of ancient humankind. In this chapter, therefore, we shall not only take

---

*As the *Hermetica* explains: "For man is a being of divine nature; he is comparable not to the other living creatures upon Earth, but to the gods in heaven. Nay, if we are to speak the truth without fear, he who is indeed a man is even above the gods of heaven, or at any rate he equals them in power. None of the gods of heaven will ever quit heaven and pass its boundary and come down to Earth. But man ascends even to heaven and measures. And what is more, he mounts to heaven without quitting the Earth. To so vast a distance can he put forth his power. We must not shrink then from saying that a man on Earth is a mortal god and that a god in heaven is an immortal man."

a look at the actual composition of Man's multidimensional organism as the Ancients saw it, but we shall also consider what the different functions were believed to involve and how they came about. This will be more easily understood by those already to some extent familiar with so-called New Age concepts of Man's inner constitution. However, followed logically, there is no reason why any reasonably intelligent person cannot grasp the underlying rationale.

To begin with then, fig. 4.1 (see also 6.1) provides us with a diagram showing the various auras, or soul-bodies, that surround the individual human being. The usual assumption made by most people when seeing these is that they are all intended to depict outward extensions of the individual's consciousness. In fact, the very reverse is true. The waking consciousness of the human being was ever held to be but a tiny holographic expression of the *real* Man's nature. The latter—as we shall see in greater detail in a moment—was that of a "divine spark" whose immensely powerful and pretty well omniscient nature was to be found within what the Egyptians called the *akhet,* or Divine Soul-body. However, this is a state of perceptual consciousness that was regarded as permanently attuned to that which lay beyond the bounds of our solar system, within the sphere of our home universe, the latter being the Underworld to the liberated divine nature. It thus contained within itself all of the perception and creative power of the whole of the lowest of the seven kosmic planes of Being, with the potential to associate itself with all the other six kosmic states as well. It was, in short, a "god"—although in the case of the average human being, a god still in its infancy, whose full sense of self-consciousness (at the kosmic level) had yet to develop.

Because this god-being was of such a vastly powerful nature, only a small proportion of its consciousness was regarded as able to manifest within the lowest kosmic state, the sevenfold nature of which was held to be contained within our solar system. Hence this latter, *partial* god nature and *partial* god consciousness was to be found in the *sah,* or spiritual soul-body (frequently referred to as the "causal soul" by our own contemporaries), which is a *solar* entity in its own right, with an identifiable range of knowledge and power of its own. In similar manner, however, because the consciousness of this being was pan-solar (i.e., extraplanetary), it was too powerful to manifest directly or fully within the limited spectrum of matter provided by our own *planetary* existence, the sevenfold nature of which it contained within itself. It thus likewise projected a holographic expression of itself down into our Earth world, this replica being known to the Egyptians as the *ba,* and to we moderns as the astral soul-body.

The natural home of this latter planetary entity was what the Ancients called the "sphere of the Moon," which is actually not the Moon at all but rather the peripheral part of the Earth's outer atmosphere that magnetically holds the physical Moon in thrall. It is then within this local heaven world that we find the *sah* (which traditionally descends no lower); from it the *ba* is cyclically projected Earthward in order to

FIGURE 5.1. THE "BAPTISM" OF THE UNKNOWN GOD-MAN
(symbolizing spiritual conception; from the Temple of Kom-Ombo)
(Photo by Ernesto Herrero)

bring about the manifestation by birth of a human being. Each time that the *ba* does this, it appropriates to itself a proportion of the local matter of the Earth's atmosphere, which then becomes its *ka* (a literal vehicle). Into this it projects the potency of its sevenfold nature—which results in the appearance of the sevenfold chakra system (known to the Egyptians as the *thesu*), which in turn creates the web of etheric light around which the cellular matter of the visible physical body matter is itself gradually accumulated.* But we shall now move on to consider the subject of Man as distinct from even the soul.

*While this brief synopsis gives us a general idea of the constitution of man as a soul, as the ancient Egyptians saw him, it is quite clear from some of the almost exactly similar terminology used by them that the ancient Hindu Brahmans of India also followed precisely the same conceptual ideas.

Man as a "Divine Spark"

As already established, the Ancients regarded Man as of essentially divine origin by virtue of his consciousness being animated and driven by the "divine spark" within. But what exactly is this "spark," and why did they draw such a distinction between the inner self and the outer self? What do these concepts themselves mean? The answers to such questions provide us with many of the keys to ancient Egyptian mystic culture and they therefore need to be carefully examined. Before we proceed, however, we need to bear in mind that all ancient religions (like the Christian faith today) believed in Deity being a unity in essence, a duality in nature, and a trinity in aspect—the latter representing the universal principles of: (1) Self-willed Life; (2) Sentient Consciousness; and (3) Creative Instinct. This duality and these three divine aspects then conditioned *all* beings and spheres of existence in Universal Nature (including both the "spark" and the soul-body adopted by it), each of which thus *predominantly* expressed one or other.

In the Egyptian tradition, Man (the "spark" of Divine Purpose) was regarded as having been born "amid the tears of Kheper-Ra" once he had joined together all the members of his (demiurgic) body-form,[1] while the gods (i.e., the *neteru*) themselves were born merely as seeds from his breath. The idea implicit in this appears to have been that Man (in his highest nature) was the expression of conscious divine imagination—clearly a higher state of being than the nature of the merely demiurgic gods (the *neteru*). It is because of this that we find the fully perfected god-Man Unas* (Un-As meaning quite literally "one consciously reunited Being") described as "devouring the gods," a description that, if taken other than metaphorically, makes no sense at all. In the very name and personage of Unas, however, we find three other clues concerning Man's higher nature. First of all, the very concept of a unified being implies that which is (or becomes) otherwise multifold in nature—an indication that Unas comprised many hierarchies of Life.[†] Second, Unas was referred to as a "son of (the star)

---

*Unas was said to have been conceived by Sekhet (the goddess wife of Ptah) and by Sothis (the star Sirius, according to Budge, *Gods of the Egyptians,* vol. 1, 514 et seq.), known to the Egyptians as Sbd, a name phonetically very similar to the Sanskrit term (*sabda*) for "word"—here the "Divine Word." The name Sekhet is itself derived from *sekhem,* thus meaning the "house of a spiritual flame," of a power emanating from the divine state itself. As the "son" of Ptah and Sekhet was Nefer-Tem—regarded metaphorically as having been born by emanation from the blue lotus (Budge, *Gods of the Egyptians,* vol. 1, 520)—the inference is that what began its existence as a Nefer-Tem eventually matured into an Unas.

†Budge (*Gods of the Egyptians,* vol. 1, 120) otherwise tells us: "The region where the heaven of Unas was situated is called 'Aaru' . . . [depicted symbolically as] a mass of waving reeds." And again (177): "In chapter cxlv of the Book of the Dead according to the Theban and Saite Recensions the domain of Osiris, i.e., Sekhet-Aaru, or Sekkhet-Aanre, contains twenty-one pylons." These thus clearly represent the seven substates of the three highest planes or states of the solar world beneath that of the solar heaven itself—that is, $3 \times 7 = 21$.

FIGURE 5.2. OANNES

Sirius;[*2] and third, Unas is clearly none other than the Chaldeo-Sumerian Oannes, described by the historian Berosus as the divine being who (again, metaphorically) as half-man, half-fish, emerged from the Great Sea (i.e., of space itself) in the most ancient times to teach humanity the arts, crafts, and sciences.

The gods (*neteru*) were regarded as hierarchies of divine being that expressed some particular (universal) principle in Nature, aspects of which could be pictorially characterized and magically invoked. Thus the concept of One Being (Unas) who—through self-evolution—combined in himself all these universal principles would indeed be regarded as "devouring them all" and rising above and commanding them. So far, so

---

*Budge (*Gods of the Egyptians* vol. 1, 58) asserts: "Though he [Man] is the son of God he is also the child of Sothis, and the brother of the Moon." In other words, Sirius (Sothis) must have provided certain superior hierarchies of soul-bodies, while the Moon provided correspondingly less evolved ones. Note otherwise the mouth of the fish, which is clearly symbolic of the crown chakra, while the fish body similarly symbolizes the principle of *kundalini*—the electrical power of the Kosmic Mind, which enables Oannes to travel through space by thought alone.

good. But at this point we usually begin to run into those people who—lacking any true sense of the spiritual nature having a factual existence as real as (or even more real than) the physical—cannot bring themselves to believe that Beings from Sirius could have been anything other than an intellectually and technologically advanced super-race who visited Earth long ago in spacecraft. This, however, is a sadly materialistic travesty of what was originally believed. But, we have already, to some extent, considered the role of Sirius in earlier chapters and will thus dwell no further on it here. We need to deal with a few more basic issues first, starting with the seven divisions or planes of our sidereal-terrestrial Nature in which Man and man are to be found.

The Seven and Twelve Divisions of the Subjective-Objective World of Man

As already indicated, it is altogether impossible to understand the Egyptian metaphysical system as obscurely outlined in the Book of the Dead and elsewhere without first understanding the ancient metaphysical concept behind what Egyptologists call "the twelve divisions," but which we would today call "the seven (solar) planes of being and consciousness," through which the consciousness of Man was deemed to constantly cycle. In chapter 4 we saw the seven *kosmic* aspects of the great god Ra (the Demiurge). However, the "divisions" of Egyptology refer to what lies *within* the lowest and most objective kosmic state. It is then within and from the spectrum of matter of this latter sevenfold state (provided by the *solar* Demiurge) that Man gathers the materials needed to create his various "vehicles" of consciousness and through which he must return to his originating heavenly home. It should also be noted—as symbolically depicted in the picture of the "seven cows of Ra" (see fig. 4.5)—that the world of man's psychological, psychic, and physical natures, created out of lesser *neteru* existence, is to be found comprising the substance and creative nature of the three lowest of these solar states.

1. Divine Being—the solar heaven world (Aaru)
2. Semidivine Being—the Field of Peace (Sekhet-Hetep)
3. Pure Spiritual Being—the Field of Grasshoppers (Sekhet-Sanehemu)
4. Spiritual soul consciousness—the Field of the Seven Hathors (Het-Heru)
5. Psychological consciousness
6. Psychic awareness
7. Physical sensitivity and corporeal being

Correspondingly, within each and every one of these states/planes of being, there existed seven substates. Consequently, as one might imagine in view of the hylozoistic principle, the constant interaction of all the associated bodies, beings, and unorganized matter that comprised these states and substates produced a huge psychospiritual complexity. It then became the fundamental task of the initiate in the Mysteries to be able not only to recognize and discriminate between them, while (consciously) in an out-of-body state, but also then to pass back and forth freely through them without being in any way affected by their magnetisms and incessant volatilities—something that could only be safely achieved by his personal purity of mind. Once he had achieved this, he became a Ptah-Seker-As'r. However, before we get to the point of considering the advanced human individuality that is so far along the spiritual Path, let us have a look at the raw material from which that individuality was originally shaped.

The *Neteru*, the *Neferu*, and the *Akhu*

The Ancients drew a very clear distinction between the gods and Man. In the Hindu tradition of the Brahmans of ancient Indo-Persia, the gods of Nature became *suras* and *devas,* while Man—the rebellious angel—became an *a-sura.* In the Greek and Near Eastern traditions, the distinction between the *suras* and *asuras* became that between angels and daemons, the latter actually being the term for a guardian spirit, not a devil. However, the essence of the distinction was that the gods or *suras* were representative of the instinctive consciousness of the Logos and were thus only capable of reexpressing his faculty of Divine Memory, by constant repetition of the status quo. They thus possessed no sense of option.* Man, the *asura* (the "spark" of higher Divine Purpose), however, was different, for by his very raison d'etre, he developed the power of choice. But let us explain in a little more detail.

In order to understand the multiple nature of Man, we need to understand the fundamental difference between his divine nature, his spiritual nature, and his psychic or elemental nature, because these words—divine, spiritual, and elemental—are commonly used in very cavalier fashion, usually without realizing that the distinction is immensely important, dealing as it does with three qualitatively quite distinct fields of being and consciousness. Now, while the many hierarchies of beings of the angelic or deva kingdom were given the generic name *neteru* (the elemental kingdoms of Nature being their progeny), the Egyptian name for the originating "divine spark" in Man was *akh,* the origin of which we shall discuss in a moment.

---

*A point confirmed by Hermes Trismegistus in the *Hermetica* (337), where he is made to say: "But the gods are made of the purest part of matter and have no need of reason and knowledge to aid them; and, accordingly, through their immortality and the vigour of their everlasting youth, are mightier than any wisdom or knowledge. Yet in place of knowledge and intelligence, God appointed for them an ordered movement determined by necessity and prescribed by Eternal Law."

The *akh* itself was regarded as the expression of Divine Purpose and its fall into the lowest sphere of kosmic existence was therefore seen as the Mind-borne Will of the Logos, endeavoring to impress itself upon the material nature of its *neter* vehicle. But in line with the triple nature of creative existence, the fall of the *akh* itself became triple—that is to say, the originally unified stream of *akhu* separated into three streams. One of these (retaining its kosmic nature) fell into and remained in the highest part of the solar heaven world, thereby revivifying and reorganizing the demiurgic nature of the *devas* or gods of the divine state. As this then resulted in the creation of a duality of existence (i.e., of Spirit and Matter) *within* the sphere of being encompassed by the Demiurge, the second group fell into the field of spiritual nature (and thus became a truly *solar* entity), while the third fell into the lowest world of purely terrestrial existence and became known as the *set-akh,* or Setekh. The task of the second group was then to assist the third group toward a self-motivated reintegration with its own nature.

The gradual self-coordination of the third group as a discrete psychospiritual being in its own right then gradually evolved that sense of independent existence that we find progressively in the plant, animal, and human kingdoms. Thus this evolutionary progression toward an awareness of the overshadowing nature of Man, the spiritual being, eventually resulted in the development of an equivalent *self*-consciousness in the archaic human type (millions of years ago). But the progression from here on to the spiritual Path proper made of this entity within man's reincarnating nature a *nefer,* a word significantly otherwise used within the Egyptian army to mean a "recruit"[3]—thus here a "spiritual recruit," or neophyte in the Mysteries.

The Primordial Nature of Man the "Divine Spark"

The paradox in the Creation process is that each "divine spark," the primordial emanation of Divine Purpose inseminated into the auric sphere of the sidereal world system-to-be from a kosmic state beyond it, was regarded as possessing no immediately appropriate body form of its own.* As a consequence, it was depicted as a complete and unified hierarchy of divine spirits under the name of the ever unseen god Khem, whose vehicle was an ark, guarded by the figure of Apuat. This, however, is but the anglicized version of the Egyptian *akh*—itself apparently derived from *a-kh-hem,*† meaning an individual group of divine spirits, or "sparks," a fragment of the Kosmic Mind seeking to impress itself upon Universal Matter.‡

---

*Hence Plutarch's pithy observation in *De Placitis Philosophorum* that "an idea is a *being* incorporeal, which has no subsistence of itself, but gives figure and form unto shapeless matter, and [so] *becomes the cause of its manifestation*" (quoted by Blavatsky in *Secret Doctrine,* vol 1, 622; italics added).
†The suffix *hem,* as in the Semitic *him* (e.g., Elohim, or Al-him), means a collective or group entity.
‡In the Pyramid Texts of Unas (para. 1760, utterance 624), the *akh* is described as "imperishable" and also as a "star."

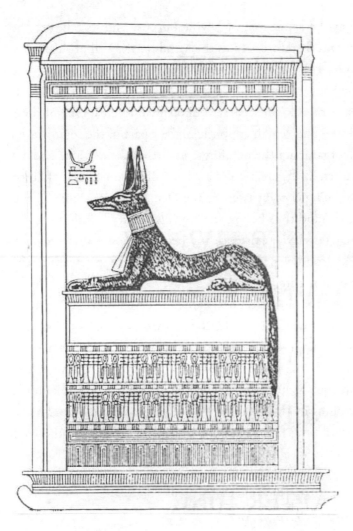

FIGURE 5.3. APUAT GUARDING THE ARK

The highest solar state into which these *akhu* fell thus became their local home—the *akh-het,* or *akhet.* Although commonly translated as "horizon," a better interpretation would be "(invisible) heavenly firmament," the latter divine state immediately enfolding the Demiurge-to-be within its auric embrace. Consequently, the next stage of unfoldment within the local sidereal system involved divinity becoming semidivinity. Now the primordial state of being of the Demiurge was known by the root word *as*—from which the names of Osiris and Isis (i.e., As'r and As't) were derived. Thus the full union of the fallen "divine sparks" with this state of divine solar being produced the *akh-as,* which is synonymous with the Sanskrit *akas(a),* meaning a primordial (prespiritual or semidivine) state from which all ordered knowledge emanates. Consequently, it is this state that is the source of all *solar* Creation. Hence we might say that the *akh,* by uniting itself with the primordial demiurgic state, was reigniting the self-willed expression (from prior cycles of experience) of the Logos behind our sidereal scheme. In short, the *akhu* were the harbingers of the divine karma of the Logos and also the agents provocateurs of Divine Memory.

Interestingly, we find widespread mention of the *akh(u)* principle elsewhere in the world. In the Ugaritic texts of ancient Chaldea we find the *okelim*—that is, *akh-elhim*—divine beings sent by the supreme god El to fight and conquer Baal (i.e., the Demiurge). In Phoenicia, they were correspondingly known as *aquqim*—probably derived from *akhu-khem*. In furthest Polynesia we find the *ahu*, the giant standing statues of Easter Island, and in Bolivia we find it concealed within the sacred name of Tihuanaco—itself derived from *ti-vahan-akhu*, meaning "Heaven Vehicle of the Divine Spirits." Within the Greek tradition the name mutates into Iaho, the illegitimate son of Zeus and Demeter, the goddess of fertility, while in the Hebrew it is Iao. In the Celtic world, the singular form was found as Oc or Og—thus their own heaven world became Ti(r)-nan-Oc, while the Celtic language in the southwest of France was originally the source of the name given to the region of the Languedoc.

The Ashemu

Now, just as the *akh* was derived from *a-khem*, so the demiurgic solar vehicle into which the *akhu* fell was the *as-hem*, or *ashem*,* this latter word meaning "the form in which a god is visible."[4] Thus the *ashemu* really means a hierarchy of divine soul beings (*neteru*); and from this same hierarchy of *as-hemu*, As'r (Osiris) and As't (Isis) became the *outwardly* manifesting principle of duality—that is, the spiritual soul-body (*sah*) and the astral soul-body (*ba*) respectively. At the climax of the *inward* returning, or evolutionary cycle, however, we have the Herculean Man-god figure Un-as becoming the "*ashem* of the *ashemu*"[5] and thereby absorbing the demiurgic nature entirely within his own in such a manner that he becomes greater than the very gods who conceived and gave birth to him.

In order to understand the protracted sequence by which this occurs, however, we need to remember that the phenomenon of duality resulting in objective Creation comes about *within* the sphere of demiurgic existence through the two emanations that occur, yin-yang fashion, from the twin poles of the semidivine (*akas-ic*) state, as depicted in fig. 5.4 (page 140). In this, the higher yin influence is that of the Osiris nature, which falls into a merely intermediate or secondary heaven world state—that of the spiritual soul. The more materially dominant yin influence, however—that involving the night cycle of the god Atum-Ra—falls yet further into the very depths of Matter in the Underworld, taking with it the goddesses Isis and Nephthys. However, right at the very bottom of this greater involutionary cycle—where Ra is metaphorically described in the sacred texts as "old and

---

*The heavenly home of the *as-hemu* (themselves seemingly synonymous with the *asu*, or divine breaths of the Hindu pantheon) was the *as-het*, which the Egyptians symbolized in the form of the *persea*, the Tree of Life in which the Great Cat Ra-Mau hid when attacking and decapitating the serpent Apep (Budge, *Gods of the Egyptians*, 61). Here also we find the root idea behind the sacred grove—the *as-ram* (ashram) in which the Mystery teachings were given out by sages to their disciples.

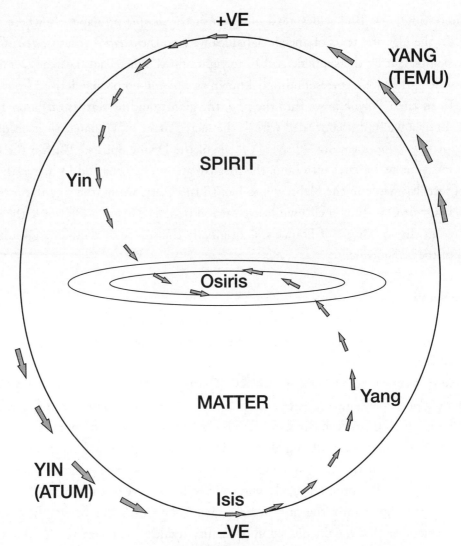

**FIGURE 5.4. TWO EMANATIONS FROM THE TWIN POLES
OF THE SEMIDIVINE (*AKAS-IC*) STATE**

tired"[6]—the Isis yang influence (that of the *ba*) kicks in and takes over.* But, encumbered with the burden of lesser Matter it has gathered up en route, it begins to climb back to the merely intermediate spiritual state, while the Ra influence now mutates into Ra-Tem and continues on its way, yang-fashion, back to its point of origin in the higher heaven world.

The Function of the Fallen "Sparks"

As elsewhere indicated, the self-centered instinct of the lesser "sparks" in Nature to accumulate matter for their own (subjective and objective) body forms was depicted by the

*Hence Isis being symbolic of the astroterrestrial (or planetary) soul nature that understands the secrets of *objective* Nature.

Egyptians as the politically acquisitive greed of the god Set. But the Set principle was dual, there being a kosmic Set—regarded as an entirely beneficent god, aiding human spiritual evolution in conjunction with Horus the Elder—and also a terrestrial, or mundane, counterpart. It was then the latter who symbolically "killed" his brother-god Osiris and temporarily appropriated the lower world kingdom (Egypt) for himself, until Osiris's son Horus the Child (representing the self-conscious, spiritually *oriented* nature in man) regained control.*

Returning to the question of the (holographic) duality produced by the very Creation process, it followed quite logically that every *akh* or "spark" intent upon expressing the Divine Will and Purpose of its parent Logos found itself able to do so only by projecting a relatively small part of its own nature (sparklets?) even further downward into yet more densely material existence (thus repeating the fall in microcosm). But, as we have just seen, this scattered emanation of lesser points of heavenly light is ultimately reabsorbed upward, back into its own true state of Being. This makes complete sense if we but remember the metaphysical principle that the point within the circle is itself a circle to a lesser point—which we might regard as one definition of Infinity. So, Creation—as seen by the Ancients—was ultimately a never-commencing, never-ending process, while the fall from Grace was likewise regarded as an incessantly repetitive cycle of differentiation on every single possible plane or state of Being.

The Sequence of Evolving Consciousness in Man

What has been described so far only involves the downward or involutionary cycle of the expression of Divine Purpose. This correspondingly had to be followed by an upward or evolutionary cycle involving the development of an increasingly individualized consciousness.† However, the names given by the Egyptians to the consequently developing sense of self resulting from the latter were quite different, reflecting the fact that this upward cycle involved a series of mutually cooperative recombinations, resulting in different stages and associated qualities of perceptive intelligence.

The earliest stage of egohood was known by the Egyptians simply as *ren*—"the

---

*Thereby bringing about a union of the spiritual and mundane natures in man, symbolized as the duality of Upper and Lower Egypt.

†When comparing these ideas with modern anthropological theory, we might say that in relation to the form-building and lesser instinctual life in Nature, the Darwinian theory of evolutionary development might appear partially to correspond. However, to the Ancients, only the divine and spiritual natures were capable of endowing man with self-conscious intelligence. The Egyptian system recognized this fact in its depiction of the interrelationship and interreaction between the lowest fallen "spark" (symbolized by the *terrestrial* Set) and Horus, son of Osiris (representing the principle of self-consciousness). For it was only when these principles had become sympathetically united in man that the Horus nature was allegorically shown as taking charge of Upper and Lower Egypt.

name"—the principle that was considered utterly crucial to the Egyptian's continued existence as a spiritual individuality. However, as this embryonic psychospiritual growth continued to develop, its mature form became known as a *nefer*—apparently signifying the coordinated intelligence of the individual. The mass of lesser "sparks" that thus coordinated their efforts to become one unified individuality in man thereafter had to create a bridge of consciousness spanning the mundane and psychic worlds before they could literally transfer themselves en masse into the spiritual state and thus forever quit the lesser Wheel of Necessity (i.e., the human cycle of reincarnation).

Now, because the god Tem(u) represented the expansive upward cycle of growth of the Atum-Ra cycle, when the *nefer* had reached the stage of actually beginning to penetrate into the upper spiritual world proper (i.e., on the Path of Initiation), he became known as a *nefer-tem,* a name closely associated with the symbolism of the lotus, as we shall see in a moment. The sequential follow-on from this was that when the *nefer-tem,* or initiate, finally emerged as a fully born individualized entity within the spiritual world (i.e., as an initiated adept) he became known as an *un-nefer,* or as Osiris *un-nefer,* the prefix *un* signifying that very same self-achieved individualization. Finally, when the *un-nefer* had developed yet further and regained in full self-consciousness the awareness of first the semidivine state and then the divine state itself (the *as*), he became Un-as, a fully individualized divinity or god-Man—a perfected "Breath."

Esotericism of the Lotus Metaphor

As we have just seen, when the human consciousness had become properly developed as a *spiritually* conscious individuality, it was called a *nefer-tem,** born (upward) into the field of direct spiritual awareness and perception via the self-engendered evolution of a mystically and occultly developed consciousness. Thus the Egyptians had Nefer-Tem(u) depicted as a child-god emanating from a sacred blue lotus—a symbol of self-generation (and of the rising Sun). For those unfamiliar with this plant, the metaphor relates to the fact that it has its roots in the mud of the river or lake (synonymous with the murkily objective world-state of objective human existence), and a very long stem,† which works its way up from the depths through the waters (i.e., the "waters" of the psychic and psychological worlds), on the surface of which (synonymous with the spiritual world itself) it then blooms to produce a beautiful, floating flower. Hence it was that the hierarchy of Nefer-Temu (the progeny of Ptah and the goddess Sekhet) was self-born *from out of the human state* amid the

---

*The Egyptian word *tem* meant "complete." Thus the *nefer-tem* was the initiate—one who had completed his spiritual probation.

†An image that has its very clear correspondence in the Hindu concept as the *antahkarana,* the "Way (or Path) of consciousness," of which it is said: "Thou canst not travel on the Path before thou hast become that Path itself" (Blavatsky, *Voice of the Silence,* 26).

FIGURE 5.5. NEFER-TEMU

a-t(e)mu, or *atma**—the pure spirit or fragrant effulgence of the lotus—a visual metaphor for the radiant and *semi*perfected Purpose of the Deity, which the thus-evolved mind and consciousness of man expressed as a spiritual adept, en route to (much later) Buddhahood.

The very close similarity between the words *neter* and *nefer* will doubtless already have occurred to the reader and we can say with some certainty that the similarity was no

---

*As *(a)temu* or *atmu* is synonymous with the Sanskrit *atma,* meaning Divine Breath, the name Nefer-Tem(u) actually indicates a hierarchy of Mind-born beings (hence "Man") emanating as the spiritual exudation of the Demiurge from one of the chakras floating on the "lake" of the kosmic *ka*. Rather interestingly, the lotus seed is sevenfold in organization and, in addition, the bud swells to its full size underwater, before it emerges through the surface of the lake and then bursts open to reveal the three concentric rows of petals of the flower itself. Hence the lotus became the symbol of Man's developing mentality and latent spirituality, which together expand enormously before actually flowering within the field of consciousness of the spiritual plane itself.

mere coincidence. The Egyptian concern with the meaning and pronunciation of words because of their magical associations was legendary. In fact, we can perhaps go so far as to suggest here that—by virtue of the word *neter* meaning a divine principle in Nature (i.e., as expressed by the *deva*/angelic hierarchies)—*nefer* actually signifies an initiated Man-being regarded as having evolved itself to be on a par with the angelic hierarchies within the spiritual world-state. It is otherwise interesting to note that the pyramid of Unas at Saqqara was itself called *nefer-asu*. *As* meaning "a state of being" and *asu* in Sanskrit meaning "breath," the literal translation should thus perhaps be something like "initiate(d)-being(s)," or "spiritual initiate(s)," or "individualized Breath."

The God-Man Unas

While Unas is regarded by Egyptologists as a pharaoh of an early (fifth) dynasty in the Old Kingdom, it seems pretty clear from careful consideration of the phraseology and contexts in the sacred texts—those found in the pyramid of Unas at Saqqara—that the name was in fact a generic one, used for a high initiate. The tradition that he was said to have been conceived by Sekhet and Sothis (Sirius) and later united to the goddess Mut, the World Mother,[7] surely confirms this. But let us take a brief analytical look at probably the best-known part of the texts, which is well worth quoting at length and reads as follows:

> The bones of Aker tremble and those who are ministrants unto them [the stars and sky] betake themselves to flight when they see Unas rising . . . like a god who liveth upon his fathers and feedeth upon his mothers. Unas is the lord of wisdom whose name his mother knoweth not. The noble estate of Unas is in heaven, and his strength in the horizon is like unto the god Tem his father; indeed, he is stronger than his father who gave him birth. . . . Unas is the Bull of heaven which overcometh by his will, and which feedeth upon that which cometh into being from every god, and he eateth of the provender of those who fill themselves with words of power and come from the Lake of Flame.[8]

It is as a result of "eating the bodies of the gods" that Unas becomes "the Great Sekhem, the Sekhem of the Sekhemu" and the "Great Ashem of the Ashemu," for "the power which protects Unas and which he possesses is greater than that of all the *sahu* in the heavens, and he becomes the eldest of all the firstborn gods . . . indeed, the power which has been given to him as the Great Sekhem makes him to become as the star Sahu, i.e., Orion, with the gods."[9]

Anybody who seriously believes that this text was merely prepared for a single, vainglorious pharaoh, rather than indicating a highly advanced stage of initiateship, has clearly missed the whole plot of what ancient Egyptian mysticism was all about.

The Alternative God Metaphor of the Ancient Egyptians

Now so far we have discussed that more or less direct approach to the teaching about Creation from the viewpoint of the initiates in the Mystery School. What we are going to look at next involves the same area of consideration from the viewpoint of the main allegorical myths and god metaphors made available to the lay population in general. This then involves the sacred Ennead of gods headed by Atum-Ra, Tefnut, Shu, Nut, Geb, Horus the Elder, Osiris, Set, Isis, and Nephthys—normally associated with the city and sacred Academy of Heliopolis (Anu).

The Genesis of the Lesser Gods and Man

As we have already indicated, primordial divine Man (the *akh*) appears properly only in the lowest of the seven kosmic divisions or planes of being—that contained by the god Atum-Ra—where, although of kosmic origin, he becomes by default a *solar* being. Atum—

FIGURE 5.6. THE SEPARATION OF NUT AND GEB BY SHU

Note: In the picture we have the two barques of Ra. On the left is the night barque and on the right is the day barque. The day effectively started at midnight and the barque commencing this half of the twenty-four-hour cycle was under the influence of the god Atum-Ra. Thus the barque of Atum's alter ego Temu-Ra completed the second half of the journey back to the celestial horizon, between midday and midnight. It should be remembered that, while we might imagine the "night" to commence at dusk and finish at dawn, the ancient Egyptian mystic cycle of the god Tum-Temu was rather different, because it involved a passage downward into material existence from a celestial heaven world in which the stars were seen as at the zenith, *not* the physical Sun, as is generally supposed.

as we saw at the end of the last chapter—although depicted in the Egyptian tradition as a mound of Matter arising from out of the waters of space (i.e., the Abyss of Nu), became associated elsewhere with the phallically shaped lingam, or omphalos, itself the natural extension of the tum-ulus, or man-made hill. That is because Matter itself—once energized by the *akhu*—possessed the instinct of creative self-organization. But let us go back one stage to the sequence actually involving the appearance of Atum.

As outlined in the last chapter, within the Heliopolitan tradition Nu-Nun—the god of the "great waters" (of metaphysical space)—was described as taking on the undulating form of the great (kosmic) serpent of many coils, Nehebkau, while within the coils of this great serpent principle Atum was depicted as lying in a state of dormant potential. However, as the greater kosmic Impulse reached and was sensed by Nehebkau, he developed five heads—symbolic of the five universal elements—just like the Hindu serpent-god Vasuki.* The associated form of the Heliopolitan tradition otherwise has Atum-Ra, after evolving into the great cat

FIGURE 5.7. ATUM-RA, AFTER EVOLVING INTO THE GREAT CAT RA-MAU, CUTTING OFF THE HEAD OF THE SERPENT, THEREBY PERMITTING THE GROWTH OF THE GREAT WORLD TREE

---

*In the Hindu tradition, the *suras* (the "gods" who unchallengingly follow the old Divine Plan) and the *a-suras* hold between them the five-headed (symbolizing the five elements of objective Creation) cosmic serpent, the Naga-King Vasuki, and use it in a tug-of-war against each other. The *asuras* hold the head end while the *devas* hold the tail end. In the center, the serpent's body is coiled around Mount Mandera—the Indian version of Mntw-Ra—which is itself surrounded by seven island continents separated from each other by seven seas. This metaphysical symbolism (incidentally very similar to Plato's description of the island of Atlantis; see *Timaeus and Critias,* 129 et seq.) quite unmistakably refers to seven (kosmic) states of Being, animated by the *devas* and *asuras.* Thus it is their combined activities that actually create and maintain the sevenfold universe in its forms and workings. However, the churning of the kosmic ocean brings to the surface fourteen lost or concealed gifts of great value, which exactly correspond to the fourteen disembodied and scattered parts of the body of Osiris. Thus the seven cosmic physical states of Mount Mandera plus these fourteen other states make up the twenty-one subdivisions of the three lowest kosmic planes of being.

Ra-Mau, cutting off the head of the enfolding serpent, thereby permitting the growth of the great World Tree, the Persea,[10] but this is a mere extension of the same allegory.

Now it is within this encapsulated mass of Atum-ic matter (i.e., our local kosmos) that a first objective duality arises, this having been depicted by the Egyptians as the lion-headed god and goddess Shu and Tefnut. Although generally defined as meaning light/heat and moisture respectively, these appear actually representative of complementary principles of *polarity* (i.e., energy and inertia), which Tum is shown as "emanating into the embrace of his *ka*." Tefnut and Shu in congress then produce their natural offspring Nut and Geb, depicted respectively as the inner firmament or arch of the sky (which contains the stars) and the human-looking god of the Earth.

But the meaning is actually rather more subtle and extensive. In the first place, Nut and Geb are described as "born in congress with each other" and thus, as divine and semi-divine Matter united, have to be separated by the active aspect of solar polarity, that is, Shu, who thereby—by the use of his force—appears between them as the god (or principle) of light. It is only when this enforced separation (i.e., of Spirit and Matter) occurs that the stars appear in the body of Nut, who is thus seen as the passive aspect of sidereal Nature—that is, the inner sheath of the crystal sphere of the demiurgic firmament. Geb then is the *active* aspect of sidereal Nature. Of these two, however, it is perhaps paradoxically the "male" Geb who "lays the egg of the (immediately local) universe"—that is, the solar system; it is within this that the appearance of both Man and his associated god-principles come about, as we shall now endeavor to describe.

The Osirian Hierarchy

The divine offspring of Nut and Geb within the solar system are five in number. They are Osiris himself (As'r), Horus the Elder (Heru-ur), Set (Setekh), Isis (As't), and Nephthys (Nekhebet); these five represent the five active principles and elements—aether, fire, air, water, and earth—which together constitute the subjective and objective nature of man as we know him. They can perhaps be better classified in terms of the following principles of function:

1. Nut (divinity)—the passive, divine nature of the solar Demiurge
2. Geb (semidivinity)—the active, creative nature of the *akhu,* united with the solar Demiurge
3. Osiris (aether)—the principle of pan-solar vital Being (the Hindu *atman*)
4. Heru-ur (fire/light)—the principle of spiritual sacrifice and transmutation
5. Set (air)—the principle of form-building and self-centered independence (Ego)
6. As't (water)—the principle of fluid vitality
7. Nephthys (earth)—the principle of inertial balance

While these are general principles, it is the way in which they work out in Man's subtle constitution that is perhaps of greater and more immediate interest to most people. To begin with, then, let us look at the subtle "vehicles" to which these principles give rise. We can then apply these to the Osirian tradition in order to better understand their operation and the *unfolded* nature of human consciousness.

3. Osiris—the unrestricted perceptual awareness of the spiritual nature
4. Heru-ur—the fallen causal consciousness within the spiritual soul-body (*sah*)*
5. Isis—the *ba*, or astral soul-body
6. Nephthys—the *ka*, or etheric double
7. Set—the *thesu* or chakra system and the associated sensory functions

The Allegorical Myth of Osiris

It is only through understanding the underlying myth (allegory rather) of the death and resurrection of Osiris that we can have any real hope of appreciating the subtle nature of the concealed meaning behind the story as a whole, for the latter deals with the very basis of our own multiple subjective solar nature, how the various aspects of the latter come into being, and how they interact with each other in a manner that we can perhaps begin to recognize. Because the story is itself so well known, we can perhaps go through it at some speed, concentrating upon the underlying meanings instead. First, however, we should mention one tradition that had the Osiris and Isis principles, while still within the womb of Nut, themselves conceiving and giving birth to Horus the Elder.† This appears to have intended to suggest that it was the primordial interaction of the two soul principles that gave rise to the appearance of the principle of psychospiritual consciousness that unites them. As Horus the Elder plays such a critical part in the story, it is important that his function as the very principle of consciousness is clearly understood.

Now the main tradition itself has all five god and goddess children of Nut and Geb depicted at the outset in the heavenly state, all being in mutual harmony. This is the divine "pre-fall" state within the solar scheme. Upper and Lower Egypt do not yet exist as a duality and Osiris—the fourth and central figure in line of the seven gods—is thus made

---

*Diodorus Siculus describes two famous columns erected near Nyasa in Arabia, one to Isis and the other to Osiris. The column to Osiris bore these words: "I am Osiris . . . the eldest son of Geb. I was born of a brilliant and magnificent egg and my substance is of the same nature as that which composes light" (Hall, *The Secret Teachings of All Ages*, 60, quoting from Diodorus Siculus). The egg in question is of course the World Soul (of the solar system in its vast entirety) and the god Geb who lays it is himself described as "one of the porters of heaven's gate, who draws back the bolts and opens the door in order that the light of Ra may stream in upon the world" (Budge, *Gods of the Egyptians*, vol. 2, 98).

†Another tradition had Osiris having an even earlier son called Baba, but, as we shall see in the next chapter, this appears to be a reference to the appearance of the World Soul by dint of the double use of the word *ba*.

ruler over the whole of the metaphorical land of Egypt—*not* Heru-ur, it will be noted. Set, representing the sense of personal desire (of the Logos) for independent responsibility, then decides to create his own kingdom. So he first of all lures the ruling Osiris principle into trying out a coffin, which he and forty-two accomplices then throw into the River Nile. It thereafter floats down from Upper Egypt to Lower Egypt and then to Byblos on the sea coast, eventually becoming trapped in the roots of a tamarisk tree, which grows up around it and enfolds it within its trunk. The tree is later chopped down and its trunk used as the main supporting beam for the local king's palace. Isis, using her magic powers, locates the divine body within the beam, persuades the king to let her have it, and thus releases the body of Osiris, which she then hides away in the Delta. Set—who has by now taken charge of the kingdom—hears of this and upon finding the body hacks it into fourteen pieces, which, for good measure, he then scatters around Lower and Middle Egypt.[11]

Now, what does all this mean? Well, let us begin by reminding ourselves that the sevenfold solar system is itself internally septenary. Thus there are forty-nine substates in all, the highest seven of which comprise the divine heaven-world, which eternally remains in status quo. It is the other forty-two substates that are involved in the process of solar Creation and it is therefore the forty-two accomplices of Set who represent them.* Osiris himself represents that creative aspect (i.e., fire, or light) of the god-king principle in the divine heaven world that—through naive inexperience—is made to fall ineluctably into the cycle of Creation. Set is the universally self-centered, creatively accumulative instinct.

The Nile, in this instance, represents the "winding waterway" of all the substates of *sidereal* being within the field of Creation, the Delta being the last and lowest series of seven substates. Isis (the maternally enfolding soul principle) finds the Osiris principle inertly caught up in the material forms of the world—symbolized by the tamarisk tree—and, liberating the inert and inactive principle, she conceals it. The meaning here is that the lesser "divine spark" of the Osiris principle is temporarily set aside within the lower states of Matter where, nevertheless, it still cannot function properly. However, the Set principle now takes a hand again and chops his brother's body into fourteen pieces,† which he then scatters. This, esoterically interpreted, merely means that the latent power of the Osiris nature in Creation is divided into fourteen substates and it is these that Isis (the astral soul)—aided by Anubis (representing the principle of the intelligently operating senses)—has first to find and then—guided by Tehuti (representing the Universal

---

*Hence the nome districts of Egypt between the First Cataract (at Elephantine) and the Mediterranean being forty-two in number.

†The number sixteen is used by some authors but this seems to arise from confusion with the fact that the temple priests symbolically used sixteen different amulets to put back together the various body parts of Osiris (Budge, *Gods of the Egyptians,* vol. 2, 126). The number sixteen would itself appear to derive from the sum of two octaves, as each octave contains a septenary system within itself (as in music). Thus the symbolic use of sixteen to recombine fourteen seems quite (metaphysically) logical.

Mind principle)—reassemble and bind them together in an interwoven body of experience (symbolized by the funeral wrappings around Osiris) and then to unite this with herself, thereby coordinating the three lowest states of solar matter and so conceiving from it one unified entity—that is, the human being.

The Parentage of Anubis

It is worth noting that, although Anubis was supposed to be the son of Set and Nephthys, one tradition had it that he was in fact the son of Osiris and Nephthys by a supposedly unwitting liaison of which Osiris and Isis only later became aware.*[12] As Anubis metaphorically represents the principle of sympathetic interest in man—which runs back and forth, sniffing out its prey, like the dog or jackal itself—it is not surprising that the Isis principle (the *ba*) is shown as training and harnessing his loyal affections to her use in helping find the missing body parts of the Osiris principle.

The Missing Osirian Phallus

The *metaphorical* phallus of Osiris (the missing fourteenth piece representing the re-creative instinct and function) is replaced by Isis with a facsimile made up of the material (symbolically described as wood) of the Delta—representing the most highly evolved product of the lowest state of Creation—and used to impregnate her. As a result, she conceives and gives birth to Horus, who (once grown to youthful manhood and otherwise with the assistance of Anubis) sets out to avenge his father and subjugate the further selfish activities of the Set principle. As a result, Horus (the Younger) eventually becomes master (king) of both Upper and Lower Egypt (the spiritual *and* psychophysical realms).[13] In other words, the self-conscious spiritual nature in the individual human being becomes predominant. And when this happens, the Osiris nature (the dominant spiritual principle within him) is shown as being completely liberated and now able to go off on his own exploratory travels in the upper heaven world.

The Multiple Horus Nature

In the ancient Greek tradition, all the heroes were the offspring of the union of immortals with mortals. Thus the mass of humankind was seen as providing an environmental seed bed for the insemination of divine or semidivine principles, which thereby provided the role model and incentive for evolutionary development in humanity's own general social attitudes—or as a warning against their debasement. The word *hero* was itself seemingly

---

*This apparently uncertain area in the myth actually looks to be quite deliberate, intending to show that—notwithstanding the "marital unity" of the *ka* with the *thesu*—the overshadowing spiritual nature of the Osiris principle remained instrumentally involved in the creative process on the objective physical plane as well and is thus able to impregnate the field of lesser being merely by the projected power of its overshadowing influence.

derived from the Egyptian *heru,* signifying consciousness itself, that acutely perceptual faculty that was able to soar above and look down upon the mundane plane of being—hence the esoteric metaphor of the hawk's head on a human body in which guise Horus is usually found.*

We have so far mentioned only two of the many Horus types found in the ancient Egyptian tradition. However, there appear to have been some sixteen altogether—which may also have some sort of association not only with the sixteen stars in the constellation of Draco, but also with the fact that the priests used sixteen amulets in the ritual reunion of the body of Osiris.[14] Nevertheless, as Horus represents the various aspects of unfolding and evolving human consciousness in the round, we should perhaps spend a little time dealing with some of them in turn, as follows, although not in any particular order.

Heru-ur (Horus the Elder, or Ancient One)

While we have already mentioned two traditions that had Heru-ur as the son of either Geb and Nut or of Osiris and Isis, the mainstream tradition had him as the son of Atum-Ra and Hathor, which seems much more clear-cut, for Hathor (the faculty of generalized spiritual awareness) was herself Hat-hor, the "house of Horus." Heru-ur—most often depicted as a hawk-headed god—was also seen as the twin of the kosmic aspect of Set and the two of them were held to be responsible for providing the ladder for the revitalized Osiris to climb up to the higher heaven world. The most important shrine to Heru-ur was at Sekhem and here he was called Lord of the Utchati[15]—Lord of the Two Eyes of Ra—which again makes complete sense for the deity representing the principle of perceptive consciousness. Here at Sekhem he was also represented as a lion god, while also being closely associated with Shu, the god of light—and thus vision.

Heru-ur otherwise had a major shrine at Kom Ombos, which he shared with the crocodile god Sebek, himself a close associate of the kosmic Set. As Sebek represented the acquisitively outreaching Mind principle and Set represented the acquisitive principle of selfhood, we can again see the logical connections. In addition, Horus was known as the Face of Heaven-by-Day, while Set was the Face of Heaven-by-Night. Finally, there was a Heru-ur of the South and also one of the North, thereby yet again supporting the interpretation that he represented the perceptual faculties of both higher and lower (individualized) consciousness.

---

*The traditional interpretation of *heru* adopted by Egyptologists is "he who is above" or "that which is above," although there is, as Budge (*Gods of the Egyptians,* vol. 1, 466) tells us, an immediate association with the Egyptian word *hr(a),* meaning "face," and also (by derivation) the modern English word *hair.* The implicit association appears to be that, just as the hair was the emanation from the head through which the Mind expressed itself, so—in symbolic terms—the consciousness of the individual was also an emanation from the Mind principle. Hence the four children of Horus were said to have their abode among the tresses surrounding the "Face of Heaven."

Sidereal Genesis—
The Origin and
Nature of Man

151

Heru-pkhart (Horus the Younger, or the Child)

This particular form of Horus was regarded as having been born prematurely and thus lame through being deformed or malformed in his lower limbs. That, however, appears to be symbolic of the emotionally and intellectually undeveloped human consciousness rather than signifying physical defects per se.

Also known as Harpocrates to the Greeks, Horus the Younger was representative of the early rays of the Sun. He was, rather confusingly, the son of yet another Horus god by the goddess Rat-tauit, who took the form of a hippopotamus, like the goddess Ta'Urt.[16] Interestingly, there were seven subsidiary forms of Heru-pkhart, which, although appearing to confuse matters even further, actually confirms what he stood for—that is, the principle of perceptual consciousness on all the seven subplanes of the *solar* physical plane—for he always appeared in full human form, although with a variety of headdresses.

FIGURE 5.8. HORUS THE YOUNGER

Heru-khenti-khat

Here the Horus principle has the head of a crocodile on which again sit the horns of Khnemu, plus the triple crown and plumes.[17] The crocodile head—associated with Sebek—and the horns appear to symbolize an association with the demiurgic consciousness, *khat* being the physical body form and *khenti* meaning "at the front of." Hence the implied meaning appears to be that of the principle of *intuitive* consciousness, or its lower correspondence, *instinctive* consciousness.

Heru-khenti-an-maati

This is the blind or sightless form of the Horus the Elder principle,[18] born simultaneously with Osiris, Set, Isis, and Nephthys. It accordingly appears to signify a state of total subjectivity, or otherwise of the immediately post-natal state in which all perceptual faculties are temporarily lost by the incarnating Intelligence. The fact of Ma'at being involved in the name implies that the very nature of consciousness becomes subsumed within that of Divine Purpose, or Law—the *dharma* of the Hindus.

Heru-merti

Here the symbolism is again under the form of a hawk-headed god above which are the wavy, lateral horns of Khnemu and the solar disk encircled by the *uraeus,* while in his hand he holds the two Utchati.[19] The name *merti* appears in one sense to signify "death," but here it would appear to represent the faculty of intuitive consciousness entering the sphere of the dual Mind principle and thus "dying."

Heru-neb

Here the god is depicted as a hawk, seated on the horns of an antelope, which Egyptologists regard as signifying his victory over Set.[20] However, the antelope represents swiftness while the spreading horns appear to symbolize mental growth. In addition, Heru-neb was described as the son of the sevenfold goddess Sesheta. So what is really represented here appears to be intellectual-cum-cultural development within the sevenfold nature of the Mind state; it is this that ultimately overcomes the lower Set nature.

Heru-khuti (Horus of the Two Horizons)

Khu-ti means "spirit-heaven" and this form of Horus is generally regarded by Egyptologists as representing the Sun in its daily course across the skies between sunrise and sunset.[21] The essence of the idea, however—in terms of human consciousness—seems to have been that this particular form of Horus represented the *combined* (or coordinated) perceptual consciousness of the two soul-bodies—the *sah* and *ba.* This would itself indicate the achievement of *spiritual* self-consciousness, and for that reason, he was here directly

FIGURE 5.9. HERU-KHUTI (HORUS OF THE TWO HORIZONS), WITH SICKLE

associated with the god Temu, who himself symbolized an upward evolutionary progression, and Khepera, who symbolized the capacity to regenerate the self at will. For this reason this triple combination of Ra-Temu–Khepera–Heru-khuti was specifically associated with the Sphinx at Giza,* while Heru-khuti's own main shrine was at Heliopolis (Anu).

Horus-Set

This strange, dual form of the entirely opposite principles appears to signify the lower form of self-consciousness in man—that of the maturely disciplined attitude of mind that has learned to integrate the faculty of self-consciousness with that of the potently organized sense of personal individuality. In other words, it is symbolic of the integrated personality

---

*This form of Horus also sometimes carried a sickle, thereby denoting the faculty of concluding a cycle—again, symbolic of the power of the Will over material existence and thus transcending the illusion of physical death.

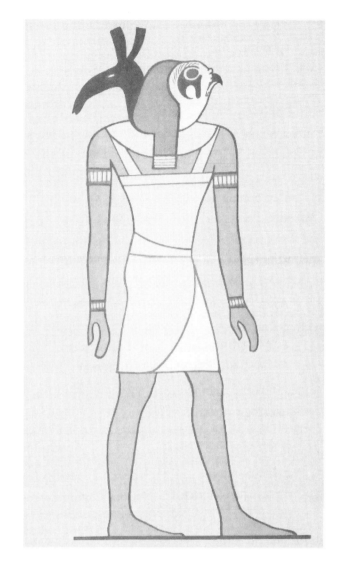

FIGURE 5.10. HORUS-SET

of man. The fact that the ancient Egyptians were able to resolve the duality of Horus and Set in this way itself clearly confirms that they were originally not paranoid about Set at all as some form of devil figure, as were the later peoples of the New Kingdom dynasties.

Heru-sma-taui

In this form (sometimes hawk-headed, sometimes serpent-headed) as the "uniter of the Two Lands"[22] (i.e., of Upper and Lower Egypt) we see the principle of integration of the higher (divine) with the lower (spiritual) faculties of perceptual consciousness. As Budge tells us: "In this form, Horus was believed to spring into existence out of a lotus flower which blossomed in the heavenly abyss of Nu at dawn, at the beginning of the year."[23] As Nu represents the ocean of Chaos, what is symbolized here is the appearance of a far higher form of perceptual consciousness than that of the purely human faculty. The abyss of Nu actually represents the first of the higher kosmic planes of Being, beyond that of merely sidereal existence. Consequently, the Heru-sma-taui principle was involved both macrocosmically in the coordination of kosmic and sidereal consciousness at the universal level of Being and also microcosmically in man.

Heru-hekennu

Heru-hekennu is usually depicted as a hawk-headed man with the solar disk over his head and encircled by a serpent.[24] It would appear that the associated form of perceptual consciousness is that of the imagination, for *hek(a)* is the word for "magic." The *ennu* suffix appears to be related to the *anu* or *annu* soul principle, thus also corresponding with the symbolic serpent surrounding the solar disk.

Heru-Behutet

Probably the most dynamically powerful of all the forms of Horus, this one was often depicted as the winged solar disk, an associated form of the great god Ra himself, thus symbolizing the overwhelming force of the pure divine or semidivine nature. The primary temple of Heru-Behutet was at Edfu,* where he is described in one of the wall texts as the self-regenerating power of light, which drives all before it.[25] In fig. 5.11, he is hawk-headed, holding a club in his right hand (denoting raw power) and a bow and arrows in his left (denoting the shafts of light of his nature). His immediate associates in the Egyptian tradition were the Shemsu-Heru—the Companions of Horus—who were symbolically described as blacksmiths.† These initiates of higher degree (adepts) were in fact those who had literally achieved the self-conscious faculty of being able to manipulate solar light-force, in pursuit of the fulfillment of Divine Purpose.

As already shown earlier on (see fig. 2.10), Heru-Behutet was often otherwise depicted in his boat, driving his spear down into the head of a hippopotamus while holding it with a linked iron chain in his left hand. He is also frequently shown spearing crocodiles, both these animals of course being followers of (the kosmic) Set. Both are thus symbolic of the highest forms of consciousness that enable Man to bring about final and complete dominion over even the most powerful aspects of Nature in our local universe. Thus Heru-Behutet was representative, in the higher Egyptian Mysteries, of Man as a pure Spirit.

---

*A further form of Horus was Heru-ma'at-taui, the son of Horus of Edfu and Hathor. He was also known as Ahy (Budge, *Gods of the Egyptians,* vol. 1, 469 and 495)—which bears a striking resemblance to the Indo-Tibetan Ahi, that hierarchy of the solar Demiurge responsible for initiating *objective* Creation.

†Interestingly, the Companions of Horus, or Shemsu-Heru, were also otherwise known as the Heru Seshta (Budge, *Gods of the Egyptians,* vol. 2, 341)—thereby signifying that they were organized in seven groups, probably corresponding with the seven *thesu* in the (kosmic) *ka* of the manifesting Logos of our solar system. It is also worthy of note that the Egyptian root word *her*—from which we appear to derive our word *hair,* signifying the emanation (of consciousness) from the head—also appears to be of Sanskrit origin, as the dual Visnu, god of love and relationships, was otherwise known as Heri (Wilford, "On Egypt," 370 and 448).

**FIGURE 5.11.
HERU-BEHUTET**

The Higher Egyptian Mysteries

As already indicated, the Egyptian Mysteries—like the Greek—were organized in a triple sequence. The lesser Mysteries—open to all—involved the allegories of Creation and the death of Osiris, his reconstitution by Isis, and the birth of Horus the Younger. The second and third Mystery sequences followed on directly from this, more specifically involving various aspects of the Horus principle. However, we shall touch further on this in chapter 12 and will thus go no further here.

SIX

MAN, THE MULTIPLE BEING

If we were to point to one outstanding difference between the modern and the ancient consciousness, it would be this: that whereas the modern consciousness feels that it contains within itself an inner world, the ancient consciousness felt itself to be surrounded by an inner world. And whereas the modern consciousness feels that objects are contained in external space, or at least separated from each other by a space that is "between" them, the ancient consciousness felt that objects contained, and therefore could reveal, an inner metaphysical space. It was this experience of a non-subjective, inner dimension to the world that nourished and sustained the ancient symbolic worldview.

JEREMY NAYDLER, *TEMPLE OF THE COSMOS*

In order to understand the nature of ancient Egyptian thought regarding both humankind and the very nature of Matter and manifest existence, we have to commence from their perception of there being a fundamental distinction between an organic entity and the many-faceted spirit that animated it. As far as they were concerned, the spirit was an emanation of divinity itself and was therefore both eternal and incorruptible. The organism, however—on whatever plane(s) of being it existed—was made up of a multiplicity of spirit natures, gathered together within a spectrum of soul entities, like the very cells in our own bodies. It was these latter that, when brought together by the principle of Mind, produced the organic entity that was subject to the process of Life and Death. Thus we are told in the *Hermetica*:

You must understand that every living body, be it immortal or mortal, rational or irrational, is composed of matter and soul . . . and there is likewise soul by itself, laid up in the Maker's keeping, for soul is the substance of which Life is made. How then can the life which is in the immortals be other than the life which is in mortal creatures?[1]

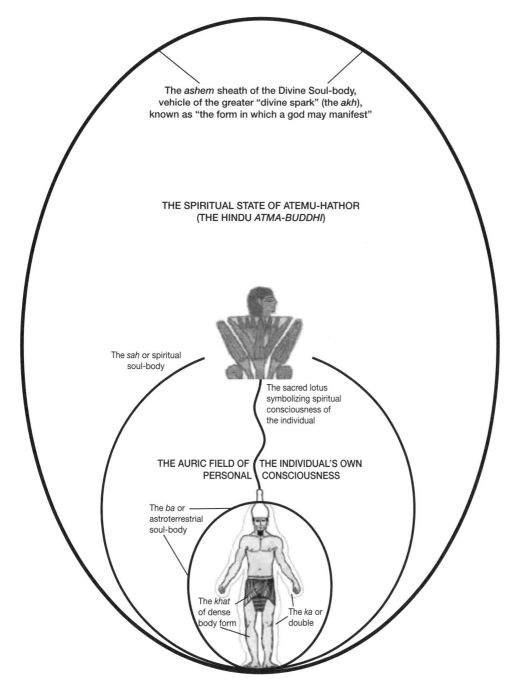

The *ashem* sheath of the Divine Soul-body,
vehicle of the greater "divine spark" (the *akh*),
known as "the form in which a god may manifest"

THE SPIRITUAL STATE OF ATEMU-HATHOR
(THE HINDU *ATMA-BUDDHI*)

The *sah* or spiritual
soul-body

The sacred lotus
symbolizing spiritual
consciousness of
the individual

THE AURIC FIELD OF   THE INDIVIDUAL'S OWN
PERSONAL   CONSCIOUSNESS

The *ba* or
astroterrestrial
soul-body

The *khat*
of dense
body form

The *ka* or
double

FIGURE 6.1. THE ANCIENT EGYPTIAN VIEW OF MAN'S SUBTLE ORGANISM

As regards the overshadowing (kosmic) Mind that brings together the many soul types
to produce either the mortal or immortal entity, we are otherwise told:

The Mind cannot naked and alone take up its abode in an earthly body. A body of
Earth could not endure the presence of that mighty and immortal being; nor could so

great a power submit to contact with a body defiled by passion. And so the Mind takes to itself the soul for a wrap. . . . Mind, which is the keenest of all things incorporeal, has for its body Fire, the keenest of all the material elements. Mind is the maker of all things and in making things, it uses Fire as its instrument.[2]

Arising out of this latter statement we then find the basis of *instinctive* Intelligence as a homogeneous principle in Universal Nature:

The Kosmos also, Aesclepius, has sense and thought; but its sense and thought are of a kind peculiar to itself, not like the sense and thought of man, nor varying like his, but mightier and less diversified. The sense and thought of the kosmos are occupied solely in making all things and dissolving them again into itself. . . . It is the swiftness of the movement of the kosmos that causes the diversity of births. For the kosmic Life-breath, working without intermission, conveys into bodies a succession of qualities and therewith makes of the universe one mass of life.[3]

The reason for providing the above three quotations from the gnostic or esoteric teachings of the Egyptians is that they provide us with a basic rationale for understanding their view of Man as a multiple being—in both his macrocosmic and microcosmic personae—whose Mind utilizes both soul and the two poles of Spirit Matter through which to express itself. They also awaken us to the fact that the Egyptians very definitely saw the universe around us as having a dynamic and ever functioning rationale of its own, which clearly does not coincide with modern man's inevitably rather self-centered view of things. The latter of course provides a fertile source of constant conflict in our own subjective nature—that is, until we realize what we essentially are (in spiritual terms) and why such conflicts arise.*

In the last chapter we looked at Man predominantly from the viewpoint of his divine and semidivine natures, and we also looked at the sequence of unfoldment of his consciousness from these elevated states of being, down through the various planes of solar existence. In this chapter, we shall take a rather closer look at some of these aspects or principles and the way in which the ancient Egyptians adapted their social and religious beliefs and customs so as to ensure their properly sympathetic association with the structure of the inner Man. First, l then, let us summarize the various aspects as follows:

1. The *(a)kh*—the divine spirit
2. The *sekhem*—the emanating power of the *akh*

---

*The Ancients took the view that while Universal Matter was entirely subservient to the Will and Purpose of the Logos as expressed, via the focused and *spiritually* self-conscious Mind of Man, mankind's *unconscious* subjective activity is the source of all problems.

FIGURE 6.2. THE WINGED DISK OF KNEPH

Over the temple doorway in this picture we see the double serpent-headed, triple-winged solar disk that the ancient Egyptians called *kneph* (the Greek *cnophis*). This archetypal image is symbolic of the threefold eternal Spirit and the dual soul supporting the sphere of individualized Being, the name itself apparently being derived from the combination of *k* (or *kh*) and *nef*—the latter being the first part of the word *nefer* (from which the Hebrew *nephesch* is also derived). Now, as Nefer-Tem was the son of Ptah and Sekhet, and Ptah was himself born immaculately from an egg that emerged from the mouth of Kneph, the symbolic relationships appear self-evident. The fact that the *kneph* symbol was always to be found over temple doorways is indicative of the fact that only the Spirit was regarded as being able to pass back and forth between different soul states (thus different rooms).

A clear distinction needs to be made between the symbol for Kneph and that for Heru-Behutet. The latter was also represented as a winged disk, but without the double-headed serpent. The glyph for Ra himself was the solar disk, encircled by the single serpent, Khut. This indicated the single directional cycle down into the Duat and back to the point of celestial origin, which Ra and his entourage incessantly followed throughout eternity. The double-headed serpent, however, indicated both this and the higher evolutionary soul cycle, within the upper, kosmic planes of existence.

3. The *sah*—the spiritual (or causal) soul-body
4. The *ba*—the astral soul-body
5. The *khaibit*—the shadow
6. The *kha*—the vital principle (within the human being)
7. The *ka* and *thesu*—the double and its system of chakras
8. The *khat*—the physical body

In addition to these, we shall also consider:

9. The *ab*—the heart
10. The *ren*—the name

The *Akh,* or Divine Spirit

Strictly speaking, the ordinary Egyptian root word for "spirit" appears to be just *kh*. However, the muted *a* is put as a *prefix* to the *kh* when associated with the "divine spark" that is emanated into the highest state of solar Being from the Kosmic Mind, but as a *suffix* to the *kh* when signifying the lesser but still vital emanation into and from the human *ka* within the lowest state of merely solar existence—which makes it akin to the Hindu *prana*. Thus the plural *akhu* and *khu* meant two quite distinctively different things—the actual significance behind this fact having seemingly escaped the attention of many scholars.

It is otherwise worth remembering that the radiance of the *kha* or *khu* vitality in man is entirely due to the functional activities of the lesser groups of *set-akhu* found within the human *ka,* responding to the influence of the *ba*. In a very real sense, the pranic *kha* is thus the liberated energy of the *set-akh*. Both the *akh* and the *set-akh* remain entirely subjective in themselves. They are known merely by their respective emanations. The lesser *akh* emanates the radiant *kha,* while the higher *akh* emanates the *sekhem*.

The *Sekhem*

As Wallis Budge tells us, the word *sekhem* literally means "to have power over something."[4] But that which had such an apparently irresistible mastery over something else had perforce to contain it and from this we may logically speculate that the *sekhem*—otherwise described as a "spiritual flame"—had to be something of that order. Now the *sekhem* was directly associated with the goddess Sekhmet, or Sekhet (Sek-het), who was the wife of Ptah (Buddha). He, as we have already otherwise seen, was the fully evolved Creator-Man-god, the highest archetypal aspect of Man's divine nature, while she was described usually as lion-headed, but also as a crocodile-headed goddess "wading in the blood of mankind." The underlying metaphor seems at first bizarrely obscure but the suffix *hem* denotes a group or collective, and the root word *sek(h)* appears to indicate a meaning roughly equivalent to "the release of Life-force" (metaphorically akin to igniting a flame or the letting of blood). It seems not impossible that our English word *segregate* is derived from it—here meaning the "detachment" of part of the collective from the main corpus.* Hence the "'divine sparks" manifest as one combined hierarchical group—that is, as and within the Divine Flame, a metaphor also otherwise found in the Hindu sacred tradition.

From the Egyptian love of words with double meanings we can see that this same word is also derivable from either *sek-hem* or *sek-khem*. Now as Khem was the ever unseen "god of the dark face" (a term also used for Ptah), meaning the "divine spark" on its own wholly subjective plane of being, the *sek-khem* could well logically infer the meaning "segregated group/subgroup of divine beings"—that is, thereby becoming *semi*divine beings. It was then these, seemingly, that fell yet further into generation and informed those hierarchies of *sahu,* or spiritual soul-bodies, which were seen as overshadowing the individual human being and providing him with his self-conscious intelligence.

The *Sah(a)*

Egyptologists have for well over one hundred years referred to the *sah* as the "spiritual soul" and indeed that is precisely what it appears to be. However, its function needs to be rather better understood, and also its sequential place in the overall scheme of things. As elsewhere mentioned, there appears to be a direct correlation between this part of man's subjective makeup and the constellation of Orion, which was itself called Sahu. The associated implication—because Orion was specifically connected with Osiris—is that the spiritual soul contains the *manifesting* divinity—that is, the fallen god-king in man.

The sacred texts all spur the individual initiate on to become an Osiris figure in his own right, thereby attaining the title of Osiris-Un-Nefer. And of course it is Osiris who was regarded as king of the Underworld—the three lowest planes or states of the sevenfold solar scheme within which the human being naturally functions. Thus Osiris—whose higher heaven world is to be found anchored to the *fourth* solar plane—is causal to the cycle of both human reincarnation and the instinct to human evolution. Consequently, the spiritual soul state that Osiris symbolizes represents the "staging post" between merely human self-consciousness on one side and divine Self-consciousness on the other. It is on the fourth solar plane of the system that we find the Seven Hathors—the seven *groups* of Horus beings, which also have a specific association with the Osiris principle. Not

---

*Which is again almost certainly why we find that Nefer-Tem—i.e., the *spiritually* individualized identity in Man—was regarded as the son of Ptah and Sekhet (Budge, *Gods of the Egyptians,* vol. 1, 520).

surprisingly, therefore, the individual initiate who achieved the attainment of consciousness of the spiritual soul became a Companion of Horus—one of the Shemsu-Heru and a *pir* of the Egyptian realm.

It is perhaps worthwhile to reflect briefly once more on the fact of Osiris's Egyptian name being As'r, while that of Isis was As't. While the root term *as* appears to signify a state of primordial solar being from which the two god-principles originate, the final letter of each name distinguishes the actual *function*. Thus whereas the *t* in As't (perhaps synonymous with the Sanskrit *asat,* meaning "non-being," in the sense of being detached from the primordial, divine state) produces a flat vocal consonant in which the tongue comes to final rest, the *r* in As'r produces a continuing vibration of the tongue. The symbolic inference is that, while the Isis nature (representing the female or astral soul nature) becomes completely passive, the Osiris nature (representing the male or spiritual soul nature) remains functionally capable of emanating a sustained degree of divine *sound*.

Interestingly, we find this same latter principle of the vibratory sound in the name Ak(e)r, given to the double-headed sphinx figure found in the fifth division of the Duat— that is, the fifth solar plane, which embodies the function of the Mind principle. If we then recall that the primordial plane or state of solar being—in which all potential solar knowledge exists—was called the *akas(a),* we can perhaps better understand the functional distinction between the two root words *akh* and *as.* The latter represents a state of *passive* semidivine being and knowledge, while the former represents a state of *active* semidivine being and *purpose.* Thus the name Ak(e)r—which is closely associated with that of As'r— itself represents the vibratory sound (or resonant echo) of that same Higher Purpose, within the lower register.

The *Ba*

As already established, the *ba* was the equivalent of the astral soul-body—that which contains the world of sevenfold terrestrial being that the human entity represents as the microcosm of the World Soul. As also otherwise seen, the sevenfold terrestrial state comprises the lowest of the seven solar planes of being. Thus Isis, as the Egyptian representative of the *ba* principle, was the goddess of all magical knowledge related to the purely objective world. She was supposed to have obtained this knowledge direct from Ra when he was "old and weary"[5]—a metaphor for the fact that the kosmic Life principle in the lowest realm of Matter becomes very sluggish in its operative function. In other words, the Great Cycle passes very slowly within our merely human field of perceptual experience.

The *ba,* however, not only contains the sevenfold terrestrial world within itself but

FIGURE 6.3. THE *BA*, WITH A HUMAN HEAD ON THE BODY OF A BIRD, SYMBOLIZING THE CAPACITY FOR SELF-CONSCIOUSLY INTELLIGENT ASTRAL TRAVEL

also acts as the foundation of the seven purely solar states, the lowest three of which comprise the lesser Underworld. Consequently, between her nature and that of the Osiris principle on the fourth solar plane, there are two intermediate solar planes, comprising fourteen subplanes. But it is these that were allegorically made to comprise the fourteen parts of the body of Osiris, which the divisive Set principle had made out of the previously unified spiritual consciousness (of Man). Consequently, it was through the reuniting (or rather, reintegrating) of these fourteen substates *and then uniting them with herself* that Isis was symbolically able to conceive the son of Osiris—Horus the Child. He it was who was born "premature" and "lame in his lower limbs." In other words, by the astral soul's own work in coordinating the astral and mental faculties in empirical fashion through pure experience, it reunites the higher and lower nature and knowledge of the Demiurge that Osiris and Isis jointly represent. However, it is only through the creation of a magical phallus—an esoteric metaphor for the crown chakra in man—that the *ba* is fertilized by the descending vitality of the higher spiritual nature and thereby conceives the lesser Horus principle—that of the integrated human personality consciousness that permits normal human self-conscious function.

The *ba* was depicted with a human head on the body of a bird in order to symbolize the capacity for self-consciously intelligent astral travel. While aurically containing the human entity during the day—thus providing it (via the *ka*) with the faculty of wakeful consciousness—the *ba* was deemed to leave the body behind at night, thereby inducing sleep in the latter. It then traveled within the psychic states according to various, mostly non-personal tasks imposed upon it by either karma or the will of the overshadowing spiritual nature—thereby accumulating dreams. It then reunited itself with the spiritual

FIGURE 6.4. THE TRIPLE FIEND AMEMET

nature (within the sphere of the Moon),* so inducing the sympathetic response of deep sleep in the physical body, to which it eventually returned with its freshly defragmented memory bank, ready to reawaken the hitherto unconscious human entity and start a new day.

At the end of each lifetime, the *ba* finally parted company with the physical body form with which it had been associated during the cycle of objective experience on Earth, thereby causing its death and subsequent corruption. Before being constrained to return to Earth for another, later cycle of incarnation, however, the *ba* had to go through a period of purgation, or catharsis, in which its memory bank of experience was assessed (in the Hall of Judgment). Here the positive and spiritually useful elements were separated from the remainder, the latter being thereafter rejected and dispersed to the mass unorganized fields of the lowest three solar states, these being symbolized by the triple fiend Amemet in the Chamber of Judgment scene. The accepted positive part of the *ba*'s experience was then assimilated by the Horus the Elder principle (spiritual consciousness) and then presented to the (fallen semidivine) Osiris nature. But the *ba*—the ever-virgin soul—was now made ready to return to Earth for a fresh cycle of human incarnation in which the whole process would be repeated, until the spiritual experience it had garnered had (over dozens of lifetimes) engendered an automatic sense of spiritual individuality that was itself capable of reanimating and then liberating the Osiris nature on its own plane. Then—and only then—was its work regarded as complete.

---

*Interestingly, there was also a lesser god called Baba who appears to have been synonymous with the astral soul of the world. Supposedly the firstborn son of Osiris, Baba was "he who feedeth upon the entrails of the mighty ones upon the Day of the Great Reckoning" (Budge, *Gods of the Egyptians,* vol. 2, 91; *Egyptian Religion,* 177). In other words, the World Soul gathers up within itself the discarded aspects of Creation at the end of the cycle.

The *Khaibit*

The role of the *khaibit* appears to be as murky as its synonym "the shadow."* In fact, it seems to be synonymous with the Sanskrit *kama-rupa,* the ephemeral "desire body," born of the residual emanation of the *kha* from the *ba.* Constituted of ethereally elemental matter and combined with the *ka* (the double), the *khaibit* was effectively an energy interface between the lowest quality of solar matter and the higher qualities of terrestrial matter. However, once the *ba* finally departed the physical body at death, the *kha* ceased to be manifest. The *khaibit*—the residue of the interface—and the *ka* then began a natural process of divorce and consequent dispersal into the latent sea of Matter contained within aura of the World Soul. But, where the emotional or desire life associated with the *ba* during the lifetime had been particularly strong, the *khaibit* remained potently coherent for some considerable time after death—sometimes for many years—even though the *ka* itself had by then completely disintegrated and faded away. Thus it is undoubtedly the *khaibit* (initially in conjunction with the *ka*) that is responsible for the ghostly (doppelgänger) phantoms found around haunted houses and graveyards, using correlations of other ambient psychoterrestrial matter to partially remanifest itself as an ethereal form once the *ka* itself has dissipated.

The *Kha*

As already indicated earlier, the *kha* is literally the spiritual exudation or emanation of light-energy from the *ka.* It is the returning psychospiritual Life-force that the *ba* has itself projected into the *ka,* thereby causing the animation of the physical body and its capacity for apparently sensory experience. Perhaps paradoxically, the inward emanation of the *ba* is the dark or invisible aspect of the *kha.* That which was visible was only the returning or *outward*-flowing emanation, reflected by the *ka,* which thereby became imbued with a subdued form of ethereal light. This liberated energy thus constituted the personal surplus *prana* given off by the healthy individual, conditioned by its experience within the *ka.* It thereby gave rise to the auric magnetism of the individual. For that reason it was specifically associated with the breath and the capacity of the high initiate (such as the hierophant or pharaoh) to bestow his blessing merely by breathing out upon or over the recipient.

The *Ka*

Generally known simply as "the double," the *ka* was that mass of elemental matter aurically isolated by the *ba* and inseminated with its own conditioning Life-force (*kha*). It

---

Shadow is derived from *shadu,* the plural of *shadim* in the Judeo-Babylonian system—hence the Greco-Roman "shades."

thereafter became a permanently rechargeable "battery" of lesser (i.e., psychic) Life-force. The imposition of the inherently septenary nature of the *ba* in turn gave rise to seven primary centers of force appearing in the *ka*. These were the *thesu*—what we know today as the chakras. Associated with these would be forty-two subsidiary *thesu,* all of them creating between themselves a literal, living web of energy around which the material of the objective physical body then gathered and remained more or less coherent during the lifetime. Following death, however, the *ka* lost its coherency and fairly quickly disintegrated.

The *ka* was constituted of matter of the fourth *terrestrial* state, itself the fourth substate of the seventh and lowest solar state. Thus the fourth solar state was considered to be the *ka* of the *kosmic* Osiris in which the seven groups of Horus beings correspondingly formed the *kosmic thesu*. It was undoubtedly because of this association between the merely psychoterrestrial *thesu* and their spiritual counterparts that the *ka* was regarded as having such (relative) importance—particularly in the later Egyptian dynasties. However, by then, public understanding of the subtle nature of man had so given way to ignorant superstition that there seems to have arisen a silly paranoia that the (natural) destruction of the terrestrial *ka* would result in sympathetic effects in its higher counterpart, so that man would thereby lose his spiritual individuality.

As a consequence of this altogether foolish notion, it became the normal custom to provide all sorts of "*ka* offerings" in the tomb of the deceased, in order to ensure its continued coherency.* There is also a suggestion that a form of psychospiritual necromancy was being practiced in this manner, through the *ka* of the deceased being used as a means of the living telegraphing their hopes and wishes to the deceased, who—already on the other side of the veil—would hopefully send back good luck influences or otherwise make beneficial advance arrangements for them with the gods. Such superstitious misunderstandings undoubtedly played a major part in the final fragmentation of Egyptian religious culture and its eventual takeover by Coptic Christianity.

As seen in fig. 6.5, the *ka* was symbolized by a pair of upstretched arms, which itself symbolized passive receptivity—a characteristic of the goddess Nephthys, twin sister of Isis. The sacred traditions of the Egyptians showed these two as almost always functioning in tandem, particularly when in association with Osiris. This is not surprising given that Isis (representing the *ba* principle) was the active partner and that the *ka* could not function independently of the *ba*—except by necromancy.

---

*According to Budge's *Egyptian Book of the Dead* (lix–lx), "Though its normal dwelling place was in the tomb with the body, it [the *ka*] could wander about at will; it was independent of the man [i.e., the physical body] and could go and dwell in any statue of him. It was supposed to eat and drink, and the greatest care was usually taken to lay abundant supplies of offerings in the tombs lest the *kas* of those who were buried in them should be reduced to the necessity of leaving their tombs and of wandering about and eating offal and drinking filthy water."

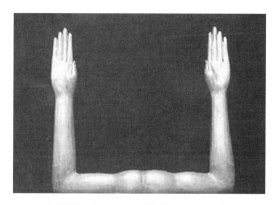

**FIGURE 6.5. *KA*, SYMBOLIZED BY
A PAIR OF UPSTRETCHED ARMS**

The *Thesu* (Chakras)

Relatively little direct mention of the *thesu* in man appears in texts, such that even Wallis Budge found the association obscure and was left drawing visual comparisons with "either the vertebra or some internal organ of the body which resembles a tied knot or knotted cord."[6] However, even this description is sufficiently graphic and bodily location-specific enough to confirm that the word *thesu* is synonymous with chakras.

While there has been insufficient retranslation of the texts by those with an accompanying knowledge of either Sanskrit or even of New Age terminology to take discussion much further, certain additional points may be added by direct implication. First of all, the incandescent bulbous projection on top of the head seen in so many paintings is clearly symbolic of the crown (*brahmarandra*) chakra. The lotus symbolism—also found artistically in profusion—seems to be directly related as well, as it is in the graphic symbolism of the Hindu and Buddhist schools of psychospiritual thought. However, in the Egyptian system, the lotus symbolism appears largely directed toward the representation of evolving (spiritual) consciousness.* It is found not only in temple and tomb wall paintings, but also in the architectural device of the capitals at the top of the temple pillars, depicting the various stages of petal opening.

The *Khat*

Khat (hence perhaps our English word *gut*) was the name given to the physical body form—the corpse—which, created and maintained by the *ka* at the behest of the *ba,*

---

*By virtue of so much symbolic imagery showing man emerging from the lotus in a spiritual context, it seems reasonably clear that the Egyptians saw it as having a higher (kosmic) counterpart. Thus these lotus *thesu* in the subtle body form (*ka*) of the god Tem (an aspect of the Solar Logos) necessarily resulted in a direct psychospiritual connection between the consciousness of god and man.

became corrupted with age and eventually disintegrated following death and the separation of the *ka* from it. Although it played but a very minor part in the Egyptian mystic and occult tradition, we ought perhaps to comment a little further upon it in relation to burial practices—which differed quite widely between the earliest and the later dynasties.

No tombs from the very earliest dynasties have actually (indisputably) been found and it seems quite likely—as the spiritual traditions were properly understood in the most ancient times—that there were no such tombs, because cremation was generally practiced. It is true that some earlier graves have been found with the skeleton curled up in the fetal position, facing east, and that in others the bones have been scattered around following apparent dissection (sometimes in association with cremation). However, such customs do not appear consistent with *mainstream* Egyptian cultural thought of the earliest dynasties. Although mummification also appears not to have been generally practiced in the very earliest dynasties, the use of it clearly grew and expanded down the millennia from about the Fourth or Fifth Dynasty. It then became increasingly available to all who could afford it and who no longer abided by the understanding of the original traditions in which the *khat* was seen of little consequence—and really of no concern whatsoever to the deceased.

The *Ab*

Although interpreted merely as "the heart" by Egyptologists, the *ab* clearly meant a great deal more to the ancient Egyptians than just the physical organ.* Remembering their fondness for wordplay, producing variations of meaning, the first thing to note is that *ab* is the reverse of *ba*. Thus it would appear that the heart was considered to be the *reflection* of the consciousness of the astral soul nature, or perhaps it would be more accurate to regard it as its manifest expression. This is unsurprising bearing in mind that the heart has, from time immemorial, been associated with the true nature of human feeling and perception. The fact that it was also the heart of the individual that was weighed in the balance in the Hall of Judgment clearly indicates that the heart contained the essence of the individual's personal achievement in any particular lifetime. However, the organ itself was, undoubtedly, merely symbolic of the quality of consciousness of the heart chakra. Thus in the Hall of Judgment, Horus the Elder (representing the spiritual consciousness of the individual) is shown addressing Osiris (the spiritual soul), saying: "I have come unto thee, O Un-nefer, and I have brought unto thee the Osiris Ani [the

---

*For example, Abtu was one of the two pilot fish that swam in front of the barque of Ra (meaning the greater Life cycle or Life wave of the Logos), guiding it on its way through the Duat. They were thus symbolically responsible for bringing into being that which was intended (Budge, *Gods of the Egyptians,* vol. 1, 324; vol. 2, 209). Hence in the human context, it is the heart that guides the decision making leading to personal experience.

candidate for initiation]. His heart is righteous, and it hath come forth from the Balance. . . . Thoth hath weighed it according to the decree uttered unto him by the company of the gods; and it is most true and right."[7]

The heart was of course weighed in the balance against the feather of Ma'at, itself representing truth, honesty, righteousness, and so on. Thus the human consciousness of the individual had to be "light-hearted" due to there being no sense of guilt or shame that would weigh it down in the sight of man's own higher sense of conscience.

The *Ren*

Generally translated as the "name" of the individual, *ren* also meant a great deal more to the ancient Egyptians; we can perhaps come rather closer to understanding why by looking closely at the root nature of the word. Thus, the serpent-headed goddess Rennenet* (who was responsible for both nursing and gestation) was always to be found in association with the goddess Meskenet (the goddess of conception).[8] The prefix word *renen* meant "to suckle," while the suffix *nennet* is one (curiously also found among the Chinese) meaning "nanny" or "nurse."[9] In addition, the Egyptian god and goddess Nun (or Nen) and Net were associated with the "womb" of space and the related principles of enveloping darkness and light. Thus the name Ren-nennet (sometimes morphing into Ren-nen-nut) appears to have signified the gestation or accretive development of "the name" within the dark womb of the Underworld. However, the concept of "the name" also otherwise implies some form of individuality and, from that viewpoint, must be regarded as having at least some sort of close association with the reincarnating ego in man. In fact, there is reasonable reason to suppose, from the contextual use of the word, that the Egyptians actually meant precisely that—that is, the evolving sense of selfhood.

The essence of the concept—as we saw in an earlier chapter—is that egohood was derived from that consciously united sense of being achieved by lesser groups of "divine sparks" (*set-akhu*) during the process of human incarnation. Thus those "sparks" that (as the *setekh*) evolved together as a united group upward from the foundational consciousness of the *ba* were seen as eventually achieving an intermediate point of individualized development (within the Mind-state of the individual). This, however, stopped just short of being able to penetrate the upper, spiritual heaven world. The parallel esoteric metaphor of the lotus bud forming just below the surface of the lake again immediately springs to mind.

However, by virtue of their literal and compulsive reliance on the principle of sympathetic magic—in which what was done at the physical level was supposed to create similar effects within the psychospiritual world—some of the later (spiritually ignorant) Egyptians

---

*The fact of being serpent-headed indicates that this goddess was also associated with the *ba* soul principle.

came foolishly to believe that by merely expunging a person's written name on a funeral plaque or mummy, or pylon, they would cease to exist. Consequently, overelaborate precautions were increasingly taken to ensure that this did not happen either by accident or design. And it was almost certainly for this reason that prayers continued to be said ritually for the deceased long after actual death, to ensure that his good, untarnished name accompanied him all the way to the spiritual world. Unfortunately, because of a failure to appreciate the inner aspect of what the *ren* actually stood for, orthodox mainstream Egyptology has signally failed to grasp this fact.

Subtle Bodies and Their Associated Positioning within the System

Having thus dealt to some extent with man's various subtle bodies and subjective principles, let us next take a look at how the ancient Egyptians saw these as fitting in with their concept of the sevenfold structure and dynamics of being and consciousness within the solar system. This itself may help to resolve some of the puzzles faced by Egyptologists when dealing with man's association with the god Ra during his nightly passage through the "twelve hours of the night" and the associated twelve divisions of the Duat. However, let us begin by looking at the sevenfold system of planes of solar consciousness in slightly greater detail, as follows.

As we saw earlier on, the whole of the solar scheme of being in the Egyptian system comprised seven planes, comprising forty-nine subplanes or substates. The highest plane (and thus the highest seven substates) comprised the divine state. Thus the six lesser planes and their forty-two lesser substates comprised the world of progressive solar manifestation—via the Duat. Hence there were deemed to be forty-two Judges of the Dead because the forty-two substates involved the temporary "death" of the manifesting divine being. These six planes of solar being then comprised the duality of Spirit and Matter, the former expressing itself through the second, third, and fourth planes, and the latter through the fifth, sixth, and seventh. Consequently, the interface between the fourth and fifth planes or states—regarded as a place or river of fiery being—was of crucial importance.*

---

*We find the same idea in the biblical rendition of the seven days of Creation described in Genesis. Here, after appearing on the fifth day of Creation and thereafter being hunted down by the archangel Gabriel (i.e., the hierarchy of Kabiri-El), the great serpent-monster Leviathan was slain and his body skin "made into a tent wherein the righteous might dwell and also a covering for the walls of Jerusalem" (Budge, *Gods of the Egyptians,* vol. 1, 278, quoting Eisenmenger's *Entdecktes Judenthum*). The "skin of Leviathan" is the *sah,* or spiritual soul-body, which acts as the separating and connecting interface between the fourth and fifth *states* in the septenary system, the latter itself disguised metaphorically as the seven "days" of Creation.

Angels, Man, and the Islamic Tradition

Now, rather interestingly, the Islamic tradition concerning the angelic hierarchies is clearly derived from the ancient Egyptian concept—although few imams would be at all happy to entertain such an idea. To begin with, the Islamic concept holds that those angels born on the second day of Creation (a metaphor for the second solar plane/state) are eternal, but that those born on the fifth day are mortal and will, as a consequence, eventually cease to exist.[10] As we have already seen, the second state is that of solar semidivinity (the *akh*); so it is entirely consistent that this—being the first manifest expression of the divine solar state—should remain eternally at one with it. The fifth state was that of the *ak(e)r.*

As Budge tells us (again confirming the Egyptian connections), according to Islamic tradition, "nineteen angels are appointed to take charge of hell fire (*Sura* lxxiv) . . . two [other] angels are ordered to accompany every man on earth, the one to write down his good actions and the other his evil deeds; and these will appear with him at the Day of Judgement, the one to lead him before the Judge, and the other to bear witness either for or against him."[11]

As already indicated, man functions within the three lower solar planes/states of being, these comprising twenty-one substates that together make up the lower Underworld—described by Islamic theologians as Hell—and hence it is here that we find these same lesser angels who were created on or immediately after the fifth Day. But heading these twenty-one are two particularly important substates. The highest represents the actual interface between solar Spirit and solar Matter, which we have just mentioned. It is synonymous with the psychospiritual state in which is to be found the modern Spiritual Ego, or the biblical "angel with the fiery sword" who stands before the gates of heaven, or paradise. The second is the purely personal ego (and the sense of conscience), which in one sense bears a relationship to the Spiritual Ego akin to that between the semidivine state and the divine state. Consequently, the lesser nineteen angels appear to be those *deva*/angelic entities whose consciousnesses themselves comprise the nineteen lowest solar substates.

Egyptian Cross-Correspondences

Rather interestingly, we find a direct parallel with this symbolism in the organization of administrative nome districts in Egypt, for the twentieth and twenty-first nomes were those of Upper and Lower Memphis—the capital city of Lower Egypt, supposedly created as a man-made island by Menes, the theoretically first pharaoh of the Old Kingdom dynasties. Heliopolis, on the other hand, was the city of the nineteenth nome and it was there, also very logically, that the process of higher learning was undertaken under the aegis and within the grounds of the sacred Academy. The remaining eighteen nome cities were located in the Delta itself, each associated with one or another of the seven mouths of the Nile.

Budge again goes on to tell us: "Muhammadan theologians declare that the angels [i.e., those comprising these same substates of the triple Underworld] are created of a simple substance of light, and that they are endowed with life, and speech, and reason; they are incapable of sin, they have no carnal desire, they do not propagate their species, and they are not moved by the passions of wrath and anger; their obedience is absolute" and "Curiously enough, some are said to have the form of animals."[*12]

The God Sokar/Seker

This somewhat unusual god was depicted, usually, with a hawk's head (signifying an association with perceptual consciousness) and a mummified human body. In the Book of the Duat, he inhabited a part of the Land of the Dead, to which even Ra appeared to have restricted access. The sacred texts themselves indicate that "Osiris became Seker," but as Budge says, this was clearly no mere assimilation of one god by another.[13] What appears to have been quite clearly intended was that Seker represented a metamorphosed facet of the Osiris principle *within* the Underworld.

The name Seker is clearly derived from the same root as *sekhem* and *sekhet*—that is, signifying the act of separation or discrimination. The texts otherwise show that Seker inhabited a place called Ra-stau within the fifth of the divisions of the Duat,[†] and it was here in this fifth solar state (that of Mind-consciousness) that the "house of Seker" was described as containing the "efflux of Osiris." As mentioned in *Land of the Fallen Star Gods,* Seker appears to be synonymous with the Sufi word *zhikr,* meaning a spinning dance performed on one leg by the whirling dervishes. Now it appears that this is itself a dynamic esoteric metaphor for the cycle of reincarnation, which accompanies a progression through the signs of the zodiac—another (cosmic) form of the Duat. Hence we may perhaps suggest that Seker actually also represents the reincarnating impulse of the egoic nature in man—that is, that which is particularly associated with the separation of the nineteenth and twentieth solar substates. In connection with the latter concept, our attention should be drawn to the sym-

---

*This surely confirms what was suggested earlier on, to the effect that the angels/*devas* represent the instinctive memory function of the Logos and thus have no sense of either choice or real individuality. As a result, they can only be what they are or represent. There is no sense of alternative—hence the fact that "their obedience [to Law] is absolute." Man, on the other hand, does have the faculty of choice, the essence of passion, and the capacity and will to re-create himself by propagation. Because the *devas*/angels are the generators of form, the ancient tradition had it that their own distinctive consciousness produced an archetypal form of animal head. Hence it was that the Egyptian *neteru*—where not in direct association with man—were all depicted with animal heads.
†In the Islamic theological tradition, we find the word *saqar* meaning the fifth stage of Hell (Sykes, *Who's Who in Non-Classical Mythology,* 168).

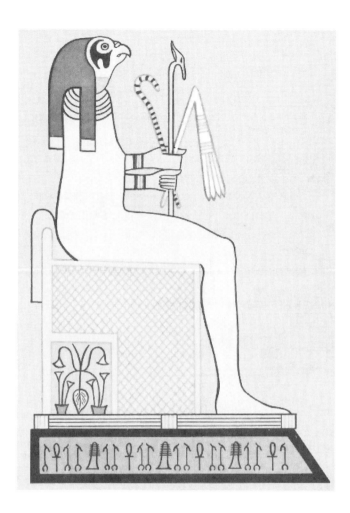

FIGURE 6.6. THE GOD SEKER

bolism associated with the "Seker boat" (otherwise known as the Hennu boat), which played a highly important role in certain of the most sacred ceremonies throughout Egypt—but perhaps particularly at Memphis. Budge describes the Seker boat for us as follows:

> It was not made in the form of an ordinary boat, but one end of it was very much higher than the other, and was made in the shape of the head of some kind of gazelle or oryx; the centre of the boat was occupied by a carefully closed coffer which was surmounted by a hawk with protecting wings stretched out over the top of it. This coffer contained the body of the dead Sun-god Af, or of Osiris, and it rested upon a framework or sledge which was provided with runners. . . . The ceremony of placing the Seker boat upon its sledge was performed at sunrise, at the moment when the rays of the sun were beginning to spread themselves over the earth."[14]

The thoroughly bizarre appearance of the Seker boat—added to the fact that it was positioned on a sledge rather than a proper keel—makes it quite clear that it was intended

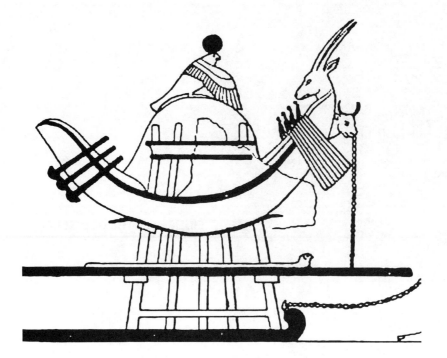

FIGURE 6.7. THE
SEKER BOAT

to symbolize a "dragging" through and across the terrestrial (under)world rather than sailing free in the waters of spiritual space. The metaphor of the boat was itself intended to symbolize a voyage, in the sense of a repetitive cycle, and it was used widely. Thus there was the Sektet boat, one of the barques of Ra*—the "boat of millions of years"—as well as the Seker boat, the latter being quite distinct from the former. Hence the Seker boat, with its casket containing the essence of a god, clearly symbolized the purely human cycle of reincarnation.

Rastau: The Dual Way

Now, because so much attention has been focused in recent years on the word *rastau* in connection with the prospect of a concealed chamber under the Sphinx,[†] it is worth examining the background issues a little more closely to note some of the (several) misapprehensions that have arisen in relation to it. For a start, Rastau is conceived of by some Egyptologists as a shrine and by others as a doorway. R. O. Faulkner, however, who translated the Pyramid Texts, described *rastau* as "the term for a ramp or slide for moving the

---

*The two barques of Ra were the Matet boat and the Sektet boat. In the first Ra is hawk-headed, in the other he is man-headed.

†Sometimes referred to as Rostau but clearly derived from Ra-*stau,* apparently signifying the "staying (or stopping) place(s)" of the god Ra. This is of particular interest in relation to Giza being associated with both Rastau and also the three stars of Orion's Belt, the middle star of which appears to have been specifically related to the Sphinx.

sarcophagus into a tomb, transferred to a region of the Beyond."[15] And when we consider some of the wall paintings symbolizing the various divisions, levels, or planes of the Duat, we certainly see a "way" leading through them, with angled sections (looking like ramps) down which coffins or sarcophagi are being lowered into the lower levels. However, as we have already seen, the coffin or sarcophagus was also a metaphor for the soul-body—whether divine, spiritual, or astroterrestrial.

One thing is quite plain. Rastau itself provided direct access to the Underworld. However, as another philologist, the German Egyptologist Adolf Erman, tells us: "Whoever enters the realms of the dead by the sacred place of Rostau has, as we learn from a map of the Hereafter, two routes open to him, which would lead him to the Land of the Blessed, one by water, the other by land. Both are zigzag [i.e., winding, or helical] and a traveller cannot change from one to the other, for between them lies a sea of fire. . . . Also before entering upon either of these routes, there is a gate of fire to be passed."[16]

Quite clearly then, Rastau led in both directions—down to the Underworld and up toward the "land of the Blessed," the latter being the divine and semidivine states of solar being. Therefore, the inference is that Rastau was indeed the name given to the gate of fire that provided access to the "winding way," passing through the realms of Spirit and Matter and the veil separating them. This duality seems to be confirmed in the following extracts from the Coffin Texts: "I am Osiris; I have come [evidently downward from the upper heaven world] to Rastau to know the secrets of the Duat,"[17] and, on the reverse cycle, where the initiate is attempting to ascend toward the intermediate and then the upper heaven worlds of Osiris: "I shall not be turned back at the gates of the Duat; I ascend to the sky with Orion (Sahu). . . . I am one who collects his efflux in front of Rastau."[18]

The Efflux

This word *efflux* is one chosen by Egyptologists and it is not an altogether happy choice, because its applied meaning is so apparently obscure. In fact, it means a continuous, accumulative emanation or discharge—in this case, seemingly of psychospiritual light—or some such. However, as we know that the Seker boat (also located in the fifth division) was made to contain the "efflux of Osiris" and that the initiate is himself an "Osiris-Ani," it would appear that the two effluxes are actually one and the same. Therefore, the fact that the initiate had to "collect his efflux" before continuing through the gates of the Duat at Rastau and then proceeding toward the upper heaven world indicates that it really means his own personally evolved essence. Again, there springs to mind the parallel visual metaphor of the lotus bud developing just beneath the surface of the lake (here the lake of the Duat itself). In conjunction with this latter idea, however, we next come into contact with the god Aker and (yet again) the duality of the Mind principle.

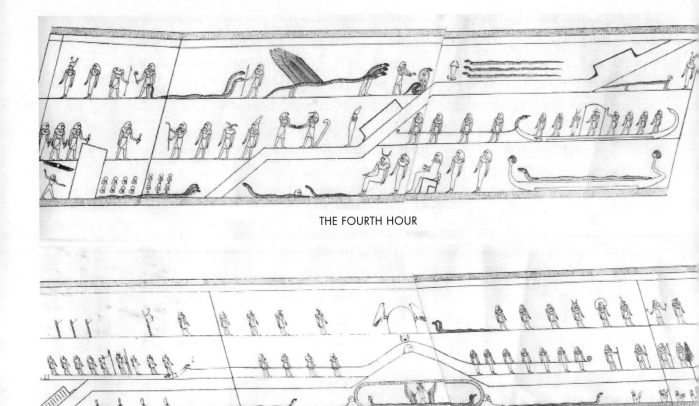

THE FOURTH HOUR

THE FIFTH HOUR

FIGURE 6.8. THE FOURTH AND FIFTH HOURS OF THE NIGHT

The God Ak(e)r

The Babylonian *simurgh* or fiery spiritual eagle was also known as an *akr*. The Egyptian Ak(e)r, however—one of the oldest of the lion gods of Egypt—was a double-headed, back-to-back sphinx figure, guarding (from either end) a tunnel or way leading to and from the Duat. As we can see from the fifth hour of the night part of the picture in fig. 6.8, the tunnel itself is formed by the outline of a (also double-headed) serpent body, the left end of which has a man's head, while the right end has three serpents' heads, one holding an ankh in its mouth.* Actually within the tunnel itself is the Horus-headed, semihuman figure of Seker, holding fast the outstretched serpent's wings. The whole composite is then enclosed within a triangular mound or hillock, capped by the solitary head of a man, facing to the right.†

Elsewhere, we find the back-to-back Akeru supporting between them the shape of the

---

*Thus this double-ended serpent form almost certainly represents the psychically conjoined *ba* and *sah* respectively.

†Interestingly, we find a curious parallel in the Celtic festival of Lughnasadh, in August, where a ritual head is placed on top of a hill—and then trampled on by someone dressed as the god Lugh, evidently representing a higher form of light (MacNeill, *Festival of Lughnasa*, 426).

horizon with the Sun's disk resting upon it—a visual metaphor implying that the Sun represents the *sah* being supported by two aspects of the Mind principle.* In fig. 6.8, however, four other points need to be taken into consideration. First of all, the right-hand (i.e., spiritual) end of the tunnel is symbolically resting upon water; second, the figure of Seker within the tunnel is shown restraining the serpent's wings; thirdly, the solitary head at the top of the triangular section is shown as involved with the formation of a mound, caused by pushing up the floor of the division or plane above it; fourthly, the ends of the divisional levels are set at an angle.† By virtue of the fact that the central area has a passing resemblance to a pyramid shape, added to the apparent association of Rastau with Giza, it has been suggested that there is an underlying implication of a concealed chamber under the Sphinx itself. However (whether or not there is such a chamber under the Sphinx), the meaning of the symbolism here looks to be quite different, for the following reasons.

First, while the two pictures display the seven divisions of the solar world, the third, fourth, and fifth take precedence in symbolic importance and are thus shown as the widest, while also containing a variety of additionally symbolic figures. Of all the pictorial representations of the twelve hours of the night, however, only the fourth and fifth hours contain the ramp imagery, along with the descending coffin or sarcophagus. In the fourth hour, the latter descends to the fourth division or plane. In the fifth hour, it descends to the fifth solar plane and takes on a semblance of semipermanency at the very left-hand edge of the picture. But the supposed "pyramid" only appears during the fifth hour, within the fifth plane—while also causing a tumescence to form in the floor of the fourth plane.

The implied symbolism is that the "divine spark" passes down through the various planes of being and consciousness in its "sarcophagus" of spiritual light, eventually coming to rest at a point where its angled position can obviously go no further but where it also simultaneously overshadows both the upper and lower parts of the fifth division, and also the whole of the sixth division too. While the left-hand half of the latter is shown as dry and arid, the right-hand end is symbolically shown as filled with water—signifying vitality. The central part of the tableau, however, is dominated by the back-to-back Aker, plus the Horus figure and the solitary head above.

The suggested interpretation is that the dual heads of Aker represent the two aspects of the Mind principle, which face the past and the future—that is, the world of

---

*Interestingly, the Egyptian word *aqer* meant "understanding." Consequently its intentionally close phonetic association with the name *aker,* the fifth division/plane, and the Mind principle is fairly self-evident. Aker guarded the gate of the dawn through which Ra passed each morning (Budge, *Gods of the Egyptians,* vol. 2, 360). Aqen, however, was the "keeper of the boat" (of Ra) (Naydler, *Temple of the Cosmos,* 233).

†In addition to all this, it is only in the fourth and fifth hours that the figures in the three main divisions actually lean (backward) at an angle. In the fourth hour, they lean to the right—signifying their instinctive spiritual orientation while facing leftward (toward material existence)—while in the fifth hour they face to the right but lean backward to the left.

material experience and of spiritual opportunity respectively. The seamlessly coiled and double-ended serpent that they support represents, it is suggested, the capacity of the human mind to generate its own personalized field of creative thought and being. The Horus-headed figure of Seker would then represent man's emerging self-consciousness, or Ego, with the serpent's wings symbolizing the fact that his creative soul consciousness has developed the tools of (imaginative) flight, but that the Seker principle holds these firmly under his control. Finally, the lone head (again, facing to the right) above the mound would correspondingly appear to represent the fully developed and individualized Mind faculty raised to prominence within the fourth division—that of spiritual consciousness itself. It is also worth pointing out that the head rests on a linear profile that is itself formed from the fusion of *two* lines—that separating the higher and lower aspects of the fifth division and also that separating the fifth division as a whole from the fourth division/plane.*

The Chamber of Judgment

Although this subject was dealt with to some extent in *Land of the Fallen Star Gods,* where particular concern was paid to the symbolic objects and figures involved in the "weighing of the heart," our concern here is rather more directed toward explaining why the symbolism involves more than just a postmortem experience. To begin with, Egyptologists have found very few tableau examples of the Chamber of Judgment scene—without drawing any distinction between the considerable differences within and between them. One of these tableaux involved the individual known as "Pepi" and the other an individual known as "the scribe Ani," accompanied by "his wife Thuthu," as shown in fig. 6.9.

It has been assumed by one and all that these were actual personalities who had died and whose after-death progressions were being ritually pictured. In fact, although the central principle remains the same for all passing through the postmortem state, the tableaux can otherwise be interpreted (and were almost certainly intended) as outlining the characteristics of the *initiatory* sequence within the subjective state of the individual—that is, in trance or deep meditation. However, to explain.

First, there appears to be a definite symbolism in the names of these two individuals. Whereas the generic name given to those who had not yet set their feet upon "the Path" was Bebi (or Babi), that given to the probationary aspirant was Pepi. Bebi was in fact the

---

*Rather interestingly, this bears a remarkably close resemblance to the modern theosophical concept of a higher and lower mind principle, the Spiritual Ego then being located at the junction of the fourth and fifth states. The Celtic Lugh, the god of light, trampling upon the head itself seems to symbolize a higher (i.e., spiritual) state of Being or consciousness, superimposing itself upon an egoic state, which had itself been raised up (Hutton, *Stations of the Sun,* 328). The parallels with the Egyptian symbolism could hardly be seen as mere coincidence.

FIGURE 6.9. THE CHAMBER OF JUDGMENT

firstborn son of Osiris,* the word-name itself meaning an "eddy" of either water or air.[19] Hence the symbolism referred to one who was unable to make anything other than the slightest impression upon the psychospiritual atmosphere. Pepi, on the other hand, was referred to as the "lesser Eye of Ra,"[20] meaning the principle of perception in the lower Underworld. He thus represented the first conscious spiritual reorientation of human consciousness. The name Ani, however, is derived from the root word *anu,* meaning "soul entity," A-Nu meaning that (first form) which is derived from out of Chaos and so manifests the principle of Knowledge-Consciousness. It would seem that the *i* suffix to each of these names is pretty well equivalent to our modern use of the letters *y* or *ie* as in familiar names such as Tommy or Debbie.† Ani's wife Thuthu, however, appears to be a merely symbolic appendage, as described further on.

The Differences of Symbolism

Now, as we can see from the smaller of the two tableaux, Pepi is being led into the chamber by a large Anubis figure, god of the Underworld, while the smaller Apuat jackal (his clothing unmarked) merely adjusts the Balance. The figures of Tehuti and the monster Amemet are also both devoid of markings. On the Balance itself, the jar holding Pepi's heart is tiny, as is also the feather of Ma'at on the other side. The right-hand Pepi figure being introduced

---

*Hence our modern English word *baby,* which itself appears to have arrived from Egypt via Scotland.

†The name Anu, from which Ani is derived, means "soul-body" and was also that given to the sacred college at Heliopolis. Hence the *ani* was one who had already commenced the process of progressive psychospiritual education.

to Osiris by a (bareheaded) Horus figure is the same size as the Pepi figure at the left of the tableau. The figures of the overshadowing gods of Judgment and also of the four sons of Horus all face leftward—that is, symbolically toward the Underworld, and there are no vertical hieroglyphs separating the various parts of the chamber from each other. In fact the chamber (of the Pepi individual's inner consciousness) is as yet undifferentiated, undoubtedly due to his lack of spiritual perception and experience. Consequently the body and clothing of the Osiris figure too lack any markings.

When we come to inspect the larger "Ani" tableau, however, we find that it is much more complex, because it represents a far more developed initiate consciousness. The gods of Judgment at the top of the tableau are now all facing to the right; there is but one much enlarged Apuat figure who is now (on the right side of the Balance) holding a vessel containing the essence of Ani's righteous life deeds and thoughts; the canopic jar holding his heart is hugely enlarged, as is the feather of Ma'at; both Tehuti and Amemet now have markings on their bodies or clothes; the right-hand Ani is immensely increased in size, as is also the (now crowned) Horus figure; a third Ani figure now becomes apparent, kneeling before a well-marked Osiris in front of whom also the four sons of Horus are now facing to the right as well. And so on. It is also worth pointing out something else in the tableau, which rarely (if ever) attracts attention. It is that, although a clearly definite sequence is being depicted, that same sequence, in the Ani tableau, is broken down into a series of definite stages, which represent a chain of consciousness. To explain.

The Sequence of Antechambers

In the outer antechamber (on the far left) we have the initiate (initially described as the scribe Ani and later as Osiris-Ani) with his wife Thuthu, who rather importantly holds a *sistrum,* which was commonly used in Egypt (and by Tibetan and Bhutanese shamans even today) for magically invoking the attentions of the psycho-elemental world. It is suggested, therefore, that she is herself merely symbolic of man's (and the initiate's) elemental senses.* So Ani and his senses are here apparently representative of his objective human persona and thus of the physical world as well—the lowest of the seven *solar* states of being and consciousness.

In the second chamber, however—which we would sequentially expect to represent the sixth solar state—there occurs the separation of the various component principles that

---

*The name Thuthu appears to be a deliberate pun on the name Tutu, which was a form or aspect of Shu, the god of light. As this same aspect was also known as Her-ka (Budge, *Gods of the Egyptians,* vol. 1, 463)—meaning "the sensory consciousness or secondary light of the *ka*"—the implication is that Thuthu represents that aspect of Ani (the etheric double) that has been left behind in the physical world to maintain the autonomic vitality of the physical body while his spirit travels onward within the psychospiritual realms of being. The *sistrum* would thus be symbolic of the functional sensitivity of the *ka,* which maintains a secondary, telepathic contact with the astrally traveling spirit.

make up the persona of Ani himself. Rather importantly, there are—at the upper level—*twelve* sets of hieroglyphic columns,* arranged in sets of seven and five. Under them, on the left, standing closely side by side, are Meskenet and Rennenet, the respective goddesses of conception and gestation/fortune. Their significance is that, without them, sustained involvement of the higher principles within the physical body is impossible.† Above these two is the *ba* bird, representing the astral soul itself, and to its right we have the *ren,* symbolized by the sphinx-headed casket. Below the *ren* is the now pharaonically attired but much smaller form of Ani—symbolizing the evolving god-king—while next to him is of course the *ab,* contained in the canopic jar on the scales.

In the next succeeding chamber, we have the figures of Tehuti—the Recorder—and Amemet the triple monster, which is depicted as eating the residues of the *ab* following the weighing and judgment, but which actually symbolizes the restitution of waste material back to the three lowest solar states. This chamber is itself representative of the *lower* fifth solar state and it is noteworthy that there is no representation of Ani here at all. It is purely associated with the phase of registration and discard—that is, involving the principle of organizational discrimination that we find in the impersonal *lower* mind principle.

The next chamber is—perhaps expectedly by now—representative of the *higher* Mind principle and state. In it we see the figure of Ani reappear, this time, however, much increased in stature and now being led by Horus the Elder with the Double Crown of Upper and Lower Egypt on his head. Horus the Elder, as we have indicated before, represents the *spiritually* oriented aspect of Man's consciousness, and in confirmation of that symbolism, Horus is shown extending his arm forward into two of three vertical sections of hieroglyphs, representing the three highest subplanes of the fifth solar state.

The fifth and final chamber is symbolically dual, thereby apparently representing the union of the fourth and third solar states—akin to the Hindu *atma-buddhi.* In the former, we have the clearly spiritualized Ani (with his crown chakra evidently active) kneeling in submission and making offerings to the god Osiris (representing his own Higher Self—the *atman*), who is symbolically seated in his mummified costume within a throne tent. Very importantly, the dais on which the throne sits is shown as being pegged down next to Ani—*that is, it is secured within the fourth solar state.* The underlying symbolism here appears to be that the throne tent or chamber of Osiris (himself representing the principle of divinity or semidivinity in Man) displays itself in a transcendent glory of spiritual light, which nevertheless is far too ethereal in itself to have a permanently fixed existence within the mere scheme of human consciousness. It is

---

*Thereby indicating a zodiacal association.

†Because Mesk-enet represents the principle of union, while Ren-nenet represents soul-fostered growth or development.

correspondingly suggested that the presence of Isis and Nephthys behind Osiris is symbolic of the union of the kosmic *ba* and the kosmic *ka* within which the *solar* divinity (Osiris) is manifesting.

The Upper Heaven Worlds

Having so far looked at the general (sevenfold) structure and psychological dynamics of the Egyptian solar world scheme, plus the sequence by which Man's individuality was regarded as being evolved through the lower states and then tested before it could pass on to the higher (i.e., spiritual and divine) states of being, let us now finally consider the latter in rather more detail. Here again, however, we unfortunately find mainstream Egyptology coming up with a completely literal interpretation of all the associated metaphors and allegories and thus rather missing the plot.

While the Underworld comprised the three lowest states in the septenary scheme, the heaven worlds were distributed through four primary solar states—the divine, the semidivine, the spiritual, and the lesser heaven world of the *sahu*. The name associations are not always completely clear in the texts (in fact the very reverse, which is probably exactly what was intended) and the metaphors also vary quite considerably according to the associated function or context. However, the following is believed to be fairly close to what was intended in terms of the picture presented to and used by the general populace outside the initiated priesthood.

The Divine and Semidivine States

The divine world of Aaru—in which lived the imperishable gods themselves—was that of the Demiurge, the Ashemu, containing the "Lake of Aaru in which Ra washeth himself."[21] Depicted symbolically by a mass of waving reeds, it remained forever subjective—at least, as far as the lower solar world was concerned—but the individual who managed to achieve access to the "barque of Ra" was regarded as having also attained an automatic and eternal right of entry to this exalted state of consciousness, forever afterward existing in a body of light and eating the same "food" as the gods themselves.

There also existed in this state three classes of *akhu* beings, the *akhemu-seku, the akhemu-betesh,* and the *akhemu-sesh-emau,*[22] who were regarded as eternal and in no way subject to either age or decay. They in fact bear a strong resemblance to the three types of Buddha in the Indo-Tibetan tradition, each of whom had responsibility for one or another of the three lowest kosmic planes of being of our home universe.*

---

*These were, respectively, the Dharmakaya, the Samboghakaya, and the Nirmanakaya, each group containing (in corresponding sequence) the whole of the fifth, sixth, and seventh *kosmic* planes of existence within their (group) consciousness, on behalf of our planet.

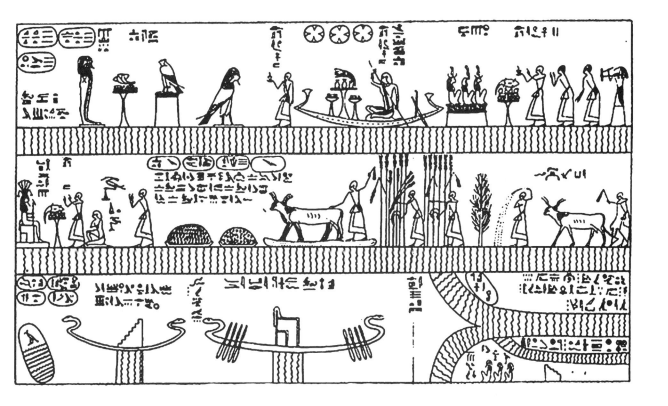

FIGURE 6.10. THE SEKHET AARU (THE HEAVENLY FIELDS)

Of particular note in this picture is that the third and lowest of the three solar states shown involves a symbolically bifurcated river or waterway, leading both upward to the higher states and also downward to the lower states of the Duat. The two boats displayed in the same third state have no crew or passengers, one containing a flight of steps (but having no oars) and the other a seat and six pairs of oars. Both boats have serpent heads at either end, clearly indicating that they are symbolic of soul-body vehicles. Here then, one might suggest, is the simultaneous point of embarkation and debarkation of the "divine sparks" involved in the greater cycle of manifest solar existence.

The semidivine state was regarded as having somewhat of a dual nature, one aspect relating to the outgoing beings and the other to the incoming ones. Hence these were known respectively as Sekhet-Hetepet (the Field of Offerings) and Sekhet-Hetep* (the Field of Peace), the latter being symbolic of the fact that, once this state of consciousness was reached by the advanced initiate, he was no longer bound by the need to return to the cycle of human existence, for he had achieved the hugely advanced state of awareness and power of a demigod and was thus in direct touch with his own true Source.

Remembering that each of these solar states was itself sevenfold in nature, the Egyptians' love of detail shows itself further in the symbolic depiction of the Sekhet-Hetepu, as illustrated in fig. 6.10. It is from this that Egyptologists seem to have primarily derived their

---

*It is worth noting that *hetep* is actually derived from *het* (i.e., house of) and *ep,* which is the reverse of *pe.* The inference is that the "city of Pe" was merely the reflection of this state.

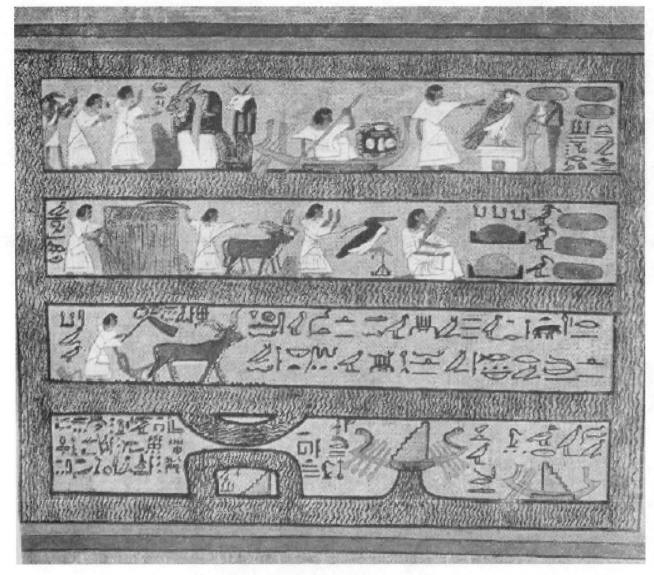

FIGURE 6.11. THE SEKHET-AARU
(from the Papyrus of Ani)

This scene appears to cover the higher four solar states and we can see that in the lowest of these we have one serpent-headed boat, double-prowed and with six pairs of oars, containing a flight of stairs and being carried upward by a symbolic wave, toward the third solar state. The other boat, although smaller, also contains a flight of stairs but only has two sets of oars. In addition, it sails flatly upon the river surface. Note also the yet smaller flight of stairs contained within the lower "island" bounded by the "river" of the fourth state, and the smaller "island," which leans toward it from the third solar state. These too are indicative of the principle of spiritual development.

ideas of all the ancient Egyptians—regardless of class or intellectual perception—having a decidedly materialistic attitude to what they wished to find in their heaven world. While it is possible that this sort of distorted view of the highest inner worlds may have become commonplace in the New Kingdom dynasties, it certainly does not appear to have been the common perception in earlier times—or in fact at *any* time among the priesthood.

The third solar state was known as Sekhet-Sanehemu—the Field of Grasshoppers, the latter seemingly being a metaphor symbolizing the densely populated and extremely energetic nature of this field of (spiritual) being, doubtless resulting from the direct emergence of incarnating spiritual beings from the immensely powerful semidivine state. Within this third solar state were located the Lakes of the Duat and the Lakes of the Jackals, another duality—this time apparently symbolizing the outflowing "waters" (of dark Spirit) and the correspondingly inflowing "waters" of spiritual light.

The Two Spiritual States

The fourth and lowest of these upper solar states—that of the *sahu*—also appears as a duality, incorporating (on behalf of our world scheme) the metaphorical "cities" of Nekhen and Pe. It was thus because of the souls or watchers of Pe that the individual himself originally emerged as a Pepi, through being seen by those above as one on spiritual probation and therefore facing one or another of the initiations on the Path. Thus we find in the texts: "O mighty heaven, stretch out thy hand to Pepi Nefer-ka-Ra, for Pepi is thy divine hawk. . . . Pepi hath come to the place where he is, and he (his father) granteth to him to rise like the sun, and he establisheth for him[self] his two divine *utchats*."[23] This fourth solar state, however, only took on the semblance of an intermediate heaven world by virtue of being united to the third solar state—which was itself the emanation of the second or semidivine state. Thus, although the seven Het-Heru were to be found here, acting as a focus for the evolutionary process taking place in the Underworld below, it was essentially a false heaven—a merely spiritual transit camp.

In Conclusion

It should now be reasonably clear from all this that the ancient Egyptians possessed a very definite and sophisticated perception of the psychological as well as the spiritual makeup of the human constitution, for what has been described in outline in these last two chapters indicates that their original concepts involved a vision of human life and death as one seamlessly continuous experience—that is, until broken by man's own self-generated and self-consciously chosen departure from the limitations of merely human existence, on his way to becoming a god.

That then concludes the first two parts of this book, dealing with man's celestial origins and his subjective nature. Somewhat inevitably, what has been touched on provides only a sketched outline of the more salient parts of the overall scheme of things as seen by the ancient Egyptians. However, it is hoped that the reader will by now possess a reasonable sense of the *mode* of Egyptian mystic-metaphysical thought, as well as understanding something of the associated form. In the next section of the book, we shall take a more historical look at the suggested origins of Egyptian spiritual culture and the factors that ultimately led to its degeneracy and demise.

PART THREE

EGYPT'S HISTORICAL BACKGROUND

SEVEN

THE RIVER NILE AND ITS SYMBOLISM

The greater part of all this land, as the priests told me, and as I judge by what I saw, is an accession of land to the Egyptians. For the plains that lie between the mountains above Memphis seem to me to have been formerly a bay of the sea, like the level lands about Ilium and Teuthrania and Ephesus and beside the river Maeander, to compare small things with great, for none of the rivers that have carried down the earth to make those regions can be compared with any one of the mouths of the Nile. . . . Now if the Nile were to turn his stream into the Arabian Gulf, what could hinder him from filling it with earth in twenty thousand years. Nay, I believe it would fill it in ten thousand years. Would not then a gulf even larger than this have been filled up in the ages before my time by so great and busy a river?"

HERODOTUS, *THE HISTORIES*

It has long been recognized that the River Nile—the Great Winding Waterway—was the central and most important feature of everyday ancient Egyptian life, not only in a geographical sense, but also in both a practical and mystical sense, for it was seen by some (at least in part) as the terrestrial counterpart of the star-strewn Milky Way in the night skies above. By others, it is thought that the ancient Egyptians considered it to represent the undulating ecliptic path through the zodiac. But in order to understand its mystical significance properly, one needs to consider it in its entirety, extending from the Delta in the north to its sources in the far south as the White and Blue Niles, themselves originating within the Great Rift Valley of East Africa and the Abyssinian highlands of the Horn of Africa.

The way in which the Nile then unfolds (through what is now the Sudan) can thereby

FIGURE 7.1. VIEW TOWARD THE SECOND CATARACT
(taken from a nineteenth-century lithograph)

be seen to give rise in an esoterically sequential manner to the country known to us today as Egypt. In very ancient times, however, Egypt was probably far larger in extent—at least in a southerly direction, as we shall shortly outline. Before going any further in this direction, however, it ought to be made clear that this chapter will of necessity deal only with general issues relevant to our main theme. To cover the Nile and its environs in detail would necessitate at least two volumes—a magnum opus in its own right, which this author at least is at present unwilling to contemplate.

The Geological Sources and Characteristics of the River Nile

As described in greater detail in *Land of the Fallen Star Gods,*[1] the valley of the Nile was progressively formed by extreme geological pressures affecting the whole landmass of eastern and northeastern Africa, commencing several hundred thousand years ago, at a time when Egypt and the Horn of Africa seemingly formed a continental island, with the Atlantic (merged with the eastern Mediterranean) lapping along its southern coast all the way across what is now the Sahara Desert, to marry up with the Indian Ocean.

The River Nile
and Its Symbolism

191

As a result of these geological upheavals, a severe fracture occurred running from the Rift Valley in the south right up to Asia Minor in the north, the Nile Valley itself actually being a subsidiary fracture. Thus the Rift Valley, acting as a vast rainwater catchment, drained mainly northward via a series of great lakes into what was to become the White Nile.

The same huge geological pressures also caused the raising up and corrugated folding of mountainous regions farther north in the areas around the widening mouth of what is now the Red Sea. As a result, these high mountain ranges—of modern Abyssinia and Ethiopia—were able to trap and tap the heavy rain-bearing clouds of the annual monsoon that blows up from the Indian Ocean to the south. The huge precipitation that ensued fed mainly westward and became the Blue Nile, with its several tributaries, which married up with the White Nile at the modern city of Khartoum;* it is here, really, that the formation of ancient Egypt might truly be said to commence. The qualitative distinction between the two merging rivers was, however, very considerable, as Wallis Budge described for late nineteenth-century tourists in his immensely detailed guide book, *The Nile: Notes for Travellers in Egypt.*

> The White Nile is so called because of the fine, whitish clay which colours its waters. It is broader and deeper than the eastern arm and it brings down a much larger volume of water. The Ancients appear to have regarded it as the true Nile. There can be no doubt, however, that the Blue Nile and Atbara are the true makers of Egypt, for, during their rapid courses from the Abyssinian mountains, they carry down with them all the rich mud which, during the lapse of ages, has been spread over the land on each side of its course.[2]

This duality of the Nile would have been of considerable mystical significance to the ancient Egyptians for what it symbolically came to represent in metaphysical terms. In that sense, the White Nile and its clay content represented the constant flow of purely material existence. However, the cyclical return of the nutrient-rich, alluvium-bearing (and thus life-giving) floodwaters of the Blue Nile and Atbara were seen as expressing the (necessarily masculine) re-creative urge of the Deity. Both of these aspects are of course necessary in universal Creation to provide form and function—the female and male aspects of both kosmic and mundane existence. Thus it was that the Egyptians depicted the great river god Hp(i) as the light and dark duality (symbolically associated with Spirit and Matter) that enabled the foundations of material existence to be laid down.

*The name Khartum was probably derived from Kha-Tum or Ka-Tum.

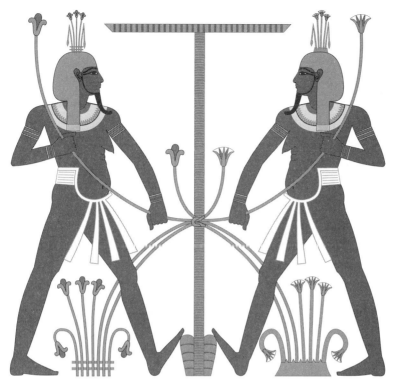

FIGURE 7.2. HP(I), DUAL GOD OF THE NILE
(Illustration by Jeff Dahl)

The God of the Nile

Although Hp(i) was chiefly associated with the River Nile, his deific remit actually extended rather further in Egyptian mystic and occult lore, as we shall see in greater detail later on. This is rather more easily understood, however, if he is perceived as a principle in Universal Nature.* Thus, we are told:

---

*Like Apuat, Hpi was regarded as being associated with Asert, the Tree of Life, which (astronomically) extended down through the Pleiades from the celestial pole in Ursa Minor (Budge, *Gods of the Egyptians,* vol. 2, 43). The name Hp(i) is phonetically the same in both the Chinese—as the river god Ho-Po—and the Sanskrit—that is, as Apah, the goddess of the celestial waters. In the ancient Babylonian it is found as Apsu, the primordial male principle depicted as the consort of Tiamat, the goddess of the ocean of kosmic Chaos. The Sumerian Apsu varied only slightly from this, being representative of the eternal and uncreated Abyss of divine water, associated with which we find the goddess Nammu, who bears a striking phonetic resemblance to the Egyptian god of the cataract, Khnemu. In the ancient traditions of west African magic, we find the name of the local witch-doctor or wizard being Obeah—which, on the face of it, looks to be a corruption of Hp-Ea. As Hp and Ob appear to be phonetically synonymous terms for the god of the raw power in elemental Nature, while Ea was the Chaldeo-Babylonian equivalent of Visnu (i.e., representing Universal Consciousness), this supposition would make completely logical sense. Interestingly also, the sacred black ibis—messenger of the god Tehuti (who himself represented the Universal Mind)—was called Hab(i). This linguistic similarity with Hp(i) can be no mere coincidence, as the ibis is a wading bird known for its great faculty of killing and then swallowing small snakes (a.k.a. souls) whole.

The god of the Nile was addressed as the "Father of the gods" and we are told in a hymn that if he were to fail, the gods would fall down headlong and men would perish"; his majesty was considered to be so great that it was said of him, "he cannot be sculptured in stone; he is not to be seen in the statues on which are set the crowns of the South and of the North; neither service nor oblations can be offered unto him in person; and he cannot be brought forth from his secret habitations; the place where he dwelleth is unknown . . . no habitation is large enough to hold him; and he cannot be imagined by thee in thy heart."[3]

Bearing in mind that the singularity of the Nile passing through Egypt was clearly seen as the living expression of this great deity (or Universal Principle), the impossibility of any sort of artistic depiction whatsoever must surely be seen as rendering the invisible but implacably powerful current in the river as symbolic of no less than the very livingness of the Unknowable Logos himself, as manifested not only in the lowest elemental Matter, but also in the highest states of active Being.

In apparent contradiction of what has just been said concerning the impossibility of depicting or confirming Hp(i)'s habitation, the Egyptians puzzlingly did appear to do so in relation to what they referred to as a deep underground cavern beneath the First Cataract. From this emanated, so they averred, a powerful wellspring, which gave the Nile its huge force and momentum within the land of Egypt. However, what they were referring to is not quite what the modern Egyptologist believes it to be. Referring to the plan-diagram shown in fig. 7.3, we can see that there is an auric zone of influence running through the location of the First Cataract, this actually symbolizing the *ba* or astral soul of Egypt. It is thus an organic emanation welling up from within *this* to which the Egyptians were actually referring—hence the symbolism of the cavern, which was itself a commonly used metaphor in ancient times for the soul. And, as Isis was synonymous with the *national ba,* which had to be impregnated with the Osirian influence in order for the Horus influence to be conceived, it is not altogether surprising that we find that the temple of Philae (dedicated to Isis) contained a dedication to childbirth of the Unknown God.

The Cataracts

The prime set of mystical associations of the Nile are to be found in the cataracts, of which there are six, the effective seventh being the confluence of the Blue and White Niles at Khartoum. Now, as already indicated, seven was a highly significant number to the Ancients. In fact, as the very structure of ancient Egyptian spiritual culture was founded on the sacred number seven, there is, at the very least, a strong suspicion that the six cataracts

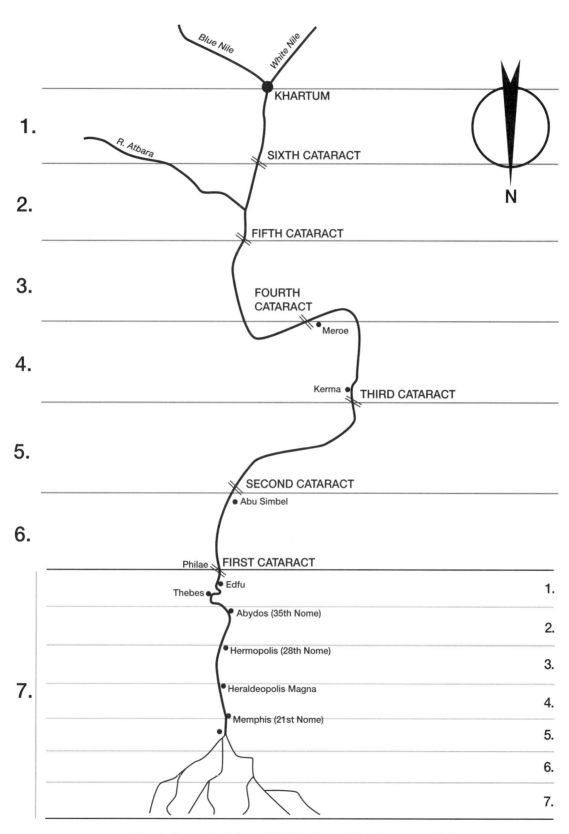

FIGURE 7.3. THE SEVENFOLD DIVISIONS OF THE RIVER NILE

were actually man-made,* rather than being merely natural geological phenomena—although most would probably describe the numerological association as being mere coincidence in this particular context. However, bearing in mind that the Nile at this point is more than 1,200 feet above the height of the First Cataract between Elephantine and Philae and would have produced a constant destructive torrent in Upper Egypt had such cataracts not been in place, there is every reason to believe that the Egyptians had due cause and capacity to create them for practical as well as mystical reasons.†

The Egyptians are known to have been brilliant hydrological as well as civil and structural engineers (among their many other remarkably developed faculties), of whose works we are told by Wallis Budge: "If we accept the statements of Strabo, we may believe that the ancient system of irrigation was so perfect that the varying height of the inundation [some forty-five feet at Khartum] caused but little inconvenience to the inhabitants of Egypt."[4] However, there are three other references that tend to support the suggestion that the Egyptians were quite capable of undertaking even more massive hydro-engineering projects in order to bring the Nile under a reasonable degree of control, while otherwise still ensuring that the results of such workmanship remained entirely in conformity with what was regarded as its kosmic counterpart.

First then, in his *The Nile,* Budge advises us: "About thirty eight miles north of Aswan . . . the channel at Silsila does not represent the original bed of the Nile, for it is only a branch of it; the true channel, which was nearly a mile wide and fifty feet deep, lies on the right side of the hill in which the quarries are and is now buried under mud and silt. There never was a cataract at Silsila."[5]

The Delta and Lake Moeris

The second reference comes from Herodotus when, in talking about the five actively functional mouths of the Nile in the Delta (there were seven in all in ancient times), he says:

For the Nile, after the [First] Cataract, flows through the middle of Egypt towards the sea, cutting the country in two. It flows thus in one channel as far as the city of

---

*The six cataracts and confluence of the Nile might also perhaps be considered to have a parallel association with the seven main chakras in the human etheric double—the Egyptian *ka*. Considering greater Egypt as the equivalent of a unified psychospiritual organism, as the Egyptians themselves doubtless saw it, the parallel correspondences in terms of function are really too close to draw any other conclusion.

†As the inundation from the Blue Nile used to cause an increase in height of some forty-five feet at Khartoum, one can imagine the constant annual devastation that would have been caused within Egypt itself by the floodwaters—if steps had not been taken to contain or at least slow it down. The topography of the area between Khartoum and the First Cataract also suggests that, without the cataracts, the actual course of the river would have been quite different and more direct, or would have dispersed westward.

Cercasorus and there it separates into three. The channel that runs eastwards is called the Pelusian mouth; the second, running westwards, is called the Canobic mouth; but the one that runs straight on where the river comes to the apex of the Delta and cuts through the middle of it into the sea is called the Sebennytic mouth and it is not the smallest nor the least famous part of the river. Two other mouths diverge from the Sebennytic and lead to the sea; these are the Saitic and the Mendesian. The Bolbitinic and Bucolic are not natural mouths, but have been made by digging.[6]

Although Diodorus Siculus, Strabo, and Pliny all commented on it as well, the third reference again comes from Herodotus and concerns the great Faiyum depression (to the west of Memphis) in which stood Lake Moeris and the temple of Crocodilopolis, originally known as Arsinoe*: "But a greater marvel even than this labyrinth is the lake called Moeris, besides which it stands. The circuit of this lake measures three thousand six hundred furlongs, as much as the whole sea coast of Egypt. That it was artificially made and dug out is evident, because almost in the middle of the lake there are two pyramids, both standing in fifty fathoms of water and built as high again above the water and on the top of each is a colossal stone figure seated on a throne."[7] But more of Lake Moeris later on.†

FIGURE 7.4. HERODOTUS

---

*The Egyptians called it the Faiyum Ta-She (the Lake District). However, all that is left of the originally vast Lake Moeris is the modern (albeit still large) Birket-al-kurun, now closely surrounded by villages.
†Diodorus Siculus also confirmed that Lake Moeris and the canal connecting it to the Nile at Memphis had both been hand-dug.

Engineering projects of such a fantastic size and nature would be regarded as altogether formidable in our own time. But for them to have been conceived and undertaken in a period prior to recorded history (i.e., over 5,500 years ago) generates all sorts of suggestions about the sophistication of ancient civilization that modern archaeology and science would find uncomfortable—to say the least. Taken side by side with the delicate placing of blocks of stone weighing more than two hundred tons in the building of the Sphinx temple at Giza—which no modern crane could achieve—it lends increasingly firm support to the idea that we really have no idea who the true ancient Egyptians really were and when they carried out such vast projects as these and the building of the pyramids at Giza.

The Metaphysical Symbolism of the Cataracts

However, to return to the subject of the cataracts and their esoteric symbolism, the implicit idea seems to have been that the distance between each represented a plane or state of kosmic existence—of which there were, of course, seven. Thus it is only when (traveling northward) we arrive at the First Cataract between Philae and Elephantine that we find the commencement of the formal nome districts of Egypt. But why should this have been so when the formal southern boundary of Egypt was to be found much farther south, near Wadi Halfa, the original location of the temples of Abu Simbel, before the area was flooded by the new Lake Nasser? The answer to this again lies in the esoteric meaning and associations of the number seven, which we find appearing again and again, not least of all in the fact that Egypt had seven oases in the desert as well. One is left wondering if these too were the results of ancient engineering schemes, all arranged in such a manner as to conform with the universal septenary principle.

When we look more closely at the septenary principle here, we again see the principle of concentricity tied up in it. In other words, the seventh and lowest division of a major sequence of seven itself gives rise to a semi-autonomous and distinctively different sevenfold subsystem, as within itself. By way of confirmation, the Nile from the First Cataract northward to the Delta has forty-two nome districts (i.e., six times seven). But adding to these the seven mouths of the Nile in the Delta makes up, with them, a total factor of forty-nine (seven times seven). However, taken as one system in its entirety, the area north of the First Cataract can be regarded as representing but one-seventh of the greater land system that stretches from the Mediterranean to the confluence of the White and Blue Niles at the city of Khartum.*

---

*This perception actually only occurred to me some time after *Land of the Fallen Star Gods* had been published. Consequently, fig. 8.2 in that book needs to be adjusted slightly to show Elephantine and the First Cataract as the culmination of the metaphorical divine state in the lowest kosmic dimension, while the seven mouths of the Nile in the Delta correspondingly represent the seven lowest substates of the seventh and lowest kosmic state.

Sacred Places with Foreign Associations

Taking this into consideration, one might suggest that the *original* location of the Second Cataract effectively represented the junction of the fifth and sixth kosmic states, counting downward (see fig. 7.3), while the Third Cataract—located close to a town rather fascinatingly called Kerma*—correspondingly represented the junction between the highly important third and fourth kosmic substates. That importance, as we saw in earlier chapters, derives from the numerologically significant fact that the fourth state in any septenary sequence represented an intermediate or secondary heaven world from which the cycle of incarnation (and associated karma) within the three lower states always began and to which it ultimately returned. Not surprisingly perhaps, it is here between the Third and Fourth Cataracts that we also find the sacred island and city of Meroe, whose name that—as Meru—we find in the Hindu and Greek mystic cultures and also that of the Polynesian islanders. In these traditions, Meru too seems to have represented a *secondary* heaven world—like Olympus.[†]

In approaching the Fourth Cataract, the Nile moves sharply eastward and this in itself throws into vivid relief its waywardly looping bend between the Second and Fifth Cataracts. Although it might seem extraordinary to suggest it, this huge bend out of the otherwise gently winding south-to-north course of the river also seems to have an underlying esoteric significance. As pointed out in an earlier chapter, the highest two substates in any septenary system were regarded as divine and semidivine, whereas the third, fourth, and fifth were regarded as their triple expression relative to the sixth and seventh (counting downward). In the Hindu system this is synonymous with the upper (spiritual) triad of *atma-buddhi-manas*. Consequently, the whole area to the east of the Nile between the Fifth and Second Cataracts might reasonably be regarded as of very considerable ancient importance, although in quite what manner this may have been expressed is not yet altogether clear. This same area—largely off-limits these days because of the tense political situation in the Sudan—was quite extensively checked over by the British in the late nineteenth and early twentieth centuries when it was known as the Island of Meroe. Rather interestingly, too, the soil-saturated River Atbara joins the Nile just south of the Fifth Cataract, thereby adding to the potential significances, for the fifth chakra in the human organism (i.e., the throat) is where the inhaled atmospheric medium meets the psychoneural system and combines with it.

---

*Thus, that which lay below this secondary heaven world became subject to the universal Law of Karma (cause and effect), as imposed upon it by the hierarchical influences emanating from within the fourth kosmic state.
†In further confirmation of relations with ancient India, Budge mentions an eleventh-dynasty pharaoh active in this area whose Horus name was Sankh-Taui and whose forename was Sankh-ka-Ra, strikingly reminiscent of the great Indian sage Shankara-charya (Budge, *The Nile,* 36).

The Sacred Land of Meroe/Marawi

Otherwise known as Meru in several ancient cultures, the name of this area appears to derive its name from the Egyptian root word *mer,* meaning "death"—paralleled in the Sanskrit by the root word *mri,* meaning "to die," and also associated with being "mortal." However, these associations seemingly derive from the fact that Meroe symbolically represented the fourth *kosmic* state—dedicated to the goddess Net, who gave birth to the Net-heru (i.e., *neteru*) gods who fell into the Underworld and were thus regarded as having died (at least temporarily) through having lost their immortality.

Herodotus refers in his *Histories* to "the great city of Meroe, which is accounted the capital of all Ethiopia," and he goes on: "The inhabitants of the place worship no other gods than Zeus [i.e., Amen-Ra] and Dionysus; these are given great honours and an oracle of Zeus is established there."[8] The ancient civilization that once existed there is, alas, no more. Wallis Budge—writing during the latter part of the nineteenth century—was only able to describe the remnants of its ruins. He rather interestingly also, however, described the existence of literally dozens of pyramids there, thus: "At a distance of about forty miles from the mouth of the Atbara . . . a visit may be made to three groups of pyramids [about 112 in all] commonly called the Pyramids of Meroe, . . . also called the Pyramids of As-sur [i.e., Osiris]."[9] Elsewhere he adds, "At Nuri . . . seven and a half miles from Marawi on the west bank of the Nile are the remains of thirty-five pyramids."[10]*

The somewhat fragmented modern historical view concerning the land of Meroe was that, during the early dynasties, it either formed part of Egypt or was an uncolonized area to which the Egyptians sent periodic foraging parties to mine the prodigious quantities of gold and precious stones found there, or to bring back large amounts of timber from its extensive forests. According to this view, Meroe was later taken over by invading "Ethiopians" and others who eventually made it their capital within the kingdom of Kesh or Cush and then themselves adopted the practice of Egyptian mystic culture and sacred architecture wholesale. However, this scenario seems full of holes and blandly unargued assumptions, which thus seem highly suspect. Given the mystic and metaphysical significances attached to the Blue and White Niles, their sources and the cataracts, and so on, it seems very much more logical and probable that the territories of ancient Egypt *in predynastic times* extended southeast all the way to the Indian Ocean, perhaps incorporating the whole of the Horn of Africa.

As outlined in *Land of the Fallen Star Gods,* the modern inhabitants of Ethiopia are clearly a historically interbred mixture of the peoples of the Indian subcontinent with local African tribes.[11] In predynastic Egyptian times (and probably even during the Old

---

*The numbers 112 (16 × 7) and 35 (5 × 7) add up to 147 (21 × 7)—which would undoubtedly have had some appreciable esoteric significance, although what that might have been is today not so immediately obvious.

Kingdom as well), the likelihood is that they were all of pure Indian extraction. The kingdom of Kesh itself seems to have derived its name from the northwest Indian region of Kashmir (i.e., Kesh-mir), to the northwest of which lies the Hindu Kush mountain region, at the western end of the Himalayas. Immediately to the south of Kashmir and also lying across the River Indus is then to be found the region of Punjab, an area historically famous for its agriculture, particularly in the field of spice production. Hence, it is suggested, it was to here—as Herodotus tells us—that the later dynastic Egyptians used to send trading parties to buy spices. In those days, however, Punjab was merely known as the land of Pun(t), where lived the *eastern* Ethiopians. Thus the western Ethiopians of the Horn of Africa were merely expatriates who had set up an autonomously separate kingdom of their own, ultimately extending their influence northward into Egypt itself at a time when, so it would seem, its *original* civilization had at least partially collapsed, leaving something of a political vacuum.*

To proceed any farther south than Meroe into the modern Sudan would be somewhat impractical, given the very limited amount of knowledge available concerning the area. At that point, therefore, we shall leave the further historical aspects of this scenario to the next chapter and about-face, recommencing our descriptions of the sequential Nile areas as we progress northward, this time, however, commencing at the First Cataract between Philae and Elephantine.

Circumpolar Star Associations

Returning to the subject of the occasionally strange geographical shape of the Nile, we should not pass without mentioning the section between Philae and Diospolis Parva. As described in rather greater detail in *Land of the Fallen Star Gods,* the Nile here takes the shape not only of the Apuat instrument used in Egyptian ritual to "open the mouth of Osiris," but also of the circumpolar constellation Ursa Minor, the Little Bear. While there is no implied suggestion (at present) that this shape was actually the result of yet another ancient Egyptian engineering project, they were certainly sufficiently aware of the shape to place the seven major temples of Elephantine, Kom Ombos, Edfu, Esna, Thebes, Dendera, and Diospolis Parva along it in positions exactly matching the relative locations of the seven stars. But that in itself implies that they must at the very least have had scale maps of the whole of Egypt—perhaps not so strange an idea in light of confirmed knowledge

---

*Edward Pococke in his book *India in Greece* (206) confirmed the Brahmin tradition that the Ethiopians were originally an Indian race, forced to emigrate because of regicide and general sacrilege. Pococke also confirmed his own research-based belief that the Pali-speaking people of the River Oxus region, to the southwest of the Hindu Kush and next to Kashmir, were the selfsame Hyksos people who swept down into northern Egypt (circa 2250 BCE) and conquered it, thereafter settling in Palestine—hence Pali-stan. It would seem, therefore, that the incentive behind this quite extraordinarily distant invasion itself arose from the knowledge of the Hyksos that their own countrymen had already invaded and taken over Egypt from the south.

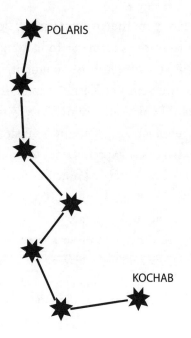

FIGURE 7.5. THE SEVEN STARS OF URSA MINOR—THE "HANDLE THAT TURNED THE QUERN" OF OUR UNIVERSE

that they were great cadastral surveyors and mathematicians as well as brilliant land and water engineers. As Robert Temple has also otherwise confirmed in his book *The Crystal Sun,* it is now quite clear that the ancient Egyptian surveyors must have used some sort of theodolite.[12]

The seven stars of Ursa Minor—as the "handle that turned the quern" (grinding stone) of our spheroidal home universe—symbolized the seven principles or powers of the overshadowing Logos of the system. Hence the seven main temples of Upper Egypt, where the Nile's course follows the same shape, were also to be regarded as manifesting these same kosmic principles *within* the system, by a process of transfer akin to the use of a magician's wand. However, the "wand" in Egypt was the *apuat* tool, directly symbolic of Ursa Minor, which thus acted as the Opener of the Ways—in both directions. Thus these seven temples had a very particular importance, with Thebes itself acting as a sort of spiritual crossroads in the process.

Mixed Esoteric Metaphors

As we have previously associated Philae and the First Cataract with the star Polaris in the constellation of Ursa Minor—and remembering carefully that we are here talking in terms of the *kosmic* environment—we might also mention the metaphorical cosmic plug regarded by the Ancients as being positioned here "in order to stop the waters of Chaos from welling up and overflowing the world." The astral soul was also the irrational World Soul (the *baba,* or Bebi), which had to be brought under the control of the spiritual nature of the god before the manifestation of ordered existence could take place. Consequently, the same waters here referred to are (in the lower register) representative of the chaotic astral feelings that provide humankind with its entirely self-oriented emotional nature.* Not surprisingly perhaps, we see here in the immediate area of the First Cataract a simultaneously operative variety of esoteric metaphors, uniting the kosmic environment with the local world environment, in a manner that merely serves to confuse the uninitiated into believing that the ancient Egyptians had a very chaotically organized (or disorganized) system of mystic thought. Nothing could actually be further from the truth.

Symbolism of the Major Temples North of the First Cataract

On the inner side of this zone of influence, then, with the First Cataract separating the two, lay the island of Elephantine, which was dedicated to the sevenfold goat-headed god Khnemu, responsible—in conjunction with the great god Ptah—for creating the manifest world system. Thus we again see the progressive sequence of Egyptian thought at work here, for after the mystic conception of the unnamed child-god had taken place at Philae (see fig. 5.1.), it followed logically that the process of creating an ethereally objective body form for him had to be undertaken. This form was that of the ovoid-shaped, consciousness-bearing soul vehicle (thus depicted metaphorically as an egg, a metaphor also associated with the gods Ptah and Geb) within which the sevenfold scheme of solar existence then unfolded.

The next stage, embodied in the temple at Kom Ombos (which was simultaneously dedicated to the gods Horus the Elder and Sebek), involved the *consciousness* of the incarnating god being pulled down into manifestation—that is, "falling." This was then anchored in the temple at Edfu (dedicated to the god Horus-in-the-Horizon), where the underlying esoteric metaphor involved the Companions of Horus, as blacksmiths forging and welding together the radiant streams of spiritual energy—the bones of Osiris—comprising the body of light (the *sekhem,* the spiritual counterpart of the *kha*). The objectively organized form of this (the *sah*) of the god was then symbolically produced, again under the aegis of the god Khnemu (this time as the Piscean fish), at Esna, while at the outstandingly multi-dimensional Thebes (under the zodiacal influence of Aries) we find the Higher Mind and Egoic nature of the incarnating god in evidence at Luxor and Karnak respectively.[13]

Progressing northward on the east bank, Coptos (under the aegis of the god Min) then took the part of the incarnating god's *lower* mind nature (in man), with Dendera (clearly under the influence of Taurus, in the guise of Hathor) on the west bank thereafter generating his *human* astral nature, and finally Diospolis Parva, also on the west bank (and known simply as Het in the Egyptian tongue), under Gemini, generating man's (dual)

---

*Hence Baba or Bebi being considered the first son of Osiris rather than Horus. An interesting parallel lies in the biblical tradition where the first son of Adam is Asmodeus (As-Ma'at-Dhyaus), through his union with Lilith, before Eve was created.

physico-etheric nature. Unsurprisingly, the geographically next great temple—that of Abydos—was regarded as the primary point of entry to the Underworld itself.[14] Hence it came under the zodiacal influence of the constellation of Cancer, the glyph of which represented the twin souls of man symbolized by Osiris and Isis—the *sah* and *ba* respectively.

The Great City of Thebes

Seven-gated Thebes was regarded as the greatest and most politically powerful city of all Egypt. Bearing in mind that it was only one of the seven cities with major temples between Diospolis Parva and the First Cataract, we should spend a moment considering why this should have been so—and also why it was itself triple in nature. In doing so, we should bear in mind that it was the fifth of the seven primary nome cities.*

As we have already seen, the fifth stage in any septenary sequence (as with the fifth division) represented the multi-aspected Mind principle—the highest expression of the lower triad of divisions or planes in the sequence. Simultaneously, however, it was also within the highest aspect of this that the essence of the overshadowing Logos was dropped or seeded from above. Consequently, *east*-bank Thebes—involving the great temples of Luxor and Karnak—respectively expressed the involutionary and evolutionary duality of the logoic nature. Thus the temple of Karnak was dedicated to the manifesting Divine Trinity of Being—the Will-to-Be, the Will-to-Know, and the Will-to-Create—symbolized by the triad of Amen-Ra, Mut, and Khonsu. Karnak's influence then extended southward (still via the east bank) to Coptos,† which appears to have symbolized the reincarnating Egoic nature of mankind.

The Initiatory Nile Crossover at Thebes

The initiatory progression from the Underworld—progressing back toward the world of spiritual existence on the Path—correspondingly moved southward along the west bank from Abydos, through Diospolis Parva and Dendera toward *west*-bank Thebes, the Place of the Dead. Here in the great temple and library complex known (absurdly) to us today as the Ramesseum (after the vainglorious Rameses II), the initiate completed his worldly knowledge and prepared himself for the conscious realization and perception of something, previously inexplicable, beyond it. But from here, once having passed the associated

---

*The Egyptians evidently saw the expression of Thebes's own higher counterpart in the great temple center of Napata, within the fifth kosmic division, between the Second and Third Cataracts. For when the great priestly brotherhood of Thebes was temporarily disempowered (during the reign of the heretic pharaoh Akhenaten), elements of it repaired to and resettled in Napata, where the temples—also dedicated to Amen-Ra—were also of considerable size (Budge, *Gods of the Egyptians*, vol. 2, 22–23).

†The origins of the name Coptos are not altogether clear, although—bearing in mind the infusion of other names of Sanskrit origin—it is not altogether impossible that it derives from the word *gupta*, which means, "esoteric" in the sense of "spiritual."

FIGURE 7.6. THE RUINS OF THE RAMESSEUM
(Photo by Steve F-E-Cameron)

This temple sanctuary was known at the time of the visit of Diodorus Siculus as that of (O)Simandius. However, in the nineteenth century it was given the name Ramesseum by the French Egyptologist Champollion, by virtue of the name having been interpreted as supposedly derived from User-Ma'at-Ra—one of Rameses II's titles. In fact, it looks much more likely (phonetically) to have been derived from either As'r-Man-Dhyaus (Osiris the god of Mind) or As'r-Mntw—the suffix *os* or *us* having been added by the Greeks, as was their wont with linguistic assimilation. As can be seen from fig. 7.6, the temple facade was fronted by figures of Osiris (As'r), which would seem to support the suggestions made here, rather than those of current Egyptological orthodoxy. According to Diodorus, the sanctuary "was surrounded with a golden circle, 365 cubits in circumference and a foot and a half thick. In it were described, from cubit to cubit, the 365 days of the year, the course of the stars and what they signified to Egyptian astrology." As one of Mntw's primary functions was associated with the cycle of the barque of Ra and Osiris was associated with the Underworld cycle of Man's personal existence, the connections seem quite self-evident to anyone other than those fixated with the flimsy evidence of Rameses II's supposedly prolific architectural developments.

tests, he (now the initiate of the third degree in the Mysteries) had symbolically to cross over the Nile, to the other side, in order to receive the recognition of the *piru* (the spiritually trained cadre of initiates) of the realm as one of them—albeit at the most junior level. In so doing, he was regarded as having died and been reborn, his consciousness now firmly and irrevocably anchored within the spiritual world. However, his day-to-day responsibilities still remained with the temporal administration of Egypt—in accord with spiritual principles.

The ruins of the temples of Luxor and Karnak are still in sufficiently visible condition today to enable us to realize just how extensive they were and, more or less, what they looked like. The west-bank temple complexes, however, are in such poor condition that only fragmentary ruins now remain in the form of the twin Colossi of Memnon, down within the floodplain, and—at some distance from them, higher up the hillside—the altogether inappropriately named Ramesseum. Beyond these, within the folds of the background hills themselves, lie the underground mortuary tombs of the pharaohs and the apparently much more recent temple of the female pharaoh Hatshepsut at Deir-el-Bahri. However, as our concern here lies merely with understanding the general nature of the underlying spiritual function of each area, we shall move on northward and not linger over such considerations.

The Nile of the North and the South

Corresponding with and in addition to all this, the Nile within Egypt was considered to have yet another major duality associated with it. The Nile of the South (known as Hp-Reset)[15] was considered to extend from the First Cataract to a point near the modern Asyut (just south of Abydos) where the over three-hundred-mile-long Al-Biruni Canal to the Faiyum commenced. From the same point to the Delta was then the Nile of the North (known as Hp-Mehet).[16] These two halves of the river were themselves represented by two forms of the god Hp(i), as shown in fig. 7.2. The Hp(i) of the South had five lotus plants on his head—thereby suggesting the emergent spiritual nature commonly associated with the lotus in ancient times and even today in India—while the Hp(i) of the North had five papyrus plants on his head—thereby symbolizing the all-purpose material nature of existence.

The number five in the ancient occult systems always represented the five elements—of aether, fire, air, water, and earth. Thus the five papyrus plants represented these elements in the terrestrial world while the five lotus plants represented them in the spiritual world—the quality attributable to each state being quite different. The fact that Hp(i) otherwise—as we have already seen—symbolized the unstoppable current of Life, with all its consequent eddies and whirlpools, serves to reinforce the idea of the huge power of the elements if controlled and tapped. This, of course, is precisely what the Egyptians were concerned with achieving in all their scientific and engineering endeavors.

Thus, commencing at Abydos (under the zodiacal sign of Cancer, the gate to the Underworld) we find associations of some temples no longer just with states of being but also with specific chakra centers in the body of the drowned (i.e., fallen) god Osiris. In that respect, the suggestion was made in *Land of the Fallen Star Gods* that Heliopolis represented the base of the spine chakra of the god, while Memphis represented the sacral chakra. Here we might further suggest that the throat-center-related city and temple were at Lycopolis (modern Asyut) while the heart center of the god was to be found at Hermopolis Magna and the solar plexus center at Herakleopolis Magna, just to the southeast of the Faiyum. But before we take a closer look at these great city and temple centers, let us briefly examine the great canal of Al-Biruni.

The Al-Biruni Canal

Although this bit of ancient hydrological engineering is rarely, if ever, considered to be of any great significance, it forms part of the system by which the excess waters of the Nile (when in flood) were channeled away for retention, rather than being allowed to cause excess flooding damage to the agriculture of the lands on either side of the Nile—particularly on the west bank. Nobody knows for sure when the original three-hundred-mile length of this canal was built. However, there again appears to be an associated mystical significance as well as a purely practical purpose, as outlined in *Land of the Fallen Star Gods*. The canal itself originally fed surplus waters from the annual inundation of the Nile into the Faiyum, which acted as a vast reservoir. Then when the river fell below a certain level, or failed to reach a certain flood level during the times of inundation, the Faiyum waters were gradually (or periodically) released via a second canal system back into the main river course at Memphis.* The parallel association with the function of the human bladder and kidneys is therefore pretty obvious, particularly when one takes into account the story of how Memphis itself came to be built, as we shall see in a moment.

Upper, Middle, and Lower Egypt

It is worth remembering that while the real Lower Egypt mainly comprised the area of the Delta, it also extended as far south as Memphis. Middle Egypt, however, correspondingly seems to have extended from Memphis to Abydos. The reasoning behind this lies in relation to the combination of the nome district scheme and the sevenfold structure behind all Egyptian organization—whether considered in either occult or merely sociopolitical terms. As shown in fig. 8.2 in *Land of the Fallen Star Gods,* the first twenty-one nomes—and thus the expression of the three lowest solar states—concluded at Memphis. Correspondingly, the next fourteen nomes—and thus the expression of the next two sevenfold solar states—concluded at Abydos. The true Upper Egypt then commenced from

---

*In fact, Herodotus (*The Histories,* 153) tells us that the excess Nile waters were cyclically channeled into the Faiyum reservoir following the annual inundation and then partially released, as a matter of course, during those months when the river flow through the Delta was its lowest: "The water in this lake [Moeris] does not spring from the soil, for these parts are excessively dry, but it is conveyed through a channel from the Nile and for six months it flows into the lake and for six months out again into the Nile."

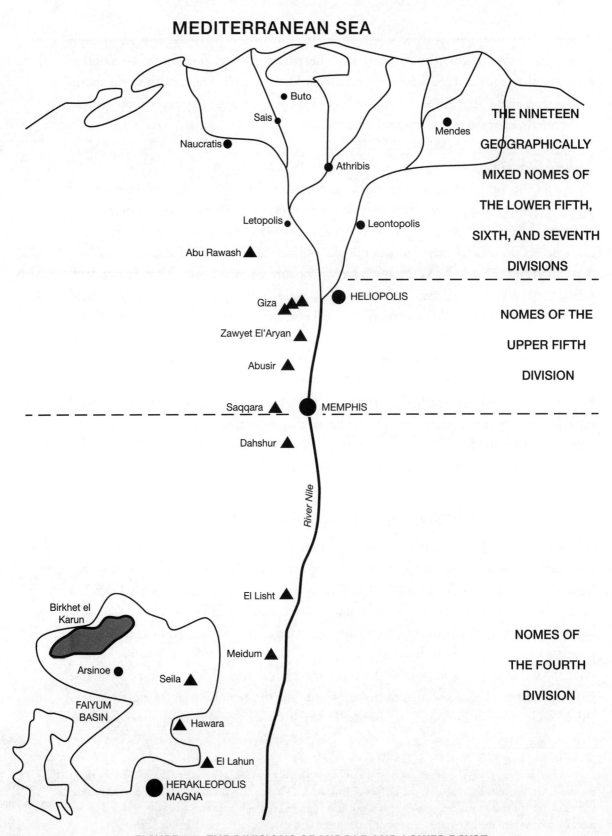

FIGURE 7.7. THE DIVISIONS OF MIDDLE AND LOWER EGYPT

Diospolis Parva and continued on southward. In general terms, however—because there were forty-two nomes in all in Egypt up to the First Cataract—Upper Memphis, being the twenty-first nome, was regarded as the halfway point and thus also as the point at which Upper and Lower Egypt were joined. What is clear, however, is that the fourteen nomes and their temples immediately south of Memphis definitely possessed a very different psychospiritual function and quality from those to the north. It is this suggestion then that we shall consider next—at least in general outline.

The Most Important Nomes of Middle Egypt

Although such an idea would be considered anathema by orthodox Egyptologists, the area of the Nile north of Abydos is perhaps best understood if we stick with the idea suggested in *Land of the Fallen Star Gods* of superimposing upon it the body (between the head and the pelvis) of the drowned Osiris. Using this as a backdrop, certain of the textual traditions concerning the nature and activities of the deities of the various main nome temples then make far more sense. For example, the head of Osiris was supposed to have been buried at Abydos[17] and it is here also that we find the Egyptian "entrance to the Underworld"—a clear metaphor, in mystic terms, for the crown chakra of this deity. It is also worth pointing out that the Egyptian name for Abydos—Abtet—is akin to that for one of the two fishes (Abtu) that guided the barque of Ra on its nightly journey down through the Underworld of the Duat and then back to his heaven world.

The nome temple correspondence with the brow chakra of Osiris appears a little uncertain but looks most likely to be at Athribis, near Akhmim and modern Sohag. The throat chakra correspondence, however, appears to be quite definitely associated with Lycopolis (originally known as Saiut and now as modern Asyut), which not only was dedicated to the god Apuat—the Opener of the Ways—but is where we also find the beginning of the Al-Biruni canal.

From its previously northwestern direction, the channel of the Nile now changes to due south and moves toward the next main nome temple at what the Greeks called Hermopolis Magna, capital city of the twenty-eighth nome. This was originally known as Khemennu—possibly derived from Khem-Anu, meaning the soul-body of the god Khem, although it was also sacred to the hare-headed god Un,* husband of the goddess Un-nut. This nome temple appears to be very obviously associated with the Osirian heart chakra, for it was traditionally here that, on the day that Ra first rose from the watery abyss of Nu, he first established himself—*before* the "pillars of Shu" were set up.[18]

---

*The association of the hare-headed god appears to involve an esoteric metaphor for the natural capacity of the human mind to accelerate to great speed from a standstill and to stop again just as quickly (just like the hare). It is interesting to note that the constellation of the hare is to be found immediately between what are generally considered to be the legs of the constellation of Orion. However, it may well be that the ancient astrologers actually had other ideas more closely related to Orion's head.

Just as importantly, the primary god of the nome was Tehuti himself, presiding over a *pauat* of eight frog-headed gods. As we have already dealt with Tehuti in chapter 4 to some extent, we will not merely repeat ourselves here. However, it is clear that Tehuti's role as the Mind-led divine recorder of all human experience is itself synonymous with the faculty of intelligent perception always traditionally associated with the heart. The association with the frog-headed gods appears to be symbolic of (a) the four compass points in a higher and lower register (i.e., in spiritual and material terms) and (b) the capacity of the heart to spawn endless strings of psychospiritual (heartfelt) responses, which reflect the soul nature itself—also described as a luminous ovoid.

The next temples of concern to us are adjacent to each other at Kom El Ahmar (ancient Hebena) and Thina (known to the Greeks as Akoris) and almost certainly associated with the twin-headed sphinx god Aker. These temples are, however, on the *east* bank of the river—a fact of great significance, particularly as we find a pyramid at Hebena. As we have already seen, the east bank of the Nile represented the *involutionary* cycle of Creation—the field of the gods—whereas the west bank comprised the *evolutionary* path traveled by Man. Thus, by inference, this particular temple complex appears to be associated with the spleen chakra, into which the pranic energies of the solar *devas* are traditionally regarded as being drawn for distribution and circulation around the physical body organism.

The Location of Tell-el-Amarna

Now it is highly interesting to note that the heretic pharaoh Akhenaten built his brand-new city of Tell-el Amarna on the *east* bank of the river, almost opposite Khemennu, but very slightly farther south. This can have been no arbitrary decision. As the Aten was the Sun and the Sun was seen as at the center of the solar system, Akhenaten was clearly making a very sharply defined politico-religious point of attempted one-upmanship. Unfortunately, his personal confusion about the true nature of the solar deity, plus his clear ignorance of (or willfully blind refusal to accept) the metaphysical basis of Egypt's geomantic harmony and geospiritual symmetry, merely served to accelerate the degeneracy of Egypt's spiritual culture, even though the priesthood of Thebes ensured the complete destruction of Amarna following his death.

Continuing on our way northward—this time returning to the west bank—we eventually come to the nome city of Herakleopolis Magna, known to the Egyptians as Sutenhenen, or Henen-su, which lies slightly southeast of the Faiyum depression. This temple complex was again of immense importance and, for reasons to be explained in a moment, just as clearly to be associated with the solar plexus chakra of the god Osiris.

The chief god of the temple here was Her-shef* (apparently a form of Khnemu), whose

---

*The figure of the god Her-shef rather oddly had four heads—one of a bull, one of a ram, and the other two of hawks. Above them were depicted the horns of Khnemu, surmounted by two plumes and four knives (Budge, *Gods of the Egyptians,* vol. 2, 61).

FIGURE 7.8. AKHENATEN AND HIS QUEEN

Akhenaten and his family are here seen dispensing spiritual beneficence to the supposed initiates of his form of solar religion, which clearly saw "the royals" as actually incarnate solar deities, rather than their mere agents on Earth.

goddess counterpart was Atet (otherwise known as Mersekhnet), who, in the form of the great cat Ra-Maou, cut off the head of the great Underworld serpent Apep, the mortal enemy of Ra.[19] The name Her-shef implies both consciousness and bravery, or emotional power and strength[20]—characteristics quite clearly associated with the energies of the solar plexus chakra. Here, in the same temple, there also existed a shrine to the goddess

Neheb-kau, another great serpent and female counterpart of the god Nau.[21] Her primary role was to provide spiritual food (i.e., made of light) for the initiate on the southward path. Curiously, however, the sanctuary at Henen-su was called "the place where nothing groweth" and it was traditionally entered by a door on the south side called Ra-stau,[22] which, as already indicated, lay in the fifth division.

Now, by tradition it was at Henen-su that the Bennu (phoenix) bird normally lived and where Ra was said to have risen for the first time when the heavens and the Earth were created.[23] Here also Shu separated the Earth from the sky. It was otherwise to this place that Set retreated after his defeat by Horus and where the goddess Sekhet waded around in the blood of mankind on the Day of the Great Slaughter[24] (see appendix E). Yet close

FIGURE 7.9. HER-SHEF, HERE SHOWN WITH A RAM'S HEAD

to here apparently lived the god Heru-sma-taui, the Uniter of the Two Lands[25]—a fairly clear metaphor for that aspect of consciousness that blends spiritual ideals with material necessities.

Immediately to the north of Henen-su lay not only the vast Faiyum reservoir and the great temple of Crocodilopolis (ancient Arsinoe) but also a variety of pyramid complexes extending all the way to (and just past) Giza itself. Now such a proliferation of pyramids in this area had to have a good reason behind it and the primary clues to that reason lie between Giza's association with Orion on the one hand and, on the other, Arsinoe's name being apparently synonymous with that of the chief star (Alcyone) in the Pleiades.[26] In addition, because Henen-su and Memphis were respectively expressive of the solar plexus and sacral chakras of the god Osiris, this whole area within northern Egypt could reasonably be regarded as the place (or field) of Divine Desire, as objectively manifest on Earth.

The effective result, if this suggestion is accurate, would be that this whole geographical area to the west of the Nile was intended to be the representative expression on Earth of a specific part of the heavens—that part, in fact, in which our own home universe was deemed to be located and which was thus the evolutionary "playground" of Mankind. And, as we saw in the early chapters of this book, because our home universe was deemed to lie within the constellation of Taurus, this whole area became directly associated in one way or another with the cult of the bull god, known to the Egyptians as As'r-Hp(i), which the Greeks later turned into Serapis, the great funerary Serapeum center of this cult (itself a functional part of the Egyptian Mysteries) being at Memphis.*

It becomes increasingly certain that the various pyramids in the area were intended to be specifically representative of stars in the Pleiades, the Hyades, and Orion. However, to attempt to draw detailed attributions between specific stars and specific pyramids in general would be a monumental task, well outside the scope of this book. But there is one issue that we should perhaps touch on concerning the pyramids in general before moving on to deal with Memphis itself.

Stellar Orientations as Seen from Earth

It should by now have become apparent to most (if not all) readers of this book that there is a distinct oddity about the suggestions already made concerning the location and

---

*The bull cult of As'r-Hpi seems to have been based upon the idea that Hpi was "the life of Osiris" and thus became the "Bull of the West." But Hpi was also regarded as "the second Ptah" (Budge, *Gods of the Egyptians,* vol. 2, 195). Unfortunately, by the later pharaonic dynasties, the whole underlying esoteric metaphor had become so thoroughly misunderstood and debased that each and every sacred white bull was being individually mummified and preserved by the priesthood in the vast underground Serapeum to the west of Memphis, designed and constructed apparently just for this purpose (ibid., 196).

directional associations of the various Nile pyramids and temples. Put very fundamentally, it is that while the circumpolar stars and celestial pole star (Polaris) are—currently at least—to be seen by us in the *northern* sky, the attribution in this book has the seven stars of Ursa Minor in the *south* of Egypt. Furthermore, the constellation of Orion is to be seen clearly by us in the *southern* sky, whereas the associated pyramids at Giza are located in the *north* of Egypt. How then can these associations possibly be accurate? Well, the answer appears to lie in the factor of the Great Year cycle and our Earth's orientation within the solar system, relative to it.

Referring back to fig. 2.4, it will become obvious that, as our solar system orbits around Alcyone, at one end of the Great Year cycle (i.e., at the celestial summer solstice) we face directly northward toward Polaris as our pole star. This is how matters stand today. However, at the other end of the Great Year cycle (i.e., at the celestial winter solstice) the pole star is Vega, close to the head of Draco, at the other end of the circumpolar ellipse. At that time, Ursa Minor's *apuat* shape, it is suggested, is seen apparently "cutting off the head and neck" of the Great Celestial Serpent or dipping close to the head of Orion, thereby symbolizing the reawakening of Orion and simultaneously heralding the imminent return of the solar gods. Thus, one might suggest, the shape of the Nile as we know it was intended to provide a permanent visual record of this cyclically longed-for moment of the Great Return, a sympathetically magical, geographic metaphor that was so large that it could itself be seen from beyond the Earth's atmosphere, in solar space. Correspondingly, the pyramids and Nile temples were also positioned by the ancient Egyptians in concord with the visually apparent locations of the various stars at that time. Drawing these various ideas together, let us take a closer, albeit relatively brief look at the area between the old capital city of Memphis and Heliopolis, incorporating the Giza plateau, before we move finally to the Nile Delta itself.

The City Capital of Memphis

Memphis—the "city of the white wall"—lay at the point where the Nile was regarded as beginning its separation into two streams just before reaching the Delta. In fact, the city was built on a man-made island, supposedly the brain-child of the early pharaoh Min or Men-kau-Ra, who reputedly had the course of the Nile physically altered here at around the time that he also united Upper and Lower Egypt,[27] as well as building the smallest of the main pyramids at Giza—a modest man indeed! Nevertheless, the very name of this individual clearly indicates that he was an entirely metaphorical heroic figure, even though the river's course was changed by the ancient Egyptians. Bearing in mind the suggested association of this city with the sacral center of the god Osiris, however, and the dual sexual and urinary functions associated with this part of the human body, the division of the Nile's waters at this point is perfectly logical—as is the underlying symbolism (as the kidney duct) of the man-made canal linking the river here with Lake Moeris.

Memphis was regarded as the capital of Lower Egypt*—undoubtedly because of its powerful magical associations with the sacral chakra of the god—and it is noteworthy that it is the only city in the whole of Egypt that had *two* nome districts. As otherwise already suggested in *Land of the Fallen Star Gods,* there is a numerological symbolism in the fact that the nome of Lower Memphis was the twentieth in the series, while that of Upper Memphis was the twenty-first.[28] Remembering that the fourteenth to the twenty-first substates comprised the fifth solar division of consciousness, and that the upper fifth division was sacred to the god Sokar (in conjunction with the god Aker), it is not altogether odd to find both Ptah and Osiris allied with him at Memphis as the compound god Ptah-Seker-As'r. Nor is it surprising to find that immediately adjacent to Memphis, to the west, is the Plain of Saqqara—a name clearly derived from Seker-Ra.

The temple at Memphis was rather significantly dedicated not to the great god Ptah himself, but to his double.[29] Now bearing in mind the previous suggestion that Ptah and Buddha are synonymous, this raises the interesting suggestion—in line with the Indo-Tibetan system—that the double of Ptah might in fact be intended to mean the bodhisattva, or manifest earthly expression of the Buddha. Perhaps this too is related to the fact that Memphis was the old capital of Lower Egypt.

Giza and Heliopolis

Giza, its pyramids, and the Sphinx are touched on elsewhere later in this book. As they have otherwise been dealt with almost to death by many other writers over the past century or so, we shall say nothing further here and instead move straight on to deal with Heliopolis.

Known as Anu by the Egyptians, Heliopolis was the place where the twin sycamore trees of Nut grew, at the foot of which the terrestrial serpent Apep was slain by the great cat Ra-Maou.[30] It was also where the god Geb, husband of Nut, originally laid the great egg of the world,[31] which contained the Bennu (phoenix) bird, said to return there every five hundred years and to immolate itself every 1,461 years[32]—a tradition that clearly relates it to the cycle of the star Sirius. The Bennu was otherwise regarded as having come forth from the very heart of Ra himself and to have taken up the job of acting as the guide of the gods in the Duat.[33] In all respects, then, Heliopolis seems to have been associated with fire, destruction, and regeneration, in a manner not quite seen elsewhere. From that viewpoint alone, there seems to be strong case for its having been seen as representative of the spine base chakra of the solar deity.

As the capital city of the eighteenth nome, Heliopolis represented the third subplane

---

*There is at least a possibility that ancient Egypt had more than one capital city, by virtue of wishing to synchronize the expression of earthly rulership with whatever astrological cycle was current.

in the fifth solar division. In the esoteric tradition, as we have already seen, the fifth division is symbolic of the multi-aspectual Mind principle. The five lower subplanes of this then represent the mental aspects of the five worldly elements—the fifth acting as the synthesis of the other four. The general idea is as shown below.

1. Upper Memphis—the abstract mind, the faculty of perceiving spiritual relationships
2. Lower Memphis—the reincarnating ego and sense of self-discriminating individuality
3. Heliopolis—the organizational and synthesizing mind faculty (element of aether)
4. Letopolis—the rationalizing, distributive mind faculty (element of fire)
5. Athribis—the adaptive, speculative mind faculty (element of air)
6. Leontopolis—the principle of mental balance (element of water)
7. Hermopolis—inertial mind, the principle of basic memory (element of earth)

Thus it was that the ancient Egyptians appear to have seen Heliopolis as symbolizing that subjective state within the mind of man where the higher (intuitive) impulse fuses with the fourfold lower mind to produce the principle of an actively coordinated, spiritually oriented, rational intelligence. In consequence, it was here that the great Sacred College was

FIGURE 7.10. THE *BENBEN* STONE

founded, the foremost in all Egypt for its range and depth of knowledge in both the philosophical and practical fields of human spiritual and mental endeavor. Correspondingly, here in the temple lay the *benben* stone, apparently made of meteoric iron, which had fallen from the heavens in the form of a blaze of light (like an intuition) and, in its fall, had been transformed into a shape roughly equivalent to that of the pyramidion—which is itself not unlike the shape of a modern space capsule.

The Nile Delta

We turn finally (and briefly) to the great Delta of the River Nile, where the vast majority of Egypt's agricultural produce has been grown and gathered since time immemorial. As we have already seen, the Nile used to have seven branches (at least two of which were man-made) flowing northward through the Delta, out to the Mediterranean Sea. The two main natural branches, however, are still known to us today as the Rosetta (Rashid) and the Damietta (Dumiyat).

The Delta area was itself split into eighteen separate nome districts, each of which had its own capital town, situated on or close to one or another of the seven river branches.* Of all the nome towns in the Delta, Sais is probably the best known historically because it was the first main town encountered by visitors (like Herodotus) sailing up the western tributary—the Rosetta. In addition, Sais was itself the seventh nome—which must have been for good and important reason.

The archaeology of the various Delta towns is still being pursued today, but from our viewpoint here, the area is of only relatively minor interest in terms of what it represented esoterically to the ancient Egyptians. Its political and socio-economic importance was, however, considerable throughout Egypt's long history, not just because of its agricultural fecundity and the prosperity this brought, but also because it was here that so many expatriates and invaders from other countries actually settled and became absorbed into the daily rituals of Egyptian life. It was through these same incursions that knowledge of Egyptian culture originally spread around the ancient world, but it was also partly because of them that Egyptian civilization and culture eventually crumbled—as we shall see in the next chapters.

From what has already been suggested, it may by now have become apparent that the physical River Nile in its entirety has to be considered as representing rather more than just the plane of the galaxy, as some have proposed.

---

*The eighteen nome towns or cities—like the eighteen lower substates of solar consciousness employed by man, the human being, within his objective body form and subjective personality—were scattered throughout the Delta.

The River Nile and Its Symbolism

217

EIGHT

THE ANCIENT
COLONIZATION OF EGYPT

The dynastic Egyptians . . . appear to have been the descendants of an invading race who entered Egypt in the predynastic period and conquered the country and then intermarried with the indigenous people whom they found in possession of the Nile Valley. The original home of the invaders was probably Asia. . . . There is no evidence to show that the invaders of Egypt were kinsfolk of the Babylonians, but there are very strong probabilities that the civilizations of both peoples sprang from a common stock.

E. A. W. BUDGE, *THE NILE*

Nobody seems to really know who the ancient Egyptians were or where they came from. One thing is, however, quite clear: they were not of any of the central or southern African native races, nor did they have the Mongol features of the peoples of northeastern Asia. Second, it is quite clear from the earliest temple paintings that their facial features were of a distinctively Caucasian type, although their skin color was depicted as coppery, or reddish—that of the "Iron Race" type—rather than any shade of white or brown. One tradition reported by Diodorus Siculus was that their ancestors had come from the far west, "from the land of the setting Sun."[1] A second tradition, however, recorded by Herodotus and others, had it that Egypt had been colonized from the east, from what is now Ethiopia.[2] But which is true? Or are both these traditions true, separated only by the factor of time?

In order to try to find an answer to this question, this chapter will take us (for a while at least) right off the beaten track in order to explore some of the prehistoric background of the civilization and culture of the Middle East in the millennia before the fourth millennium BCE. Bearing in mind that it deals with the Caucasian origins of the peoples of

FIGURE 8.1. THE CORRIDOR OF ANCIENT CIVILIZATION

the Middle East as a whole—including both the Indo-European and the Semitic types—and that these are quite distinctively different from the Sino-Mongolian and African Bantu types on the northeastern and southwestern flanks. It almost inevitably brings in the perennial question of Atlantis. However, we shall leave that to one side for the moment while we examine the hows and whys of the Caucasian ethnic type making its appearance at all in the first place and then dispersing southward and westward into Indo-Persia and western Europe respectively.

First of all, then, there is general consensus among scholars and scientists (largely by a process of linguistic deduction) that modern Middle Eastern and European culture seems to have originated (no one has the slightest clue as to why) somewhere in or around the Caucasus Mountains, between the Black Sea and the Caspian Sea. This area extends southward to the Persian Gulf, taking in ancient Chaldea and Babylonia (modern Iraq), and also eastward into ancient Indo-Persia,* flanked in the north by the River Oxus and in the east by the Hindu Kush range, part of the mighty Himalayas. But why should a Caucasian type evolve in this particular area immediately adjacent to the Mongol-featured peoples of Tibet, Ladakh, and China, whose facial characteristics are actually so much closer to those of the native African and South American types? Science has no really satisfactory answer to this any more than it has as to why the Egyptian and Sumerian civilizations should apparently have surfaced so suddenly, ready made, and with no background history indicating a cultural "learning curve."

The Dating of Egyptian Civilization and Culture Generally

The integrity of the basis (or bases) on which modern scholars and scientists have tried to date ancient Egyptian culture—in particular the architecture and statuary—is a highly important but rarely debated one. In fact, very few Egyptologists since the nineteenth century have even raised the question. What has historically happened, in fact, is that the Victorians—basing their ideas on a mixture of supposed biblical chronology and geological deduction (in that order)—decided that the earliest Egyptian and Chaldean civilizations suddenly appeared at about 4500 to 5000 BCE, "fully clothed" as it were. Twentieth-century Egyptologists, however, commencing with Flinders Petrie's pottery dating, have gradually whittled this away until the present commencement of ancient Egyptian civilization—according to them—began much more recently, between 3000 and 3250 BCE. However, let us begin at the beginning and work our way forward to the

---

*Nearly all European languages are derived from Sanskrit, the sacerdotal language of the most ancient Indo-Persians, whose direct cultural influence once spread from Asia Minor beyond the eastern borders of India, even to Thailand and the islands of Indonesia.

present day so as to see what anomalies might be present in their methods of calculation.

The first real reference point for any dating of ancient Egyptian culture is Manetho's king list, produced (already very retrospectively) in Ptolemaic times, about two thousand years ago. Manetho's figures ostensibly take us back some twenty thousand years to the time of "divine dynasties." However, Manetho's figures were themselves tampered with by Eusebius, one of the early Christian bishops of Alexandria, who, disbelieving an even greater stated antiquity, drastically reduced them. But when we take into consideration the priests of Heliopolis indicating to Herodotus that their astronomical records went back well over fifty-two thousand years, it not only casts Manetho's figures in a different light, it throws up an implicit but immediate suggestion that Egyptian civilization (and thus its architectural environment too) had to have been in existence by then as well. Taking human scientific knowledge even further back, we find that the Greek Hipparchus—supposedly the first discoverer of precession—was himself apparently aware of much more ancient astronomical knowledge, for we find in the *Commentary on the Timaeus:* "The Assyrians have not only preserved the memorials of seven and twenty myriads [270,000] of years, as Hipparchus says they have, but likewise of the whole apocatases and periods of the seven rulers of the world."[3] Now scholars have just blithely disregarded these (and many other) statements and traditions, although handed down by men whose intellectual and moral integrity was considered, even in their own time, to be beyond question. Why? Simply because they just do not fit with the limited amount of other historical, archaeological, and paleontological evidence available today, even though much of this, not very surprisingly, is very self-conflicting.

What appears to have happened is that at some time approximately during the post-war period of 1945 to 1965, the scholarly and scientific mind-set of the West suddenly hardened to produce an orthodoxy that insisted upon using certain criteria allied to random rural archaeological locations as fairly inflexible reference points for all future research, notwithstanding the potentially associated major conflicts arising out of adopting such a stance. Notably, all these reference points were to be found at a serious distance from known main centers of ancient urban culture. But by a deft intellectual sleight-of-hand it was then *assumed* that the ancient urban centers must have been later developments—a proposition that has never been clearly articulated or fully justified, or seriously questioned. However, using the assumption as a foundation and quickly building the footings of modern orthodoxy on top of it (thereby disguising its dubious structural integrity), modern research has come up with those parameters that now condition all associated mainstream thought in these areas. Rather interestingly, the hardening of intellectual orthodoxy has been very closely paralleled by the development of (and dependence upon) merely technological methods of dating, notwithstanding their known limitations. Consequently, the following equation actually applies:

$$\begin{array}{r} \text{arbitrary choice of location} \\ + \quad \text{technological dating} \\ + \quad \text{disregard of tradition} \\ \hline \text{modern orthodoxy} \end{array}$$

A Completely Different Approach

We have described the case for the Ancients' view that the whole process of evolution is the result of a fundamentally *spiritual* drive in Nature, organized via the subjective nature in Man in a manner quite different from that suggested by Darwinian theory. Having adopted that standpoint, there is obviously little point in trying to discuss the advent of the Caucasian racial type as merely the result of an inexplicable environmental conditioning, as anthropologists are wont to do, on the basis that any other form of assumption must by self-definition be "unscientific." Therefore we shall look at the subject from the (necessarily speculative and scientifically unprovable) view that each such radical ethnic type is itself but the *objective* expression of the manifesting consciousness of a particular *subjective* (or archetypal) principle in Nature—that is, in a manner of which the ancient Egyptians themselves might have approved as fitting in with their own sequentially operative system of metaphysical thought, and as otherwise confirmed by ancient Hindu tradition. First, then, let us look at the question of what influence apparently acts as the motor behind all evolutionary change on our planet—again, at least, as far as the Ancients were concerned.

The Spiritual Guardians of Our World

It is implicit within all that has been suggested before that there is some form of highly intelligent organization in Nature that clearly comprehends its underlying principles and has both the knowledge and power to bring about their evolutionary expression in all its various kingdoms, including the human. The Ancients were of the belief that such knowledge and faculty was in the hands of living gods and demigods, highly advanced beings (i.e., intelligent spirits) who had already long since passed through the human stage of development and had arrived at a point of evolution in which they were able to access (in fact become) that part of the consciousness of our *solar* Deity (thereby joining Ra in his boat of millions of years), which enabled them to perceive, stimulate, and guide the underlying subjective dynamics of our planetary Nature in a manner needed for its proper expression and fulfilment.* The instinctive nature and propensities of man (for both good and evil) then became responsible for all the rest of what subsequently eventuated as *objective* culture and civilization.

This author, at least, has no intellectual problem with accepting—in conjunction with

---

*Which itself then becomes a major conditioning factor for all human souls subsequently involved in the process of objective reincarnation, irrespective of their personal evolutionary standing.

the Ancients—the possibility (nay, probability) of such an active hierarchy of divine or semidivine Intelligences, notwithstanding the fact that they (understandably) do not make themselves generally available to satisfy mere human curiosity.* In fact, to accept that the universe maintains its hugely complex and dynamic equilibrium *without* such active, intelligent involvement by beings of an inordinately more developed nature would be far more difficult. Nevertheless, the ancient traditions indicate that even these great beings are themselves so constrained by the sense of Universal Order and Harmony (Ma'at in the Egyptian tradition) that their own activities are necessarily tailored entirely in coordination with astrological cycles. However, in conjunction with astrology, a sequentially operative numerological factor had also to be taken into consideration in the expression of Divine Purpose—as the Ancients again recognized.† But, bearing in mind that the universe is indisputably an organism, one would surely expect no less.

Bodies of Light

That perhaps the majority of such gods and demigods—the original Ur-Shu or Shu-Khan (inverted in Egypt as the god Khonsu)—might have their natural bodily existence as soul beings in forms of hypertenuous light substance—as the Ancients also believed—seems quite logical when considered in conjunction with the tradition that man's own soul is a body of light that aurically contains and maintains his physical organism, as well as acting as the true repository of his consciousness and sense of knowledge. The logicality of the idea extends to the fact that—through eventually coming to realize the limitations of merely human existence—man was regarded as becoming a being who likewise developed the faculty of self-consciousness *as and within the god-soul nature,* in its own full state of being. As says the *Hermetica:*

> This then is the difference between an immortal body and a mortal body. The immortal body consists of a single kind of matter; the mortal body does not. The immortal body acts on other things; the mortal body is acted on. The immortal body has the mastery and the mortal body is mastered. For everything which puts forces in action has the mastery . . . and that which has the mastery is free and takes the lead; but that which is mastered is in its servitude and is passively borne along.[4]

This liberating spiritual development then took man a large part of the way to the further and later conscious realization of his own innate divinity. However, the crossing of

---

*Sadly, the current proclivity toward channeling (the modern form of spiritualism) has turned this whole subject into something of a circus sideshow, with all sorts of individuals claiming to be the direct agents of such divinities, who are presented either as "ascended Masters" or "super-intelligent extraterrestrials" (from Sirius et al.). Sic transit gloria supramundi!

†Hence the Pythagorean view that God manifests as Number, in association with their maxim "God geometrises."

such thresholds of advancement was also regarded as necessarily subject to the natural exigencies of astrological cycles, themselves the very expression of Divine Law in the kosmos.

The Law of Operative Cycles in Nature

While physical science already accepts the principle of cycles in certain areas, it is as yet only able to formulate opinions (and laws) about the direct *effects* of those of relatively short and thus easily measurable duration—for example, the four seasons of our Earth year. It is also recognized that the movement of our planet around the Sun and the movement of our Moon around the Earth produce coherently measurable effects upon the forms and consciousnesses of species in our various kingdoms of planetary Nature. Is it not rather more than a little illogical to presume (as science does at present) that there can be no such corresponding effects of a different magnitude and progressively qualitative nature, affecting whole races, resulting from man's involvement in the *greater* sidereal cycles—just because science has not yet found the technique of perceiving and measuring them?* What is sauce for the goose . . .

As we saw in the first chapters of this book, the astronomical and astrological dimension was seen by all the ancient wisdom traditions as providing the key to the transitional manifestation of Divine Purpose in our local universe and thence upon our planet in particular. Consequently, we cannot in all seriousness divorce ourselves from at least the possibility that there is some measure of likely truth in this. Astrophysicists are all too willing to tell us that the influences emanating from other star systems are far too weak for astrology to have any basis in fact. Yet the generally applicable principle behind the capacity for reception, modulation, and onward transmission of an energy or force (whether in a human being or a radio) is actually dependent upon wavelength and resonance—involving the actual tuning *of the mechanism of reception*—and has very little to do with the physical power of an outside influence trying to force its way in.

With that in mind, and regarding man's soul organism as a form of energy transducer, it would not be difficult to conceive of the idea of *each* individual or ethnological type of consciousness perhaps naturally expressing or being naturally responsive to a particular psychospiritual wavelength. On such a basis, the various types, once developed and brought into communion with one another, would together provide the full range of receptivity necessary for our planetary Life as a whole to benefit in evolutionary terms. This would naturally include the other kingdoms of Nature, as well as the purely human.

---

*Scientists already glibly talk about how plants, animals, and humans propagate through wanting their genes to be spread, completely oblivious of the fact that they are in fact describing a form of semi-intelligent response and sense of purpose in cellular substance. But it seems not to have occurred to them that man is a multiple being living out his (temporary) existence in a variety of states *simultaneously*. Hence even the physical man is a veritable conurbation of different entities that, in active co-relationship, provide him with a single, intelligently organized form through which his higher consciousness may experience their nature and faculty.

The Science of Ethnology and Its
Spiritual Counterpart

Now ethnology has absurdly become somewhat of a taboo subject since the simple-minded rise and mental infection of political correctness over the past twenty-five years, on the grounds that to compare racial distinctions is immediately to criticize and thus invite abuse. This is a ludicrous attitude, more often than not spread by little-minded and unself-confident (or holier-than-thou) people who are more concerned to ingratiate themselves with others and thereby increase or otherwise safeguard their own social or political standing than anything else. However, it is so prevalent that we shall just have to push out our own boat regardless. But in so doing, we shall come at the subject from a perhaps unusual angle, as follows.

As with the Sphinx in Egypt and the Kabiri Bull in Assyria, the Ancients distinguished mankind's *celestially* based consciousness from that of our local planetary Life, symbolically by depicting a human head on an animal body.* Conversely, the consciousness of the *neteru* hierarchies—representing the higher instinctual forces in Nature—were symbolically depicted as having human bodies with animal heads. The factor of consciousness affecting the form and type was thus seen as crucial; it was because man's intelligence was seen as essentially the expression of the consciousness of a *higher* god that the depiction in temple and mortuary art of the human head on the human body (as opposed to the animal head on the human body) was seen as so important.

Now, if Man and his spiritual soul vehicle are intrinsically celestial entities, as the Ancients believed, it follows that purely human ethnic characteristics must logically be morphically derived from a series of soul types (*bau*) specific to our own Earth-world. Thus objectively apparent differences in facial (i.e., ethnic) characteristics would have to be regarded as mere effects of causes inherent in the nature of the World *ba,* the astral soul of the planet itself. On this basis, it would appear that the primordial appearance of any racial prototype must necessarily begin with a prototypal generation of bodies of light, which, only after much evolutionary development, could themselves produce an objectively different human stock from their own nature—via the normal processes of human birth.† If this is indeed so, the first generation of what we might regard as proto-Caucasian stock must have been *ethereal* beings (and not physical ones). However, Nature being entirely

---

*Taurus and Leo represented the two (higher and lower) points of commencement of the "fall from Grace." But whereas the Sphinx represented the fall of the psychospiritual consciousness of the lesser gods into the *lower* cycle of the zodiacal Duat, the Kabiri Bull represented the consciousness of semidivine Man already fallen into the higher, celestial environment of the Taurean Demiurge.

†Perhaps the same principle applies as in the case of morphic resonance as described in the theories of the biologist Dr. Rupert Sheldrake (*A New Science of Life*). Here, changes in faculty brought about by environmental conditioning produce a subjective response, which is telepathically transmitted to all other members of the same species, irrespective of where else in the world they might actually be.

sequential in her operations, there must otherwise have been some subsequent link with the geographically closest groups of the preceding (Atlantean?) racial subtype. So let us take a brief closer look at how the ancient Egyptians might have seen this issue.

As we saw in an earlier chapter, the ancient concept had it that Man the "divine spark" was born into a Divine Soul-body when originally falling into the realm of our local universe via the impulse emanating from the Kosmic Mind of the overshadowing Logos of our system. Within the Divine Soul, a dual polarization of consciousness then took place, resulting in the appearance (still within its aura, but in a non-locational sense) of the *sah* and *ba*—the spiritual and astroterrestrial soul organisms. However, the ancient Egyptian system being fundamentally septenary, there had to be seven primary spiritual soul types—depicted by them as the Seven Hathors—each type emanating subaspects of itself in cyclical rotation, always following a septenary sequence, which, as we also saw, necessarily resulted in a progression associated with the influences of the zodiacal Duat. Something of this is depicted in fig. 8.2.

It follows quite naturally and logically from this that if each and every incarnatory sequence commenced in the soul nature, the first or prototypal ethnic types also had to be ethereal or semi-ethereal beings. The Indo-Tibetan system of thought on this subject has it that the astroterrestrial soul, or *ba*, emanates from itself by an act of will (*kriyasakti*)— under the impress of the *sah*—seven centers of force, or chakras (*thesu* in the Egyptian). These then generate from their own emanations a substructure or living web of light to which local matter is systematically attracted and thereby gradually evolves into cells, tissues, organs, and so on, which make up the objective body form of the infant child in the womb. Now while this may be what follows in the average human birth cycle once the primary conditioning influences have been set in place, it would appear that the Ancients also saw the very same general principles being followed in the case of racial prototypes, until the ethnic type-to-be had been properly developed.

Lemurians and Atlanteans

In her remarkable work *The Secret Doctrine,* H. P. Blavatsky* revealed some of the ancient traditions still held in the Far East concerning the first appearance and unfoldment of humanity on this planet via a series of what she called "Root Races," beginning with the Pitars or Pitris—the "Ancestral Fathers."[5] The consciousness of each of these Root Races (its development extending for millions of years) represented the unfolding or evolving state of perceptual awareness of the demiurgic Deity of our particular planet. In her description, seven such Root Races were scheduled to appear—coinciding with the greater

*Regarding the much (and foolishly) maligned H. P. Blavatsky and some of the extraordinarily radical concepts (including that of the Root Races) that she reintroduced to the West from Oriental sources, the reader is directed to her monumental work itself.

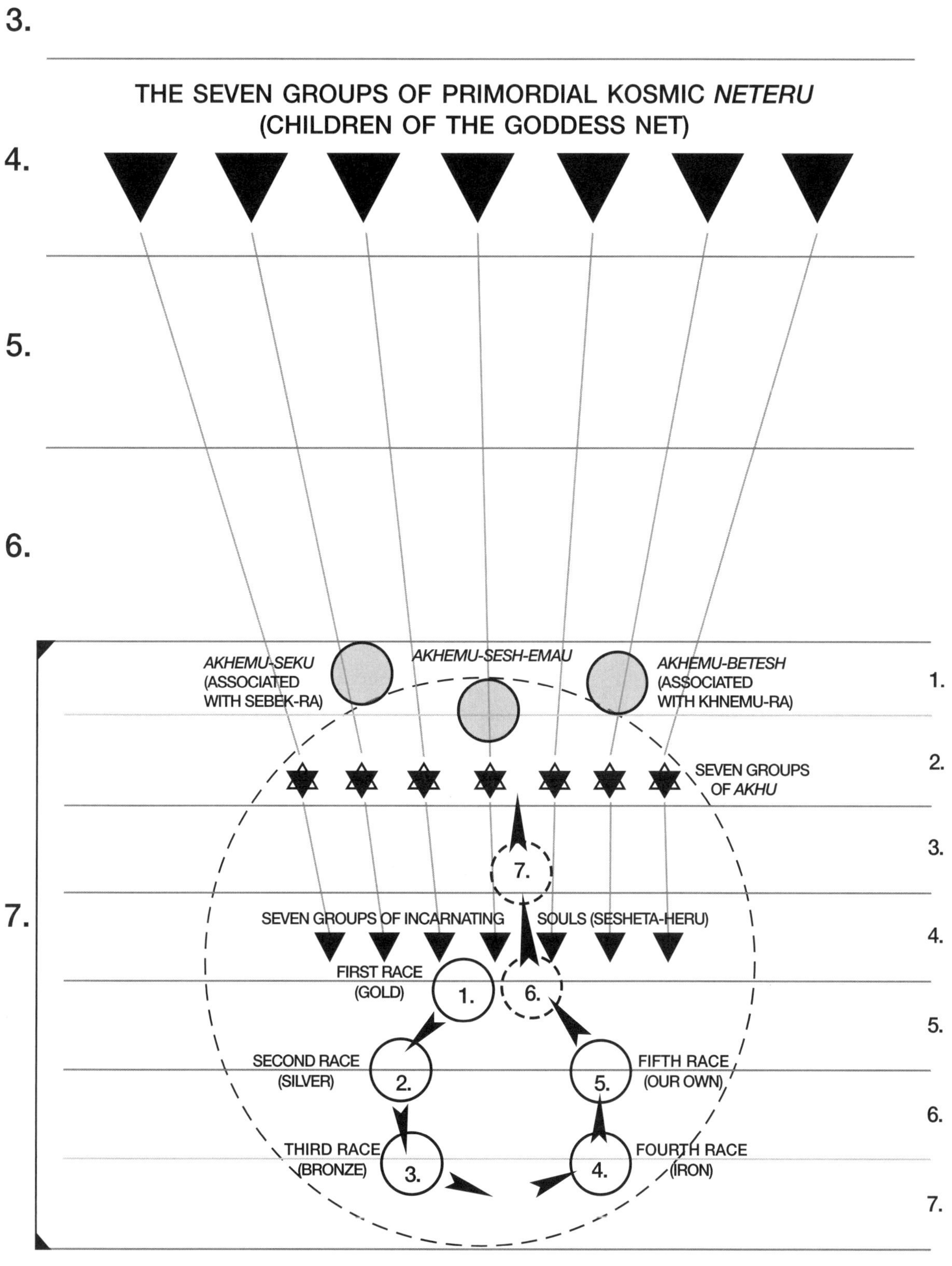

THE SEVEN GROUPS OF PRIMORDIAL KOSMIC *NETERU*
(CHILDREN OF THE GODDESS NET)

AKHEMU-SEKU
(ASSOCIATED
WITH SEBEK-RA)

AKHEMU-SESH-EMAU

AKHEMU-BETESH
(ASSOCIATED
WITH KHNEMU-RA)

1.

2.

SEVEN GROUPS
OF *AKHU*

3.

7.

SEVEN GROUPS OF INCARNATING   SOULS (SESHETA-HERU)

4.

FIRST RACE
(GOLD)

1.

6.

5.

SECOND RACE
(SILVER)

2.

FIFTH RACE
(OUR OWN)

5.

6.

THIRD RACE
(BRONZE)

3.

4.

FOURTH RACE
(IRON)

7.

FIGURE 8.2. SEQUENTIAL UNFOLDMENT OF MANKIND'S CONSCIOUSNESS
(and the associated rationale of a series of world races)

Yuga cycle of the Hindus—of which only five have yet done so.* Of these five, the first two and a half apparently possessed an ethereal form of consciousness, with the later Third Race (the Lemurian) being the first to begin developing a childlike intelligence, which then evolved further during the two succeeding races, the Atlantean and the Caucasian, in a manner corresponding with the development of the individual today.

The Sequence of Unfoldment

To try to define the progressive sequence involved in Divine Intelligences first creating a particular quality of soul-body by an act of will (the Hindu *kriyasakti*) and then investing it with a consciousness and sense of self-motivation might appear intensely problematic to the Western mind, although not to the Oriental way of looking at things. But it would seem that the ancient Egyptians did conceive of Creation in this way, within the nature of the gods Ptah—whom we have already suggested as being but a differently spelled form of the Indo-Tibetan Buddha—and Khnemu.

In the Buddhist tradition, the self-attained Buddha nature is certainly that of a planetary or even a solar god who, through prior experience in the human kingdom, has learned how to expand his consciousness to the point where it becomes so all-inclusive of all the kingdoms of our planetary Nature that it is indeed ultimately able to emanate lesser soul aspects (or correspondences) of them from its own soul nature at will. Thus Ptah was depicted as producing the auric "egg" of each soul entity in conjunction with the god Khnum, for it is the greater Mind principle alone that contains and so induces the lesser soul form's self-generation, ex nihilo, the latter then proceeding to evolve each karmically distinct human form.†

This then all comes back to what was suggested earlier about all acts of creation (whether divine or human) inescapably generating an innate duality within the created soul form. Thus, as the universe is alive, each aspect of such a duality would itself necessarily (and automatically) become a living entity. Hence it is that the god nature constantly re-creates itself ex nihilo. However, that itself must surely result in an objective progression in the manifest field of Creation. As evolutionists tell us, there is a visually evident sequence of evolutionary development in the forms of the animal kingdom, notwithstanding the fact that all the various types thus produced now exist and function together in an ecologically balanced system. But if there is a progression of species' forms within the

---

*In the ancient Greek and other traditions, we also find this concept of five races of mankind—the gold, silver, bronze, mixed bronze and iron, and iron (Graves, *Greek Myths,* 12)—all treated by modern scholars as merely empty myth, rather than as metaphor.

†But it is already accepted by anthropologists that man has possessed the same bodily physique and also upright stance since at least the beginning of the Quaternary period, some 1.8 million years ago. Although fundamentally a geological age, its beginnings seem to have initiated a wide variety of changes throughout all the kingdoms of Nature.

animal kingdom, why not also within the human? And why should this intrinsically make one human ethnic type worth more or less than another?

The Principles of Ethnological Differentiation

On that hypothetical basis, therefore, within the present Fifth Race—and following the numerological progression already suggested—each aspect of this duality would then each have produced out of itself a triple form of self-expression, resulting in a number of ethnic subtypes, as follows*:

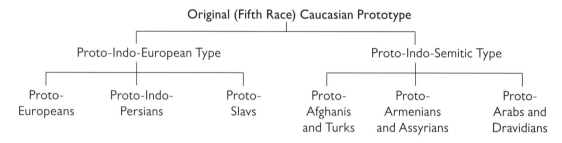

As we saw in chapter 4, the ancient sevenfold view of the world had it that the amalgam of a triple duality of soul types within a common environment produced the appearance of a mediating fourth principle. The latter then embodied that fusion but still retained all the various preceding characteristics. Following the same principle within human society, mutually interactive commerce and culture arose, naturally giving rise to physical interracial fusion as well as jingoistic aggression and open warfare. It is these inevitably chaotic latter cultural fusions and separations that anthropology and archaeology have then allowed themselves to believe in as the real cause of modern ethnic differentiation.

Now there is at least one tradition that has it that the *original* African and Sino-Mongolian stock were actually Atlantean, as were the "native" Amerindian types of both North and South America. Whatever the truth of the matter, the facial features of each type are quite clearly very distinctive. Indeed, their features are much more closely related to each other than they are to those of the Caucasian type—whether of Indo-European or Semitic stock. The point of mentioning this, however, is to highlight the fact that the common focus of the two former types was the Atlantic Ocean, whereas that of the Caucasian was some eight thousand miles away and in a much more northern latitude of the planet's surface. Therefore, there are perhaps some grounds for supporting the argument (outlined in greater detail in *Land of the Fallen Star Gods*)[6] that the original Sino-Mongolian type was a refugee (via Alaska and the Bering Straits, during a cyclic period of ice free polar

---

*It must be realized that these are very generalized classifications. The original ethnic types have become so intermixed that it is virtually impossible at this stage—particularly with the Semitic types—to be more specific.

zones) from Atlantean colonies in North America* and that the original Caucasian type was a hybrid somehow produced from that same stock, in Central Asia, over one million years ago. But the next problem to be considered is how the later ethnic Caucasian types might have recombined socially with the earlier ones to produce the civilizations and cultures of the ancient, post-Atlantean world scene.

How Long Ago Did It All Happen?

The problem one always comes up against in trying to calculate the age of any ancient civilization or culture lies in which of several reference criteria one uses. Modern orthodoxy on this issue starts (and finishes) with the standpoint that *Homo sapiens* is an entirely modern phenomenon that appeared (none know why) between 100,000 and 150,000 years ago, having gradually evolved from the anthropoid ape to become a hunter-gatherer and then an urban settler only about 10,000 to 15,000 years ago. However, as described here and in *Land of the Fallen Star Gods,* the ancient traditions took the very different view that intelligent mankind and its culture were literally millions of years old, man himself being a *spiritual* entity in origin, with a multiple soul organization, while the anthropoids were, contrary to Darwinian theory, merely Nature's degenerates.

The Brahmins of northern India—the descendants of the great Indo-Persian priesthood of Aryavarta—say that their written and oral traditions confirm that their sacred knowledge (including astronomy and astrology) was handed down to them by gods and demigods well over a million years ago when Atlantis was in its later heyday. The Puranas also speak of the then contemporary great island continent in the far west, in the mid-oceanic area, which quite clearly resonates with the idea of Atlantis. Even Herodotus mentions that the astronomically oriented Chaldeo-Sumerian civilization had flourished for over 470,000 years before the time of Alexander the Great.[7]

Yet, from all of these, all that we have left to us today, just over a mere two millennia after Alexander, are a very few relics, which tell us almost nothing about the Aryavartans and even very little about the much later Sumerians themselves.[†] But that in itself surely tells us something about the speed and cyclical consistency of degeneracy throughout Nature *as a general principle*. This is highly important because our concern here is to consider the possibility that Egypt might actually have been colonized from both the West and the East *at different times*—the last main occasion being from the East. But before we do so, there are one or two other matters to be looked at.

*Thus supporting the research of the American archaeologist Virginia Steen McIntyre, indicating that Native Americans were around well over two hundred thousand years ago—a discovery that, when made public, resulted in the destruction of her career in academia for having the temerity to so radically question the then current orthodoxy.
†Not altogether surprising in view of the great ancient libraries and millions of books and manuscripts burned over the last two millennia or so by a barbarically minded mixture of Romans, Christians, and Muslims.

Cultural Degeneracy as a Normally and Naturally Operative Principle in Nature

It seems strange to have to even mention this principle, as (orthodox) historians have spent so much time and effort in chronicling it in relation to every major civilization and culture in recorded history—and several minor ones too. As a result, we now know that such failures (in the objective world) result from disease, famine, war, and natural cataclysm. Such appears to have been the fate of the Lemurian and Atlantean races of untold millennia ago and the vast majority of their peoples. Now, when we reach the relatively recent fourth to fifth millennia BCE, we come across an apparently very large hole in the immediately preceding historical record, for both the highly sophisticated and urbanized Chaldeo-Sumerian and Egyptian civilizations and their accompanying cultures seem to have sprung into sudden existence without any apparent learning curve. However, as the supposed transition from a hunter-gatherer to a highly sophisticated urban culture would unavoidably have had to take literally thousands of years with at least some cultural evidence of its gradual evolution being found somewhere in the vicinity, why is it that absolutely nothing of such a nature appears yet to have been found? Well, there are a variety of possible reasons, or a combination of them all, as follows:

1. The evidence is already available but archaeologists have just failed to interpret or date it correctly.
2. The evidence lies buried under either modern construction or previous ancient construction, or the dust of ages, still to be discovered.
3. Archaeologists are looking in the wrong places.

A Gauntlet Thrown Down in Front of Anthropological Science

The view of humankind's culture being far, far older—in fact, by several millions of years—has been reinforced from the scientific viewpoint by Michael Cremo and Richard Thompson in their formidable work *Forbidden Archeology*. In it they document findings of numerous human artifacts and even buildings lying under layers of coal, rock, and sediment, which are themselves millions—in many cases literally *tens* of millions—of years old.[8] The quite separately derived fact that the *Homo sapiens* of the early Quaternary period (between 1.5 and 1.8 million years ago) were actually appreciably taller than today's average, with very sharply defined modern features, and an appreciably larger brain,[9] itself indicates that—as with everything else in Nature—some principle of cyclical degeneracy and renewal indeed operates in the racial type, just as it does in the animal and plant species. Modern science, however, weighed down with the inflexibly ponderous Darwinian theory of natural selection (purely by survival of the fittest), can conceive of no alternative principle that might be at work behind the scenes, because (a) it takes no account of the soul principle being a practical reality, (b) it has discounted the possible rise and fall of human intelligence as a cyclical phenomenon, *and* (c) it makes no fundamental distinction between man and animal, because of regarding consciousness as a merely evolutionary supplement of physical nature.

Modern science as yet, alas, has materialistically empirical theories and assumptions in abundance, but no guiding philosophy—because it refuses to accept even the possible existence of the parallel psychic and spiritual worlds of being, on the grounds of their being unnecessary. Thus any rational attempt to discuss ancient systems of philosophical and metaphysical thought with these self-blinded scholars and scientists is doomed from the outset by their own prejudices. Similarly, because of carbon 14 and other techniques of dating of bones, pottery, and old clothes found in graves, anthropological and archaeological sciences have assured themselves that the earliest permanent townships could only have come into being about 10,000 to 12,000 years ago. The present assumptions are quite clearly unfounded and misplaced.

The Assistance of Cyclical Periods of Cataclysm

Nature has its own mechanisms of promoting natural degeneracy in order to get rid of old forms so as to allow new evolutionary developments; even modern science recognizes that cataclysms play a significant role in this regard. However, whereas scientists currently tend to believe that cataclysms are entirely spontaneous and due to constantly changing environmental circumstances that are largely beyond our and their capacity to predict, except in the very short term, the Ancients would doubtless have regarded such a view as fundamentally flawed. The reason they would have done so lies in the fact that they saw all terrestrial phenomena as the result of premeditated intent on the part of the various demiurgic hierarchies of Intelligence responsible for operating and maintaining order in the universe in general, and on our planet in particular.

As far as they were concerned, all major terrestrial events were the result of causes operating in the spiritual worlds in response to, or in accordance with, the Divine Plan. And as the Divine Plan was principally operative in the area of constantly changing celestial relationships, it followed that all such events could be looked for in relation to astronomical and astrological cycles—these being seen as one and the same in ancient times. Thus, in exactly the same way that we now know that the Sun has a twenty-two-year cycle during which there occur two eleven-year sunspot subcycles, when tremendous surges occur in the amount of solar energy discharged, so in the 81,500-year cycle mentioned in chapter 2, there are two roughly 41,000-year subcycles (already well known to science), which somehow appear to give rise to really major cataclysms on Earth. The last such cycle seemingly peaked about 12,500 years ago.

As yet, mainstream science has not put two-and-two together in regard to this matter, possibly because it is afraid to extrapolate such correlative ideas from the rather fragmentary information currently at hand and possibly also because the sense and practice of interdisciplinary relationships between astrophysics and geology are still in their infancy. Notwithstanding that, the ancient concern with understanding all the possible ramifications of astronomical cycles for the benefit of human society becomes increasingly more understandable. However, there is another subliminal factor at play in bringing about the cyclical disappearances of civilizations and their cultures.

The Original Continent of Atlantis

Very briefly recapitulating what has already been suggested, it would seem that at least several hundred thousand (and more likely many millions) of years ago, there existed a major civilization and culture in or around the mid-Atlantic area, with colonies in what now comprise west and northwest Africa, far western Europe, and also the Americas.* This then, seemingly, was the fabled Atlantis. Over a vast period of time, however, predominantly due to volcanic and earthquake activity, this appears to have broken up into a mass of smaller island groups and island continents, most of which subsequently also disappeared for the same reasons.

As also otherwise described in *Land of the Fallen Star Gods,* the main effect of these cataclysms seems to have involved dispersions of Atlantean humanity both eastward and westward, to produce the ancestors of the African Bantu in the east and the various native American Indian types in the west, the latter giving rise (much later) to the Eskimo and Asiatic Sino-Mongolian types, as a result of crossing the Bering Straits westward into Asia[10]—*not* the other way around as mainstream archaeology would currently have us believe.

The Flight of the Atlanteans

That the somewhat dramatic idea of Atlanteans fleeing from the rising oceanic waters in the tropics directly northward into America and Iberia perhaps involved a much later exodus is to some extent supported by the known fact that much of what now comprises

---

*Commencing around 850,000 years ago, it seems that a major shift of the Earth's magnetic/polar orientation was taking place—lasting probably well over 200,000 years, thereby giving rise to progressively vast changes in the shape and extent of continents, rivers, seas, and oceans. One of the most dramatic of these changes seems to have involved a westward twisting of the equatorial region of the Earth's crust, in the opposite direction from the upper and lower hemispheres—a phenomenon that must have resulted from the imposition of external celestial influences, perhaps affecting our solar system as a whole. The main result of this torque action on the Earth's geology, it is suggested, appears in the sudden sharp bend of the mid-Atlantic Ridge, the volcanic mountain range that extends from the north to south polar regions—a phenomenon that must have had a devastatingly cataclysmic effect upon any mid-Atlantic continental landmass and its associated civilization(s) and culture(s).

continental Europe was itself largely under water between one and two million years ago. Whatever the truth of the matter, it seems that a (perhaps deliberately) isolated pocket of late Atlanteans eventually took refuge on or around the high plateau of Tibet, north of the Himalayas,* some only much later moving progressively westward as the oceanic waters receded, until they eventually adopted the sheltered valleys of the Caucasus and the foothills of the Hindu Kush as their homelands. This is by no means, however, a suggestion that all other Atlanteans living farther south or even in the Atlantic Ocean area itself died out or perished under the rising oceanic waters. For it is reasonably certain that it must have been their descendants who progressively gave rise to the native peoples of central and northern America over the course of the last several hundred thousand years.

Taking it for granted that some such psychospiritual evolutionary process and associated guardianship might indeed have taken place, we need to consider what might have occurred once the period of assimilation and change had been completed, resulting in the final proto-Caucasian mutation of the late Atlantean type. This must have been something in the order of one to one and a half million years ago, by which time continental Europe had itself perhaps already begun to appear above the oceanic surface. Clearly, we can know very little if anything of the first cultures and the civilizations of the new Caucasian stock, but it seems almost certain that, at some stage, they would have become progressively drawn into cohabitation with still extant Atlantean communities on the western seaboards of Europe and northwestern Africa. If the Chaldeo-Sumerian and Chaldeo-Assyrian civilizations were already in existence over 250,000 and 470,000 years ago, respectively, as we heard earlier on, it seems not unlikely that the earliest known stepped pyramids (the ziggurats of the later Chaldeans) were in fact the product of prior contact with Atlantean culture. But of the details of this, we can as yet know nothing at all.

The Appearance of the Atlanto-Caucasian Type and Its Architecture

In her book *The Secret Doctrine,* H. P. Blavatsky reported the ancient Brahmanical tradition that, after the natural dispersion of the early Caucasian tribes from their natal homeland in Central Asia about a million years ago, some traveled far to the west and, having first fought and then intermarried with the remaining Atlanteans of the northeastern Atlantic shores (of Iberia, Brittany, and so on), generated a new hybrid ethnic type.[11] From these, it seems, emerged the later Celts and Nordic types, plus the Berbers, Moors, and

---

*There are a variety of ancient traditions dealing with this. Perhaps the best known is that of the Hindus, involving the Kumaras who settled on the Sacred Island in the middle of what is now the Gobi Desert. These much later gave rise to the Khmer, who built solar- and star-oriented temples all over southeast Asia, including those at Ankhor Wat and Ankhor Thom. However, the Chinese story is very similar because their Atlantean island (Maligasima—hence perhaps Malaga in southern Spain and Malacca in Sumatra) was sunk and the king—one Piru-un—then escaped through a warning from the gods and two idols and with his family subsequently peopled the whole of China.

Tuaregs of northwestern Africa and the Guanche people of the Canary Islands. According to Blavatsky, it was from this hybrid race that the original migration to the newly emergent land of Egypt later occurred (about one hundred thousand years ago), at a time when it was part of a great island subcontinent incorporating the Horn of Africa and western Saudi Arabia. At that time, the eastern side of Arabia must still have been under the waters of the Indian Ocean, while the Red Sea had not formed properly as we know it today.

Although it may not be possible for us today to draw a clear picture in our minds of what the original Atlanteans or the later hybrid Atlanto-Caucasians looked like, we can perhaps draw certain inferences about them and their type of consciousness from the form and scale of their architecture. The most ancient form of building—now unfortunately classified under the generalized term *Neolithic* (but actually far earlier)—involving subtly coursed stone walls made of huge blocks several hundred tons in weight (such as those at Cuzco, Sacsayhuaman, Ollantaytambo, Gozo, and Tyrens), but with no clearly defined raison d'etre, appear to be the oldest and thus most likely to be of pure Atlantean origin. The much later Indo-Caucasian style of architecture, however, is much more defined and artistically sophisticated. But between the two—for example in the Egyptian (particularly evident at Giza and Abydos)—we find a rather interesting amalgam of both. While we shall look a little more closely at this subject in chapter 9, it might perhaps be regarded as a useful pointer to the transitional development of the creative *intellectual* nature in man, as opposed to the as yet largely aspirational or idealistic mass consciousness of the Atlanteans.

The Religious Culture and Mind State of the Original Atlanteans

While there appear to have been few clear traditions handed down telling us much about the original Atlantean forms of culture, one notable tradition concerning them is that their religion was based entirely upon magic, which although originally benign, became tainted with selfishness and thus ultimately turned self-destructive. Now, as this word *magic* has a very specific meaning in our present day and age, it is necessary for us to pause a moment and explain that, in relation to the Atlanteans, it meant "the Great Knowledge"—that is, of Nature's own underlying techniques, as effected by the *deva-neteru* hierarchies.

As we have already indicated, the Ancients took the view that there was a corresponding progression of everything in Nature; hence—man being a celestial entity—each succeeding race of mankind was the (naturally sevenfold) expression of the progressively unfolding consciousness of the (solar) deity of our world system—that is, Ra in the Egyptian tradition. The principle worked in exactly the same way as with the young human being's consciousness, which naturally unfolds in seven-year cycles. Therefore, just as the Indo-Caucasian type is the predominant expression of the organizing intellectual principle, which correspondingly unfolds in us during the ages of fourteen to twenty-one, so the Atlantean was the predominant expression of the often volatile and naturally self-concerned astral (or emotional feeling) nature, which unfolds in us between the ages of seven to fourteen.

On this basis, then, the main forms of self-expression in Atlantean times would have involved the development of idealism and devotional attachments incorporating the capacity for great love, dedication, and respect, as well as self-sacrifice and a sense of duty. However, so the ancient traditions again have it, in those halcyon days, early human-kind's parents—the great demiurgic hierarchies of the gods—moved visibly among human beings, the elemental forces of Nature being their powerful (although childlike) servants. Consequently, the Atlanteans learned by example all about the natural magical powers in Nature and how they could be manipulated by knowledge of ritual. However, it appears that some of the later Atlanteans, who prematurely began to develop the intellectual principle, began to utilize such powers for their own self-centered designs, thereby dethroning the gods and putting man on a par with them. From that point it was but a relatively short step to all sorts of selfishly motivated interference with Nature.

The latter description bears an interesting resemblance to the approach of some contemporary scientists who, seemingly oblivious of Nature's capacity to fight back, with often devastating results, rather naively believe that they too should be allowed to go on playing with their more dangerous scientific experiments without constraint—all supposedly in the name of furthering greater knowledge to the betterment of the human condition, but actually more to satisfy their own curiosity and intellectual vanity. Yet such exploitation comes at a price, because our planetary Nature, according to the Ancients at least, knows only the principle of harmonic balance and thus cyclically brings all distortion back into line by enforced means—that is, through cataclysms that reduce all mankind's artificial creations to rubble and dust.

Rise and Fall of the Atlanto-Caucasians

One might reasonably speculate that the advent of the early Caucasians must have reenergized the pure Atlantean stock, itself isolated and progressively depleted in the wake of earthquake and volcanic cataclysms that had continued for tens of thousands of years after the great polar shift of around eight hundred thousand years ago. The conquering early Caucasians may even have been able to reorient the Atlanteans to a more spiritual approach to life. As the oceanic waters receded, however, it would have become possible for the fast-expanding new hybrid sub-races to colonize the freshly emergent lands (of modern continental Europe) farther and farther afield. Yet, at some stage or another, the old self-centered and self-indulgent tendencies of the Atlantean nature clearly began to reassert themselves, thereby causing a deep schism among the population. Things could well have deteriorated to such an extent that some felt the absolute need to distance themselves fundamentally from this worsening cultural environment by emigration—in a manner not dissimilar to the Pilgrim Fathers setting sail for North America in 1620 CE. Hence, so it would appear, there occurred a great exodus to the new island continent of greater Egypt about one hundred thousand years ago. It was this that must have enabled the fugitives to set up from scratch an integrated culture and civilization with a wholly spiritual orientation, in which all magical ritual was rigorously dedicated toward reflecting the Will of the celestial heavens.*

Plato's Atlantis

The power and influence of the Atlanto-Caucasian race seems, however, to have continued developing for some tens of thousands of years, if we are to accept the story told by the high priest of Sais to Solon, as recounted by Plato.[12†] For it would seem from that story that the peoples of the central and eastern Mediterranean (including the Greeks and Egyptians) were being constantly harassed by the territorially aggressive "Atlantes" in the tenth millennium before his own time—that is, 12,500 years ago. It was then only due to another major outbreak of volcanic and earthquake activity, in and around the geologically volatile coastal area of northwest Africa, that the central island base (Poseidonis) of the Atlantes was destroyed in a cataclysm that must have inevitably torn the very heart out of their civilization—as would happen today if London, New York, or Tokyo, for example, were suddenly without warning to suffer the same fate.

It is interesting to note that the series of really major cataclysms that destroyed Poseidonis seems to have coincided not only with the Egyptian Zep Tepi—the zodiacal point in the 25,920-year cycle of the precessionary Great Year that is opposite to where we stand today and which the Egyptians referred to as the time of the "Return of the Gods"—but also to the climax of the last 41,000-year demi-cycle of displacement of the ecliptic pole. To what extent this could be put down to pure chance is of course infinitely arguable. But it would have to involve an extraordinary confluence of coincidences.

---

*It seems not altogether impossible that some of the migrating Atlanto-Caucasians departed northward toward Brittany, Ireland, and the British Isles, rather than southward to Egypt. Perhaps this is why there traditionally appear to have been curiously strong connections (not just of a merchant trading nature) between Egypt and Britain even as late as three thousand to five thousand years ago and why the Druidically arranged standing stones of Carnac in Brittany appear to be named after Karnak in Egypt.

†The Atlantis actually mentioned by Plato in the *Timaeus* is quite clearly a metaphor for our solar system and definitely not the series of concentrically organized, *geographical* land masses he describes. However, that does not vitiate the actual existence of a geographically and geologically real Atlantean land mass facing the Pillars of Hercules from the west side. It seems as though Plato was (deliberately) running several metaphors and allegories together with real ancient history. But his knowledge of the date of the major geological cataclysms affecting the area in question is clearly confirmed as accurate by modern scientific research, as one can quite easily confirm from a visit to the library of the Geological Museum in London.

With no central or historic core left to their culture, it is suggested that the remaining Atlantes—the ancestors of the modern Guanche, Berber, and Tuareg—eventually settled naturally into a parochial tribal system of self-government, the structure of which can still be seen today. It exists, interestingly, in tandem with an almost institutionalized sense and practice of sympathetic magic, which is at the very core of the Berber and Tuareg cultural belief systems. Yet in this we find the clear legacy of the original Atlantean culture, although the literal application and extent of it, even today, would perhaps be difficult for the average objectively oriented and Western-educated mind to appreciate.

But What Happened in Egypt Itself between 100,000 and 5,000 Years Ago?

The history of Egypt during this prolonged period must itself remain largely (if not entirely) within the field of speculation and conjecture, even though we have the outline record of the divine and semidivine dynasties of Manetho to fall back on as a general guide. In that respect, the one thing we can depend upon is the importance that the ancient Egyptian religion placed upon integrity and accuracy (from the outset) in every single aspect of their cultural existence. Hence, we can surely otherwise rely without undue anxiety upon their records of the contact they maintained with the "land of Pun(t)"—the "land of the gods"—from which they imported spices. Although some Egyptologists have concluded that Pun(t) must relate to Ethiopia, there are no records of spices having ever been grown (in sufficient abundance for commerce) in that part of Africa, whereas northwestern India *was* famous for them. Pun(t) appears almost certainly to be synonymous with the lush valley and delta of the River Indus leading up through the delta province of Sind into the Punjab and thence to Kashmir. The latter lies in the foothills of the western Himalayas and the Hindu Kush range where Apollonius of Tyana apparently went to study with the fraternity of spiritual adepts or rishis—who were said to live there even up to the beginning of the twentieth century. Ethiopia has no such tradition. But why should the early Egyptians have felt the contact with Pun(t) to be of such importance?

In answer, human nature being as it is where tradition is concerned, we can perhaps rely quite strongly upon a probably instinctive wish by the emigrant Atlanto-Caucasians to reignite and subsequently maintain the link with the land of their original spiritual and genetic origin. By so doing, they would have been able to infuse in themselves a constant sense of proximity and contact, which could provide considerable support to their new civilization, founded as it was on entirely spiritual and metaphysical principles. But perhaps even behind this there are further intelligently constructive purposes at work.

Spiritual Geography and Reconstructed Ethnic Links

If one considers a map (see fig. 8.1) of the area extending between Egypt and the high plateau of Tibet, it is interesting to note that the angle of orientation is roughly similar to that of the plane of the ecliptic relative to the celestial equator. While this might seem to be pure coincidence, there is no denying the fact that this same corridor incorporates the whole cradle of modern civilization around three major rivers, each with deltas—that is, the Nile, the Tigris-Euphrates, and the Indus. At the top of this same corridor lies the Gobi Desert and the high plateau of Tibet, where the gods—according to Indo-Tibetan tradition—were supposed to live, in the fabled Shamballa.* Next down lie the valleys of the Hindu Kush, adjoining Kashmir and Pun(t)jab, where the adept demigods, or rishis, traditionally lived; then next in line comes greater Mesopotamia (incorporating ancient Chaldea, Babylonia and Sumer), while fourth and last down the chain lies Egypt, itself regarded as the Land of (the reflection of) Heaven on Earth.

The Four and the Seven in Terms of World History

In the ancient metaphysical tradition, four (hence also the square) was regarded as the number associated with objective manifestation of the double within a septenary system. But, remembering that we are considering the historical interaction and transition of evolving consciousness between the Atlantean and the Indo-Caucasian races, is there more (or less) to this than meets the eye here? How open are we to the suggestion that even the geographical positioning of great civilizations and cultures might perhaps be intelligently premeditated in line with sacred metaphysical principles, according to some greater Divine Purpose, or Plan? Well, let us speculate a little, as follows.

If we take a look at fig. 8.3, we shall see that it is presented as two parallel diagrams, each having fundamentally the same meaning. On the left, we see the sevenfold system incorporating—within its upper half—the fourfold sequence we have just described, extending between the Gobi and Egypt. Each of the four upper planes represents the associated consciousness of the groups already mentioned in connection with them (that is, divine, semidivine, and so on). The lower three planes (of associated consciousness) then refer to the consciousness of the Fourth (Atlantean) Race type.

The right-hand diagram, however, shows the interaction between the Fourth and Fifth Races in terms of an evolutionary Life wave of developing consciousness. At the end of the sevenfold Fourth Race cycle a natural schism or polarization occurs, because the race's primary potential has run its gamut. Consequently, the evolutionary "cream" of the Fourth Race type separate from the rest—both culturally and geographically—by moving from

*The name Shamballa appears to be derived from a combination of *dhzyan* (the Tibetan form of *dhyan,* meaning "meditation," and *b'Allah,* meaning "of God"—hence "the place of the meditating gods" responsible for the guidance of our planetary Life.

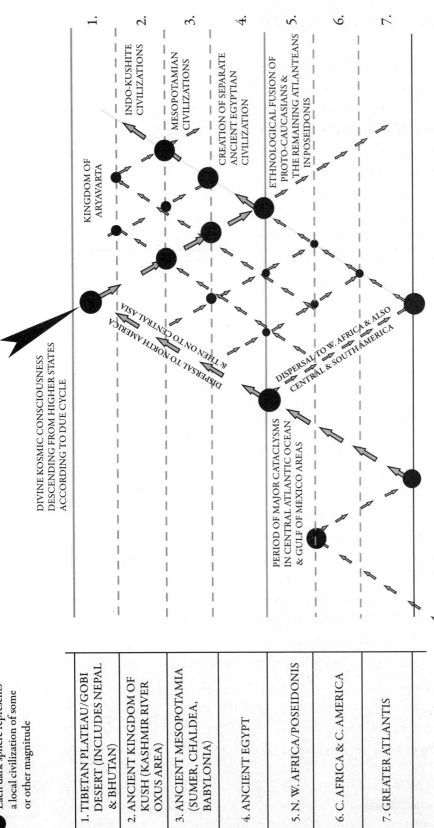

FIGURE 8.3. GEOGRAPHICAL AND METAPHYSICAL CORRELATIONS OF THE FOURTH AND FIFTH WORLD RACES

Note: The fundamental concept depicted here in diagrammatic fashion is that the cultures that give rise to civilizations are themselves the products of cylically operative changes taking place within the spectrum of consciousness of the Logos of our system. Hence, within the seven levels of his range of (kosmic physical) awareness, cultures and civilizations are constantly appearing and disappearing in order to fulfill the varied expression of what we might thus call "Divine Purpose," through the activities of Mankind. This "Evolutionary Wave" concept gives rise, in turn, to a dissemination of Higher Purpose *throughout* the system, with human ethnological types alternately differentiating and then re-fusing at the end of each cycle, with worn-out and degenerate stock correspondingly disappearing en route. Each ethnological type is merely the vehicle of a particular divine impulse, temporarily animated by "sparks."

North America to Central Asia via Alaska and the Bering Straits. There they continue to evolve their wholly spiritual form of self-development, eventually producing in themselves a subjective state of mind that (after tens of thousands of years) eventually draws invocatively toward itself a yet higher form of consciousness—that of the Intellectual Mind principle.* That, according to ancient tradition, takes the form of more highly developed groups of beings—"gods and demigods"—that incarnate among them. This then constitutes the true genesis of the Fifth Race, which thereafter progressively begets its new subjective inheritance upon humanity in the mass, like ink spreading in water.

The upward development just described is, however, paralleled by a downward repetition of historic Atlantean culture and civilization among the remainder of the Fourth Race types left behind. Consequently, the latter progress through a *second* sevenfold cycle, at the end of which they come into contact with the first cycle of unfoldment of the new Fifth Race type of consciousness—possibly in Iberia and Poseidonis. Before doing so, they will have progressed in total through *thirteen* historic subcycles—mirroring the thirteen rediscovered parts of the body of Osiris—before the new form of a higher (mental) consciousness descends in cultural form among them. This fusion, however, is but a temporary one, there subsequently occurring a schism between the two groups, the main caucus of Fifth Race–oriented types then going off to found the civilization and culture of ancient Egypt, while the residual Fourth Race type of culture thereafter progressively fragments and dissipates—over a very prolonged period of historical time, however, for Nature moves at her own very sedate pace.†

Over the period of the next several tens of thousands of years, one might perhaps expect to find that the various Fifth Race civilizations and cultures of Aryavarta, Greater Mesopotamia, and Egypt became steadily more closely integrated within one great and common spiritual and social culture. However, something clearly happened (latterly) along

---

*The new type of electrical brain patterns themselves doubtless causing progressive changes in the facial characteristics as a result, thereby ultimately giving rise to a completely new ethnological type.

†What we are seeing here, in terms of the evolutionary development of human consciousness across the globe, appears to be the result of mankind merely following the instinctive tendency of Mother Nature in the mass to express herself objectively (in cycles) first as a duality, then as a double triplicity of cultural potentials. However, as the natural tendency of human consciousness is to gravitate toward others of like mind and cultural interest, it is perhaps unsurprising that this should have happened in ancient times on a global scale. Different groups expressing varied but purely Atlantean forms of consciousness (hence their social tribalism) migrated to: (1) central and southern Africa; (2) the Americas; and then (3) Asia. There they created their own very different cultures, some occasionally being of great scale, and producing their own magnificent civilizations. Correspondingly, the Fifth Race produced its own preliminary duality—the Indo-Caucasian and the Indo-Semitic types, which, blending with the mid-Atlantean remnants, produced out of their fusion not only the ancient Egyptian civilization, but also the multiple basis of much of western European culture and civilization. It is then this mediating sub-racial group that (although having its own internal spectrum of differentiated consciousness) has been responsible for engineering the regeneration of a truly global civilization—our own today. Yet, notwithstanding this generalized cultural fusion, we can still see the underlying cross-cultural seams that join the whole together, which one day will doubtless be the cause of yet another great cycle of human evolutionary fragmentation.

the way, resulting in what appears *on the surface* to have been a prolonged cultural dark age, which affected both Egypt and Aryavarta, until the historically recognized resurgence of civilization and culture in the Middle East somewhere between 4000 and 5000 BCE. Curiously, it may be that this supposed dark age was a natural—and temporary—precursor to the much later cultural developments that would take place in western Europe, leading to the reappearance of a reintegrated *world* civilization and associated culture of *world* consciousness. Whatever the actual cause, Manetho's list of archaic Egyptian kings—those "gods, demigods, and heroes" preceding the Old Kingdom dynasties—perhaps needs to be considered rather more carefully than it has been to date.

Each reader will understandably tend to form his or her own view as to the underlying probabilities (or lack of them) inherent in what has just been speculatively suggested. As no hard evidence can be adduced to support the concept, it must necessarily remain just a conceptual theory—albeit one that holds its head above water with as much aplomb as modern mainstream anthropological theory. Nevertheless, we must move onward, turning several as yet blank pages of history to areas of known and generally accepted association with ancient Egypt—more specifically involving the ancient kingdom of Kesh.

The Ancient Lands of Kesh/Cush and Pun(t)

As Wallis Budge tells us: "Kesh or Cush was the ancient name for Ethiopia."[13] And he then also adds: "In the earliest times, the descendants of [the kingdom of] Cush appear to have had the same religion as the Egyptians."[14] But as we saw earlier, there seem to have been direct socio-anthropological connections (as well as trading relations) between the Ethiopians of the kingdom of Kesh—which lay beyond the First Cataract—and the Eastern Ethiopians, as Herodotus called them, of the land of Pun(t), the latter clearly meaning modern Punjab, which lies between Kashmir and the delta of the River Indus. It was the northern Kashmiris (or Kesh-miris) from the area of the River Oxus who invaded Egypt during the third millennium BCE, probably joining ethnic kin whose resettled location was already known.

Now, Kesh-mir was evidently a very large kingdom, which (originally) seems to have stretched from the Black Sea and the Mediterranean right across northern India, toward southeast Asia, thereby forming the basis of what was later to become the greater Indo-Persian empire of the early peoples following the Hindu religion.* Sir Flinders Petrie himself claimed that there appeared to be definite trading connections between ancient

---

*What actually seems more probable (at least to this author) is that the original spiritual links between (Ethiopian) Kesh and Egypt for some reason (as all things ultimately do) eventually withered, with the result that only the objective links remained—thereby giving the impression to our own later archaeologists that Ethiopian Kesh had evolved as a quasi-separate kingdom of its own accord. Egyptologists reckon that the origins of civilization and culture in Ethiopia go back only about 2,500 years, so we can perhaps suggest that its spiritual degeneracy must have occurred during the two millennia before that—which itself appears to coincide with the degeneracy in Egyptian civilization.

Egypt and southern Russia even in the Second Dynasty and also "more particularly with the Caucasus."[15] In passing interest, the southernmost state of this kingdom of Kesh, on the eastern side of the Indus, was called Yaudheya—which seems to have provided the origin of the name of that region in Palestine (Pali-stan) later called Judaea. Quite probably, therefore, the Jews of Judaea too were originally no more than colonially expatriate Semitic types from greater Indo-Persia.*

By virtue of the trading that took place between Egypt and Pun(t)—quite certainly extending well back into what we would today regard as prehistory—it would be surprising if no immigration were to have taken place between them. In fact, it seems very probable that the connections were quite deliberately of spiritual and cultural origin, not merely the later result of commerce. There are too many fundamental cross-cultural links within the framework of the ancient Egyptian architectural-metaphysical master plan to suggest anything else.

Artistic and Cultural Differences

Curiously, the art and architecture of ancient India appears completely different from that of ancient Egypt. There are no direct correlations whatsoever. Whereas Indian art and sculpture—even where of massive size—is flowing and full of dynamic, physiologically exact and colorful detail, much of it involving considerable (and intricate) abstract symbolism, the Egyptian counterparts are both monolithic and almost psychologically static by comparison. And yet we find throughout Egyptian sacred culture Sanskrit-based names, words, and sacred allegories having a clearly common source in ancient Vedic India. It is this—plus the Brahmin tradition of the Ethiopians of Upper Egypt having been enforced Brahmin émigrés from northwestern India—that leads one to surmise that these latter expatriates—apparently between the fourth and sixth millennia BCE—found and became immersed in an *existing* ancient Egyptian culture and civilization that, by that time, was already in some degree of decline and thus vulnerably open to such incursion. But that of course still leaves open the question: "*Who* were the real ancient Egyptians and *where* did they come from?"

The wheel by now seems to have turned full circle, for as the linguistic trail left by the speakers of the ancient Hamitic language seems to have spread eastward to Egypt, via the Berber and Tuareg peoples of the Mahgreb and the western Sahara, themselves closely related to the Guanche people of the Canary Islands,[†] it seems fairly clear that the *original* ancient Egyptians—as Diodorus Siculus was told—did indeed come from the "lands of the setting Sun." But then, if these western lands were not the territories of already semi-Caucasian Atlanteans, whose were they?

---

*The name Israel, given to the (wholly metaphorical) patriarch Jacob and then supposedly to his descendants, appears to be derived from the quasi-Egyptian, quasi-Babylonian compound term As'r-El, meaning a specific hierarchy of divine beings.

†As otherwise described in *Land of the Fallen Star Gods* (62).

NINE

The Spread and Decline of Ancient Mystic Culture

We assume today in our modern arrogance, that Greece was the height of ancient culture, but it was not so. Rather, the Greeks were, as evidenced by Homer, with his rudimentary, vestigial ideas of shades and of the gods, a rather backward people whose culture was revived by the influx of Egyptian and Chaldean Mysteries. But that influx, though it reinvigorated the culture, was yet nonetheless a descent, a translation downwards which . . . represented a decline, a decline of the Mysteries manifested also in the sectarianism and fragmentation of Greek philosophy into the various schools, rather than remaining all the votaries of the Mysteries. All of this was, in any event, contemporaneous with and as a result of the fundamental loss; the loss of the primordial, hierophonic language of ancient Egypt . . . which was a manifestation of the unity, the totality that was Egyptian culture and which could not be transmitted in toto to the Greeks, or to the West.

ARTHUR VERSLUIS, *THE EGYPTIAN MYSTERIES*

Popular modern orthodoxy has it that our European cultural heritage is essentially derived from the Greeks, to some extent via the Romans. However, it was Herodotus (a cultured Greek) in the second century BCE who himself confirmed that the Greeks owed their mystic culture (the foundation of their whole culture) in its entirety to the Egyptians.[1] It is also clear that Greek architecture and statuary owed their direct origins to the Egyptians, whose ancient colonial influence seems to have extended to at least Crete.

As we shall endeavor to show in this chapter, the cultural influence of the ancient Egyptians extended much farther geographically, in all directions, where it mixed with other already extant cultures.

FIGURE 9.1. THE RUINS OF THE ACROPOLIS

Note: Although the Greeks learned (from the Egyptians) how to incorporate *pi* (π) and *phi* (∅, that is, the Golden Ratio) into their architecture, they were not at all as concerned about location for the most part—except insofar as the projection of grandeur and superiority were concerned—although the Parthenon was built on the Acropolis next to an already sacred spring. Perhaps the most self-evident difference between Greek and Egyptian temples—apart from the fact of non-enclosure—is that the Greeks built theirs in often arbitrarily prominent locations, atop a series of steps, to heighten the idea of ascending toward the gods. The ancient Egyptians evidently saw little or no point in this because Man was regarded as already a god in his inner nature and therefore needed no merely objective uplift—which would, in any case, only succeed in distancing him from the real god nature. Consequently, the approach to Egyptian temples—at least in earlier times—tended to be on flat ground, with only minor elevation, the temple design itself being highly subjective in its psychological orientation and entirely astronomical in its geographical orientation.

Language Similarities

It is obviously a very tall order to try to show cultural cross-references between ancient civilizations in prehistoric times when modern orthodoxy says that such civilizations could not have existed because there are no documented records of them. However, a large proportion of this view—as we have already described—is based upon scholars turning a very selective blind eye to at least circumstantial evidence. The latter quite clearly shows that such civilizations and cultures had to have existed, otherwise the circumstantial evidence itself would not have been possible. Just as an example of prehistoric transatlantic cultural relations that were theoretically impossible, Charles Berlitz in his book *The Mystery of Atlantis* provides us with the following historic similarities in language:[2]

AMERINDIAN WORD	TRANSATLANTIC WORD	MEANING
Atl	Atl (Berber)	Water
Teocali	Theoukalia (Greek)	House of the gods
Potomac	Potamos (Greek)	River
Pniw	Pneu (Greek)	To blow
Mixtli	Omitchli (Greek)	Cloud
Balaam	Bileam (Hebrew)	Priest-magician
Malku	Malkuth (Hebrew)	Kingdom
Papalo-atl	Papilio (Latin)	Butterfly (dragonfly?)
Llake-llake	Lak Lak (Sumerian)	Heron

To these we can add a few more words and names specifically related to Egyptian culture:

EGYPTIAN	HP(I)	ANU	A-TUM	TA'URT	AKH(U)	HER(U)
NORDIC			Audumla	Urd		Aesir
GREEK		Ouranos	Atomos	Tartarus	Iaho	Hera
HINDU (SANSKRIT)	Apah	Anu	Atman		Ahi	(A)sura
BABYLONIAN	Apsu	Anu		Tauthe		Aura
CHINESE	Ho-po					
PHOENICIAN				Tauthe		Aura
PERSIAN	Apu	Anahita			Akhra	Ahura
BASQUE					Ekhi	
POLYNESIAN		Anu	Kiho-Tumu	Tahiti	Akua/Ahu	
MAYA/AZTEC			Atonatiuh		Ahau	Huru-kan
CELTIC	Abac	Anu			Oc	
GUANCHE	Abora					

Pan-African Fertilizations

Perhaps unsurprisingly, in view of its geographical location, we find distorted versions of Egyptian mystic names and words throughout central Africa, where they have become thoroughly mixed up with local, largely animistic religious belief systems, several of which, however, also attribute a sevenfold nature to their heaven worlds. For example, among the Yoruba tribe of Nigeria, the supreme god is known as Olodumare,[3] which, when deciphered, re-becomes El-Atum-Ra. The Bakongo tribe of the Congo/Zaire believe that their god first created the Great Breath Mahungu—that is, Mah-Ankh(u)—and then an androgynous semidivine man-being called Muntu Walunga (i.e., Mntw-El-Ankh).[4] The oracle tablets of the Shona people of Zimbabwe are called *hakata*[5]—clearly derived from the Egyptian word for magic, *heka,* the latter word being found almost exactly the same (as *haka*) even among the Maoris of New Zealand, whose international rugby football team use it today for their pre-match public ritual.

Even more fascinatingly, we find among some of the indigenous African tribes distorted versions of names and words that are of *Asiatic* origin. The word *jok,* meaning the unified spirit of the gods, is found in several variations all along the Nile and clearly had its genesis in the Sanskrit *yog(a).* The Hausa word for "miracle" is *laya,*[6] which is also a Sanskrit word, involving a process or point of magical transition or transmutation. In Benin (Nigeria) the Bendel tribe believes in a Spirit of Destiny called Ehi,[7] corresponding with the Indo-Tibetan Ahi (and the Basque Ekhi). The elemental spirit in a talisman is, according to the Ashanti of Ghana, an *asuman*[8]—a compound word derived from the Sanskrit *asu* and *man,* meaning "breath" and "mind" respectively. The Ashanti Creator of the Universe is Odomankoma[9]—phonetically recognizable as *atman-kumar(a).* The Turks used the same god-name even up to the early twentieth century for their Ottoman Empire.

The Ubiquitous God Ra of the Pacific

We have already mentioned the fact of several Egyptian god-names and mystic words being found in Polynesia, but further mention should be made of the widespread use of the god-name Ra itself. The Polynesians actually had the pure and simple name Ra for their main solar deity, as well as variations of it for associated aspects of the same deity, such as Rata, a fusion of Ra and Ptah.[10]

The Polynesians also had a cosmic octopus called Tumu-Ra'i Feuna,[11] which etymologists have translated as "foundation of the earthly heaven" but which is a very thinly disguised version of Atum-Ra. We otherwise find Ra elsewhere on the western Pacific seaboard, among the Japanese, as Ra-iden, Ra-itaro, and Ra-icho.[12] So can we in all seriousness avoid the obvious cross-cultural implications of all this?

The God Ra in the Hindu Tradition

In the Hindu tradition, the god-name Ra is also found in several guises. For example, Rama is the great (but metaphorical) solar avatar expressing the return of kosmic consciousness (like the barque of Ra in Egypt) to our solar system, while Bala-Rama (i.e., Ba-Lha-Rama)—chief god of the Nagas, or kosmic soul beings (Elohim)—is his astral-soul vehicle, which emanates from itself the thousand-headed serpent god Sesha, who holds back the great waters of kosmic Chaos until Indra (just like Horus) arrives to take command. The name Sesha is correspondingly found in Egypt as the goddess (Seshat) responsible for setting out the bounds of each temple prior to its construction and also expressing in her nature the sevenfold principle that was regarded as the basis of all subsequent Creation.

The Spread and
Decline of Ancient
Mystic Culture

247

Upon the arrival of the Jove-like Indra we find the appearance of Rudra (probably Urt-Ra originally) who gave rise to eleven sons—the Maruts—who became supporters of Indra, later becoming the ten Pranas plus Manas.[13] The whole concept is in fact an allegory of the spiritual creation of our solar system and its divine hierarchies, Rudra representing the auric sphere of the solar system and his eleven sons the number of years between the cyclical sunspots. The Maruts*—who were depicted as being responsible for holding apart the spheres of Heaven and Earth—are otherwise to be found as Merodach, the anglicized Marduk in the Chaldeo-Babylonian system. For the name of Merodach—who, like the Egyptian god Shu, separated the upper and lower firmaments from Chaos and created the world of light between them—is itself derived from Marut-Akh.

Other Southeast Asian Correspondences

We find similar distortions of Egyptian terminology—this time mixed up with Hindu religious (astronomically oriented) architecture—in Cambodia, at the great temple of Ankhor Wat, built (according to tradition) by the mysterious brotherhood of the Khmer.† As already commented upon by Graham Hancock and Santha Faia in their book *Heaven's Mirror*,[14] this temple name is obviously derived from the Egyptian Ankh-Hor, although it could be added that the Wat is just as clearly associated with the Egyptian Duat,‡ while the immediately adjacent and far larger temple enclosure known as Ankhor Thom is itself clearly derived from Ankh-Hor-Tum.

Transoceanic and Transcontinental Travel of Ancient Thought

Southeast Asia is of course two thousand miles east of Egypt, across the broad expanse of the Indian Ocean; it therefore seems less than likely, from the overriding Hindu style of the architecture and other mass religious associations, that the Egyptians were themselves directly involved in Ankhor Wat's aesthetic design. However, the linguistic and astronomical associations do show to what extent there evidently existed a shared cross-fertilization of metaphysical thought between the ancient Egyptians and the Indo-Caucasian peoples of the Indus Valley, where archaeological excavations at Mohenjo-Daro, for example, clearly indicate that their civilizations were contemporary as well as

---

*The name Marut is also found in the Islamic tradition as *marid,* the most powerful of the four classes of *djinn,* the latter word itself being found in the Japanese tradition as the suffix *jin,* meaning a "lesser god or guardian spirit."

†Found in India as the Kumaras (i.e., Khmer-Ra), and also in Crete.

‡While Duat is clearly dualistic and refers to the Underworld, Wat or Uat is just as clearly monistic and might thus be regarded as referring to the upper heaven world of the celestial vault.

being highly sophisticated in both astronomical and engineering terms. Thus we might well ask, "Which came first?"

There really can be little doubt that movement of both knowledge and commerce around the Indian Ocean and Asia generally in ancient times was very extensive. In confirmation of this, it was pointed out in *Land of the Fallen Star Gods* that mummified Egyptian corpses had been forensically proved to contain organically assimilated traces of silk[15]—clearly from China—while we now also know that China had its own pyramidal ziggurats, with specific astronomical orientations and associations, which again imply ancient cultural connections with Atlantean concepts. Baghdad was, of course, a major center on the old Silk Route to China at a time when it traversed the great Indo-Caucasian civilization that spread from eastern Anatolia to the Himalayas and right across northern India to the border with modern Burma.

Moving westward, however, it is fast becoming something of an accepted sport to show that the Americas were known to Europeans long before Columbus "discovered" them in 1492 CE. After many decades of scholarly insistence to the contrary, it is now generally accepted that the Vikings landed (and almost certainly traded) there a thousand years earlier, possibly even sailing down the coast as far as Central America, where the Aztec record indicates a tradition of blond, bearded Indo-Aryan visitors. Others of their compatriots were even then busy setting up trading stations in the east, on or close to the Black Sea—something also once thought thoroughly improbable. But bearing in mind that such wide-ranging experience would then have become common knowledge, it seems highly unlikely that it would not have been discussed with other traders interested in sharing their experiences of far-off lands and adventures. Hence we can surely speculate on reasonable foundations that a worldwide intercultural knowledge must have existed at a time unknown to modern scholars, although within the period of recorded history.

Notwithstanding this, there are plenty of other traditions indicating that transoceanic travel and relations were not uncommon in far more ancient times still. We now know, for example, that—steering by the stars and currents—the Polynesians crossed vast areas (literally thousands of miles) of the Pacific Ocean on quite large multi-hulled outrigger craft, while Phoenician sailor-traders operating from various cities around the Mediterranean, like Carthage and Tyre, appear to have circumnavigated Africa in its entirety. The Phoenicians certainly had the skills to cross the Atlantic—as well as having the ancient knowledge that a continent existed on the other side. However, the Brahmins of India have always insisted that their ancient forebears—many thousands of years before the Phoenicians—had sailed to every part of the world *and* had also accurately mapped it.

The oldest written traditions of the Indo-Aryan Hindus (such as the Puranas) also clearly demonstrate their knowledge of the many islands of the Atlantic and simultaneously confirm a tradition that a continent existed to the far west of them.[16] Consequently

The Spread and Decline of Ancient Mystic Culture

the practice and tradition of epic voyages of many months or even years can no longer seriously be considered a purely modern one and the dragged-out insistence of scholars that the issue is still unproven will undoubtedly continue to be shredded by further and better direct or circumstantial evidence, as time goes on, thereby demonstrating that the tradition of Atlantis's existence can no longer be seriously considered a mere fable.

Back to the Atlanteans

Bearing in mind the tradition that the island home of the latter-day northern Atlanteans (of Poseidonis and Iberia) had seemingly once been part of a much larger Atlantic continent, with colonies in the Americas, it is again virtually impossible that some associated traditions were not passed down to posterity amid associated folk memories. One such tradition—as we saw in the last chapter—that some of the emergent Caucasians had mixed directly with the Atlanteans and absorbed their culture itself further indicates that their own latter-day offspring—the Berbers, Guanche, Basques, and ancient Egyptians—must also have possessed such knowledge.

One is then forced to ask, how else could it have been that the priests of Sais, in their discussions with Solon, knew of historic traditions going back at least nine thousand years unless some traditional folk memory or recorded history had been maintained? How else would they have been able to teach Solon elements of the Atlantean language itself, as Plato tells us? Why is it that the very specific designation of such an ancient period coincided exactly with geologically known cataclysms in that immediate area? Why is it that the people of the Canary Islands *still* talk of their Guanche ancestral traditions as having been a part of Atlantis, prior to the main civilization disappearing in a huge cataclysm, which they believed to have destroyed all else on Earth too? Why does the neighboring Basque tradition follow suit? How is it that the countries of Central America contain so many place and other names commencing with the prefix *atl,* itself synonymous with the Welsh Celtic double *ll* prefix, as in Llandudno? And so on.

Egyptian Devotion to Absolute Accuracy

The fact of the Egyptians having retained 345 carved wooden statues,[*17] supposedly representing an unbroken succession of previous priestly hierophants, gives some small indication of just how assiduously careful the Egyptians were—even in latter-day times—to preserve and maintain an absolutely clear historic record of what had gone before. But this care was itself endemic and universally applied throughout Egyptian culture and civilization. The desire for exactitude is shown just as clearly, however, in the Hindu Brahmanic

---

*345 = 7 x 7 x 7 + 2, i.e., the total number of subplanes in the sevenfold kosmic system, plus an originating duality. Coincidence?

tradition, particularly in the formulation and expression of the ancient sacerdotal language, Sanskrit. Therefore, it is reasonable to assume that, in these two ancient traditions at least, we may treat what we hear and read with a high degree of probity and certitude as to probable accuracy.*

From the time of Egypt's original colonization (some one hundred thousand years ago), it would be reasonable to assume that the overall development of its culture (and its full separation from Atlantean culture) took quite a while to achieve—probably well over ten thousand years. Judging by the Saitic priests' indication that their historical records extended back over fifty-two thousand years in astronomical terms[18] and at least twenty thousand years in monarchical terms (according to the adjusted dynasties of Manetho), it would appear that we can safely go back at least thus far. But it is altogether impossible to hazard a guess at just how long it actually took to devise the thoroughly coherent and fully integrated mystical tradition. All we can speculate upon is that its form and content were clearly quite distinct from that of the Atlanteans, with their focus on Nature-magic. However, there are certain speculative ideas that we can draw from the linguistic side.

The hieroglyphic tradition appears to be of ancient Atlantean origin, shared as it was by both the Egyptians and the Mayan people of Central America. In the *later* Atlantean sub-races (of which the Chinese, Japanese, and Koreans appear to be but the last remaining vestiges) we find the hieroglyphic tradition losing its animalistic and artifactual orientation and taking on a much more abstract (almost shorthand) form—something that also appeared much later in the hieratic and demotic scripts of the Egyptians themselves. These variations continued with those modifications subsequently found in the (Sanskrit) Nagri script, which has a common upper line from which the ideographic letters are suspended—an esoteric metaphor for the underlying archetypal idea-forms suspended in common from the spirituo-causal plane of being and consciousness.[†]

The name Nagri is itself derived from the Sanskrit word *nag*,[‡] which—meaning "serpent"—also implies "soul." Because all knowledge was deemed to be provided by the

---

*It should nevertheless be remembered that the Ancients placed the highest importance on the use and accuracy of pure memory, by virtue of such self-discipline putting the individual in full control of his own subjective nature—an absolutely essential faculty in terms of facing the various trials of initiation into the Mysteries of the inner psychospiritual worlds of existence through which the neophyte or initiate had to pass.

†In the most ancient races of all—including the Australasian—the first real languages (like the click language of the Kalahari Bushmen and some of the natives of Borneo) were apparently agglutinative. That is to say, they comprised monosyllabically fixed and basic word-ideas stuck together in different sequences to convey different phrases or sentences revolving around the verb and the noun—only the latter, however, being of a qualitative nature. These linguistic ideas were then painted in simple pictures and patterns, first on rocks and later on loose fragments or tablets of stone. The cartouche surrounding the name (symbolic of the aurically enfolding soul-body) confirms a discriminating sense of mental organization and cultural sophistication.

‡*Nagal* was the name given to the chief magician in the Aztec/Mayan culture, as also in the Tibetan (Blavatsky, *The Secret Doctrine*, vol. 2, 213 et seq.). But the same root word is to be found in the Egyptian language as *nak*.

soul principle, the Nagri was created as an intentionally sacerdotal script from the outset and it thereby, of necessity, conformed to the rules of behavior of soul consciousness. Consequently, its highly structured form, complex grammar, and euphonic pronunciation are all absolutely balanced and harmoniously sequential in Nature—to a far greater degree than any occidental language of today.

Orientation of Egyptian Scripts

It is particularly interesting to note that the most sacred of the ancient Egyptian scripts—the hieroglyphic—was written both in horizontal lines and in columns, with the text itself beginning on either the right or left side of the page. In the case of the former, the pictographs all face to the right. In the case of the latter, they all face to the left. Hieratic texts, however, were written from right to left, although the hieroglyphs used had to be read from left to right.[19]

The main point of interest here, however, lies in the fact that the left side represented the Underworld or field of material existence, while the right side represented the spiritual world. Consequently, that which *faced* leftward and originated from the left was seemingly involved in leaving the mundane world behind and looking back toward it from the higher viewpoint of the psychospiritual worlds of consciousness. That which came from the right and faced right conversely concerned itself with issues oriented toward psychospiritual issues as seen from the world of progressively mundane existence. The Sanskrit Nagri script is written from left to right and has to be read in the same way—hence the

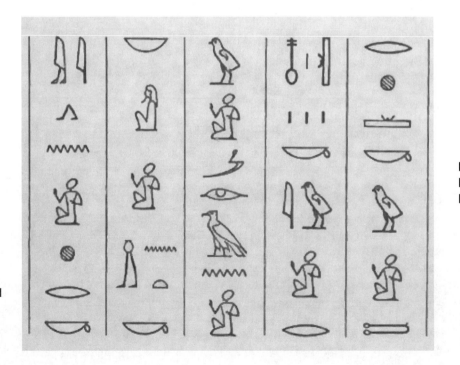

FIGURE 9.2. LEFT-FACING HIEROGLYPHS

fact that the European languages in general are written and read in the same fashion. Semitic scripts, on the other hand, are still written and read from right to left, with no distinctions as to subjective or objective orientation. The Atlantean-based hieroglyphic script, however (as found in the Chinese and Japanese), is written in columnar form, read from the top of each column downward and then, in sequence, from right to left.

Occidental Language Associations

When we come to the Indo-European languages, we find a far more fluid sense of ordered structure and priority, with the verb (i.e., the action) now becoming highly qualitative as well in its expression. As a direct result, the whole language style is far more colorfully unstable. The Hamitic language (that used by the Egyptians, the Berber, and the Guanche people of the Canary Islands), however, appears to lie somewhere in between, this probably being due to a prehistoric fusion of the Hamitic and Sanskrit *within* the Atlanto-Caucasian culture. Unfortunately, the Guanche were virtually wiped out genocidally by Spanish invasion and settlement in the sixteenth century, while the Berber tongue is even now being gradually stamped out by the cultural myopia of Arabic-speaking society in northwest Africa. What therefore now otherwise remain are the closely related Semitic language subtypes spoken by Arabs and Jewish people, although only the latter seem to have retained any associated sense of its sacred aspects and uses. Fortuitously, these have been passed down to European scholars and thus not entirely lost, while the Hebrew rabbinic tradition itself (through greater concern with politico-social issues) appears gradually to be losing interest in such arcane aspects of its own culture.

Architectural Comparisons

In the last chapter, we took a brief look at the high importance of magical ritual in the religion of the Atlanteans, something that has been passed down among the Berber people of northwest Africa in the form of intense superstition in every single aspect of life. In relation to religious culture, it appears likely that the Atlanteans were the first to build pyramid-shaped ziggurats, some fine examples of which are still to be seen in Central America and northern South America, in addition to the ruins in ancient Mesopotamia and much smaller versions in the Canary Islands.

The ziggurat, or stepped pyramid, was clearly intended as an invocatively devotional structure, oriented toward the idea of solar or sidereal worship as far as the populace was concerned (but additionally toward astronomy and astrology as far as the initiated priesthood were concerned), and probably using fire and light to great theatrical effect. The very psychological effect of the neophyte or initiate having to climb laboriously heavenward in purely physical terms was undoubtedly intended to provide a deep

The Spread and
Decline of Ancient
Mystic Culture

253

FIGURE 9.3. THE ZIGGURAT, OR STEPPED PYRAMID, OF TEOTIHUACAN
(Photo by Gustavo Von)

psychological impression of what had to be achieved in parallel subjectivity—hence the fact that the numbers of steps were to be found in multiples of seven. The angled nature of climb might also well be directly relatable to the angle of the ecliptic path our solar system follows around the zodiac—thus providing a (macro)cosmic as well as a purely personal side to this imagery.

Bearing in mind what we have already suggested about Egyptian influence possibly having had an input in the astronomical layout of the Cambodian temple complex at Ankhor Wat, it seems not impossible that it was also involved in similar manner with the layout of Teotihuacan, which is almost a carbon copy of Giza in certain respects. As indicated in *Land of the Fallen Star Gods,* this name appears to be derived from the compound Tehuti-Vahan,[20] which would make the Egyptian involvement an absolute certainty, even though these are ziggurats. Whatever the truth is concerning this matter, only the Egyptians appear to have extended the pyramid concept to produce smoothly shaped exteriors such as those at Giza, even though those at Dasshur and Saqqara are of a somewhat different shape and type. While the Egyptian pyramid, with its geometrically positioned internal passageways and chambers, was surely dedicated to complete introversion of the invocative religious idea and to the function of initiation via the concentrated influence of specific stars (as we shall see in a later chapter), it is interesting to note that neither the Chaldeans nor the Chinese nor the Indo-Aryan peoples of the Indus Valley appear to have followed suit in quite the same way. Quite why this should be so is not apparent.

The Egyptian mystic tradition—notwithstanding its scientific and engineering knowledge—was as deeply embedded in ritual as its parent culture. And that ritualized form of endeavor and expression (specifically associated with architecture) was handed down in more modern times in the Masonic tradition, principally via the Romans. But before we examine that area more closely, we shall take a brief look at the "Neolithic" mound builders and the Judaic tradition.

The Ancient Mound Builders of Europe and North America

Archaeologists have rather taken the view that the mounds found particularly extensively in Ireland and North America were a sort of unevolved or "poor man's" pyramid and that the real ziggurats and pyramids were but their later and more sophisticated counterparts. This, we suggest, is quite wrong, for the mound quite clearly had a rather different genesis and orientation, which appears first of all in recorded history in the vesica piscis shape found in the mound of Tum (in Egypt), the Eye of Ra/Horus (again in Egypt), and the body of Tiamat (Babylonia).

While there is no denying that the interior of the mounds was used for purposes of initiation and (much later) for actual burials—particularly of tribal kings—the essence of the idea was that it was within the mound that light first appeared and thus that objective Creation began. Bearing in mind that the fallen *akh/asura*/Man-angel was deemed to take on a primordial soul-body of light, which thus esoterically became its tomb or sarcophagus, and that this light was emanated from the eye of the Deity, it is not difficult to follow the mental association that led to the tribal king being returned, at death, to his point of origin in what became a burial chamber.* However, this was actually a distortion of the original metaphysical meaning of the structure and its use—in conjunction with astronomical cycles and sympathetic magic—which involved putting the neophyte or initiate into a state of isolation necessary for his consciousness to achieve or regain a direct spiritual contact or focus.

Some of the mounds to be found in both Ireland and the Americas are truly huge—the size of literal hills—and one tradition at least has it that these were actually of Atlantean origin. This is notwithstanding the fact that much smaller mounds were still apparently being built under ten thousand years ago. As the background metaphysical concept is a timeless one, however, this is perhaps not altogether surprising. But it has significant

---

*The scores of graves (*mastabas*) found in the immediate vicinity of the Giza pyramids undoubtedly owe their provenance to exactly the same sort of distorted psychology—involving a mixture of wishful thinking and attempts at sympathetic magic.

effects in throwing a very different light on the course of assumed prehistory to that popularly accepted and propounded by most archaeologists.

The Judaic Mystic Tradition

The religion of Judaism is actually only about 2,500 years old, and it was the result (based upon political necessity) of a cobbled-together mass of Chaldeo-Babylonian and Egyptian metaphysical concepts and Creation myths rather than having any truly independent existence of its own. However, the following skeletal outline of certain of the main metaphysical ideas that the founders selected indicates that there was, at some preceding time, a definite sense of an esoteric relationship existing between the civilizations and cultures of the Tigris-Euphrates Valley and the Nile.

Leaving aside the Creation story in Genesis, which has to do with the noumenal sequence of unfoldment of the kosmos of our local universe as a whole, we move straight to the allegorical story of Abram (A-Brahm—the outgoing Will of the Deity) leaving the city of Ur, following receipt of instructions from God (i.e., the Elohim).[21] Ur means "primordial," and here it appears specifically related to the circumpolar constellation of either Ursa Minor or Ursa Major. The story also has it that Ur was built by the descendants of the great hunter Nimrod (almost certainly derived from the compounded Egyptian names Khnum-'Urt), who clearly represents the kosmic Demiurge and who also seems to have been associated with the constellation of Orion.

This latter move thus actually represents a (cyclical) fall into the world of kosmic objectivity—which was naturally sevenfold. In confirmation of that we find Abram being married to his half-sister Sara,* who has already been married six times before (!), and thereafter becoming A-Braham, or Abiramu[22]—possibly derived from Hpi-Ram(u). He cannot immediately produce a primary heir through Sara (the kosmic Mother aspect), so he instead fathers a first son, Ishmael (i.e., As-Mah-El, meaning "great lord of demiurgic being"), with the bondmaid Hagar (derived from Heka—i.e., magic), who represents the lower world scheme. Only subsequently is he able to produce a second son, Isaac (As-akh), with Sara herself, despite her (metaphorically) advanced age of ninety years[23]—yet another metaphor involving the cyclical movement of the six decans of a celestial scheme. Ishmael and Isaac thus respectively represent the Elohim and the *akhu* of our local universe.†

Isaac marries Rebecca and she duly produces the twins Jacob (the Judaic Jahkubel, being derived from Iaho-Bel) and Esau (A-Sah, perhaps), this duality representing the

---

*Sara is a name meaning "union" or "confluence," as in the Hindu goddess name Sarasvati, the wife of Brahma.
†In confirmation of which, Isaac is none other than our old friend Akh-As (i.e., *akasa*) merely reversed. Consequently, we can see quite clearly that Ishmael's apparent banishment into the "desert" is actually no more than an allegory of the fact that this principle—i.e., the demiurgic hierarchies—remains in its divine heaven world, outside the solar sphere of manifestation where the action is.

two aspects of our solar system—the Sun at its center and its outer auric heaven world. Thus Esau is himself described as "red and hairy," while Jacob was "a smooth man." Jacob, although born second, esoterically (with the aid of his mother) robs his brother of his birthright by taking subjective precedence in the solar system. Later on he fights with the angel of the Lord and prevails, thereafter being given the name Israel—seemingly derived from either As'r-El or As-Ra-El. His thigh is damaged in the fight by the angel and he thereafter has a pronounced limp[24]—an allegory seemingly related to the constellation of Ursa Major (the Thigh) and its looping orbital movement around Ursa Minor. He then marries and produces twelve sons—a reference to the sevenfold (involutionary and evolutionary) planes of being within our solar scheme, which themselves have a direct correlation with the zodiacal Duat. Of the twelve sons, one (Joseph—from Jah-Suf) becomes specifically associated with Egypt (the lowest of the seven solar planes), over which he takes temporal control as the pharaoh's chief vizier.[25]

The Mystic Kabbalah

The Old Testament being of an almost entirely allegorical nature, one could go on and on with these esoteric interpretations. However, we shall instead look briefly at Judaism's gnostic tradition—that of the (originally Chaldean) Kabbalah—and note what Egyptian correspondences we can find there too. In fig. 9.4 (page 258), therefore, we see the normal layout of the kabbalistic tree. However, it is shown here as enclosed within a triple aura, which corresponds with the universally held ancient concept of seven states of being/ Creation held within an enfolding (triple) soul nature—the three lower planes of the kosmic universe. In relation to the latter, the word Ain is the same as the Greek Aeon (meaning the god of duration), while Soph—from which we have the Greek Sophia—is actually derived from the Persian *suf,* meaning "divine breath"—thus the Sufi tradition. *Aur* is probably associated with the Egyptian root word *her* or *hor.*

Although kabbalists usually pay great attention to the "lightning flash" progression between the various *sephira,* the diagram shown here describes two interfacing spheres of existence of being—thus producing between them the triplicity of Spirit-Soul-Matter with which we are perhaps more familiar. It also simultaneously depicts the seven kosmic states within the system, thereby very elegantly combining several different metaphysical concepts (not all mentioned here) within an overall dynamic unity. Within the seven planes shown in the diagram, we have a number of other Egyptian associations. For example, Kether is the same as Kheper(a), the self-generating god principle. Geburah is equivalent to Geb-Ra, and Da'at would appear to be synonymous with Ta'Urt. Chokmah is a straightforward combination of Shu-Kumar(a), and Netsah—the "woven body of light"—is arrived at from a combination of the Egyptian goddess of weaving (Net/Neith) and *sah,* meaning the spiritual soul-body.

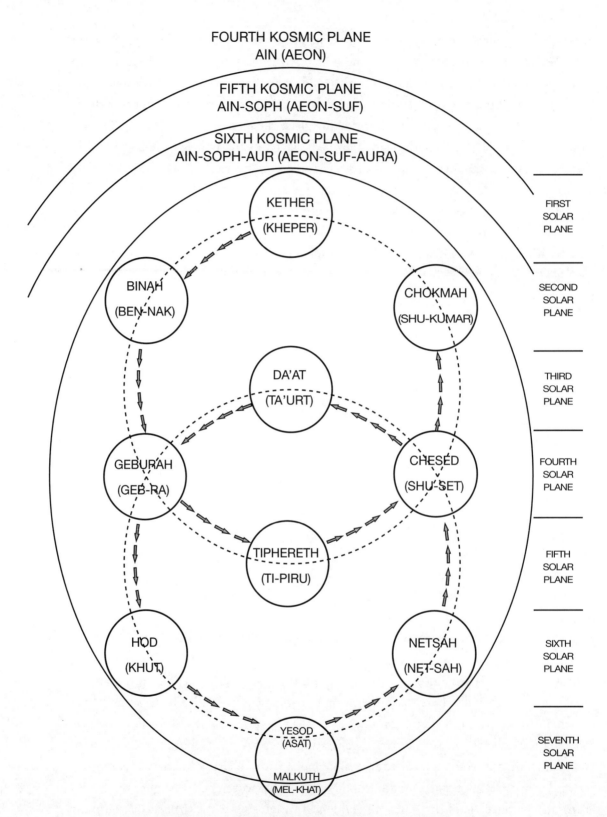

FIGURE 9.4. EGYPTIAN RELATIONSHIPS IN THE KABBALAH

Freemasonry and Its Origins

Modern Masonic tradition (of the last millennium) has a dual nature, inasmuch as its orientation has become split between those who practiced the merely theoretical aspect (the "speculative Masons") and those who—as architects, surveyors, and building artisans of various types and skills—practiced "the Craft" in their daily working lives (as "operative Masons"). While the former are a relatively modern phenomenon, appearing among the social milieu of English gentlemen in the mid-seventeenth/early eighteenth century, the latter—who provided them with the foundation for their ideas—had roots clearly going back to their forebears, the architect-surveyors and craftsmen of Egypt. But to understand how this actually came about, we have to pursue a little more history, as follows.

Although the Greeks probably drew the inspiration for their Ionic and Doric architecture from the Egyptians and had it designed and built by their own (Egyptian-trained) "Dionysian architects," it was Roman civilization that spread the associated knowledge even farther northward. In the first place the Roman army followed the Greeks in taking over the mastery of Egypt in the wake of the followers of Alexander the Great, some two thousand years ago, long after its decline had commenced in the third millennium BCE. While the Greeks were great builders of classical architecture for themselves, the Roman military were great civil engineers and administrative organizers (like the Egyptians), and their empire spread a great deal farther across Europe as well as right around the Mediterranean. As a consequence, their construction professionals not only picked up a great deal of highly useful architectural and engineering-related knowledge while in Egypt;* they also inevitably picked up much of the associated ritual and *some* of the accompanying knowledge concerning the initiatory process.

The Circulation of Sacred Masonic Knowledge

Because of the wide and constant circulation of military personnel that took place within the Roman Empire, the construction knowledge and ritual of the Craft, plus the associated structure of the Brotherhood of the Craft, not only passed back to Rome itself but also traveled to the wider outposts of the Roman Empire, including Spain and Gaul, as well as Britain. The Romans used that knowledge to construct their great municipal buildings—principally in Rome—but with the gradual dissolution of the empire in the wake of invasions by the Goths, Huns, and so on, and the decreasing availability of funds, the practical need of the skills diminished quite radically and reoriented itself around maintenance and repair rather than much new construction—except in the building of monasteries and small churches for the growing religion of Christianity.

---

*Hence the first great modern literary masterwork of classical architectural theory and design produced by the Roman Vitruvius.

It was not until the wealth of Byzantium (principal city of the eastern empire) began to filter back to western Europe via the merchants of Venice and the Knights Templar that things began to change, for a fascination with ancient knowledge also accompanied the treasure trove. This occurred not only through the agency of the Knights Templar—who constructed their own buildings of increasing size and grandeur—but also due to the influence of the old sacred knowledge passing simultaneously through their hands and through the new (Moorish) universities in Spain. It appears then to have been the fusion of the two influences, coming from east and west respectively, that led directly to the sudden eruption of classic (Gothic) cathedral architecture in France, under the Compagnonnages of operative Masons[26]—a name that immediately resonates with the Companions of Horus, the "master Masons" of ancient Egypt.

The Factor of Jewish Influence

Due to the influential involvement of Jewish scholars in the early translation and understanding of ancient metaphysical texts—remembering that their own Semitic language had itself been evolved from the Hamito-Semitic, which was then still generally in use among the Berber and Moorish peoples—the Masonic tradition of today does tend to have (in places) a decidedly Old Testament flavor.* However, the material is quite definitely of Hermetic-Egyptian or Atlanto-Egyptian origin. We can confirm this from the use in Masonic ritual of a whole variety of esoteric metaphors, including the following few:

1. The term Great Architect of the Universe (G.A.O.T.U.).
2. The All-Seeing Eye of the Deity (i.e., of Ra, or Ptah).
3. The allegory of cutting and polishing the *ashlar* (from *as* and *lha*), a metaphor for the development of spiritual individuality and character in man, derived from the previously amorphous spiritual nature of elemental existence in Nature—symbolized by the geological rock mass.
4. Although now regarded as of late origin, one of the most important Masonic mottos is *Ordo ab Chao* (Order from Chaos).[27]
5. A Masonic Lodge is regarded as an Ark, a repository of wisdom and secrets.[28] This, however, is clearly the Egyptian *akh* and not the Mosaic form of *ark* (although the

---

*One should remember that the Jewish merchants who traveled the Mediterranean area in early historic times were actually expatriate Indo-Persian Phoenicians—i.e., Punicians, originally from Pun(t). By virtue of having major trading operations based at Tyre in Palestine, in Egypt itself, and at Carthage (where they were known as Pani or Peoni), they were closely involved in linguistic and trading terms not only with the indigenous peoples of the whole southern Mediterranean area, including the Mahgreb—where we find the Berbers and Moors—but also with the Templars themselves. In *A Dictionary of Hinduism* (Stutley and Stutley, 219), we find the Pani described as a merchant class of caravan traders (despised by the Brahmins), who in one tradition came from Babylonia and whose descendants were the Phoenicians.

FIGURE 9.5. EYE OF RA

latter was undoubtedly derived from the same metaphor in a kosmic context).

6. The use of the Hiramic legend, another allegory related to the Spiritual Ego in man, which is overpowered by man's lower three aspects—the physical, astral, and mental natures—depicted metaphorically by the "three hired apprentices," the fellow craftsmen who "killed" Hiram*—himself a distorted version of Horus, that is, as Her(u)-a—the head of the Dionysian Architects.[29]

7. The use of a sarcophagus or coffin from which the Master Mason is "raised up" from the dead.

8. All Master Masons are esoterically known as Sons of a Widow, the symbolic meaning being that they are initiated Heru (Heroes), children of the astral soul (the *ba*, symbolized by Isis) that bore them.

9. The use of two pillars, one of which is "broken," corresponding with the fallen or leaning Djed Pillar of the Egyptians.

There is a great deal of further association between the ancient Egyptian mystic tradition and the Masonic tradition, in both historical and ritual terms.† One such example

---

*The "three hired apprentices" in the Masonic tradition were supposed to have killed Hiram with three artifacts corresponding with their respective trades—the plumb, the level, and the hammer. They, however, respectively represented the characteristics of the elements of air, water, and earth, and also of the three corresponding lowest solar planes of consciousness—the mental, astral, and physical. In addition, Hiram was hit by them at each of the three doors to the temple, which reinforces the point concerning the inbuilt esoteric metaphor. The three apprentices thus merely represent the triple personality nature of human consciousness, which indeed appears to "slay" the guiding Spiritual Ego—the true "Master Mason."

†The Masonic degrees of initiation are themselves derived from the concept of an achieved freedom from the various states of material existence in the septenary scheme of things. Thus the modern Master Mason is "raised up" (from "the dead") at the 3°—which represents the third plane of solar matter (counting upward), synonymous with the Egyptologist's fifth division and the Mind state. However, there is a further progression in the same line, for the 33° in the Ancient and Accepted Rite series of initiations clearly refers to the final conquering of the four lower septenary states of solar matter, *plus* five substates of the fifth ($4 \times 7 + 5 = 33$). Thus this supremely advanced initiate would have been deemed to have overcome the five solar elements in their five dimensions as a whole and thus to have achieved the status of a self-conscious demigod. Today's appropriation of these same later ritual degrees shows just how far ignorance as to their real nature has prevailed over ancient knowledge.

involves the word *cowan,* used by Scottish Masons to describe the (junior) administrator of one of their lodges. This is actually a distorted version of the original Shu-khan (prince of light), which became *chokhan* in the Tibetan tradition, *chohan* (adept teacher) in the Egyptian—as Herodotus confirms[30]—and *cohen* (the priestly sect) in the Hebrew.

Interestingly, the original sacred meaning of the term itself seems to have become distorted among Masons quite some time ago, for the *cowan,* who was responsible for the cutting of the rough blocks of stone—a metaphor for the *chohan's* responsibility for selecting and gathering from the general mass those intended for the Path of Initiation—latterly became a very junior member of the Masonic Lodge. However, our attention must now turn to the actual decline of Egyptian mystic culture and civilization, or rather, to the reasons behind it.

The Beginnings of Corruption and Decline

It is obviously rather difficult to put one's finger on the actual moment or period of the beginning of the decline of any culture or civilization, and it is all too easy to attribute such decline to foreign invasion or influence, although these certainly began in Egypt during the second millennium BCE. However, coming at it from a somewhat different angle, we can perhaps suggest a few pointers that seem to indicate fundamental changes taking place in spiritual attitudes, in far earlier times. To begin with, we shall follow the assumption that the decline began after the last of Manetho's demigods and adept-heroes had handed over the governance of the country to mortal rulers—or rather, to lesser initiates—something in the order of six thousand years ago, around the time of the change from the Age of Gemini to the Age of Taurus. Such a handover would, of course, have been one of great moment, fraught with some anxieties on the part of the inexperienced new regime, by virtue of lacking the spiritual insights and other powers of their mentors. Even so, what probably happened involved the adept-teachers themselves taking an advisory backseat rather than merely disappearing altogether from the scene.

Bearing in mind that Zen masters and highly advanced yogis or rishis of this last millennium seem to have adopted a common policy of retiring to monasteries and other secluded places well away from general public gaze, in order to carry on their work for humanity at large behind the scenes, it seems not altogether unlikely that the origins of this approach had their genesis around the same time as the Egyptian handover took place—not just in Egypt, however, but also in Chaldea. The suggested reasons for the handover were explained at greater length in *Land of the Fallen Star Gods,*[31] but in general terms it would appear that it had to do with allowing mankind its own period (corresponding with the due astrological cycle) of learning how to take full responsibility *for* itself, largely *by* itself. After all, to have mankind governed directly by gods, demigods, and heroes all the time would make any sort of general spiritual evolution ultimately impossible. To learn and understand the self-discipline necessary to achieve spiritual adeptship and the leaving behind of the limited human nature, it was of course necessary to experience what self-rule was all about.

Three of the original cultural traditions that appear to have been extant at the time of the handover involved (a) the cremation of all dead bodies, (b) the morganatic succession of the royal family of Egypt, and (c) exclusion of all males from the ownership of landed property.* With regard to the former, Egyptologists have found no mummies of a period earlier than the Third Dynasty of the Old Kingdom (almost certainly due to the general practice at that time being that of cremation, as in the clearly related ancient Brahmanic tradition of the Hindus).†

The Practice of Mummification

Now mummification is a practice not generally found as such in the Middle or Far East, except among the Sufis and Tibetans, who reserve the practice solely for their high initiates, regarded as saints, believing that the dead body form must retain at least some of its holiness and associated power of automatic linkage with the heaven world. It has been confirmed, however, as common among the Guanche people of the Canary Islands (believed by some to be the descendants of Poseidonis, Plato's island of Atlantis) and also in parts of northern South America. It thus remains a moot question as to where this imported tradition actually came from. One possibility—derived from the suggestion that the demigods and heroes (i.e., high initiates) had by this time apparently retired to seclusion from public life—is that the custom was imported in order to maintain a Sufi-type sequential linkage with the spiritual world of existence through the person of the (now purely human) pharaoh. But this is pure speculation.

It follows that if such forms of spiritual uncertainty or inadequacy (plus political

---

*All landed property descended strictly in the female line from mother to daughter (Murray, *The Spendour That Was Egypt,* 100). The deliberately disenfranchised males were thus perpetually reminded that their role in both the family and society at large was a *spiritual* one and not one in which considerations of material ownership should become their concern.

†As the Egyptologist Margaret Murray (*The Spendour That Was Egypt,* 185) tells us: "Mummification was introduced into Egypt in the IIIrd dynasty as also the building of mastabas for the nobility. These traditions arrived complete." It is interesting that no mummies from the Old Kingdom have ever been found—almost certainly because the Egyptians had previously practiced cremation. Egyptologists now believe that from about 2250 BCE (i.e., the commencement of the Middle Kingdom of Egypt) the democratization of funerary beliefs and practices, supposedly guaranteeing the individual an afterlife, resulted in wealthy members of society outside the nobility gaining access to these ritual concepts. Thus the details of the original sacred texts became accessible to a wider spectrum of Egyptian society, and seem also to have been added to, eventually resulting in their subsequent use—in conjunction with those (perhaps later) texts known to us as the Coffin Texts and the Book of the Dead—for purely funerary purposes.

corruption) became current at the very highest levels of Egyptian society, then the disease would automatically have been passed down via succeeding generations to the rest of the body of Egyptian society. And this is precisely what seems to have happened, for with the change to a male succession in the royal line, we also find the practice of mummification extending first to other members of the royal family, then (doubtless as a special honor) to members of the aristocracy and the royal court, and so on, until, in the final absurd analysis, in the much later dynasties of the New Kingdom, every Tum, Dick, and Heru who could afford it had variously elaborate forms of mummification and associated ritual organized for their own funeral—and those of pet animals too! Sic transit gloria demimonde.

The Issue of Dynastic Succession

In the case of the royal succession—originally through the female line of the royal household—each new king appears to have been chosen from among the *piru*, the initiated (spiritual) "peers of the realm." His eldest daughter by the queen—who was herself the eldest daughter of the preceding king—then became next in line to the throne, and so on. The name *pharaoh* (itself derived from *piru*) as king of Egypt is not to be found in the earliest records.* However, the spiritual quality of the *piru* had evidently declined quite quickly after the purely mortal kings had taken over, because by about the Fifth Dynasty, the kingly succession had already begun to pass directly from father to son.

It is perhaps worthwhile commenting in passing that the whole point of the original form of succession and heredity of landed property was that it was seen to follow a similar general principle in universal Nature. The female principle was that which generated and guaranteed continuity of type or form and it therefore represented the soul. The male principle, on the other hand, represented the "divine spark" (the Osiris nature), itself expressing the revitalizing evolutionary Purpose of the Deity. As a consequence, it was essential that the king was specifically chosen by the *piru* from among themselves (rather like the selection of a new Pope in the Roman Catholic Church)—perhaps confirming the personal choice of the last king himself. Only in this way could the highest spiritual quality of kingship be guaranteed, along with the maintenance of a perpetual link between the land of Egypt and the spiritual state of being in which the gods and demigods were to be found. Similarly, as women were seen as representing the principle of continuity in Nature, with the male principle being the source of all natural

---

*The (plural) term *piru* appears to be derived from a Sanskrit root *p(i)r*, as in *p(u)rusha* (i.e., *piru-sha*, meaning "pure spiritual being"). *Sha* (hence the Indo-Persian god-king, the Shah) is the singular form of Shu, the Egyptian god of light. Thus the *piru* were perfected spiritual beings, capable of self-generating and wielding the energy and force of light itself. Interestingly, Herodotus (*The Histories*, 150) confirms that in his time (second century BCE) the high priest was called a *piromis*—a term clearly derived from *piru-meskh*, the initiate-uniter of different qualities of light-being. The term is found in English among the old nobility as "peers of the realm."

aggression, property interests were very sensibly taken out of male ownership altogether.

Other forms of corruption also followed in the wake of popularization of the mummification process and acceptance of dynastic nepotism. Among other things, Ra lost his position (to Osiris) as the defining senior deity in the cycle of life and death. Along with the growing fascination with death and a cozily happy afterlife existence that seems to have overtaken the peoples of the New Kingdom dynasties, the funerary arrangements and accoutrements became ever more elaborate. For example, *ushabtis* were placed among the funerary wrappings, along with sundry magical spells or invocations, in order to enable the deceased to recruit a variety of elemental entities to do any necessary work on his behalf in the spirit world.

Pharaonic Vainglory and Administrative Laziness

Yet another form of spiritual corruption that began to take place occurred in the form of the defacing (by alteration) of sacred hieroglyphs on public monuments by succeeding pharaohs for the purpose of their own self-aggrandizement and glorification. Such a practice would have been completely unthinkable on the part of the original rulers of Egypt, whose concerns were held (of spiritual necessity) to be completely impersonal. To have altered that which was true is fundamentally dishonest. And as dishonesty intrinsically involves the corruption of spiritual self-discipline, the very act would have set a precedent throughout Egyptian society, thus encouraging all sorts of moral decay and carelessness in its wake.* Such activity had reached rampant proportions by the time of Rameses II (ludicrously accepted by Egyptologists as a great pharaoh from his own court's written records), who seems to have had it done extensively on his own behalf, particularly at Abu Simbel and Thebes—although, rather interestingly, not at Giza.

From the later Old Kingdom period onward, we find Egypt becoming increasingly rich and wealth-oriented through international trade and territorial aggrandizement; as this wealth grew, so the offerings to the temples became more and more lavish until, by the New Kingdom period, the priesthood was the wealthiest class in the land. As such forms of largesse are themselves a clear indication of the growing reorientation of social values away from the abstractly religious to the profoundly material, it is not altogether surprising to find corruption as an immediate by-product. A close parallel in more modern times is to be found in the growth of the monasteries in England in the wake of the Crusades and of the Church in Spain in the wake of the discoveries of the New World treasures across the Atlantic.

Egyptologists are already well aware of the fact that the Old Kingdom came to a

---

*The later priestly scribes clearly failed to understand the real importance of the sacred hieroglyphs because, as Budge (*The Egyptian Book of the Dead,* xxviii et seq.) confirms, by the intermediate dynasties they were making mistakes in copying old texts, which originally would never have been allowed.

very sudden end, supposedly around 2250 BCE, the reason for this generally being considered as very probably due to political machination—although there is insufficient evidence as yet to confirm this beyond doubt. However, it appears that there were also severe droughts affecting the country at that time—very probably coinciding with the change from the Age of Taurus to the Age of Aries and the end of the prolonged climatic wet cycle of some six thousand years, which had, for millennia, allowed many surrounding desert areas to flourish, thereby making possible widespread savannah farming. The fact that administrative degeneracy was also taking place on the political scene cannot have helped to alleviate matters or to encourage the population as a whole to pull together for the benefit of all.

There are also some current archaeological suggestions that the Faiyum lakes at this time had been allowed to fall far below their normal safe levels, with the consequent result that farming in Lower Egypt suffered catastrophically from lack of adequate irrigation, on which the people's very livelihoods depended. Consequently, severe famines occurred and general political paralysis led to invasion of the Delta area by Hyksos tribes who had journeyed all the way from northeastern Indo-Persia. All these depredations led to a complete change in the ruling pharaonic family setup, and with the dawning of the intermediate dynasties, it appears that father-to-son succession in the royal line became fully institutionalized. At the same time the whole structure and organization of Egyptian upper class and political life appears to have undergone a fundamental change as well.

The Intermediate and New Kingdom Dynastic Period

During the First Intermediate Period, it appears that the various provincial governors of Egypt became princes, while most of the legal and financial duties of the pharaoh became delegated to a grand vizier acting as his deputy. Consequently, these functions, which previously had a mystic association as well as a social one, became purely administrative and political in nature. The intensely personal relationship of the pharaoh with the people of Egypt continued until the arrival of the Greeks, who made the state the owner and political supervisor of the whole country, with the pharaoh taking the role of a mere chief executive. As a result, there developed a huge bureaucracy and the whole mystic-religious system progressively fell apart through lack of a common and continuing sense of communal involvement between the governors and the governed.

As previously suggested, with the example of the greatest self-discipline and spiritual humility at the top of Egyptian society, the unquestioning response of the Egyptian public at large to the following of ritual in all areas of life and to equally unconscious moral rectitude followed as a matter of automatic instinct. It was only when spiritual indiscipline and self-indulgence were allowed to creep in at the top of their society that the whole structure and fabric of Egyptian society began to fall apart—hence the extraordinarily prophetic words of Hermes Trismegistus:

> O Egypt, Egypt, of thy religion nothing will remain but an empty tale which thine own children in time will not come to believe; nothing will be left but graven words and only the stones will tell of thy piety. And in that day, men will be weary of life and they will cease to think the universe worthy of reverent wonder and of worship. . . . As to the soul and the belief that it is immortal by nature, or may hope to attain to immortality, as I have taught you—all this they will mock at and will even persuade themselves that it is false.[32]

Over the period of the next two millennia, we find the progressively complete disintegration of Egyptian civilization and culture through a mixture of internal political intrigue and invasion (of and from other countries—from both north and south), concluding with the Macedonian Greeks and the Romans. Thereafter, with the rise of Islam in the seventh and eighth centuries, Mohammedanism—along with the westward migration of increasing numbers of ethnic Arabs—spread like wildfire westward across northern Africa, finally sealing the fate of the last vestiges of the ancient Egyptian Mysteries, until rescued by Sufi influence and thence transmitted (in part) to Europe via the Templars and the Moorish universities in Spain, which were open to Muslims, Jews, and Christians alike. This fortunately happened before the advent of the Turkish Ottoman Empire, which completely suffocated any form of spiritual vitality for centuries, before it too was driven out by the French and British in the nineteenth and early twentieth centuries.

The Orphans of Ancient Egyptian Mystic Tradition

Notwithstanding these depredations, one finds the threads of ancient Egyptian mystic thought—albeit in somewhat distorted garb—surviving in other cultures long after its own national demise, as, for example, in the Mandaean sect, which seems to have originated in Jordan and then migrated in the second century CE to southern Mesopotamia (present-day Iraq). As Yuri Stoyanov tells us in his excellent and highly readable recent work *The Other God,* the Mandaeans were gnostics with a pronounced dualist culture in which "the creation of the world and man was seen as the work of a demiurge, Ptahil, who was originally a light being but came to cooperate with the demonic spirits of the 'Master of Darkness' and was consequently banished from the Lightworld. As the body of Adam was motionless, his soul was brought from the Lightworld to animate it."[33]

There are in fact two Egyptian traditions here, melded into one. First of all, Ptahil is (after allowing for the addition of the Arab *el* as a suffix) none other than Ptah, who certainly cooperated with the curly-horned Khnemu, god of the cataract, to create and animate the forms of the kosmic Underworld. In addition, Ptah was himself known as the dark god (like Khem) because his primary remit was from the Unseen Logos (hence the Master of Darkness), whose noumenal existence placed him above and beyond the merely sidereal universe. Second, "the motionless body of Adam," which had to be reanimated by his returning soul being brought from the Lightworld, is clearly none other than the Egyptian Osiris.

The preoccupation of the Mandaeans with the soul's journey back up through the demon-infested upper spheres before it reentered the Lightworld is itself a virtual carbon copy of the Egyptian metaphysical perception—as also of the Tibetan. Mandaeism, however, somehow managed to produce within itself an inimical dualism between the later and actually historical figures of John the Baptist and Jesus in which the former was seen as the messenger of the King of the Lightworld, whereas Jesus was merely "a kind of apostate Mandaean, facing the trial of purgatory."[34]

Also during the second to third centuries CE we find an early and evolving Christian theology that, although almost entirely imported from Egyptian Coptic sources—themselves by then already based upon a very partial and merely Osirian tradition of the god figure risen from human death (involving the lesser Egyptian Mysteries)—was already developing its own distorted and apocalyptic versions of esoteric tradition and ritual. Fighting what sometimes appeared to be a losing battle with neo-Platonism and Hermeticism—themselves true and gnostic forms of the same ancient wisdom tradition followed by the early Egyptians—Christianity proved the victor purely because of Constantine's use of it as a political tool to bring to heel the chaos being caused in the Roman Empire (and Rome itself, particularly) by a proliferation of mystic sects, which had already undermined the religious basis of Roman culture that itself gave sanctity to the administrative and social tenure of the emperor and the Senate.

Other Examples of Distortion of Original Ancient Concepts

According to Origen, one of the early Christian bishops, the revived souls of the dead—following the Last Judgment—would have an ethereal, spherical body form.[35] This, clearly repeating the ancient Egyptian concept (as carried forward by Hermeticists), was condemned by the Church Fathers of the time as heresy—probably because it too closely matched the dreaded spiritual independence of neo-Platonic concepts with which the politically fixated Church had already had to do battle. Much later on, in the twelfth century CE, we find a recrudescence of the common pre-Christian teaching found throughout the Middle East as to man having two souls—the *ba* and the *sah* of the Egyptians. The idea was clearly carried forward by the Bogomils in their teachings, for in 1140 CE a synod at Constantinople (modern Istanbul) posthumously anathematized the monk Constantine Chrysomalus for just such a "heretical" concept.[36]

In these cameos, therefore, we have a perfect example of the way in which new mystic traditions arise out of the partial or amalgamated and serial distortions of misunderstood earlier traditions, often in combination with more recent bits of local history, in order to fit and support a modern conceptual theory that, however, lacks anything like the same depth as the original metaphysical concept. Many so-called New Age theories today generate themselves from the same technique. Intervening history throughout Europe, the Middle East, and Eurasia is also littered with such examples, all based upon overfascination with (and overemphasis of) one or two arbitrarily chosen aspects of the original Sacred Mystery Tradition by some local charismatic individual whose followers then elaborated the newer imagery and turned it into a modern belief system.

When we consider our own immediate era, we again find a proliferation of mystic and quasi-mystic sects and groups, nearly all of which are concerned with promoting and promulgating but one or two localized aspects of the ancient wisdom tradition, which they find most attractive and appealing. Is it any wonder, then, in the face of the distortion such partiality almost automatically engenders, that many of their adherents are seen by today's scholars, scientists, and the general public (in their own undiscriminating way) as woolly-minded or mentally unbalanced mystics? The whole genre has thus generated a vicious circle, thereby confirming the old adage that "a *little* knowledge is a dangerous thing."

Notwithstanding this, we shall take a look in the next chapter at how the world of orthodox Egyptology itself adopts partial, woolly-minded, and clearly self-inconsistent views within the field of ancient Egyptian architecture and statuary, where the built environment from one end of the country to the other provided one vast sequence of interrelated esoteric metaphors.

PART FOUR

ANCIENT EGYPTIAN CIVILIZATION AND CULTURE

TEN

Egypt's Sacred Art,
Architecture,
and Statuary

The Egyptian philosophers have sublime notions with regard to the Divine Nature, which they keep secret and never disclose to the people but under a veil of fables and allegories.

ORIGEN, EARLY CHRISTIAN BISHOP OF ALEXANDRIA

If anyone implies that it is disgraceful to fashion base images of the Divine and Most Holy Orders, it is sufficient to answer that the most holy Mysteries are set forth in two modes; one by means of similar and sacred representations akin to their nature and the other to unlike forms designed with every possible discordance . . . [thus] divine things may not be easily accessible to the unworthy, nor may those who earnestly contemplate the divine symbols dwell upon the forms themselves as final truth.

DIONYSIUS THE AREOPAGITE, FIRST CHRISTIAN BISHOP OF PARIS

To the initiated of the sanctuary, no doubt, was reserved the knowledge of the god in the abstract, the god concealed in the unfathomable depths of his own essence. But for the less refined education of the people were presented the endless images of deities on the walls of the temples.

ALPHONSE MARIETTE, EGYPTOLOGIST

While the quality of a civilization's culture is perhaps most readily assessable in its language, it is undoubtedly most visible in its art, more particularly in its architecture and statuary, for these are usually its most complex and long-lasting forms. Art itself has been defined and redefined in many ways, but in practical terms it is any form of expression within which the subtlest subliminal characteristics serve to stir in others a recognition of their own creative inner nature and of its extraordinary depth of perception. Paradoxically, however, true depth in art is only to be found in conjunction with humility—in the extent to which the artist (Zen-like) forgets himself in the pursuit of a perfection of his powers of both observation and reproductive technique. But these are themselves based upon a recognition of the potentials of relationship and significance that Nature herself can be induced to produce from her concealed depths.

For that latter reason, it is nearly always art with an associated sense of the sacred that brings out the greatest skill and perfection in technique and visual appearance. It is also a recognition of this same underlying principle that results in the production of classic art, the immediate and instinctive aesthetic appeal of which travels happily and convincingly across centuries and even millennia, to appeal to all civilizations and their various generations.

Our present Western world espouses a curious fascination with the crude superficiality of modern art and perhaps all too frequently derides the classical because it does not properly understand it. However, it is all too easily forgotten that artistry is the product of either a healthily balanced or a sadly unbalanced subjective nature and that the degree of health and balance is itself determined by the self-discipline and corresponding lack of self-indulgence on the part of the artist. Artistic virtuosity results from seeing things as they truly are *with the inner eye* and reproducing them in a subtle but vibrantly living manner, which sparks an instant (although not necessarily fully conscious) response of recognition in the observer. It is for this latter reason that the Ancients held there to be certain sacrosanct rules operative in all art, those rules being based upon mathematical and geometrical proportion. For what we regard as the sense of proportion is, in fact, on the inner side of the veil of consciousness, a sense of clear-sighted perspective. This otherwise highlights the fact that the Ancients viewed that which could be seen on the inner side of life as being *causal,* and therefore much more closely associated with reality than that which could be experienced using only the external senses. This is actually not too far off what modern psychology might say, although the worlds of hard science and scholarship would undoubtedly balk at it.

The Use of Visual Archetypes

Because all ancient Egyptian sacred art, architecture, and statuary was intended to be symbolic, the repetitive use of archetypes was very extensive, the only distinctions being in terms of size, orientation, and embellishment. The proportions and the actual imagery

FIGURE 10.1. THE "GODDESS" TEMPLE AT ABU SIMBEL
(taken from a nineteenth-century lithograph)

Note: The picture shows what amounts to a dual trinity of gods on either side of the temple entrance, the latter representing the seventh (or rather, the fourth) state into which or from which Man must pass on his evolutionary journey. This temple is quite different from the so-called and better-known "male god" temple at Abu Simbel, with its four giant seated god figures, two each on either side of the temple entrance. While the standard orthodox interpretation of Egyptologists is that the male temple was dedicated to Rameses II, and that this other adjacent temple was dedicated to his queen, this is quite clearly in error, even though the goddess Hathor seems to have been the temple's main focus of attention internally. As Hathor represented the kosmic *ka* of the Logos, with the entrance itself symbolizing the opening of the cave in the sacred mountain from which Hathor emerged, it seems fairly clear that the esoteric meaning and function here involved the fall and eventual reemergence of the "divine spark." From this viewpoint, there is perhaps some substance to the idea that this temple was consecrated to the esoteric union of the male and female aspects of the Deity—something that may perhaps have been symbolically reenacted by the pharaoh and his queen according to an associated (astrological) cycle.

always remained exactly the same. This is something we can see particularly clearly in relation to both temple pillars and also statues. However, we shall deal with those issues under specific headings a little later on in this chapter. To begin with we shall continue to focus on general issues.

One comes across archetypes throughout Egypt in the fields of art, statuary, and architecture. In fact, one might go so far as to suggest that—apart from some of the very crude art of the later dynasties—the idea of free artistic religious expression would have been completely foreign to the ancient Egyptian mind. The reason for this is again related to the depth of spiritual orientation of their culture. From their viewpoint, there would have been no sense in trying to conceive artistically of something that could only be purely temporary if unrelated to the reality of the inner worlds. In fact, to do so would, in their minds, have been directly subversive of the spiritual balance in Nature and therefore completely unacceptable.

In an age when occidentally conceived freedom of expression operates consistently on or beyond the boundaries of mere license and thus very quickly degenerates into pure anarchy, it might be extremely difficult for us to understand the nature of the ancient viewpoint as described. In fact, we only have to look at the still-held ancient views in China and Japan to see the horror of their ruling hierarchies at the Western idea of complete personal freedom, which they see (quite understandably) as fundamentally anarchic to social order. We see in this nothing but self-centered bureaucracy and social interference—but that is only because it has lost all its religious background and now relies merely upon the dry bones of politics to hold it together. It has, in that sense, fundamentally changed from the motivation behind the ancient viewpoint.

Now, bearing in mind the ancient Egyptian sense of exactitude with regard to all forms, it appears at first very curious that their temple and initiatory (or funeral) chamber art is so static in presentation, with the hands always artistically but quite deliberately "wrong." Why was this done? Well, the answer is given by Dionysius the Areopagite in the quotation at the beginning of this chapter. Knowing the human tendency, where religion is concerned, to allow spiritual respect and honor to degenerate into mere blind worship, and otherwise wanting to ensure that the functional messages contained in the tableaux were not easily overlooked, the Egyptians introduced a convention of quite intentional distortion. How, in the face of this, could one worship something so potently malformed? The Ancients pursued the selfsame principle in literature and storytelling—as do the Sufis even today—with their heroes saying and doing things that were quite often plainly absurd but which nevertheless contained a paradoxical germ of wisdom to those who cared to look beneath the merely surface expression.

Everything in formal Egyptian art of the Old Kingdom and even much of the Middle Kingdom dynastic periods was concerned with conveying a message containing a psychological or spiritual truth. Only with the gradual degeneracy of the original culture in the later dynasties did this inviolable principle become compromised and eroded, more or less beginning with Akhenaten's time when it was cast aside altogether in blatantly devotional tableaux aimed at deifying the pharaoh and the royal family. Thereafter the rot set in progressively until it became so extensive that sacred art became virtually a mere adjunct to funerary practice and so, eventually, lost its soul altogether.

The Foundations of Classical Architecture

It is by now well established that the ancient Egyptians were highly skilled in both mathematics and geometry, and in their use in the fields of architecture, engineering, and optics. They had a perfect understanding of the nature of the point, the line, and the properties of the circle (as well as all the other geometrical figures), because they saw all of these as expressing fundamentally metaphysical relationships in universal Nature. Thus the unseen point that defines the limits of all structures and forms was itself seen as an esoteric metaphor for the creative "divine spark," while straight lines were indicative not only of emanating rays of light generating relationships between the points but also of the principle of Ma'at. Correspondingly, curved lines were related to the soul principle and thus also the enfolding nature of the *deva-neteru* hierarchies.

In classical architecture, curves and points are usually either implicit or merely partially expressed, while only straight lines are always fully explicit. The actual positions of straight lines, however, were determined by the unseen curves of the related soul principle, those positions then expressing specific meaning as well as having an associated musical relationship. By way of illustration, the twelvefold segmentation of the circle—which parallels the Egyptian mystic concept of the "twelve hours of the night" or the "twelve divisions of the Duat"—can be seen in reference to the progression of major chords, sharps, and flats in the musical octave.*

The Basic Egyptian Unit of Measurement

One cannot go very far in Egypt without coming into contact with the sacred cubit. In line with their wish to ensure that all of man's creations were exactly in proportion and harmony with the greater celestial environment, the Egyptians made an absolute science of the art of measurement—hence their profound interest and skill in geometry and mathematics. Thus also the sacred cubit was made to have a direct and very exact relationship with the circumference of the Earth and also with the cycle of the giant star Sirius.† But these same relative proportions are to be found everywhere, including in the dimensions of the temples and also in Egyptian statuary, as we shall see in a moment. The ancient Egyptians built into all their architectural creations the mathematical proportions of both *pi* (π)—the relationship between the septenary principle and the circumference of a circle—and *phi* (φ)—the profile of a regular spiral or vortex, or

*A Pythagorean concept for which I am indebted to my old friend, polymath artist and television producer Malcolm Stewart.

†In his book *The Great Pyramid* (chapter 7 and appendix A), Peter Le Mesurier confirms that each base side of the Great Pyramid is 365.24 cubits in length. But this is also the number of days in an Earth year and thus the axial revolution and circumference of the planet are in direct proportion. Additionally, the sum of the four sides is 1,461 cubits—1,461 years being the cycle of the star Sirius.

line of perspective relative to visual distance, often referred to as "the vanishing point." Consequently, nothing in their architectural designs (or statuary) was arbitrary in terms of either size or relative proportion. Regularity was as all-important as the associated sympathy of the symbolism.

Architectural Angles

The exact accuracy of angles in Egyptian architecture and statuary was also of great importance because of the macrocosmic relationships they signified and through which relationships were thus made possible. The primary angles were related to:

1. The four cardinal points
2. The rising and setting of the Sun and of particular stars and constellations
3. The angle of the Earth's annual orbital path relative to the Sun's equator
4. The angle of the ecliptic—that is, of our solar system's orbital path in space around its own parent star

As we now know, these angles varied within certain specific parameters over given lengths of time—that is, involving sidereal cycles. For example, the sides of the Great Pyramid are set at an angle of 52.5°, whereas the Ascending and Descending Passages are set at angles of about 26.25°. The latter represents the maximum angle of tilt of the Earth's magnetic pole relative to the plane of the celestial equator, whereas the 52.5° angle seems to be associated with the ecliptic path.

One considerable architectural curiosity in relation to the angles is the fact that, while all other temples were built to a rectangular peripheral plan, those at Thebes—Luxor and the Ramesseum—were not. Both these were built as skewed parallelograms. The maverick archaeologist Schwaller de Lubicz devoted much of his life to studying the temple of Luxor and came to the conclusion that its skewed plan was due to the architect's intention that it should resemble the human body in forward motion from a statuary position like that of Menkaura, as found with the *kouros* statues copied by the Greeks (as shown in fig. 10.2, page 278). However, the fact that this architectural anomaly is found only at Thebes (on both sides of the Nile) must itself be highly significant, perhaps having an association with that sidereal skew known to us as the ecliptic pole.

Perhaps also there is some association with the fact that Thebes was the principal city of the *fifth* nome of Egypt, the fifth division in the Book of the Dead (and the fifth stage in any septenary sequence) having to do with both the cycle of life in the Underworld and also the plane of mental perception—which is itself constantly at variance with the plane of the spiritual world. So it was here that the initiate had to turn and move forward—crossing from the west bank to the east bank, and then turning away from the majesty

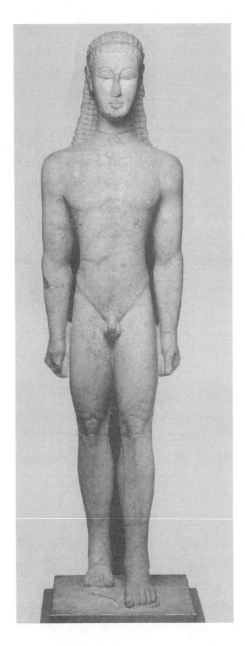

FIGURE 10.2. *KOUROS* STATUE WITH THE LEFT FOOT FORWARD

of the lower world (symbolized by Karnak) toward Luxor and the higher states of being represented by the great temples extending from Esna to Philae.

General Issues Related to the Great Nile Temples

Notwithstanding their having been built according to an original master plan that covered the whole of greater Egypt in ancient times, tens of thousands of years ago, many of even the most important temples had been allowed to fall into a state of severe dilapidation by the time of the later pharaonic dynasties. Consequently, these in particular came under a scheme of restoration by the Greek Ptolemies, who saw the regeneration of the original Egyptian religious sense among the populace of the country as politically as well as socially crucial to the survival of the state and their own political power and influence.

However, as a result of the extensive rebuilding and renovation that was carried out—not all of which was done to a high standard—considerable confusion now exists among Egyptologists as to the actual age of the temples—notwithstanding an *apparent* consensus on the part of mainstream orthodoxy. One of the best examples is to be found in the great temple of Hathor at Dendera, where the wall carvings are of two completely different types. The older type involves the figures actually standing proud of the general stone surface—an incredibly sophisticated and difficult technique to master. The rest of the friezes are merely carved into the stonework surfaces. Here also some areas of the stonework are quite clearly considerably older than others.

It appears that the farther south one goes, however, the general quality of masonry repair and carving gets better—perhaps because the southern temples were much farther away from the cosmopolitan cities of the south (like Alexandria) with their laissez faire and more degenerate ways. Thus the priests of the south were able, for far longer, to ensure the maintenance of high standards of workmanship in proper accord with strict religious and artistic criteria. Unfortunately, once Christianity and Islam appeared on the scene, temple preservation ceased and active despoliation took place instead.

The Main Forms of Egyptian Sacred Architecture

Egyptian sacred architecture fundamentally consisted of four main archetypal forms:

1. The pyramid
2. The temple pylon
3. The temple itself
4. The obelisk, or stele

Each form had its own very specific symbolism. We shall now take a look at each of these in necessarily quite generalized terms. After that, we shall also take a look at Egyptian sculpture in the round.

The Pyramid

To begin with, then, the pyramids—in themselves and in their location—appear to have represented those stars in the heavens that the Egyptians regarded as being associated with initiatory development. As mentioned, certain groups of pyramids—particularly those between the Faiyum and Giza areas—seem to have been directly associated with the

Pleiades and the Hyades nebulae and also the constellation of Orion. Yet, as we have also drawn very specific correspondences between the stars of Ursa Minor and the seven temples between Diospolis Parva and the First Cataract,[1] we should perhaps spend a moment considering the fundamental differences between the two areas of symbolism, as follows.

It might be said that, whereas the pyramids were symbolic of Man reaching back up to the stars—and therefore involving the process of spiritual initiation—all temples were intended to ground a specifically associated sidereal influence on Earth and thereby set up a permanent rapport for the *downward* transmission of Divine Purpose, resulting inevitably in the constant regeneration of human social culture. In a certain sense, this is fundamentally rather similar to the originally intended purpose behind the Christian church building (the architecture of medieval cathedrals having been extensively based upon that of the Egyptian temple, as modified by Greco-Roman thought), or a Buddhist or Hindu temple. However, most of these tended to become sadly degenerate during the twentieth century, due to a focus on materialism on all fronts having produced a corresponding lack of general faith and confidence in the practice of religion. The sense of the sacred has so far departed that modern church architecture is almost completely functional and has no invocatory design or atmosphere about it at all, even the building's orientation now often being considered immaterial.

The Egyptians called the pyramid by the generic name *aakhu-t,* which is actually derived from the multiple *a-akhu-t*—clearly confirming its derivation from the "divine sparks" or divine spirits that had their home in the stars. Rather interestingly, we find in the Pyramid Texts of Unas the statement: "As for anyone who shall lay a finger on this pyramid and temple, which belong to me and my double, he will have laid his finger on the mansion of Horus in the firmament."[2] This is a very specific, as well as dramatic, statement, which needs to be considered most carefully—in the light of sympathetic magic—because the "mansion of Horus in the firmament" is another way of saying "the higher soul-body in which the principle of self-consciousness resides."

The Pyramid as a Celestial Vehicle

As we saw earlier, there appears to have been, in the Egyptian mind, a direct association between the pyramid and the *benben* stone—the meteorite—that falls to Earth like a veritable phoenix, in a blaze of light, and winds up as a pyramidion-shaped lump of highly magnetic iron. This lump of celestial rock was considered to be from the bones of Osiris, the Osirian "bones," however, being of celestial light itself, the substance of the stars. Now the pyramids were obviously man-made—of either stone or, in some cases, even brick*—and were built up from the Earth's surface, with the "asteroidal tail end" facing the heavens. The clear inference from this, it is suggested, is that the ancient Egyptians wished to *simulate* on

---

*For example, the pyramid of Zoser is built in seven tiers out of small bricks, while the neighboring pyramid of Meidum is built in three tiers out of stone.

FIGURE 10.3. THE SPHINX AND THE GREAT PYRAMID
(as seen from the Khafra Pyramid causeway)

the ground what existed in the heavens in the way of particular stars or star groups. Then, by aligning various passageways with the actual movement of particular stars relative to each other, the pyramid itself would have been considered to fulfill the role of a stellar double.

Initiation in the Pyramid

It follows quite naturally from this that, if the Egyptians were also able to position a prospective initiate within the pyramid in such a way as to be in the direct or indirect line of the thus focused celestial emanations from a particular star, that individual would—through the workings of sympathetic magic—be directly exposed to those same concentrated influences. It would appear that, in the same way that modern fairy tales sometimes have astral souls ascending "on a moonbeam," the ancient Egyptians believed such a thing actually to be possible. Hence the (spiritual) soul of the higher initiate (not merely that of the pharaoh) would, in a sense, literally become a star, through temporary absorption while in the deepest meditative state of spiritual contemplation.

However, as the highest aspect of Man's own nature was regarded as being permanently resident in the stars anyway, it may have been that the Egyptians saw the whole process instead as one of direct "celestial seeding" of the lower soul nature by the higher, in a manner that accelerated a natural process of evolutionary development, which would otherwise take unnecessarily long to achieve. Whatever may have been the associated details of the matter, there can be no doubt whatsoever that the pyramids were not intended as the tombs of vainglorious pharaohs, the vast majority of whom were quite happy to have their bodies entombed far underground in the hills of the West Bank, at Thebes.*

Now, although there were only seven (at the most nine) solar initiations in the ancient occult system, there are a great many more pyramids in Lower and Middle Egypt than this. So, the obvious question arises: "Which pyramids were used for initiation and what were the other ones used for?" Well, the suggested answer comes back to the issue of the sevenfold stellar sequence that trails through Orion, the Hyades, the Pleiades, and so on, en route to the circumpolar stars. As already suggested in *Land of the Fallen Star Gods,* the "homeward trail" commenced at Giza, with the five initiations to be taken in the three pyramids there, which ultimately brought forth the Risen Master Mason—a spiritually self-conscious adept, who had attained the summit of purely human achievement. But beyond that, to the immediate south, lay the pyramids of Saqqara and Dashur, some of them even bigger than the Great Pyramid at Giza and of different shape and material.

Bearing in mind that the central idea of the Egyptians involved eventual spiritual liberation *for all,* it seems not unlikely that the other pyramids were used not only for different aspects of the higher initiations—leading to kosmic consciousness—but also for invocative purposes. That is to say, at cyclically opportune times, these pyramids would perhaps have been occupied by the higher initiates in the country for purposes of telepathic contact with the higher realms of being, for such purposes as attaining to yet greater knowledge, mainly through intense and prolonged contemplation, but not involving initiation per se.

*In support of that, one can imagine the psychological reaction of a proud court retinue at the suggestion that their monarch should be ignobly buried underground when previous pharaohs had had the honor and dignity of a pyramid as their public mausoleum. The continuing insistence by Egyptologists upon willfully ignoring this self-evident fact makes their own viewpoint increasingly farcical. When one bears in mind the incarceration of the dead pharaoh's body in a mummy coffin, which is necessarily of far larger proportions, it is quite clear that the whole job could not be fitted into the stone sarcophagi actually found in the pyramids anyway. These only just fit the height of a tallish man.

FIGURE 10.4. THE THREE PYRAMIDS AT GIZA

The Temple Pylon

Often mistakenly regarded as triumphally inscribed archways on behalf of vaingloriously successful, warmongering pharaohs,* the Egyptian pylon is a rather curious architectural feature to which little attention is usually paid. It basically involves a colossal wall—much higher than any of the other temple walls—immediately in front of the outer entrance to the temple. That wall is itself dual in nature—as one can see from the photograph in fig. 10.5 (page 284)—with a central, flat arched gateway, the size of which also varied according to the temple in question.

The essence of the concept seems to have been that of impressing upon anyone approaching it a psychological enhancement of the idea that external access to the temple was massively confrontational, thus acting as a barrier to be penetrated with due forethought and solemnity. In that sense, the pylon would have symbolized the gate of the soul of the temple, which had to be penetrated in order to gain access to the field of knowledge held within. The fact that the ancient sacred texts frequently refer to (metaphorical) sequences of twenty-one pylons appears to confirm this.

The underlying geometry of the pylon's architectural design, however (see fig. 10.6, page 285), provides a very distinctive additional dimension. The important thing about this is clearly that the *non*-physical geometry was intended to have a perhaps even more important subliminal effect upon the soul consciousness of the individual and the masses

*As Budge (*Dwellers on the Nile,* 93) confirms for us, "The history of Egypt shows clearly that the Egyptians, as a nation, were wholly lacking in military spirit and that they abhorred war." But, bearing in mind the extreme sense of spirituality found in their religion, this is surely unsurprising. What is surprising is that Egyptologists go on, generation after generation, retailing an orthodox prejudice that is plainly in error.

FIGURE 10.5. THE MAIN TEMPLE PYLON AT EDFU

of the populace than the objectively visible pylon itself. The location and direction of the various architectural lines and points, including the great entrance gate, appear—as we can see from the diagram—entirely derived from the natural internal meridians arising out of the intertwined equilateral triangles (and the sacred tetraktys) within the circle or sphere. This bears a strong resemblance to the same principles described and commented upon in *Land of the Fallen Star Gods*[3] in relation to the geometry of the Great Pyramid.

The exterior facade of the pylon was, as we can also see, covered with carved scenes and hieroglyphs, which were doubtless (originally) intended to enhance the visual sense of grandeur, mystery, and importance, but which also conveyed a specific message concerning the characteristic nature of the particular temple for the initiate and the associated priesthood. Even here, however, we find archetypal imagery in some profusion, for the largest carved impression was usually that of the initiate—dressed as the king of Lower Egypt—smiting his foes with a great club. However, this is *not* suggestive of a historic battle fought

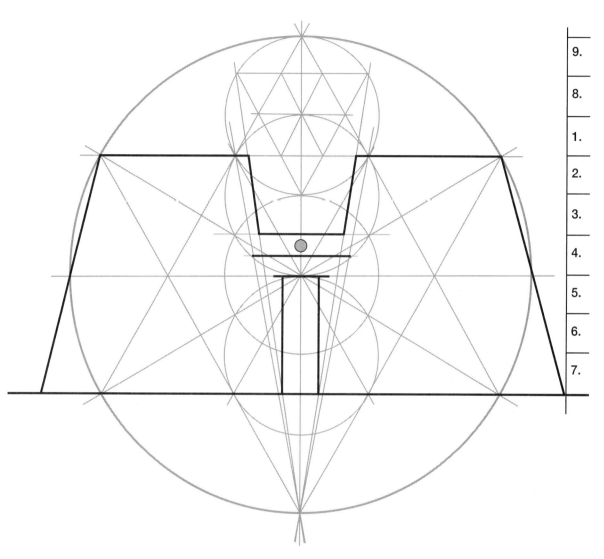

9.

8.

1.

2.

3.

4.

5.

6.

7.

FIGURE 10.6. THE UNDERLYING GEOMETRY OF THE TEMPLE PYLON

Note: The overall depth of the circle that enfolds the pylon geometry is measurable to a factor of twelve. That part that then stands above ground level and actually constitutes the structure of the pylon stands to the circle in the proportion 6:12, while that part below ground level stands to it in the proportion 3:12, and effectively represents the Lower Underworld. The height of the great porch or entrance gate at the center is half the overall height of the pylon, and it also represents the three lowest planes of solar existence through which man passes on his evolutionary way. The next and fourth plane is symbolically represented by the gap between the top of the great entrance door and the bottom of the "valley" at the top of the pylon. This is divided in half, with the upper part depicted as containing the winged solar disk-body of Kneph (found over all temple doorways in ancient Egypt). This is the plane of spiritual soul (*sah*). The next two "divisions" (symbolically invisible to our objective sight) are, respectively, the plane of emanating Spirit and the semidivine plane within which is to be found the *akhu*. Above this are (1) the highest solar plane and (2) the sixth and fifth kosmic planes.

by a particular pharaoh and his armies. It was intended to depict the initiate subduing his own lower desires and thoughts before entering the sacred precincts of the temple. The idea of physical warfare being depicted upon the walls of a temple, whose very presence was based upon pure orientation toward the higher worlds and the spiritual nature, is little short of farcical. Yet this too is the modern orthodoxy.

The Famous Battle of Kadesh

Perhaps the most famous pylon in Egypt is that of (supposedly) Amenhotep III and Meremptah at Luxor. It is generally (but wrongly) regarded by Egyptologists as being a rather one-sided record of the pharaoh's war against the Hittite tribes of the Middle East, concluding in the fantastic Battle of Kadesh, which is mentioned in various other temple complexes as well. In this supposed battle, the pharaoh almost single-handedly routs his foes. But when considered in the light of Egyptian mysticism, it becomes clear that the inscriptions were actually oriented toward the *subjective* battle in which the initiate struggles against and eventually vanquishes his own lower inner nature. This is to some extent confirmed by (a) the story being endemically absurd if treated other than as allegory, (b) the enemy being the *keta*—a word of seemingly Sanskrit origin meaning "unruly children"* (from which our own Anglo-Saxon word *kid* is probably derived), and (c) the fact that the initiated Pir must indeed leave his own "troops" (his thoughts and emotions) behind and fight the battle single-handedly, while calling upon his father-god in heaven (Amen-Ra) to aid him—as the pharaoh is shown doing. As elsewhere suggested, the whole imagery bears a distinct resemblance to the Battle of Kurukshetra found in the Bhagavad Gita.

Certain of the temples had a series of pylons placed in sequence, one after the other, with intervening forecourts. Karnak is a good example. Here there were six or seven, clearly indicating the importance of the sevenfold structure yet again. In fact, Karnak is the only temple known to have two primary axes, one being east-to-west and the other north-to-south. This confirms that Karnak was seen as symbolizing a very real spiritual crossroads for the initiate once he had crossed over from the west bank of the river. Having approached in the first place via the west-east axis, from the river, he now had to make a choice involving following the other axis either northward (back to the material world scene) or southward (toward the higher reality whose influences began in the temple of Luxor). However, bearing in mind that the temple of Luxor is known to have been representative of the *spiritual* conception and birth of the initiate (i.e., the pharaoh, according to orthodox Egyptology), and that the final battle with the lower self of man had to be completed in the Mystery Tradition before this became possible, the esoteric sequence and meaning here is very clearly and instantly recognizable.

The pylon gateway—like the inner temple gateway, or porch—was of course specifically

---

*The unruly children being one's own constantly errant, elemental thoughts and desires.

positioned in such a manner as to allow the rising Sun (or a particular star), at a specific time of the year, to direct its rays right through the central axis of the temple, so as briefly to illuminate the holy-of-holies, the innermost sanctuary of the god figure to whom the temple was dedicated. This then—through sympathetic magic—respiritualized the sanctuary (and thus recharged the whole temple) on that day each and every year.

Immediately in front and on either side of the temple pylon gateway were usually placed two statues having a particular significance and relationship with the temple in question. For example, immediately in front of the temple pylon at Karnak—after passing through the dual ranks of the giant rams—we would originally have seen two gigantic seated human figures, apparently representing gods, each with a giant stele behind it. The same arrangement is still fortunately to be found in front of the nearby temple of Luxor. But these figures were in fact symbolic of the dual polarity of Man's own higher god nature, which the initiate had to pass between en route into the temple itself. In front of the pylon gateway at Edfu, on the other hand, we find the much smaller statue of the sacred Horus hawk, overshadowing the still smaller figure of the initiate-soul, which stands on its feet, as shown in fig. 10.7.

FIGURE 10.7. IN FRONT OF THE PYLON AT EDFU, THE STATUE OF THE SACRED HORUS HAWK OVERSHADOWS THE FIGURE OF THE INITIATE-SOUL.

Egypt's Sacred Art, Architecture, and Statuary

The Temple Itself

Let us now take a look at certain aspects of the ancient Egyptian temple. As we shall see, there are many, each with its own sets of symbols. While the associated architectural principles remained the same for all temples, the size, orientation, and complexity varied, often quite considerably, according to the nature and importance of each temple itself. This is important and needs to be carefully borne in mind.

The Great Forecourt

Upon passing through the outer pylon gateway, one emerges into a truly gigantic courtyard where one might imagine that the masses of the populace would gather, awaiting the emergence of the priests from within the temple to minister to them. From this one passes into the temple itself, through the great doorway and then between the rows of huge pillars thronging the hypostyle hall and leading the individual onward toward the various sacred chambers in which the priests carried out their devotions.

The Temple Roof and Pillars

It can be imagined just how dark, gloomy, and fearful the interior of the temple might have seemed were it not for the ancient Egyptian architects' highly intelligent and creative use of their art to ensure that sunlight was able to penetrate wherever necessary. Perhaps the best example of this is the hypostyle hall roof, following the line of the central nave, a feature carried over (with some variation) into our medieval European cathedrals. This part of the temple structure appears to have been designed to convey a symbolic idea concerning the separation of the Underworld from the true light of the heavenly world above. Thus the design was intended to borrow light from above, not only to provide internal illumination but also for particularly theatrical purposes, using the camera oscura effect.*

In the case of the pillar, both ends are significant.† The number of base rings appears to have signified the number of foundational substates out of which the emanation arose. The upper capitals of the pillar, on the other hand, displayed the particular stage of psychospiritual unfoldment of Man (on the Path of Initiation)‡ associated with the particular temple. For example, fig. 10.8 shows us the capitals of the sequence of temples moving southward from Dendera to Philae.

---

*This works through the operation of light following the *phi* principle, in which a distant image is naturally rotated in proportion through 180 degrees by any lenslike aperture, even of an architectural nature.

†It is noteworthy that the temple pillars at Luxor actually taper downward, being thinner at the bottom than at the top—symbolic of the spiritual reorientation of the initiate (of the third degree) at this stage.

‡In Lower Egypt—from Abydos northward—which the Egyptians saw as esoterically symbolic of the solar Underworld, the capitals of the temple pillars were representative of the papyrus plant. At Dendera, the capitals were formed in the shape of Hathor heads, with large and protuberant ears, which were themselves metaphors referring to spiritual hearing and the capacity of the initiate of the second degree in the Mysteries to have achieved this faculty.

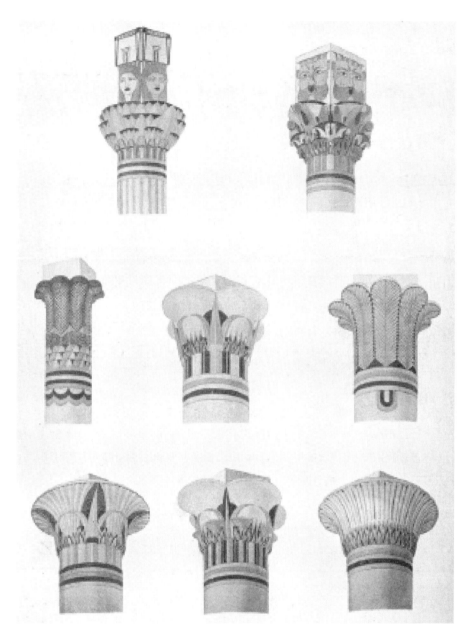

FIGURE 10.8. EXAMPLES OF TEMPLE PILLAR CAPITALS
(all located within the temple of Philae)

At Dendera—seemingly associated with the second-degree initiation in the Mysteries—the capital consisted of the head of the goddess Hathor (with protruding cow's ears), thereby indicating that, at this stage, the faculty of inner (psychospiritual, but not pure spiritual) perception had been consciously gained. At Karnak, the capitals display the fully opened buds of the papyrus plant, which, we shall recall, was symbolic of Lower Egypt and also of material existence. However, a fundamental change now takes place because the capitals of some of the temple pillars at Karnak and Luxor are those of the sacred lotus—and they are still closed. At Esna, the lotus bud—which was symbolic of spiritual development in both Egypt and India—is partly open and at Edfu it is fully open, with three inner tiers of petals having become evident. At Kom Ombos, Elephantine, and Philae, these then open out even more completely to show the fully explicit lotus flower in all its symbolic beauty.

Stellar and Solar Alignments and the Symbolic Use of Light

So much has already been written about this subject by various authors over the past hundred years, in relation to both the pyramids and the Nile temples, that it would be merely repetitive to detail them yet again here. However, there is one general assumption in connection with the issue that needs to be carefully reexamined and questioned. It relates to the rationale behind the innermost sanctuary of the temple being illuminated by the *phi*-focused ray of light from the rising Sun or a rising star.

As we shall see later on in this chapter when dealing with the subject of ancient Egyptian colossi—and as we have already seen in relation to their concept of Creation within the enfolding soul-body principle—the Egyptians' metaphysical system worked from the outside inward. Thus the gods, per se, were vast ethereal soul beings who enfolded the world of lesser being (and lesser beings) within their invisible auric nature. Consequently, that which lay at the center—while still perhaps representing the "divine spark"—would probably not have been the image of the *ancestral* god-being. This appears to be confirmed by the small and even childlike figures in the innermost chamber at Abu Simbel.

The Temple *Adytum*

Not identifying the central figure with the image of the *ancestral* god-being of course represents a very radical departure from the orthodox view of how the Egyptian temple was oriented and run. We therefore perhaps need to consider what might have been the true function of the *adytum* or "holy-of-holies,"* which certainly was still only accessible to the higher (or highest) elements of the initiated priesthood. But that itself may provide us with the answer we seek.

As we otherwise know, the primary Egyptian concern was to maintain a permanent and direct link between Heaven and Earth. But this could only be done through the agency of man—the fallen god. However, in order to be responsive to the divine influence

---

*The name *adytum* is ostensibly Greek and means the innermost sacred sanctum within the temple. However, it actually looks as though it had been derived partially from Sanskrit and partially from Egyptian, for *adi* in Sanskrit means "divinely primordial" and of course Tum was the god of the self-raised mound of objective space that rose to meet the descending fire brought by the sacred *benben* bird.

emanating from the Sun or a star, the individual in question had to have already achieved a direct and conscious sensitivity to and link with his own divine nature. In other words, he had to be a high initiate whose spiritual status enabled him to act as the de facto agent of transmission and reception of psychospiritual influences on behalf of the population at large. This leads us to the implication that it—the holy-of-holies—was perhaps occupied by the hierophant of the temple himself on these very special occasions and by no one and nothing else.

The only serious alternative solution to this question is that the holy-of-holies was in fact occupied by a statue or statues of a lesser god figure, merely representing man or an aspect of man, as found in the innermost sanctum of the temple at Abu Simbel. As we can see from fig. 10.14 (page 299), this particular temple's inner sanctum contained four small figures—from left to right: Ptah, Amen-Ra, man as high priest, and Ra-Herakte.

The two temples at Abu Simbel were of course carved into the rock face, whereas all the other main temples were built as self-supporting architectural structures. That itself would appear to symbolize the fact that Abu Simbel was quite distinctly different in representing the god nature of Man immersed progressively in matter (rock being but crystallized light). Thus the moving ray of light indicated the *sequence* as well as the fact of life-giving irradiance emanating from the solar Demiurge, while the Ptah (or Buddha) nature in Man was itself of a different (and higher) nature.

The Geometry of the Free-Standing Temples

As one can immediately see from earlier diagrams, the entrance into the temple was via a smaller sphere of being, which led into a larger sphere of being, the proportions of the two spheres always being geometrically balanced. There was never anything arbitrary about the associated sizes. The relative height above ground level of the temple floor was always the same, and the number of steps between the two (in the Greek, Persian, and Hindu versions) always apparently being in multiples of seven or five, representing the number of substates of consciousness to be crossed.* The number of pillars was always even. Odd numbers represented motive force or power, while even numbers represented fixity and form. Remembering the principle that it is always the space inside or between the forms that gives the whole meaning and importance (as is the case even with the domestic house), one can perhaps see that the internal proportions were intended to induce in the

---

*This was common throughout the ancient world. For example, the temple of Borobudur in Java has seven levels—built as a higher five and a lower two—with the top level being surmounted by three rings and a central stela. In addition, there are 1,460 friezes on the walls, which indicates an association with the cycle of the star Sirius. At the top of the seven lower levels, there are three circles of bell-shaped structures known as stupas, with one gigantic stupa in the middle. All the bell-like stupas contain a Buddha figure sitting in the meditative lotus position—apparently an esoteric metaphor symbolizing the star gods themselves in their celestial "homes."

Egypt's Sacred Art, Architecture, and Statuary

291

individual's subliminal consciousness an immediate sense of relative being, for the soul nature knows itself only by its sense of proportionate relationship.

The Sacred Obelisk, or Stele

These colossal pieces of stone carved out of a single lump of granite and in some cases weighing up to four hundred tons—and either capped by a pyramidion or ending in a pyramid shape—appear to have symbolized the four lesser elements of earthly Nature growing upward and gradually closer together, until they suddenly reach a point of common fusion with the fifth element—the aether. Usually found in pairs immediately in front of the pylon entrance gate to the temple, the obelisk might perhaps be regarded as somewhat akin to the native North American Indian totem pole. In other words, it could have represented something of the historical background of the local populace, perhaps covering a given period of time. We find the Romans following the same idea—for example in the case of Trajan's Column, covering the valorous exploits and achievements of but one Roman general-cum-emperor and his armies.

As John West points out in his guide book *The Traveler's Key to Ancient Egypt,* obelisks or stelae act like huge sun dials and would hence have permitted the astronomer-priests to use them as precise astronomical and calendrical pointers.[4] However, this was clearly not their only or perhaps even main raison d'etre.

FIGURE 10.9. OBELISK AND PYLON AT LUXOR

Egyptian Sacred Statuary

When we come to address the subject of Egyptian sacred statuary in greater detail (here we can only take a few examples), we find two distinct symbolisms, neither of which—contrary to what Egyptologists seem to think—has anything whatsoever to do with the dynastic pharaohs. The primary symbolism relates to the use of sympathetic magic, while the second is associated with the relative correspondences and distinctions between god and man (on the Path of Initiation). While we shall take a look at some examples of the latter, to see what is actually involved, let us first consider the issue of sympathetic magic. In relation to this, perhaps the best description of what was involved, or intended, is given to us by Proclus in his *Commentary on the Timaeus* as follows:

> As of statues established by the telestic art, some things pertaining to them are manifest, but others are inwardly concealed, being symbolical of the presence of the Gods, and which are only known to the mystic artists themselves; after the same manner, the world being a statue [i.e., an image] of the intelligible [state], and perfected by the father, has indeed some things which are visible indications of its divinity; but [also] others, which are the invisible impressions of the participation of being received by it from the father, who gave it perfection, in order that through these it may be eternally rooted in real being.[5]

It is well known that some ancient priesthoods actually used statues as oracles in order, supposedly, to convey the will or desire of the deity in question. However, it would seem that this only started to occur when the degeneracy of the Mystery Tradition had really gained a strong foothold and when real psychospiritual knowledge had been replaced by superstitious practice arising from intended spiritual shortcuts. Archaeologists have surmised that some of the statues in question were fitted with moving parts, which could be manipulated by the priests themselves. However, no examples of any such have yet been found and this suggestion must therefore remain in the field of conjecture.

Statuary Symbolizing Degrees of Initiation

Turning next to the issue of initiation-associated symbolism, the first example is that of the figure with the advancing left leg, signifying forward motion *toward the Underworld*. Interestingly, the stance of the initiate in statuary groups (such as shown in fig. 10.10 and found elsewhere also) evidently made a great impact upon the Greeks who came to Egypt during the later dynasties, because large numbers of simulacra—that of the *kouros*—have been found by archaeologists in various parts of Greece (see fig. 10.2). The very name *kouros* (after detaching the Greek *os* suffix) looks as though it may have been derived from the Egyptian *kau,* meaning "the divine spirit of the individual." In Greece, the *kouros* was

FIGURE 10.10. STATUE OF MEN-KAU-RA, FLANKED BY THE GODDESS HATHOR ON HIS RIGHT AND A NOME GODDESS ON HIS LEFT

always in the form of a young man in his athletic twenties. In Egypt the figure was always of a wonderfully well-proportioned but mature man in his *forties*. However, in both cases, the figure was actually an idealized, archetypal human type—never that of a particular individual—a principle adopted throughout Egypt from the earliest Old Kingdom dynasties to at least the mid-Intermediate Period.*

Menkaura Symbolism

Although the statue of Men-kau-Ra (Menkaura), shown in fig. 10.10, is generally believed by Egyptologists to be the statue of a pharaoh, it is clearly nothing of the sort. Now in the Cairo Museum, this statuary was originally discovered in the Valley Temple of the smaller of the three main pyramids at Giza†—which, as outlined in *Land of the Fallen Star Gods,* was the pyramid dealing with the preliminary rites of initiation. Thus Men-kau-Ra (meaning "Mind-Spirit-God") was seemingly the generic god-name given to that aspect of divinity overshadowing the first of the seven main initiations. The nome goddess here actually appears to represent the astral soul nature of the Menkaura initiate.

There are a number of tellingly symbolic features in the statuary group. First of all, the initiate is shown wearing the crown of Upper Egypt—signifying spiritual consciousness. Second, both the goddesses hold their inner arm protectively around him, while both of his hands (but not those of the two goddesses) are shown clenched around a tubular article, which appears to symbolize the fact that he is pulling some sort of (symbolic) vehicle along behind him. The nome district goddess is shown to be standing still—her feet being together—while Hathor's left foot is just a little forward, thereby symbolizing the beginnings of forward movement by the initiate's spiritual soul nature. The initiate himself is depicted confidently striding forward in very determined fashion—hence perhaps the old expression "putting one's best foot forward."

Closer examination of the same statuary reveals that the faces of the two goddesses are actually just the same, the sole distinction between them being their respective headdresses. Hathor's depicts the incoming solar disk, representing spiritual birth. That of the other goddess involves the feather of Ma'at and the Jackal of Set, the latter representing the directional orientation of the initiate's consciousness.

---

*As John Anthony West (*The Traveler's Key to Ancient Egypt,* 261) points out, we find very clear resemblances between Egyptian artistic depiction of spiritual archetypes (such as the human-headed sphinxes at Luxor) and those found in certain Buddhist temples (such as Ankhor Wat) in Asia. The resemblances involve distinctively Oriental features and ears symbolically placed much higher on the head than is physiologically normal. This is yet another indicator of the intercultural links between ancient Egypt and Asia described earlier in the book.

†In the Cairo Museum there are actually three such statuary reliefs, each being slightly different from the other and thus indicating a very definite sequence, or progression.

The Initiate of the Third Degree

We turn next to the statue of the supposed King Pir, found still erect in the grounds of the temple of Karnak at Thebes. As we can see from fig. 10.11, this statue involves an apparently female figure (with symbolically high headdress) standing upon the feet of a hugely larger (male) god-being. Now, in order to understand the symbolic meaning here, we need

FIGURE 10.11. THE STATUE OF THE INITIATED PIR AT KARNAK

first to take into consideration the fact that Karnak represented the stage on the spiritual Path at which the initiate became king over his own multiple mortal nature, although he still had far to go and had still not set his feet upon the final stretch of what we might call the Higher Path—that leading toward godhood itself.

Second, however, we need to take into account the fact of relative proportion between the two figures. In that respect, we can see that the female figure (representing the astral soul nature of the initiate) is—by standing upon the feet of the god-king—slightly raised up above the level of mundane being and is also thereby depicted as being under his direct protection. But the headdress of the female figure is shown as extending upward to the concealed fork of the god-king's legs, thereby describing an implicit association between the lower creative function of the god and the head consciousness of the initiate.

The Colossi of Memnon and the Ramesseum

The huge, forlorn figures of the Colossi of Memnon (see fig. 10.12, page 298), which nowadays stand alone on the west-bank floodplain, next to the road leading to the new bridge over the Nile, must once have had a pylon and temple gate immediately behind them, exactly as one finds across the river at Karnak and Luxor.* A few scattered remains of that original temple are still to be seen a little farther along the road, which itself winds slowly upward to the lower slopes of the background hills, where we find the somewhat better preserved remains of the so-called Ramesseum. The traveler Diodorus Siculus described how this latter temple and its sanctuary were "surrounded with a golden circle, 365 cubits in circumference and a foot and a half thick, while within it were described, from cubit to cubit, the 365 days of the year, the course of the stars and what they signified in Egyptian astrology."[6] He also spoke of the library attached to this same temple, which he says dealt with "the Medicine of the Mind."[7] That itself sounds like a library on the science of psychology.

There originally were three giant statues, one larger than the others and seated. Now only part of two such figures remain, both sadly toppled over and in ruins. But it was the inscription on the largest figure—"I am Simandius, king of kings. If anybody desires to know who I am or what I have done, let him outdo what I have done"—that impelled the poet Shelley to write his poem in which Ozymandias is made to say, "Look upon my works ye mighty, and despair!" The essence of the idea behind all this, however, seems to have been that the initiate, once having reached this particular point in his own psychospiritual development, had already achieved the very summit of purely human potential, in terms of the scale and magnificence of his artistic, creative genius. For him, there was nothing further of a temporal nature to be achieved or sought after. All that remained involved the pursuit of purely spiritual knowledge and faculty.

---

*It is noteworthy that, although much damaged by erosion, the smaller symbolic female figures seen next to the legs of all giant seated god figures are still to be seen beside the Colossi too.

FIGURE 10.12. COLOSSI OF MEMNON
(Photo by Marc Ryckaert)

The Temples at Abu Simbel

We turn finally to the massive statuary at Abu Simbel, where the huge god figures, some sixty feet in height, seated externally at the front (all with exactly similar features) have been ludicrously taken as representing Rameses II, with the twelve lesser female figures standing next to or between the legs of the figures supposedly representing his daughters. While the staff of Rameses II may sycophantically have had his hieroglyphic name carved upon the statuary long after its actual carving and erection, the temple is clearly far older and was intended to fulfill a mystic function as yet unrecognized by modern scholarship.

FIGURE 10.13. THE MIDDLE CHAMBER OF ABU SIMBEL'S MALE TEMPLE
(from the drawings of David Roberts, R.A.)

FIGURE 10.14. THE HOLY-OF-HOLIES CHAMBER AT ABU SIMBEL, WITH (LEFT TO RIGHT) PTAH, AMEN-RA, MAN AS HIGH PRIEST, AND RA-HERAKTE
(from the drawings of David Roberts, R.A.)

The location of the Abu Simbel temples is just north of where the Second Cataract used to be, and as we have seen, the Second Cataract itself appears to have been symbolically representative of the line of demarcation between the second and third states of *kosmic* being in Egyptian septenary macrogeography. It was thus associated with the interactive association between the Kosmic Mind nature and the Kosmic Desire nature. But the overall symbolism is only to be understood by considering all the statuary, both inside and outside the temple.

Inside the Temple

The first intermediate chamber within what is known as the "male" temple has four pairs of facing god figures (see fig. 10.13), all standing and all of the same size as the King Pir statue at Karnak. The faces of the figures are exactly the same, but those on the left side wear the crown of Lower Egypt while those on the right wear the double crown of both Upper and Lower Egypt. As the left side or leftward movement symbolically represented material existence and the crown of Lower Egypt symbolized kingship of the lower nature, we can safely say that these four represent an implicit progression, downward into material existence, by the *spiritual* nature of Man. Correspondingly, the four facing god-kings on the right side of the chamber symbolically represent dominion over material *and* spiritual Nature. That leaves the issue of the four much smaller, seated figures in the innermost chamber (see fig. 10.14). These are roughly the size of the average man, but they are depicted from left to right as (a) the god Ptah, (b) Amen-Ra, (c) our old friend Rameses II yet again (!), and (d) Ra-Herakte.

In fact the twelve god figures have to be viewed as representing a single, triple progression, almost certainly associated with the zodiac. In the same way that the Egyptian twelve-month year resulted from a downward and backward cycle through seven states, divided into three seasons, we see here the triple cycle of Man. The first four solar planes, months, and zodiacal houses (Aries through Cancer) represent the fall of the god nature into the field of spiritual existence. The second small inner group of four figures represents fourfold man, plus the next four planes in succession and the middle four zodiacal houses (Leo through Scorpio). The four standing giant figures with the double crowns of Upper and Lower Egypt then represent the spiritually self-conscious man, the upper four planes to be reascended, and the four final zodiacal houses (Sagittarius through Pisces).

Returning briefly to the four small seated figures in the innermost chamber, the symbolism concerning Man's multiple nature goes even further. At the two solstices of the year, the rising Sun sends a solitary ray that pierces the outer chamber and comes to rest first on the left shoulder of the *second* figure from the left—that symbolizing the Amen-Ra principle. It then proceeds to the third and fourth figures over a period of about twenty minutes, but it never illuminates the figure of Ptah. Ptah was the Lord of Darkness—a

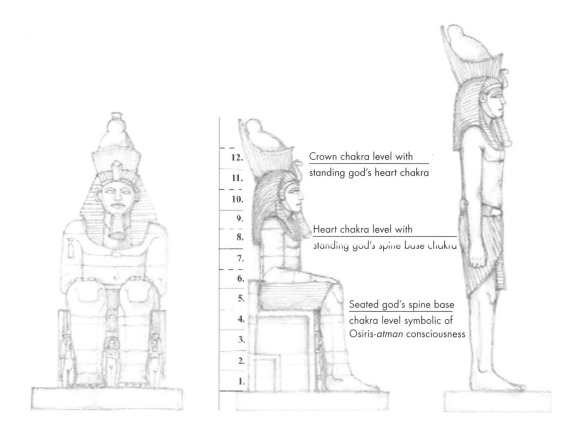

12.
11.
10.
9.
8.
7.
6.
5.
4.
3.
2.
1.

Crown chakra level with
standing god's heart chakra

Heart chakra level with
standing god's spine base chakra

Seated god's spine base
chakra level symbolic of
Osiris-*atman* consciousness

FIGURE 10.15. SUGGESTED METAPHYSICAL CORRESPONDENCES INVOLVING THE STATUES AT ABU SIMBEL

Note: The female statues to either outer side of the leg of the large male seated figures have crowns that rise to a point just above the base of level four of the sectional stonework. The female statues between the legs, however, do not possess a crown and their heads are set lower than those of the other female figures, rising to a point only halfway up level three. This then apparently corresponds with the astral soul employing the lower mind principle, whereas those that stand independently outside the protection of the large god figures represent the soul nature of the spiritually awakened person (i.e., the initiate), which is capable of extending its range of consciousness up to and even into the fourth state. Through doing this, it makes direct contact with the (kundalini) Life-force of the higher god nature into which it is then reabsorbed. It is noteworthy that the fourth-to-fifth and the sixth-to-seventh levels on the seated god figure are each carved in one unjointed section.

NB: The actual stone joints on the statues are as shown on the vertical scale, not as perhaps implied by the drawing.

name that signified his power over the waters of Chaos and over space itself. He was the Self-born Creator who remained ever in the shadows. Associated with the zodiacal sign of Leo, he—as man's own Spiritual Ego—was himself the primary fallen solar deity and thus needed no physical Sun to illuminate him. The next figure—that representing Amen-Ra—symbolized man's dual mental dynamism. The third figure represented the human being himself, while the fourth figure—symbolically that of Ra-Herakte—represented the rising, semidivinely oriented faculty of self-consciousness.

The External, Giant God-Beings

We turn next to take a look at the four external god figures in greater detail, because there is further symbolism to be seen here—again, largely oriented around the issue of proportion and posture. First of all, they all look exactly the same and wear exactly the same crown—that of Upper and Lower Egypt. All four are seated, thereby symbolically indicating that the divine principles that they represent are temporarily static. Each god figure is surrounded by three lesser, female figures, the smallest being between the legs and possessing no form of headdress at all, while the other two, on either side of the legs, are of different heights and wearing different types of headdress. Each trio, we suggest, thus symbolically represents the psychological, psychic, and physical aspects of the four aspects of the *kosmic* Man-god.

When we look at the actual stone structure that comprises the giant god figures themselves (see fig. 10.15), we see that each is composed of massive stone blocks of equal size and height. Each of these was itself symbolic, apparently representing a plane of kosmic Nature, there being twelve levels (or divisions) in all. The lower five of these represent the five elements and the lower five solar planes. Thus the upper perimeter of the seventh and highest solar plane passes across the chest of the god, where a central cartouche indicates

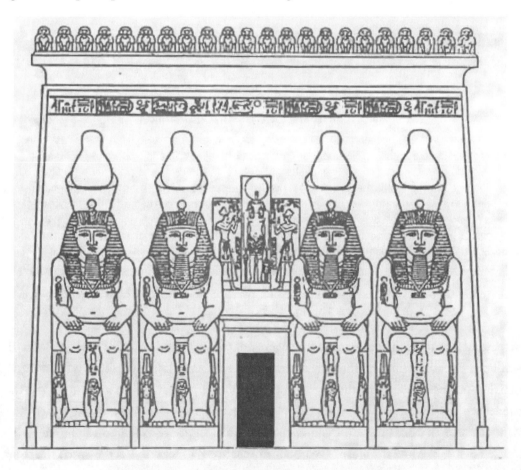

FIGURE 10.16. THE FOUR EXTERNAL GOD FIGURES

the heart chakra. The sixth and seventh planes are united within the upper body of the god but the five lower planes are dual in nature, represented by the two legs, symbolizing the outward (involution) and the inward (evolution) movement of Creation inherent in the cycle of manifest existence.

The female figures—as already indicated—symbolically represent the three material aspects of the god nature, within the three lowest planes of *solar* existence. But they also represent the developing soul nature of Man. The figure between the legs is symbolic of the soul quality of average mankind. The figure outside the left leg symbolically represents the psychically developed soul type, while the figure on the outside of each right leg, with two high plumes on the headdress, symbolically represents the spiritually oriented soul type. The top of the plumes of the third and tallest figure are at the same level as the base of the spine of the seated god-man—where lies the kundalini energy of Creation itself.

Finally, the twelve levels of the stonework of the four main figures seemingly represent the seven levels of the kosmic physical plane in their entirety, plus the five subplanes of the plane of Kosmic Desire. However, there are two further subplanes implicit, by virtue of the god figures being seated. When the god being (in Man) stands fully erect, those two subplanes become manifest—and the god consciousness thereby expresses the consciousness of the lowest kosmic planes in their entirety. His yet higher consciousness—represented by the crown on his head—then symbolically touches the lowest level of the plane of Kosmic Mind; as we have the same symbolic association with the Second Cataract, we can immediately see why this particular statuary and temple were located in this particular place.

The Supposed Involvement of Rameses II

Egyptologists tell us that the whole temple complex was built by Rameses II in his own honor, merely accepting at face value the Rameses-oriented hieroglyphs carved on the statuary. However, the facial features of the four external gods and the eight smaller internal gods are quite clearly all the same and bear no resemblance *whatsoever* to the somewhat aquiline features of Rameses II, as shown in fig. 10.17, based upon the mummified remains

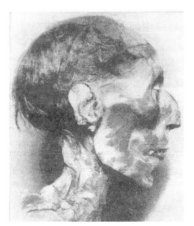

FIGURE 10.17. AQUILINE FEATURES OF RAMESES II, AS SHOWN BY HIS MUMMIFIED REMAINS

of the pharaoh himself, which are now on display in the Cairo Museum. So, Rameses-Kilroy, rest in peace!

Conclusion

It naturally follows that if Man in his divine nature is the essence of a great kosmic Thought, which is busily fighting its way back to its point of origin—within the kosmic Imagination—the symbolic *statuary* of the ancient Egyptians (but not the associated temples) would go no further than this. Hence it is that we find the *apparently* southernmost boundary of ancient Egypt at this location, even though the symbolic imagery of the Nile passing through yet higher kosmic states (in the modern Sudan) was also clearly extant in the most ancient times, as described in chapter 7.

The Egyptians were concerned with the symbolic representation of the *factual* states of existence—both kosmic and solar. They were realists, concerned with the need for absolute accuracy in their symbolism, by virtue of the fact that the automatic magical effects of sympathetic association would generate great problems of disorientation if their metaphysical perceptions were faulty. Consequently, it became essential for them to pursue the symbolism to the nth possible degree. And it is for this reason that we can look at the sacred art, architecture, and statuary of ancient Egypt and see behind and within its integrated combination a self-evident but underlying master plan.

ELEVEN

THE RITUALIZED MAGIC OF EGYPT

Magic, then, is a mysterious divine force through which the spiritual and physical universe becomes manifest, and hence a force permeating and linking all levels of reality from the highest to the most material. But it is also— and this is an especially important aspect of the way the ancient Egyptians understood magic—the means by which the human being, and ultimately all Creation, returns to the supreme Godhead, the unmanifest Source of all that exists. In both respects, Heka is intimately connected with Maat, the "right order" of the universe established at the beginning of time, to which it was considered vital to attune political, social, and moral life.

JEREMY NAYDLER, *TEMPLE OF THE COSMOS*

Because of the rites of mummification and fascination with funerary preparation for an afterlife, it has come to be commonly believed that Egyptian religion was fundamentally based upon the fear of death and that its association with magic (which they called *heka*) was largely oriented toward the associated means of postmortem self-protection and even of hopefully transcending death itself in a materialistic heavenly sense. This, unfortunately, may have been the degenerate form adopted progressively during the Middle and particularly the later New Kingdom dynasties, but it was certainly not the view or practice in much earlier times when the philosophy and practice of magic were seen as the scientific application of sacred knowledge concerning Nature's finer forces.

As we have already seen, ancient tradition had it that that the Atlantean form of religion was actually based upon magic—a natural development resulting from a time in man's much earlier evolutionary development when he was still subservient to the *neteru (deva)* forces in Nature. However, the Atlanteans—so it would appear—allowed their religion to become atheistically polarized and dominated by fascination with the control of Nature through artifice and technology for their own self-indulgence, rather than adhering to the principle of there being a greater plan and purpose in Nature to which all adhered. As a consequence, disaster overtook them. However, the basis of that disaster is perhaps worth examining a little more closely because it provides us with a better understanding of the why and how of Egyptian magic itself.

As we saw earlier in the book, Nature was originally seen as based upon material existence being formed out of a vast spectrum of living light, itself in a constant state of flux. This spectrum in turn resulted from the principle of (holographic) repetition, whereby the lesser was seen as an emanation of the greater and contained by it. By virtue of this, everything existed in some or other type of ordered association with everything else,* either being precipitated from the soul (as ethereal light) into constantly mutating forms—via the work of the elements—or the converse, thereby ensuring that the form became radiant through the indwelling life achieving liberation. But because every entity was regarded as an expression of the process of the one Life (of the Logos of the system), all beings were correspondingly seen as essentially organized in hierarchically predetermined forms of functional relationship with each other. Consequently, magic itself was based upon a knowledge and understanding of these sympathetic relationships and functions and their applications *in conjunction with Divine Purpose.*

While knowledge of these potencies and relationships in Nature inevitably became a source of power, the ability to apply that knowledge had to take place through a clear understanding of the two governing principles of activity in the kosmos—based upon energy and force, activity and inertia, spirit and matter, life and form. However, in the same way that we find still occurs in modern society, the later Atlantean general public, so it would seem, became fascinated with the use of power and the technique of its use, without bothering to understand the background rationale and philosophy.† As a direct consequence, they allowed themselves to become dependent upon it through overindulgence and it is this that fundamentally triggered the problems that inexorably led to cataclysmic disaster. It is also for this reason that human society—whenever and wherever wholly freed of cultural restraints of a religious or philosophical type—always eventually degenerates into a self-feeding morass of greed, suspicion, and superstition.

But to explain: as we have already seen, the Ancients took the view that the soul prin-

---

*Hence the words of Hermes Trismegistus (*Hermetica,* 363): "There is nothing that is not arranged in order; it is by order above all else that the kosmos itself is borne upon its course; nay, the kosmos consists solely of order."
†This is also happening today, through human society allowing itself to become almost completely dependent upon science-based technology. In conjunction with this, human creativity has allowed itself to become pressurized into domination by business acumen and success, and it is now judged almost entirely by reference to financial gain and profitability, the thoroughly fragile linchpins of modern society's very existence. But is this disastrous misjudgment just a case of human history repeating itself?

ciple was the source of all knowledge, the latter being accessible in hierarchically organized sequences. Thus the divine aspect of Man (a kosmic entity that had its place within the crystal sphere of the solar horizon) contained all knowledge concerning our solar system as a whole. Correspondingly, the spiritual soul (*sah*)—a solar entity that had its place within the crystal sphere surrounding the Earth—contained all knowledge of existence on Earth plus a fair amount about what lay farther out in the solar system as well. The astral soul (*ba*), on the other hand—being a largely passive instrument caused to emanate from the World Soul by the *sah* and having its "slate" washed pretty well clean at the end of each incarnation (before being reabsorbed into the *sah* for its next insemination of the seeds of Divine Purpose)—retained only an instinctive knowledge of all the elemental powers in *terrestrial* Nature.

Practical Magic (*Heka*) and the Spirit World

Now magic, per se, involved the ability to manipulate (or to cause change in) the living matter contained by the World Soul. This matter is what nineteenth-century Hermeticists called the "astral light," and what has been known for centuries (and refuted by modern science) as aether. However, all matter being living substance—and thus involving serried hierarchies of life—the very process of magic necessarily involved the principles of attraction and repulsion, the capacity to respectively invoke and evoke the spirit legions in Nature and then command them on their way with a properly defined purpose or activity in mind. In confirmation of this within the Egyptian gnostic tradition we find in the *Hermetica*:

> Marvellous is all that I have told you of man; but one thing there is more marvellous than all the rest; for all marvels are surpassed by this, that man has been able to find out how the gods can be brought into being and [how] to make them. Our ancestors were at first far astray from the truth about the gods; they had no belief in them and gave no heed to worship or religion. But afterward they invented the art of making gods out of some material substance suited for the purpose. And to this invention they added a supernatural force whereby the images might have power to work good or hurt, and combined it with the material substance; that is to say, being unable to make souls, they invoked the souls of daemons and implanted them in the statues by means of certain holy and sacred rites.[1]*

---

*Unfortunately, Sir Walter Scott made a cardinal error in his translation, inasmuch as many of what he generically called gods (*neteru*) were actually no more than nature spirits, or elemental entities. The translation is very misleading but it at least gives a clear indication of the fact that particular types of shamanistic practice were well known to the Egyptians.

Reading between the lines, the problem associated with Atlantean overindulgence of this latter faculty, however, doubtless derived from the fact that the elemental and other lesser spirit beings (*not* gods) thus evoked became overfamiliar with man and thus began to control him through his overdependence upon them. Because lacking in the powers of reason enjoyed by man (due to his greater knowledge of his Higher Self), these lesser hierarchies of spirit beings then ultimately ran amok in a manner strikingly reminiscent of what happened to the wizard's apprentice in the Disney film *Fantasia*. So tradition has it, all that these entities understand—if allowed out of control—is the incessant indulgence of their creative instincts, regardless of any conflicting sense of Higher Purpose in man himself. Thus man has to learn to control them on behalf of that Higher Purpose, commencing within his own organism—by *self*-abnegation and *self*-control.

The Rationale of Control Over the Spirit World

By understanding and implementing the principles of self-discipline and self-control, man was seen as liberating himself from dependence upon the self-demanding nature of these lesser entities. As a consequence, his waking consciousness developed a balance between the need to fulfill *their* cyclically operative needs within reason (recognized by the appetites of sleep, food, drink, sex, excretion, etc.) and *his own* need to maintain a sensitive equilibrium in his subjective nature, supported by the astral soul-body. If he failed in this, his *ka,* or etheric double, became oversuffused with elemental activity of one sort or another, which eventually caused some form or another of subjective imbalance or disorientation and consequent physical illness or disability, which progressively permeated his environment as a whole.

Now magic is generally thought of as involving one's own power over other things or beings. But—as we have just seen—magic was actually regarded as the power (through knowledge) to cause change in Nature by sympathetic means. However, as the old saying has it, "A *little* knowledge is a dangerous thing." Consequently, ignorance and self-indulgence were always seen as the two greatest dangers where any use of magical practice was concerned. Magic started in the mind and thus it was there, according to the Ancients, that understanding and self-discipline had to be fostered under the tutelage of a sense of Higher Purpose *before* any occult knowledge or power was allowed to be accessed. And because the dangers associated with its use were so well known (by the more experienced members of the priesthood, who knew how to control it), it became de rigueur that occult power could not be used under any circumstances for any purpose clearly associated with oneself. One who did so was regarded as taking the "Left Hand Path"—the left hand being associated with the descent into materialism.

Curiously enough, the refusal to use occult or magical power self-indulgently—notwithstanding the knowledge and capacity to do so—was known to result in the development of yet greater powers. We have a clear confirmation of this, for example, in the person of Apollonius of Tyana, who made it quite clear that it was his highly ascetic personal lifestyle that gave him control over the natural forces in Nature.[2] As the individual thus subjectively withdrew from personal association with these lesser forces in Nature, he paradoxically became aware that his own inner reserves of occult power derived from his association with a far greater Individuality of Being. Thus he became increasingly and self-consciously aware that he and this greater Being were one and the same and that the lesser forces in Nature were but the living body organisms and processes of this great and initially incomprehensible Intelligence.*

The Problems Facing the Neophyte

Now, as our world-existence was regarded by the Ancients as functioning on seven associated planes of being—with man functioning objectively and subjectively within the lower three of these—the issue of magical power was seen as having to do with the control over the elemental or psychospiritual matter and entities that comprised these three states. That control became regularized by interactive social ritual during waking brain consciousness, but during sleep the individual was largely on his own. In the case of the unevolved and average individual, this presented little problem because the subjective nature was so self-engrossed that it effectively shut out all external contact. However, in the case of the neophyte or lesser initiate in the Mysteries, it was a very different matter, because he was learning to become psychospiritually awake and thus fully self-conscious in the subtlest manner, whether his physical body was awake or asleep.

Because—as the Hermeticists have it—"energy follows thought," the wakeful attention of the individual during bodily sleep (while astrally traveling in his *ba*) resulted quite automatically in attention being drawn to his dynamic presence (like a moth to a light) by groups of various types of *devas* and elemental entities—according to the purity (or lack of it) of his own nature. His ability to pass through them without harm or distress then depended upon his natural self-confidence as a spiritual being of higher status (and thus power) than they. But because the less advanced individual was recognized as being particularly vulnerable, rituals were developed for instinctive memorization and use, not only to protect but also to help the individual recognize the subjective Path by the various signs and groups of entities he was likely to meet along the way. This, it is suggested, is the

---

*We find the same principles expressed in the ancient Vedic tradition, from the *Katha Upanishad*: "He who lacketh discrimination, whose mind is unsteady and whose heart is impure, never reacheth the goal, but is born again and again. But he who hath discrimination, whose mind is steady and whose heart is pure, reacheth the goal and, having reached it, is born no more."

FIGURE 11.1. SYMBOLIC REPRESENTATION OF ASTRAL TRAVEL BY THE INITIATE ANI, THE DOORWAY BETWEEN THE TWO FIGURES OF ANI REPRESENTING THE OUT-OF-BODY TRANSITION

real basis of the so-called spells in the Pyramid Texts, Coffin Texts, and the Book of the Dead. In fig. 11.1, we actually see what appears to be a symbolic representation of astral travel by the initiate Ani, the doorway between the two figures of Ani representing the out-of-body transition.

The Development of Physical Spirituality

The individual whose purity of motive and subjective self-consciousness were highly developed inevitably possessed an astral soul-body of considerable natural radiance and power* that automatically kept the mischievous elemental denizens at bay yet was also capable of directing them by an act of will. Additionally, because of the increasing ability to recognize the various hierarchical types of elemental and *deva* beings in this way, the individual initiate was able to call upon them to assist him in his work (e.g., healing) when back in his physical body, *in full waking consciousness.* By virtue of his training in this manner, the initiate was also ultimately enabled to maintain an unbroken continuity of consciousness between the spiritual soul state, the astral soul state, and the waking physical state. In this manner and as a direct result, his semidivine nature began to show through his purely human nature (as spirituality) and thereby radiate out into society at large. Thus by a process of self-willed subjective development, he eventually became a fully qualified spiritual adept and then, later on, a manifest demigod, with power over those processes we misleadingly call "life" and "death."

Consequently and perhaps unsurprisingly, the physical body of the high initiate was regarded as manifesting spiritually attuned forces, particularly through its primary organs, in which the psychospiritual forces themselves had become entrapped through the occult

*Qualities actually generated by the spiritual individuality contained within it, or using it as a vehicle.

discipline he had imposed upon them during his lifetime.* It seems to have been this that ultimately led to the common practice of postmortem cremation in ancient times being gradually (and unfortunately) replaced by mummification. Turning back to the direct issue of practical magic, however, there are two particular areas that generally attract modern public attention and we should perhaps spend a moment looking at these.

Words of Power, Magical Curses, and Charms

One area of practical magic involved the use of magical rituals for both attracting good luck and also issuing curses. The second involved the use of good luck talismans (*ushabti*), which the Egyptians—in the later dynasties particularly—carried extensively on their persons and also left in specific locations on the mummified corpse at the time of the funerary proceedings. The first simply worked on the principle of invoking (with incantations, sympathetically associated incenses, etc.) and then binding angelic or elemental subhierarchies to act on one's behalf according to some verbally delivered formula, in a manner that would be triggered by some particular set of circumstances. As Wallis Budge tells us: "The Egyptians believed that if the best effect was to be produced by Words of Power, they must be uttered in a certain tone of voice and at a certain rate and at a certain time of the day or night, with appropriate gestures or ceremonies."[3]

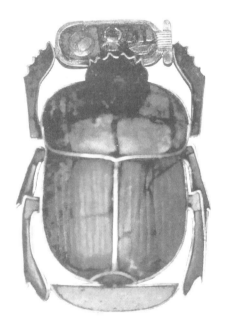

FIGURE 11.2. AMULETS IN THE FORM OF SCARAB BEETLES WERE THOUGHT TO HAVE THE POWER TO PROTECT THEIR OWNER FROM DANGER OR HARM.

---

*Consequently, the viscera of the human body—the various main organs—were also regarded as having particular occult significance. Thus, during the mummification process, they were removed and kept separate from the body itself in canopic jars dedicated to the four sons of Horus. The modern name for the internal organs is *offal*, seemingly derived from the ancient name of the guardian spirits (*ophelim* in the Hebrew) equated with physical body processes.

The traditional knowledge concerning this faculty has been passed down the millennia among witches, wizards, and shamans, but it also frequently appears quite instinctively on the part of ordinary people who somehow manage to get themselves sufficiently worked up (emotionally—and thus psychically) about some issue or another of importance to them, thereby bringing about a sustained degree of concentration and soul alignment not normally applied. It has always also commonly been found functioning (even today) as a result of (and in tandem with) extreme religious piety. However, if the Ancients were able to achieve phenomenal effects in this manner, modern attempts to achieve the same thing merely by means of uttering supposedly potent words or phrases from a magical grimoire, while lacking any attendant understanding of the supersensory effects of sound and any associated sense of dramatic intent, appear by comparison instantly doomed to failure.

This same view is expressed by Arthur Versluis in his book *The Egyptian Mysteries,* where he says: "Now, as is reiterated in the Buddhist sutras and in the Upanisads, the performance of ritual without knowledge is fruitless—the degree of knowledge determines the efficacy or power of a given rite. . . . The purpose of a ritual is to maintain a connection with the celestial realms, to keep people from falling into paths of blinding darkness, of brute secular materialism and ignorance, to remind them of their Origin and responsibility."[4]

The second, involving the *ushabti,* involved the manufacture of an abstract glyph—or a totem like the ankh, signifying the Life principle—or a god figure out of very particularly chosen materials. Whereas modern scholarship and science take the firm view that these accoutrements are all merely of a psychologically stimulating or relaxing nature, the Ancients took the equally firm view that such *ushabtis* could be potentized by a psychomagnetic or mesmeric ritual. In this, an elemental entity of a particular nature and quality was induced to enter the talisman and there remain quietly captive to serve its owner according to its nature and force.* We have something of this in the story of Aladdin and his magic lamp. But the instinctual use of such magnetized talismans and charms is actually still almost as active today throughout the world (even in the West). The only difference is that in the West, they *are* usually treated as psychological placebos even by many of the people who wear them. And, indeed, because they have never been subjected to formal ritual, that is precisely what they are.

Modern Correspondences

These days, one tends to come across all sorts of individuals offering for sale crystals and protective talismans of one sort or another, without actually fully understanding the nature of what they are about and rarely bothering with the use of ritual per se—or prior

---

*Something which the Christian Church (without properly understanding it) has also managed to trivialize in its various blessings of virtually anything its members wish to have sanctified or merely made lucky.

FIGURE 11.3. DEPICTION OF A RITUAL INVOLVING THE ANKH,
WHICH SIGNIFIED THE LIFE PRINCIPLE

purification of themselves. Consequently, the factor of potentization tends to be left up to the buyer or receiver, who either unquestioningly believes in its natural organic force (and thus achieves nothing in response) or otherwise manages to inseminate some of his own, thereby turning it into something resembling a personalized psychic battery. The projection of such mesmeric force—what the Chinese tradition calls *chi* or *ki*—for good or ill is of course widely used in natural healing and also by the Christian Church (the Roman Catholic and Orthodox Churches in particular) for sanctification by the bestowal of a priestly blessing. This author has even seen a small reptile rigidly paralyzed by its use. It has since time immemorial been used for such things as snake-charming and rendering all sorts of other animals completely docile. The "gift" is, for example, widely known among members of the gypsy fraternity, particularly where the training of horses is concerned.* It is also the very basis of what we otherwise call "charm," as well as being the root source of all hypnotic influence.

One comes across the issue of potentization (somewhat mundanely) in the form of homeopathic preparations. Here the principle involves the progressive reduction of all traceable chemicals in a fluid until all that remains is the (invisible) spiritual essence of that which is going to be used to treat like with like. The fact that the essence is not pathologically detectable leads scientists to scoff and say that there is actually nothing left, so that any medical improvement must be entirely due to a placebo effect or natural recovery. However, the ancient view was that by ritually ridding something of its lower, chaotic material nature, its remaining psychospiritual essence—having a clearly defined and instinctive understanding of its own purpose in Nature—would release its harmonizing power *intelligently* into the desired environment, thereby bringing about wholly beneficial change.

Wonder Workers

In India, various types of apparently extraordinary phenomena are produced by the best wandering magicians and fakirs, although there are very few left these days. There the assisting elemental spirits are generically known as *madan,* each type having its own nature and powers. For example, as H. P. Blavatsky described in her book *Isis Unveiled,* the *poruthu-madan* are used in all manifestations of physical force, including levitation and also the subjugation of wild animals; the *kumil-madan* is used to produce rain out

*This brings to the fore the issue of the various types of elemental beings (considered in terms of both function and quality) used by the Ancients in their *ushabtis* and their other magical or religious rituals, for, although all elementals were seen as homogeneous in their fifth essence—that of the aether—they were otherwise regarded as fourfold in qualitative function—as fire, air, water, and earth. However, each of these in turn was seen by the alchemists as triple in nature. Thus, for example, fire was found in its transformative role as (a) warmth or heat, (b) light, and (c) electricity. To complicate matters further, each of these was regarded as dual.

of thin air; the *shula-madan* is used to reproduce artifacts, again out of nothing, or to grow plants from seeds at an extraordinary rate.[5] Notwithstanding this, the more spiritually oriented of the fakirs—all self-dedicated to the god Siva, the doyen of all scientific knowledge—seemingly utilize their own auric magnetism as well to create equally or even more astounding effects.

These same phenomenal powers are still (occasionally) to be found in various parts of Africa today, although Middle Eastern and Western religion has so focused the attention of society on man's concern with material self-satisfaction to the exclusion of almost everything else that (until very recently) Nature has been largely forgotten except as a place of mere utility and extortion. Thus, because faith (based upon a very real interest in and natural understanding of natural association) is absolutely fundamental to any form of practical magic, the general attitude toward this arcane area of knowledge has become thoroughly corrupted by a desire to use it for pure self-gratification. Consequently, the sense of its underlying rationale has either been lost or been turned into black magic. However, with the rise of interest in both books and television programs on Nature and ecological science, this unhappy situation is very gradually being reversed and we may yet hope to see a general recognition of its social and psychological importance.

Turning back to the issue of charms, however, we find in ancient Egypt of the latter dynasties this same corruption of the understanding of what magic was all about, with a consequent descent into religious apathy, mass superstition, and fear of death. As a consequence of increasing affluence in the Middle Kingdom dynasties, the higher branches of society turned toward increasingly luxurious self-indulgence, which inevitably resulted in poverty appearing in other quarters in response. This in turn gave rise to the seriously problematic by-product of grave robbing for jewelry, resulting in the later use of rituals supposedly to bring down astral curses on the heads of the thieves.* Even the pharaohs regarded themselves as not immune from this—hence the curse in the tomb of Tutankhamen.

Ceremonials and Rituals

As human beings lose their *natural* faith in the fundamental reality of a spiritual continuity of existence, it is noteworthy that they always instinctively start to produce theologically based ceremonials, rituals, and artifacts to act as reminders. However, over time, the faith and its continuity in ceremonial degenerates into a mere hope and the reminders ultimately into mere historical curiosities. This then is the eventual fate of all civilizations and cultures and it is the reason for new ones constantly springing up as old forms are perceived as no longer being able to fulfill the needs of the present day. But a society without

---

*Vice and theft in society have always historically increased in direct proportion to society's own proportionately greater attribution of value to things as opposed to abstract values such as character, goodness, responsibility, and so on.

some nationally shared forms of (cyclically operative) religious or spiritually oriented ceremonial is one without any true sense of its own inner nature and structure. Ceremonial is the mass means by which human nature publicly faces up to its common spiritual faith and responsibility and thus regenerates itself, while its persistent use imbues that same society with its own psychospiritual force.

Ritual, on the other hand, is but the individual act or sequence of acts of invocation, evocation, or propitiation, carried out by an individual or group of individuals to fulfill a particular psychospiritual function in human society, for the latter's own sake. Its consistent efficacy, however—as is also the case with ceremonial—is entirely dependent upon the experiential understanding by the priest of the nature of—and his familiarity with—the various planes of being *and* his capacity to put himself in direct rapport with them by a simple act of will. This is the true essence of what we call faith. A ceremonial carried out without complete faith, and a deep and abiding sense of its own importance on behalf of society as a whole, becomes empty and dead. Thus a nation that dispenses with ancient ceremonial merely on the grounds of its supposed lack of economic, political, or intellectual usefulness sets about the destruction of its own social foundations and does so at its own peril.* And a priesthood that loses understanding and faith in the true nature and efficacy of both ceremonial and ritual is itself doomed to become a living ghost in its own time.

We can see historically that in Egypt private ritual became increasingly more important than public ceremonial and as the importance of ceremonial diminished, its degenerate forms tended to become licentious.† This occurred, for example, in Greece with the Bacchanalia, which *originally* was no more orgiastic than are our autumn ceremonies of Thanksgiving and harvest festivals.

The Priesthood and Priestesshood

We turn next to the issue of the distinction in function between the priesthood and priestesshood, remembering that, in ancient times, the idea of a priesthood without its female counterpart would have been unthinkable by virtue of the perception that the male and female principles were psychospiritually complementary. The female aspect was specifically related to the soul principle while the male was specifically related to the fallen "spark," whose task it was to re-become its father, the greater expression of the Unknowable Deity, through its association with the soul principle in its highest aspect. Hence in the Greek tradition we have the wholly allegorical story of Prince Oedipus, who became separated

---

*This is clearly evident in Western society wherever the secular or atheistic approach has become totally dominant.
†Hence the desire of the Ptolemaic dynasty to see the Rites of Isis reinstituted, in order to restore sociopolitical stability in an Egypt that by then had already become spiritually degenerate.

from his family in early childhood and after a life of much wandering unknowingly returned and married his own mother after killing his father, also in ignorance.

In the sacred tradition of both India and Greece, girls who chose to become priestesses had the choice of leaving at any time—usually in order to marry—up to a certain point. Until they left, however, they were required to remain absolutely celibate. At certain stages, they faced a degree of positive and progressive commitment to their order, on behalf of a particular god or goddess,* for the remainder of their lives. In fact, there seems a strong probability that the original practice involved all young women becoming attached to a temple as junior priestesses for a number of years during their teens and there receiving an important part of their education, while also participating in the lesser Mysteries and (in some cases only) becoming a seeress. However, the continued practicing of seership outside the confines and authority of the temple, once one retired from it, was absolutely forbidden.†

We have no reason to suppose that Egypt was any different in these respects and there are a few still extant frescoes (see fig. 11.4) that actually appear to depict senior and junior priestesses. Mention should perhaps be made at this point of the golden-hued projection

FIGURE 11.4. FRESCO APPEARING TO DEPICT SENIOR AND JUNIOR PRIESTESSES, WITH GOLDEN-HUED PROJECTIONS FROM THE TOP OF THEIR HEADS

---

*Notwithstanding this, Herodotus (*The Histories,* 107 and 116) was able to observe that in fifth-century BCE Egypt, "no woman is minister of any deity, whether male or female; all are served by men." However, he goes on to confirm that the role of the priestess was devoted to seership and divination, neither of which was generally practiced by the priests (*The Histories,* 124). Interestingly, the name *nun* given to the modern version of the priestess found in convents and abbeys appears to have been derived from her Egyptian counterpart having been a priestess of Nun.

†The fact that this occurred later on—thereby giving rise to the advent of isolated cases of witchcraft—only shows the extent to which the disciplines of the Mystery School had become thoroughly degenerate.

at the top of the girls' heads, which Egyptologists have bizarrely interpreted as incense cones, which were lit in order to perfume the hair. Found also on male figures—as in the Chamber of Judgment Ani picture—the cone is quite clearly intended to represent the burgeoning crown chakra, thereby demonstrating the faculty of seership. Bearing in mind that soul knowledge—and therefore prevision—was associated with the female aspect of Nature, it was quite natural that the human female nature should be used to access it. And as the vibration of the soul nature gave rise to *deva* speech, or music, it was again quite natural that it was the priestesses who were largely responsible for the more subtle forms of musical accompaniment.

General Role Distinctions

This is not to suggest, however, that Egyptian, Greek, or Indian male youths had no associated capacities or training. The young men undoubtedly also had to spend a proportion of their late adolescence and early manhood in temple service, again with decisions becoming necessary at various stages of commitment as to whether to remain or to return to lay life in Egyptian society. The primary distinction between the priest and priestess seems to have been that the former, representing the positive (i.e., male) aspect of the overshadowing god, had to learn the principles of esoteric and occult knowledge in *intellectual* depth, plus the active command and control of the *deva* and elemental forces in Nature. The priestesses' role, on the other hand, appears to have been restricted to non-intellectual functions, in line with the required passivity of the soul principle*—hence the involvement in seership, sacred dance, and sacred music.

Elements of this training are to be found even today in the role of the geisha in Japanese society and in attitudes down the centuries as to human society finding meekness, humility, gentleness, and devotion in womanhood a great joy and blessing. Unfortunately—as with all things human, given time—this tradition has degenerated into a form of enslavement of the female in the home to the husband and sons. This degeneracy—particularly prevalent in the Middle and Far East†️ and disgracefully institutionalized in some areas of

---

*The equivalent growth of independent shamanism (male mediumship) was evidently not seen as such a threat by virtue of the male nature being mentally rather than astrally polarized. Whereas the female response involved her becoming subsumed within the astral (feeling) nature and thereby being completely taken over by supraphysical forces—which left her unconscious of what her body was doing—the male shaman was expected to be fully aware at all times. Notwithstanding this, we see in some remote places even today the activities of some very low-grade male shamans (so-called) who allow total loss of control and whose nature thereby gradually degenerates into submission to mere animism—or animalism.

†️The tragic degeneration of the Japanese geishas and Indian *devadasis*—equivalents, originally, of the Roman "vestal virgins"—into culturally gifted courtesans owes itself to the priestess's dutiful union with the overshadowing god nature having originally been taken advantage of in a purely physical way by an increasingly (spiritually) ignorant priesthood. Originally, this would probably have been due to an ill-conceived view of the spiritual act being more potent if brought fully down to earth. Thereafter, however, the rot set in.

Islam and Hinduism—has itself resulted in a huge imbalance and distortion at the root of modern society. The tendency found in the West to go to the very opposite extreme in an effort to make women equal (rather than complementary) is clearly a natural—albeit misguided—reaction to this distortion, but itself merely compounds the problem (as is gradually being realized by women themselves) and results only in yet further psychospiritual disorientation.

In parallel fashion, ancient tradition had the man fulfilling an almost secondary or supporting role in the active ordering of daily family life (while remaining head of the family) but taking an active primary role where religion and public life were concerned. Unfortunately, this too has degenerated in many places (throughout the world, not just in tribal society) in the menfolk becoming serially lazy, self-indulgent, and aggressive, where their minds have not instead been actively turned toward the pursuit of knowledge and the creation and formulation of an artistic culture on behalf of society as a whole.

The Priesthood in Egypt

The ancient Egyptian temple priesthood seems in some respects to bear curiously close parallels to that of the Church of England—possibly through early Masonic and later Templar influence having their own origins in Egypt. The Egyptian priesthood as a whole came under the formal aegis of the pharaoh, but it would appear that the supreme hierophant at Heliopolis was himself of very considerable influence throughout Egypt too. It may well thus be that their roles were in some way functionally complementary.

Each temple had its own local chief priest (the Mer) and the main nome temple appears to have had a hierophant whose role and position were akin to those of a modern bishop—only with far more influence. As Budge tells us: "Other orders of priests were 'father of the god,' the asperger or 'pure one,' 'the scribe of the holy books' and 'the possessor of the book.' Kheriheb . . . the priest who arranged the order of service and recited or chanted specific parts within them . . . was usually a man of great learning and was believed to possess magical powers. . . . He was the chief performer in all the important magical funerary ceremonies, especially in those that concerned the 'Opening of the Mouth.'"[6]

There were of course numerous lesser priests in each temple hierarchy as well, each and all having their particular role and functions to fulfill on behalf of the god or goddess in question.* In addition to these full-time priests, there were also lay priests who fulfilled specific supporting duties for so many hours per day, or who did so for a month at a time. Thus, as in village England and France, the local temples became pretty well the central focus of both religious and social life for men, women, and children, much of the activity,

---

*Originally, during the Old Kingdom period, the Egyptian priesthood seems to have involved a quite small full-time cadre, with the rest being made up of a constantly rotating succession of lay priests. The professional priestly cadre expanded enormously only later.

The Ritualized
Magic of Egypt

319

however, being commonly of a very routine nature, as in every community throughout the world. However, the ever-present nature of sympathetic magical custom gave ancient temple society a flavor and color rarely seen in the western European Christian tradition, in any century.

Theurgy and Thaumaturgy

By virtue of woman's passive or supporting role in the psychospiritual field, any occult activity on her part much beyond that of acting as a medium or oracle (under supervision) would have been considered potentially very dangerous to both her and to society in general through sympathetic transmission of unrestrained influences. Consequently, all occult activity involving either theurgy or thaumaturgy came under the control of the initiated male priesthood—as did the actual practice of mediumship by the priestesses. The much later dislocation of the temple system resulting in women independently selling their services as mediums—like the Obeah—caused huge anxiety because of the lack of centralized control by trained priests—hence the thoroughly misunderstood biblical injunction "Thou shalt not suffer a witch to live." There was, however, no general prohibition against the use of such occult practices—*provided* that they remained entirely within the control of the established priesthood and were practiced only inside the temple.

Theurgy—from *theos* and *urgos,* meaning "god" and "will-force"—is essentially associated with the various procedures needed to invoke the Divine Will and then give expression to it through the medium of the hierophant to the congregation. It thus appears largely subjective, even though actually giving rise (if done properly) to the appearance of a distinct change in the atmosphere of the church/temple through the presence of some supraphysical (spiritual) being or influence. Theurgy thus works through the evocative use (in tandem) of the Higher Mind and spiritual soul. Thaumaturgy, on the other hand, involves quite definitely phenomenal magic such as levitation, mesmerism, telekinesis, and physical body impenetrability. It works through the use of the focused Mind principle in conjunction with what nineteenth-century Hermeticists called the "astral light" and what late medieval alchemists referred to as the aether. It is entirely based upon sympathetic association but appears no less potent for that, if carried out properly.

The Ceremonials and Rituals of the Egyptians

That brings us to the issue of the actual ceremonials and magical rituals as practiced by the ancient Egyptians—of which relatively little is clearly known. However, many are probably still with us today in the disguised form of those unknowingly practiced by the Catholic and Orthodox Christian priesthood, who borrowed them long ago from the Coptic priests when the latter switched religions in about the third or fourth century CE. Bringing with it a vast tract of religious imagery—which enabled Osiris, Horus the Younger, and Isis to be very easily transmuted into the characters of Jesus and his mother—this infusion provided the infant Christian movement with a ready-made theological basis and an associated public support, which eventually nullified the efforts of the Neo-Platonists of Alexandria and thus effectively initiated the cultural Dark Age.

Perhaps the purer part of Egyptian public religious ceremonial appears to have been absorbed by the Orthodox arm of the Christian Church, which had its primary center at Byzantium—later called Constantinople and now Istanbul. That which had already passed to Rome during the time of earlier Roman occupation of Egypt inevitably became conditioned by then existing forms of worship (and associated architecture) of other gods, such as Jupiter, Bacchus, Pan, Minerva, and so on, which were themselves merely alter egos of the Greek gods. Consequently, we see in the architecture and ceremonial of Roman Christianity an interesting mixture of both the Greco-Roman and the Egyptian, which renders it quite distinct from the more nearly Oriental flavor of the Orthodox type found today in Greece and Russia and several other countries in between.

Some Examples of Egyptian Theurgic Ceremonies

While sheer space prohibits the capacity to dwell much further on this subject, there are three well-known public religious ceremonies known to have taken place in ancient Egypt, which we might mention in passing, in order to give the whole subject some distinct flavor. The first is the ceremony that took place with the inauguration of any new temple or public building. The second is a ceremony that took place at Coptos and seemingly involved the pharaoh himself. The third is the Festival of Lights (or Lamps), which took place at Sais in the Delta.

The building foundation setting-out ceremony involved either a high official (i.e., the temple hierophant) on behalf of the pharaoh or the pharaoh himself if the occasion were sufficiently important, plus priestesses on behalf of the goddess Seshat. As earlier described, she was the goddess of the number seven, which was regarded as the metaphysical basis of all existence. Although the author is not a Mason himself, it would appear that there is (rather inevitably) a temple setting-out ritual practiced by Freemasons even today and that it also involves the use of the number seven. Furthermore, the ancient Egyptians appear to have used knotted cords in their setting-out and various other procedures, as do also the Masons.

The ceremonial at Coptos apparently involved both puppets or marionettes and a fairly frantic form of running dance by the pharaoh, waving a boat paddle[7]—not dissimilar in some respects to the rather odd biblical story of King David dancing naked and with complete abandon in front of the Temple in Jerusalem. Quite what else was involved we do

The Ritualized
Magic of Egypt

not know, but the essence of the associated symbolism seems to have been connected with the errant and often uncontrollable aspect of the Mind principle in Man (which in India is associated with Hanuman, the monkey god) and its eventual control by the Higher Mind under the aegis of the Spiritual Ego.

The Festival of Lights was held in honor of the goddess Net/Neith and it seems to have involved the hanging of candle-lit lanterns in great number throughout the house and neighborhood, all over Egypt.[8] The simple, underlying, and rather beautiful symbolism is that of the multitude of "divine sparks" acting as the points of celestial light that, when seen together in unison, constituted the underlying web of manifest existence.

Masonic Ceremonial

It would again be impossible on the grounds of space within this book to go into any detail regarding the ceremonies and rituals of modern Freemasonry, although there can be little doubt that the oldest ones have their provenance among those of Egyptian temple practice. Much historical research is still being done by Masons themselves, trying to uncover the true origins of their modern Craft tradition, aspects of which have already been found in still extant records of thirteenth-century operative Masonic craft guilds. Thus further detailed comment on this issue will have to wait a little longer. In the meantime, however, it is still possible to see how sacred imagery and allegory, plus numerology and its combinations, played (and still play) a very important part in Masonic ritual in general, even though often unrecognized within the mainstream Masonic fraternity.

The Magic of the Eye

The Eyes of Ra and Horus play such a major part in the whole Egyptian occult and mystic tradition that we cannot pass without looking at this particular issue in some detail. In the first place, however, we should perhaps make the point that the fascination with "the Eye" was entirely practical and not at all theoretical. The projected influence of the eye in all ancient traditions was seen as possessing great magical power, not only within the ambit of physical existence and experience, but also—and if anything more particularly—within the subjective realms in which the initiate or shaman was consciously able to transport himself by astral travel.* Thus we find in the Pyramid Texts: "O King . . . I have saved

---

*There is an old English expression: "The eyes are the windows of the soul." Although usually taken as artistic metaphor, the saying is factually accurate, for the soul is the vehicle of all the faculties of perception, combined in one. Thus the "eye of the soul"—when turned in any particular direction—sees with the whole of itself. And many who have experienced in full consciousness the phenomenon of astral travel will bear witness to the fact that soul vision curiously involves seeing things from the inside as well as the outside.

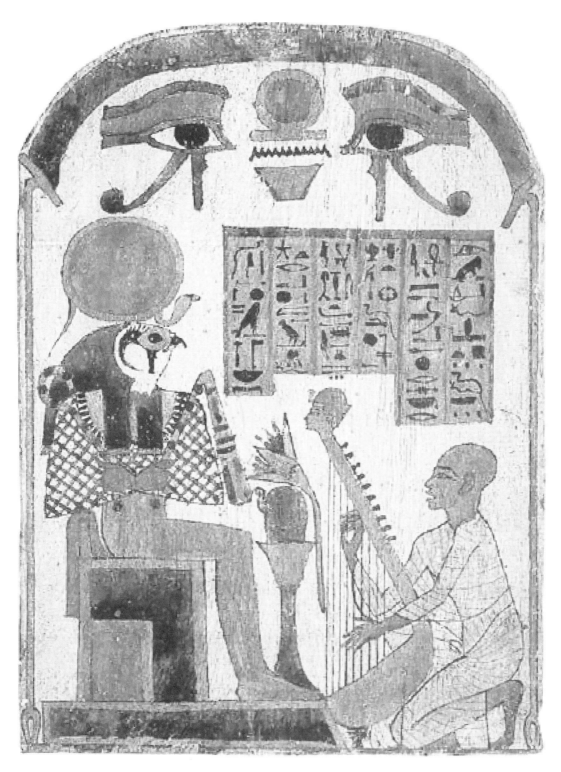

FIGURE 11.5. EYES OF HORUS, METAPHOR FOR THE FOCUSED ATTENTION
OF THE GOD WITHIN, ABOVE THE DEPICTION OF HORUS,
THE GOD THAT SYMBOLIZED INDIVIDUALIZED CONSCIOUSNESS

you from your obstructor, I will never give you over to your attacker, I have protected you . . . by means of the power of repulsion which is in my face." *Face* here, however, actually means "my focused attention."[9]

Within our mundane world, the experience of someone else watching us or of their reacting suddenly to our watching them intently is extremely common, although as yet not understood by science. The ancient tradition, however, had it that the eye emitted its own quality of light, as well as absorbing light-borne imagery, and that, given the right circumstances and training, this could be extended in its projection to quite extraordinary distances, in a manner that would appear to defy the laws of optics. The strength of the projection, according to the tradition, was entirely dependent upon the sustained *subjective* focus of the individual, allied to his will. But the principle itself operated by virtue of that universal planetary medium we have already mentioned—the Hermetic astral light, which modern science still consistently refuses to accept, notwithstanding its having recently posited the existence of a universal quantum fluid. However, "a rose by any other name . . . "

The Subjective Realm

The Ancients did not believe the subjective realm to be imaginary or insubstantial as modern science does. For them it comprised serial states or planes of being and consciousness, which possessed their own quality of light substance and associated hierarchies of animate existence. In this astral realm, Man's consciousness (symbolized by the god Horus) was not only able to travel at will (using the *ba*) but also able to create instantaneous effects, merely through conscious mental focus. Thus in the Pyramid Texts:

> O Osiris the King [i.e., the initiate], mount up to Horus [the principle of individualized consciousness]; betake yourself to him, do not be far from him. Horus has come that he may recognise you . . . he [Horus] swims bearing you; he lifts up one who is greater than he in you [i.e., the divine self in Man] and his followers have seen you, that your strength is greater than his, so that they cannot thwart you. Horus comes and recognises his father [the divine spirit] in you . . . Horus has wrested his Eye [the faculty of perception] from Set [the principle of acquisitive selfishness resulting in lack of focus] and has given it to you, even this sweet Eye. Make it come back to you, assign it to yourself and may it belong to you. Isis [the soul vehicle] has re-assembled you, the heart of Horus is glad about you . . . and it is Horus who will make good what Set has done to you.[10]

The fact that Horus "recognizes his father in you" is indicative of the fact that it was the unseen demigod within Man's higher nature that was itself the source of the potency exerted by "the Eye" of the perceptive will nature, via the Mind. Thus the very act of subjective coordination brought about the rebirth of the faculty of perceptive consciousness.

Consequently, it was entirely logical that yet greater degrees of subjective coordination brought about correspondingly greater and wider degrees of perceptive consciousness—and associated Will-force. The Pyramid Texts confirm this from a variety of angles time and again.

The Various Eyes of Ra and Horus

As already indicated, "the Eye"—whether of Ra or Horus—was intended as a dual metaphor for the focused attention and thus also the will-force of the god within. When in association with Ra, it became the Will-to-Be and the cyclical Life wave itself. When in association with Horus it became the Will-to-Know—the principle of focused attentiveness that engenders an automatically associated consciousness.* The left eye is the materially oriented one—hence the left side of the brain being associated with the purely intellectual function. The right eye is the truly creative and assimilative (or withdrawing) one, the superior director, or observer—hence the oft-found phrase "the Watchers of Pe."†

In another sense, the two soul-bodies (the *sah* and *ba*) were themselves the respectively right and left eyes of the deity, for it was through the limitations of their agency that the energy of the deity (i.e., the "divine spark") was seen as being able to manifest a proportion of itself as the radiantly objective light of consciousness itself. Thus when the tradition tells us that Set tears out the left Eye of Horus and hangs on to it, it signifies the fact that the self-centeredly acquisitive principle in man (i.e., the lower mind) has attained a certain degree of psychological perception. The fact that Horus, in response, tears off Set's testicles is, correspondingly, a metaphor indicating the development of conscious control by man over both the physical reproductive instinct and his instinctive tendency toward selfishness.

The left Eye of Horus is commonly associated by Egyptologists with the Moon while the right Eye is correspondingly associated by them with the Sun. However, these two—the Moon and Sun—are themselves respectively symbolic of the lower mind and Higher Mind principles. It also needs to be remembered that the Moon—whether in ancient magical terms or otherwise—was actually only symbolic of the *ba* of the Earth, it being merely a trapped

---

*It is important to remember that although Osiris represents the fallen nature of the "divine spark" within the *sah* and Horus represents the faculty of self-conscious perception, they are depicted as quite separate in order to maintain the initiate's distinctive sense of his true Higher Self as the unconditioned and unconditionable "divine spark," the demigod within. It is for this reason also that there is a more direct correlation between Ra and Horus than there is between Ra and Osiris. As already described, Osiris represents the spiritual *form* of Man—that is, the equivalent of the Hindu *atman*—whereas Ra represents the cycle of the Breath of Life, which is itself the co-manifestation of the consciousness of the Logos. Consequently, Horus and Ra merge at the higher levels of being into one another, although presented as different god-aspects of the same principle.

†Pe appears to denote that psychospiritual state in which the observing nature of overshadowing deity (i.e., the Spiritual Ego) was to be found.

The Ritualized
Magic of Egypt

325

reflector, having no independent nature of its own. It was thus the reflection of the spiritual energy *from above* that enabled the consciousness of the *ba* (Isis thereby being transmuted into Hathor) to mount back up to the *sah*. It is from the idea of this projected and reflected energy interplay that the Egyptians appear to have derived their symbolic concept of the "ladders" the initiate was able to use to gain access from the lower world into the higher.

The Use of Spells and Mantras

As a means of auxiliary assistance to their efforts at achieving spiritual focus, the Egyptians used a wide range of incantations of various types, in many cases using stock phraseology such as "the doors of the sky/firmament are open to you, O King" and "I travel the Winding Waterway" and "be a spirit in the horizon." The oldest of these are to be found in the Pyramid Texts. Others based on similar themes are to be found in the later Coffin Texts and the supposedly more recent Book of the Dead.

To call these incantations "spells," however, is very misleading. They were in fact invocations and evocations, uttered either by the candidate in the Mysteries or by the officiating priesthood. Their aim in either case was slightly different. Where uttered by the candidate, the overall purpose appears to have been that of orientating and focusing his mind on the immediate task at hand and preparing himself psychologically for it. Where the utterances were made by the priests, it was clearly *on behalf of* the candidate and not only supported him but also aimed to evoke spiritual powers on his behalf while keeping other non-spiritual forces at bay. An example of the former is as follows:

> O Geb, Bull of the Sky, I am Horus, my father's heir. I have gone and returned, the fourth of these four gods who have brought water, who have administered purification, who have rejoiced in the strength of their fathers. I desire to be vindicated by what I have done. I the orphan have had judgement with the orphaness, the two Truths have judged though a witness was lacking. The two Truths have commanded that the throne of Geb shall revert to me so that I may raise myself to what I have desired. My limbs which were in concealment are reunited and I join those who are in the Abyss; I put a stop to the affair in On, for I go forth today in the real form of a living spirit that I may break up the fight and cut off the turbulent ones.[11]

The Vanquishing of Apep (Apophis)

Apep was the symbolic representative—in the form of yet another serpent—of the most powerful forces of darkness* that informed the chaotic Abyss of Nu, which Ra—with the

---

*Inherent in the dissolute states of Matter within the septenary kosmic universe.

help of other gods and goddesses—had to overcome in his daily progress through the Duat; the subjugation of Apep always took place in the ninth division.[12] There Apep was trapped by one god holding on to his tail while Selkit the scorpion goddess (representing the zodiacal sign of Scorpio) pierced and pinned him to the ground in six places, with knives or swords. Now this whole symbolism had a tremendous magical significance for the ancient Egyptians and its meaning—which is multiple—needs to be clearly understood.

First of all, Apep has both a solar and a personal role to play. The former is zodiacal in association and refers to material existence in our local universe as a whole. The fact that Apep is pinned to the ground in six places means that Universal Matter within the solar system is made (by Divine Will) to segregate itself into six phases of manifest solar being. Now, as we have previously seen, the two highest solar planes are entirely subjective. It is only the third state/plane (the homogeneous element of pure spirit or aether—the Hindu *atma*) that sees the first emanation into manifest existence. So, taking this as the end of Apep's tail and counting six stages downward into the sevenfold Duat (each plane separation counting as a knife), we find that the serpent's body begins to curl back up as it reaches the seventh and lowest state. Its sixth and seventh sections thus reach back up into the sixth and fifth planes respectively, the latter being synonymous with the *ninth* of the twelve divisions of the Duat. What we are therefore seeing is symbolic of the downward (involutionary) cycle of the solar Life wave (the barque of Ra) followed by the beginnings

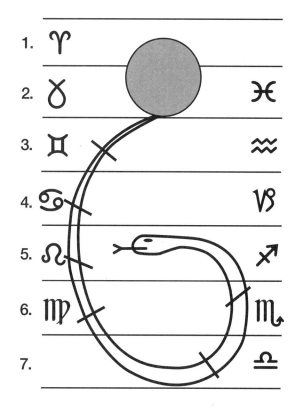

FIGURE 11.6. APEP PINNED BY SIX KNIVES

of the upward (evolutionary) part of the cycle. Apep is slain at this point by Selkit, who (like Scorpio) represents the lower (organizational) aspect of the Mind principle—found on the fifth plane—which has just dominated the sixth (astral) state of solar being.

Now from a purely personal viewpoint, because Man is a solar being and is thus himself representative of the seven planes of purely solar existence, the very same principles apply to him, *because he is Ra*. The solar Life wave is *his* life, emanating from the divine and semidivine states of his innermost being. And it is in the fifth (mental) plane of material existence that he uses his mind principle in the process of self-realization, which leads to the domination of matter and all those elemental instincts that are symbolically associated with Apep.

As previously indicated, the fundamental essence of all ritual and ceremonial is to bring about a sympathetic association between the world of objective physical existence (in which the ritual or ceremonial is made to take place) and the inner, psychospiritual worlds in which the creative powers of Nature are at their most potent. The successfully invocative act thus induces these powers to release their force and thereby set in train a creative or regenerative sequence. However, when the type of ritual involving the slaying of Apep was practiced, the original intended effect was to subliminally awaken the inner consciousness of the populace to a better perception of its own inner nature and the way in which it functioned. Unfortunately, increasing spiritual laxity and the apparent crudeness of the outer ritual seems—by the later Egyptian dynasties—to have resulted in the absurdly literal and overemotive personalization of Apep as a mere devil figure.

Ritual/Ceremonial Dress and Accoutrements

To conclude this chapter, we might spend a few moments looking briefly at some of the ceremonial garments and accoutrements worn or carried by the pharaoh, all of which were regarded as having a powerfully magical significance too.

The Red and White Crowns

As we can see from fig. 11.7, these two crowns—although doubtless able to be worn separately or together by the initiate or hierophant during private ritual—were frequently worn together in public by the pharaoh. When this was done, the Red Crown—symbolizing Lower Egypt and thus also the lower or material Underworld—contained the White Crown—symbolizing Upper Egypt and the higher Underworld, the sphere of spiritual existence. The essence of the symbolism was thus that the initiate combined in himself—through the powers of his mind—the expression of the union of all Egypt and thus of the whole of the twin realms of Spirit and Matter in the kosmic Underworld.

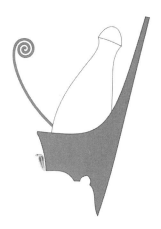

FIGURE 11.7. THE RED AND WHITE CROWNS

The crowns were worn together (as at the top) or separately (Red in the middle, White lower). The Red Crown symbolized Lower Egypt and the lower or material Underworld; the White Crown symbolized Upper Egypt and the higher Underworld, the sphere of spiritual existence.

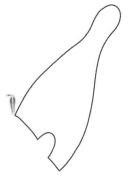

As Margaret Murray tells us:

The crowns of the south and north appear to have been another form of the two protective goddesses, being in themselves divine. The crown of the south was known as the Lady of the Dead, the crown of the north was the Lady of Spells. When the two were united into one headdress, the Double Crown, it was known as the Lady of Power, or the Lady of Flame.[13]*

---

*A quote that draws immediate comparison with descriptions of the way in which kundalini energy is said to work.

It is interesting to note that the long curling proboscis often found extending from the Red Crown is itself a facsimile of that found on the head of the common butterfly, which uses it to sip nectar from flowers. The underlying symbolism therefore appears to be that it is the lower nature (inherent in the integrated personality of the human being) that extends its faculty of *imagination* upward into the higher realms of consciousness and thus draws down the "nectar" of inspirational creativity.

The Uraeus, *the Vulture Cap, and Other Headdresses*

While the *uraeus,* or raised cobra's head, was to be found on the foreheads of both gods and goddesses (as well as pharaohs and their female consorts), the vulture cap was only to be found on the heads of goddesses and priestesses. However, the vulture's *head* was often to be found on the forehead of the pharaoh, in tandem with the *uraeus,* the latter being on the left and the former on the right. The esoteric metaphors these embellishments represent play a fundamental part in the occult side of Egyptian sacred life, which Egyptologists unfortunately (willfully) fail to recognize, notwithstanding the clues provided very clearly by the occult and metaphysical traditions of India. Briefly, they might be described as follows.

The *uraeus* was the form of the goddess Uatchet and was directly associated with the Red Crown of the North[14]—hence also the phenomenal world. It was symbolic of what in the Indian occult tradition is called the *ajna,* or brow chakra. Its function was that of providing clairvoyant sight of a purely psychic nature, plus telepathic faculty. This psychic force center was symbolically opened by the priest touching it with the instrument called *urhekau,* which took the form of a short, undulating, serpent-like rod with the head of a ram, on top of which was placed an erect cobra (see fig. 11.8). The vulture head, on the other hand, was the form of the goddess Nekhebet and was correspondingly associated with the White Crown of the South, to which were sometimes added two plumes, or feathers of Ma'at.[15] It was symbolic of what in the Indian tradition is called the *brahmarandra* or crown chakra, the latter being the "mouth of Osiris," which, when symbolically opened by the priest using the Ursa Minor–shaped *apuat* instrument, endowed the individual with direct spiritual perception and thus infallibly accurate knowledge concerning all things.

It is worthy of note that Nekhebet was also sometimes represented by the Serpent of the South, with this and Uatchet's Serpent of the North being found simultaneously on the right and left sides respectively of the winged disks (of Kneph) over temple doorways and gates.

The full vulture headdress covered the whole of the top of the head, with the wings extending down the rear sides (see fig. 11.9). Generally associated with the goddess Mut, wife of Amen-Ra, it was not indicative of spiritual protection, as Egyptological orthodoxy

FIGURE 11.8. THE *URHEKAU* (SHORT, UNDULATING, SERPENT-LIKE ROD WITH THE HEAD OF A RAM, ON TOP OF WHICH WAS PLACED AN ERECT COBRA) AND *APUAT* (URSA MINOR–SHAPED INSTRUMENT) CAN BE SEEN IN THIS ILLUSTRATION.

FIGURE 11.9. THE FULL VULTURE HEADDRESS COVERING THE WHOLE OF THE TOP OF THE HEAD, THE WINGS EXTENDING DOWN THE REAR SIDES, HERE WITH COMBINED RED AND WHITE CROWNS

too readily believes, but rather of full spiritual *perception*. It might seem strange to find the vulture synonymous with spiritual knowledge, but there is a definite and fundamental logic to the symbolic representation, for the vulture tears away the outer covering of the flesh to go straight for the guts (thereby also revealing the structural bones of the skeleton beneath) when feeding upon the bodily carcass of carrion food. The perceptual intelligence of the overshadowing spiritual nature does precisely the same thing, only we call it insight or intuition.

The distinction between the vulture cap, on the one hand, and the combined Red and White Crowns with *uraeus* and vulture head, on the other, is that of *power*. The vulture cap gave passively oriented spiritual sight to the seeress, but the crowns represented psychospiritual strength or force and were thus only worn by men. The Red Crown *contained* the White Crown, just as the powerfully trained Mind contains the intuition and can thus utilize it before its light-force dissipates naturally throughout the individual's aura. The oddly "waisted" appearance of the White Crown is itself suggestive of a viscous liquid's shape when passing downward from a point to a lower surface—which, in terms of descending spiritual energy, may perhaps be what the Egyptians wished to symbolize.

We otherwise find the Egyptian goddesses wearing a variety of horned headdresses, often containing a red sphere resting between the horns (see fig. 11.10). This sphere (sometimes oblate, or slightly flattened in shape) is usually interpreted as meaning the Sun, yet

FIGURE 11.10. GODDESSES WERE OFTEN DEPICTED WITH HORNED HEADDRESSES CONTAINING A RED SPHERE.

this seems somehow questionable, bearing in mind that the Sun was represented as a *male* principle. The horns—for example of the cow goddess Hathor—had the tips pointing either inward or outward, each having a different aspectual significance. However, their common function was clearly that of a container, rather like the rim of a modern wine glass, which also points inward or outward. What then were they symbolically containing?

Well, bearing in mind that the female nature was associated with the nature of material existence, it would appear that it was probably intended to signify the *substance* of a particular plane or state of being. In line with that, it has otherwise been suggested that the horns in certain cases might be those of the Moon, which seems not unreasonable given that the Moon was the female counterpart of the Sun and that the Moon reflects (thereby seeming to contain) its energetic Life-force. The oblate shape, however, would be more symbolic of the Earth, for this is the shape of our planet, induced by its axial spin. However, these are generalized issues. The specific meaning of the symbolically wrapped message has to be considered, in each case, in relation to other contextual indicators.

Turning back to the ceremonial clothing worn by the pharaoh, there are one or two other important symbolic features that we might also mention, as follows.

The Menat

The *menat,* hanging down the back from the rear of the collar, took the form of a long drooping and unopened lotus plant. It thus appears to have symbolized what the Hindu calls kundalini—the sacred psychospiritual fire of Creation itself, which traditionally resides within the spinal column. The magnificent ceremonial collar forming part of the *menat* (found in very similar fashion in other parts of the ancient world) appears very like the Oriental mandala. The fact that it is worn on the upper part of the body, between the throat and the heart, is itself suggestive of the angled, turning celestial wheel from within the middle of which the Tree of Life (i.e., the head and its attendant consciousness) emerges. In the picture of the god Aah (fig. 11.11, page 334), the *menat* appears to be attached to the toplock (*not* a sidelock) of hair traditionally worn by Egyptian youths before attaining manhood. Although difficult to see, the central section interestingly has fourteen separating subdivisions.

The Kilt

There appear to have been various versions of this garment. The ancient Egyptians commonly wore what in India is called a dhoti, a long piece of cotton cloth that passes around and between the legs—like a much simplified version of Western shorts. The Egyptian version of this peculiarly shaped piece of clothing looks somewhat similar, although having a rather more tailored appearance. It is also remarkably like the Greek kilt. A quite separate and purely ceremonial version worn by the pharaoh in turn bears a likeness to

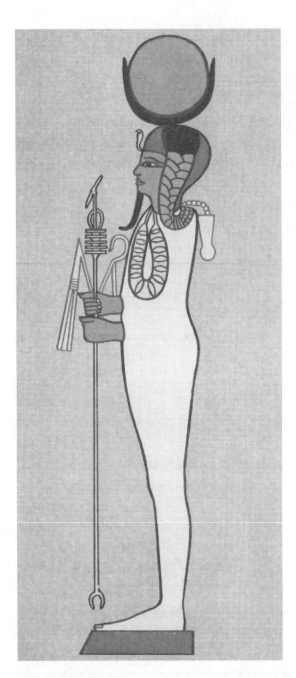

FIGURE 11.11. THE GOD AAH WITH *MENAT* IN THE FORM OF A LONG DROOPING AND UNOPENED LOTUS PLANT

the modern Masonic apron (see fig. 11.12). The occasions on which it was worn are not altogether clear.

The Apron

Somewhat reminiscent of the Masonic apron, we occasionally find pharaonic figures wearing what is pictured (in fig. 11.12, left) as a wedge or pyramid-shaped lower garment in front of the kilt. Quite what the operative significance of this is still uncertain, even though some of the details suggest the possibility of astrological associations. The Masonic

FIGURE 11.12. THE APRON (LEFT), THE FULL-LENGTH FORMAL COSTUME (CENTER), AND THE ANCIENT EQUIVALENT OF MODERN SHORTS (RIGHT)

apron derives from the practical tool holder of the craft workman, just as the Scottish *sporran* acts as a purse and general holdall of small personal effects. However, the positioning of this over the male genital area (rather than strapped at the back or to one side) otherwise implies that there might have been some implicit association or correspondence with the (contained) creative function.

The Crook and Flail

Usually held ceremonially by the pharaoh crossways in front of his chest, these two instruments—as one might very easily see—were apparently symbolic of his responsibility to act as the shepherd of his people and also their master, he who drove them forward in spiritual progress. Taken together, they represented the pharaoh's majesty and the signs of his office.

The Scepters or Wands

There were two main types of this instrument,* the feet of both ending in a skewed claw shape, somewhat reminiscent of an auger, which probably allowed them to be stood upright in either sand or soil, whereas a merely straight and pointed end would not have rendered them as stable. The "head" of each varied, however. One possessed the flower bulb of the papyrus plant, while the other possessed the head of the gazelle found on the prow of the Seker boat. The associated symbolisms appear respectively to have been material stability and psychological or psychospiritual stability—both involving the vertical straightness of Ma'at. These scepters may therefore have been symbolically associated with the equivalent of judicial hearings, or proceedings.

Having dealt in this chapter with the issue of magic, ceremony, and ritual in the broad sense, in the next chapter we shall take a much closer look at the way in which these were applied in relation to the more specific issue of progressive initiation within the Mysteries.

*See some of the pictures in preceding chapters.

TWELVE

The Mystery Tradition and the Process of Initiation

The worship of Isis associated with the Mysteries from an early period, was recognised by the first Ptolemy with the help of Manetho, an Egyptian priest, and Timotheus, a Greek skilled in the Eleusynian Mysteries. . . . It had the charm of something foreign and full of mystery. Its doctrine, supported by the prestige of immemorial antiquity, successfully opposed the mutually destructive opinions of the philosophers, while at the same time its conception of deity was by no means inconsistent with philosophic thought; and it brought to the initiated that expectation of a future life to which the Eleusynian Mysteries owed their attractive power. The ascetic side of the worship too, with its fastings and abstinence from the pleasures of sense, that the soul might lose itself in the mystical contemplation of deity, had a fascination for natures that were religiously susceptible.

AUGUST MAU, *POMPEII: ITS LIFE AND ART*

Although Herodotus in the fifth century BCE remarked upon the fact that the Egyptian Mysteries were pretty well identical with the Greek Mysteries, save only in the names of gods and godesses,[1] little concerning the origins and details of this relationship has come down to posterity direct from Egypt itself. However, that may in part be due to the fact that the Egyptians were much more "security conscious" of their mystic and occult secrets than were the naturally extrovert and loquacious Greeks. Consequently, we have a much better idea of the Greek system, although the interpretation of even this by modern scholars has managed to create serial distortions in certain areas—notably in the totally false idea that the Eleusynian, Orphic, and Dionysian Mysteries were unconnected. In fact, they clearly involved a triple progression, and in view of the remarks of Herodotus, there is every reason to suppose that the Egyptian system—which gave rise to the Greek—followed the very same sequence and esoteric tradition.

Initiatory Sequence in the Greek Tradition

The shared progression, evidenced in the Greek tradition, might be briefly described as follows:

1. The general public religion, involving the Eleusynian Mysteries. This was divided into the greater and lesser Mysteries,* the latter involving the participation of everyone in the community (including children and even guests from other communities)—excepting only murderers. These traditions involved sequences of Mystery plays allegorically dealing with the greater and lesser cycles in universal Nature, plus the cyclical separation of the dual soul principle during the initial stages of incarnation.†

2. The intermediate initiatory tradition comprising the Orphic Mysteries. This was open to all adult males who wished to participate more fully in the inner spiritual tradition, which, here, dealt allegorically with the cycle of specifically human reincarnation and Man's search for his spiritual individuality.

3. The advanced initiatory tradition comprising the Dionysian or Bacchic Mysteries. This was (originally) open to very few of the males in the community and it is the least understood of the three. Generally but mistakenly regarded in latter times (when it became thoroughly corrupted) as inciting its adherents toward the orgiastic and licentious, it was originally the very reverse—in fact, highly ascetic. It actually dealt with the highest aspect of Man, symbolized by the semidivine god figure of Dionysus, who, although torn to shreds shortly after birth at the orders of Hera,‡ wife of Zeus, was reconstituted by his grandmother Rhea, wife of Kronos—a *kosmic* god figure.[2] Dionysus was shown as having instinctive, raw power over all the

---

*The enactment of the greater Mysteries, however, took place only every five years.

†The Egyptians believed in the reincarnation of the world-system as much as they did in the reincarnation of the individual. In confirmation of that we find in one scholarly analysis of the Edfu Texts (Reymond, *The Mythological Origin of Egyptian Temples*) the following: "The first era known by our principal sources was a period which started from what existed in the past. The general tone of the record seems to convey the view that an ancient world, after having been constituted, was destroyed and, as a dead world, it came to be the basis of a new period of creation which at first was the re-creation and resurrection of what once had existed in the past." Herodotus himself confirmed that the Egyptians believed in reincarnation. Margaret Murray (*The Splendour That Was Egypt*, 212) also confirms this: "'Death is my abomination' says the man and he learns with avidity the spells which 'cause a man to return to his home on Earth.'"

‡Hera was synonymous with the Egyptian Heru principle (signifying self-conscious awareness itself); this allegory also denotes a fragmentation of the divine nature of Man.

elemental and creative forces in Nature (because of the vital influence of his divine nature) and could thus at will unfurl the "vine and wine" of Life (i.e., of incarnate existence) itself.*

From these three traditions it can be seen that only the second and third truly dealt with initiation, per se, because they were concerned with promoting a sense of spiritual evolution involving the return of the fallen god-self in Man to its rightful place within the state of Divine Consciousness. The fact that these two traditions were originally only available to adult males (as regards initiation itself) was not, however, due to a myopic desire to keep women in their place. Women were regarded—again, originally—as on a par with men in a spiritual and divine sense. But as the female principle had to do with the sacrosanct maintenance of Nature's foundational balance, while the male principle had to do with evolutionary progression—which naturally upset that balance—to allow women to participate in the higher Mysteries in an *actively* pursued sense would (from this viewpoint) have automatically involved a chaotic and unnatural disruption of Nature through the spontaneous magical work of sympathetic association, with disastrous results. This does not mean that women were not involved originally in an extremely important supporting (and thus only *apparently* passive) role, as priestesses representing the higher soul nature. That seems particularly likely in the case of those older women who had already passed the menopausal stage and were thus themselves free from the associated elemental influences.

As described in an earlier chapter, priestesses could clearly develop psychospiritual faculties of a high order. The "cones" depicted as surmounting their heads (also found on the figure of Ani in the Chamber of Judgment) self-evidently indicate that the crown center chakra was in such cases fully active, thereby giving access to the higher (i.e., psychospiritual) vision. As the Ancients believed the inner Self within both men and women was completely non-polarized as regards gender,† it seems very likely that (at least in the most ancient times) some women would have achieved a very high spiritual status indeed, thereby equating them during their Earth life with the goddess nature, just as the male initiate was to be equated with the god nature. But gender at the god level meant a very different thing than that at the human physical level. Thus the gender and role differentiation

---

*The allegorical stories concerning the semidivine Dionysus show him to be generally benevolent to mankind at large, but absolutely merciless in punishing anyone who failed to respect his worship. However, the esoteric meaning behind this relates to the fact that Dionysus (as Dhyani-Zeus) represented the highest "divine spark" in Man himself—the directly appointed agent of Divine Purpose. He was thus the supreme arbiter of human karma. Consequently, anyone who failed to abide by (and act according to) a sense of Higher Purpose in life was shown as immediately running straight into the full force of unrestrained karmic discipline.

†As Isis is made to say in the *Hermetica* (Scott, 499) to her son Horus: "The souls, my son Horus, are all of one nature inasmuch as they all come from one place, that place where the Maker fashioned them; and they are neither male nor female, for the difference of sex arises in bodies and not in incorporeal beings."

between priest and priestess was something specifically associated with the uniting and grounding of the overall Mysteries (via public ceremonial) within objective human society *as a whole*—and via that to terrestrial Nature in general.

Because reincarnation was, in ancient times, commonly accepted as the natural process underlying human existence, there was originally no serious concern at being born either male or female in any one lifetime. Consequently, as the balance of Nature and of human society in general was the primary concern, there was automatic acceptance of gender differentiation and the natural part it had to play in the individual and in the general scheme of things. Hence the role of the goddess and of womankind in preserving and protecting Nature in all its various aspects would undoubtedly have been seen as essential to any capacity of the lesser "divine spark" to achieve unity with its higher counterpart in its progressive liberation from the thrall of material existence while in a male incarnation.

In our own age when there is such widespread gender confusion, it is perhaps salutary to remember that the real Ancients suffered no such problem, because they placed the spiritual welfare of society *as a whole* firmly ahead of the self-centered instincts of the individual and thereby, through their particular form of religion, ensured the establishment of a mutually altruistic sense of social orientation and focus. It was thus only the *much later* and highly distorted sense of *intellectual* (and then physical) self-indulgence of the Greeks that caused an increasingly widespread failure to understand and abide by the originally esoteric concepts in their own seven schools of philosophy. As a direct consequence, the allegorical escapades of their gods gradually took on ludicrously literal sensual overtones, with the result that they degenerated from esoteric metaphors first into divine personalities in their own right and then into self-indulgently fickle figures of fun, several of whom supposedly practiced heterosexuality or homosexuality as the mood took them. Thus the spreading of atheism, lack of a focused communal spiritual sense and practice, too much leisure, and worship of the purely aesthetic at the expense of the inner ethic resulted—as it always historically does—in widespread social and psychological disorientation. It is highly interesting and instructive to note just how much the decay of Egyptian society accelerated once the Greeks took over the political control of Egypt in the wake of Alexander the Great's conquest.

The Egyptian Mystery Tradition

Careful comparison of the Egyptian with the Greek tradition indicates that the equivalent correspondences to the Eleusynian, Orphic, and Dionysian Mysteries respectively involved:

1. The rite of Osiris and Isis, involving the birth of the gods, followed by the death of Osiris, his bodily dissection by Set, its reunion by Isis, and her subsequent concep-

tion and birth of Horus the Younger. This rite may well have been divided in the higher and lower Mysteries, as in Greece.*

2. Rites centered on the battles between Horus and the *lesser* Set, ending in the victory of Horus and the award to him of kingship over both Upper and Lower Egypt, plus the consequent, full liberation of Osiris himself within the upper heaven world. The esoteric meaning behind the rite related to the conquest of the human personality by the Spiritual Ego.

3. Rites related to the battles of the Companions of Horus with the various higher and lower powers and denizens in Nature (related to the *kosmic* form of Set) on behalf of the winged, abstract solar deity Heru-Behutet, itself representing the highest self-conscious spiritual Individuality in Man—that is, the demigod.

These various rites would have been in accordance with the traditional ancient way of seeing the unified process of existence unfolding as an inverted triplicity, corresponding with (1) the divine world; (2) the psychospiritual world; and (3) the psychoterrestrial world. For the mass of the populace, the first rite—that of Osiris and Isis—subliminally explained the cycles and seasons of life, death, and rebirth in Nature and also gave both hope and faith in the ultimate success of goodness over selfishness. Very understandably, it focused heavily on the work of Isis and her fellow goddesses (and thus of women in general) for ensuring the restoration of the rightful balance in Nature. Not surprisingly, therefore, the Rites of Isis were regarded as supporting the very foundations of all Egyptian religion—with the priestesshood having an equivalent public importance on behalf of the community and the family, both socially and in religious terms.

The Distinction between Ceremonial and Ritual

The ancient word *rite* actually denotes a more or less public ceremonial, whereas the *ritual* per se involves a particular act or series of acts performed either within the public ceremonial or privately for alternative reasons, such as those oriented toward magic, alchemy, or divination. The aim of the rite or ceremony was to draw together the group or community in a highly significant psychological or spiritual sense and thereby provide a powerful magnetic focus of consciousness, which would theurgically draw down upon itself specific higher (i.e., spiritual) and *regenerative* influences. The separate ritual, on the other hand,

---

*In fact, the Orphic Mysteries are in part even more closely related to the lesser Egyptian Mysteries, for Orpheus—like Osiris—had his body torn to pieces, while his severed head—representing the Mind principle—was depicted as floating down the river to the sea and eventually across to the isle of Lesbos, symbolically populated only by women (Graves, *Greek Myths,* 51–52). However, Lesbos is merely the World Soul of our Earth, populated entirely by astral soul entities, among which the culturally creative Orphic mind then discarnately operates.

FIGURE 12.1. THE UNDERLYING GEOMETRIC SYMMETRY OF THE SOLAR BARQUE IMAGERY
(confirming it as a symbol of the constantly mobile, animating Life cycle of the Logos, or Ra)

had a very much more specific aim in mind, almost always of a directly thaumaturgic nature, to bring about *change*.

With this in mind, it is perhaps easier to see why the Ancients paid so much attention to the regularity and accuracy of ceremonial—whether in the community generally, or otherwise among smaller groups of initiates (of whatever status)—and also to the accuracy of ritual.* Carelessness in either would have been regarded as unforgivable—and probably unthinkable—because of the consequent effects in destabilizing the very basis of society and its spiritual connections. Is it thus any wonder that religion was to be found permeating every single aspect of Egyptian life?

Education and the Egyptian Mystery School

Turning to the issue of the Egyptian Mystery School itself, there are still fortunately enough indicators available to us today to provide a definite picture of what it was all about and how the associated educational system was practiced—that is, provided that one begins with the perception that ancient Egyptian beliefs involved a carefully and thoroughly integrated system throughout and not just the mass of conflicting sectarian ideologies that modern Egyptology would have us believe, through its own willful ignorance of the metaphysical background of the cultural and architectural facade.

As has already been described in earlier chapters, the Egyptian Mystery School was itself based upon the view that in Man was a multiple "divine spark," which—despite having fallen from a state of celestial Grace—yet retained the instinct and the creative drive to regain that state through a process of self-disciplined and ethically based psychological and spiritual evolution, which enabled its progressive liberation from the thrall of material existence and merely human incarnation. This was therefore the undoubted basis of the Egyptian educational process. The sequence of initiation and the institutions that ancient humankind designed to help achieve initiation then followed naturally in its train. But in rather more detail, what was the background of these institutions and initiations and how did they operate?

The Forms and Centers of Education

There seem to have been two associated systems of education operative in Egypt—at least during the period subsequent to the Old Kingdom. While there do not seem to have been any quite such formal educational arrangements for girl children, all boys began in the "Writing School," after which a process of streaming apparently operated. Some—evidently seen as potential "high flyers"—were trained for special careers in departmental schools, while the remainder carried on and eventually passed to one or another of the university colleges,[3] presumably unless they finished earlier in order to pursue a more mundane career as a farmer, artisan, and so on. In practical terms, the general educational system does not look like it was very different in many ways from what is practiced today. However, its orientation was clearly quite different from our own.

---

*Which is why the fundamental basis of testing in Freemasonry involves perfect memory of ritual and associated speech.

Several authors of antiquity—such as Clemens of Alexandria and Diodorus Siculus—confirm that the Egyptian educational system was based upon the forty-two Sacred Books of Tehuti. One of these actually dealt with education—"the art of causing to become" itself. The actual scope of the university curriculum in those days was clearly quite immense, as it included law, medicine, cosmography, astronomy, geometry (theoretical and practical), surveying and architecture, plus painting, writing (both hieroglyphic and hieratic), music, and ritual dancing. It seems that a special class of priest-teachers was in charge of each such subject.[4]

The various university colleges, although dealing with the broad curriculum just described, each appear to have specialized in a particular subject. For example, it seems that the applied sciences were dealt with very particularly at Memphis and Heliopolis, while places like Khemennu (Hermopolis) were more oriented toward the theoretical side of knowledge. The great ecclesiastical college of Khemennu was where, as Gosse tells us, "Tehuti taught men the science of arithmetic and mensuration, pure mathematics, the laws of music, oratory and drawing, botany, the ingenious art of painting in words and speaking to the eyes, a system of medicine and a theological code."[5]

The Great Academy at Heliopolis (Anu)

The most famous university college in ancient Egypt was at Heliopolis, the City of the Sun.* Its fame as a seat of the most profound learning spread far and wide throughout the ancient world because of the wisdom of its priest-teachers, who were called "the Mystery Teachers of Heaven." At their head was the high priest, who wore the sacred leopard skin, spangled with stars, to confirm his position as Astronomer Royal of all Egypt. The specialist subject at Heliopolis, however, seems to have been applied mathematics, approached particularly in terms of astronomy (almost certainly incorporating astrology) and physics.[6] Here also was to be found the sacred *benben* temple, the asteroidal pyramidion at the center of which symbolized the cyclical rebirth or regeneration of each great solar epoch.

Before we proceed to deal with the sacred Academy of the Egyptians in greater detail, we should bear one particular point in mind. The very fact that the Academy was built and existed (at Heliopolis†) and prepared individuals for progressive degrees of initiation in the Mysteries clearly militates against the idea so dear to Egyptologists that only the pharaoh-king of Egypt was actually able to take the highest initiations that led to becom-

---

*The university and its library were, however, transferred to Alexandria in Ptolemaic times, when Euclid was to be found in charge of the mathematics department (Gosse, *The Civilization of the Ancient Egyptians,* 19–20). However, this same transfer resulted in the inevitable destruction of the original university and temple architectural complex, which was thereafter, at some later time, demolished, its masonry being utilized for local housing and Coptic Christian or Muslim temples.

†Macrobius is reported as saying that the great temple at Baalbek in Syria was actually founded by Egyptian priests from Heliopolis (Budge, *The Nile,* 453).

FIGURE 12.2. HIGH PRIEST SHOWN WEARING THE SACRED LEOPARD SKIN

ing a god-star. As elsewhere suggested, it is almost certain that each new pharaoh-king was originally selected from among the higher initiates *by their own hierophants* as being the best available to lead the country in both a spiritual and a political sense—that is, until the degeneracy of father-to-son succession took hold and the priesthood then became increasingly marginalized as a purely religious function, with disastrous consequences for Egyptian society as a whole.

The International Reputation of the Academy of Heliopolis

Although none of the original buildings now exist—their foundations being probably somewhere under a public park near Cairo Airport—the Academy appears to have enjoyed the highest of reputations, even on an international basis, throughout the ancient world. The alumni from Greece alone, from the sixth century BCE onward, give some sort of idea of the quality of minds that came to study there. Consider for instance that virtually every great Greek philosopher was said to have travelled to Egypt, or to have been Egyptian himself. Pythagoras was said to have been taught by Oenophis of On (Anu); Plato by Sechnuphis of On; others of note connected with Egypt included Aleques, Archimedes, Apuleius, Anaxagoras, Diodorus Siculus, Euripides, Herodotus, Lycurgus, Musaus, Orpheus, Pausanius, Solon, Strabo, Thales and Xenophanes—not to mention Plotinus and Porphyry, who were Egyptian by birth.[7]

Until the founding of Alexandria in the third century BCE, we historically find no mention of any other international center of educational excellence in Egypt,* although the various temples along the Nile undoubtedly acted as the focus of early schooling, as did the abbeys and monasteries in Europe† during the late Middle Ages. It would again seem highly probable that application (within Egyptian society) for admission to the Academy came by way of instruction and recommendation by the hierophant of the local temple school to the Chancellor–Grand Hierophant of the Academy, who would have been one of the most important and influential people in all Egypt.‡

The Mystery School Curriculum

The subjects studied at Heliopolis clearly included various sciences, including mathematics, metaphysics, astronomy/astrology, engineering, surveying/cartography, chemistry, psychology, medicine/healing, art, and music—and probably much more besides. All we really know is that the philosopher-priests were concerned to know *everything* they could about every single possible branch of knowledge that existed. At what age entry to the Academy was allowed, we have no idea, although it seems unlikely that it would have been until the late teens and almost certainly involved some degree of streaming. In addition, it would seem very likely that enforced sabbaticals were taken, for work in the various Nile temples as priest-teachers, physicians, astrologers, and so on.

In short, although having a perhaps much wider curriculum and a very definite spiritual bias, the Academy should perhaps be regarded as having in some ways been equivalent to one of our very best universities—like Oxford or Cambridge—in the eighteenth and nineteenth centuries. The fact that Pythagoras should supposedly have spent twenty-two years there (even if slightly exaggerated) nevertheless indicates very clearly that its educational techniques, at that time anyway, were not oriented (as ours today regrettably are) toward competition and preparation for a mere career in Egyptian society. It would seem rather more likely that the Hierophant-Chancellor at Anu made the decision as to whether the individual would benefit from further time spent there (not exactly in the manner of a post-graduate course, however) or whether he should instead leave to take up a particular type of position elsewhere. It also seems likely that individuals would have been required to return to the Academy at various later stages—according to their general progress— to continue their studies and thereby take the higher grades of initiation, if conditions permitted.

*Herodotus confirmed in his *Histories* (95) that the most highly intelligent Egyptians were the philosopher-priest-teachers at Heliopolis.

†After the general dissolution of the monasteries in sixteenth-century England, a few survived only by evolving into public schools.

‡Yet few names have come down to us—perhaps understandably, given that personality cults would undoubtedly have been unthinkable in earlier times, before Egypt's social and religious system began to fall into decline.

This same concept of intermittent but progressive initiation (which one finds in the East even occasionally today), while maintaining one's commitment to higher education and community duties, was based upon the perception that man, while a terrestrial god *in potential,* needed to be thoroughly "rounded out" and rigorously tested before he could be remotely considered as approaching that hallowed state. Thus it was said of the nature of Man:

For Man is a being of divine nature; he is comparable not to the other living creatures upon Earth, but to the gods in heaven. Nay, if we are to speak the truth without fear, he who is indeed a man is even above the gods of heaven, or at any rate he equals them in power. None of the gods will ever quit heaven and pass its boundary and come down to earth; but man ascends even unto heaven and measures it. And what is more than all besides, he mounts to heaven without quitting the Earth, to so vast a distance can he put forth his power. We must not shrink then from saying that a man on Earth is a mortal god and that a god in heaven is an immortal Man.[8]

The Raison d'Etre of Initiation

The process of initiation (in all sacred traditions, whether ancient or modern) essentially involves a progressive expansion of consciousness and associated range of *subjective* perception. This in turn produces a corresponding increase in the sense of *inclusiveness* of all in universal Nature being part of one unified process. But that in itself implies the existence of progressive stages of *limitation* of consciousness (and thus of relative ignorance). That also in turn implies the existence of progressively sequential fields (or states or planes) of inner being to which perceptual access has to be learned or gained by developing skills of coordination of those higher subjective senses, the existence of which is not apparent to the average person. This is so even though the average person must himself already possess such faculties in embryo—little of this, however, yet being appreciated by modern science and scholarship.

The fundamental basis of the process of initiation, as understood by the Ancients (and by spiritual teachers in the East even today), consisted of three aspects:

1. Training (in terms of general education, self-discipline, and practical ethics)
2. The actual testing
3. The *subsequent* passing on of specific knowledge not available to others of lesser grade

It is implicit in this that the candidate could not be presented for initiation until and unless his own immediate teacher had thoroughly satisfied himself and the superior hierophant that the individual was up to it. The reason for that derives from the fact that the trials of initiation were quite deliberately hazardous, the individual being required to show courage and faith above all, as well as a thorough understanding of what he had previously been taught.* Were he not ready and the tests either killed him or left him insane, it would have seriously reflected upon the psychological and spiritual judgment of his teachers themselves. But the Ancients were exceptionally thorough where such things were concerned and although misadventures would undoubtedly have sometimes occurred for some reason or other, arising out of a flaw in the candidate's character, they would have been exceptional.

The Seven Initiations

To the Egyptians, Man's compound subjective and objective nature was itself already septenary, by virtue of expressing the essence and nature of all the seven solar planes comprising the kosmic physical plane. As Wallis Budge commented, the Egyptians took the view that, on this basis, it was quite possible for a man to adapt this (sevenfold) matter in order to evolve spiritually into a demigod while still in incarnation on Earth.[9] In order to do this, however—as in all such systems around the world—he had (by his own self-determination) to reach such a point of inner perception that the characteristics of any particular state of associated consciousness no longer exerted the hold of fascination over him.† As a result, the lesser "spark" within him gradually drew closer to its higher counterpart within his spiritual nature. That in turn resulted in his various subtle body forms becoming increasingly more luminous and psychomagnetically potent, as the previously chaotic elemental matter within them came under his perpetually present self-control. In this manner, he attained an inner stillness, which enabled the subtlest transmission of psychospiritual resonance between the various soul-bodies to be clearly registered. It was doubtless with this in mind that Pythagoras—himself a graduate of the academy at Heliopolis—conceived of the sounds of the stars, or what he otherwise called "the music of the spheres."

Within the later (Greco) Egyptian tradition, the seven initiatory grades were known by the following names: (1) Pastophoris; (2) Neocoris; (3) Melanophoris; (4) Kristophoris; (5) Balahala; (6) Astronomus; and (7) Manneras (hierophant).[10] They were also to be found in several other traditions, including the Mithraic, where they were symbolically referred to as follows: (1) The Raven; (2) The Bridegroom; (3) The Soldier; (4) The Lion; (5) The Persian;

---

*Various stories have come down to us regarding the terrifying experiences through which prospective candidates for initiation were put—probably by means of both artifice and auto-suggestion. But the whole point of such tests was to introduce him to the very same sort of experiences he would meet while astrally traveling on his own, without anyone there to protect him. His courage, fortitude, and sense of self-reliance were thus seen as of the greatest importance. Thus loss of courage meant pretty well instant failure.

†In some cultures where the original severity of training was relaxed, the popular use of hallucinogenic narcotics (such as mescaline in the Americas) became popular in order to speed up the mystic state but always led to neural degeneracy—as it still does today.

(6) The Courier of the Sun; and (7) The Father.[11] Although seven in number, the sequence seems to have followed in groups of three, as shown in fig. 12.3. Here we see the overlap in the third and fifth degrees between (a) the triple human world, (b) the associated inner psychic and spiritual states, and (c) the (semi)divine state. The fourth degree, however, stood alone. The first three initiations were thus seen as related to the three planes of material existence found in the nature of the human being—that is, the physical senses, the astral (psychic) nature, and the psychologically (i.e., purely intellectual) lower mental nature. When the individual had conquered all these, after a truly harrowing final series of tests, he was regarded as an initiate of the third degree and in full control of his purely human nature, as well as having a whole range of commensurate psychic powers at his command.

In Greece he was regarded as an Epoptae—one capable of seeing with the inner vision. In Egypt, this made him a Pir (something still found in the Sufi tradition today) and thus a member of the *spiritual* nobility—albeit of the lowest grade. In certain traditions, this was therefore regarded as merely the first of the true initiations of the Higher Way. The fifth degree then saw the conscious assimilation of the nature of the spiritual soul and the first of the three stages of attaining semidivinity.

According to Manly P. Hall, the seven initiations of the Mystery School were as follows:*[12]

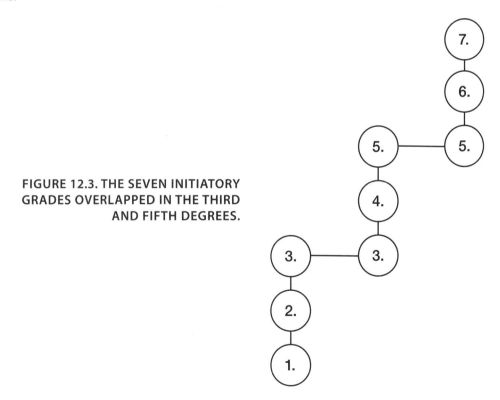

FIGURE 12.3. THE SEVEN INITIATORY GRADES OVERLAPPED IN THE THIRD AND FIFTH DEGREES.

---

*The old English Templar rite also had seven degrees—clearly derived from the Mystery Traditions of the Middle East during the Crusades in the twelfth century.

1. The Enterer of the Gate (the Recognizer of the Law of Karma/Nemesis)
2. The Self-Cleansing of the Heart
3. Descent into the Abode of the Dead (Hall says that the pharaoh officiated at this initiation)
4. The Slaying of the Medusa (an esoteric metaphor for the imagination) and the Drinking from the Cup (Crater/Grail), which represented the *haoma/soma* of Universal Life
5. The Degree of the Alchemist, symbolized by the decapitation of Typhon/Set in his cave
6. The Degree of the Astronomer, in which the initiate was instructed as to the origins of the gods and their significances, the First Cause, universal cycles, and the sidereal dance
7. The Degree of Prophet—from which the hierophants and pharaohs were chosen

The Associated Masonic Tradition

Although many Freemasons are uneasy about the suggestion of their rituals having been derived from ancient Egypt, it is quite impossible to draw any other conclusions when faced with the paraphernalia and symbolism used in their lodge ceremonials. Professor J. S. Curl—a noted Masonic writer and historian—tells us: "Euclid is supposed to have instructed the male offspring of the Egyptian aristocracy in the Mysteries of the [Masonic] Craft and there is much else [in Freemasonry] that points to an Egyptian or Graeco-Egyptian set of legends, many of which overlap, interlock, and merge with each other."[13]

A point worthy of note is that the ancient Egyptian third degree was *not* the same as the present Masonic third degree (which more nearly and confusingly resembles the fifth), in which the Mason—representing Hiram Abiff, Solomon's Master Mason and (site) architect—is raised up, as it were from the dead—that is, the Underworld kingdom. Here too, the Underworld as seen by both the Ancients and the original Masons comprised the whole of the lowest three planes/states of solar matter,* so the initiate ultimately had to make the transition from that (triple) sphere of existence into a higher one before he became a full adept, or Magus. This necessarily involved his leaving behind his purely

---

*The Master Mason thus represents the Spiritual Ego in man's inner nature, an aspect of the "divine spark" (represented by Solomon) being forced to descend into the three lower states of solar matter (the mental, astral, and physical) in order to take incarnate human form—hence the building of the Temple. Thus as Professor J. S. Curl tells us in his book *The Art and Architecture of Freemasonry* (32), "Various versions of this story [the Hiramic legend] exist, but the variant in which the Master of the Works at King Solomon's Temple was murdered by means of three blows (with a hammer, a level, and a plumb) to the head by three Apprentices . . . who were trying to obtain the secrets of the Master Mason, is the best known. Each blow was delivered at a different door of the Temple." "Each door" is of course symbolic of the vortex point of entry to each of the concentric fields of consciousness surrounding the individual, while the "three Apprentices" are themselves but metaphors for the elemental nature of these same three states.

human status, the apotheosis of which had been attained at the Egyptian third degree. Consequently, the fourth degree (again, in all traditions) involved a subjective "crucifixion" in terms of an at last clearly *direct* perception of the *actuality* of spiritual existence (at its own level of being) and thus the nature of duality itself. But it was only when the individual had been able to make the later, irrevocable decision to cross over to the other side that he passed the fifth degree and thus progressively began to unite his liberated lower "spark" with its immediately higher counterpart in the Divine Soul—the *ashem* body—the Hindu *atman*.

Elsewhere within the Masonic tradition we find the various subsequent "degrees of the royal arch"—available to those who have become Master Masons. These too refer to the conquering of various higher substates of matter—spiritual matter this time—within the septenary system. Thus the 33°—the highest theoretically available—actually appears to relate to the supposed control by the individual of all the four lower solar planes of being, plus five of the substates of the fifth plane (4 x 7 + 5 = 33). The rationale behind this is related to the correspondence between the five lower solar states and the objective expression of the five kosmic elements.* Thus when each of the five substates on each of the five lower solar planes of existence had been conquered, the individual "spark" was regarded as being reunited with its highest (semidivine) counterpart. Briefly stated, man—if capable of achieving this within his lifetime—became an incarnate demigod of the seventh initiation, with unimaginable power available to him on behalf of the Demiurgos. It would appear that this (altogether highly rare) seventh initiation in the series took the adept Magus up to the stage (in Egypt) of being a Ptah-Seker-Ausar—perhaps akin to the stage of inner realization achieved by Gautama Buddha in the seventh century BCE. However, there is little of real value that can be added here as to quite what this might involve in practical terms, although there is a strong suggestion that it involved the final retrieval of the Masonic Lost Word.[†]

The Initiatory Experiences of Osiris-Ani

Although Egyptologists have mistaken the scribe Ani for a literal, deceased personality, it seems fairly self-evident that the name was a generic one given to the candidate for initiation, who had to travel through the various subjective states in his quest for greater spiritual enlightenment.[‡] In this same quest we again see the operating principle of renunciation, for Ani is depicted as having to progress through ten pylon gates, the first five

---

*The higher counterparts of our five solar elements of aether, fire, air, water, and earth.
[†]This subject is interestingly taken up by A. A. Bailey in her various books on the background Himalayan Adept Hierarchy, well known to students of modern theosophical thought. It is also dealt with—albeit in poetic terms—in the small and deeply mystical book *The Voice of the Silence* by H. P. Blavatsky.
[‡]The name Ani itself appears to be derived from Anu (a soul being) in exactly the same way that we would today alter a personal forename in affectionate terms, e.g. from Harold to Harry, or from Anne to Annie.

The Mystery
Tradition and the
Process of Initiation

351

of which (corresponding with the five elements) are connected with coordinating and integrating aspects of his psychospiritual nature. Once he has passed through these five solar states, Ani arrives at the sixth pylon portal, associated with the higher "divine spark" and semidivinity. Very logically, therefore, the local divinity is called "He Who Has Been Joined Together."[14] Just as logically, when reaching the seventh pylon gate, associated with the highest and purest solar state (that of the enfolding demiurgic nature), he finds the local deity names as "She Who Clothes the Feeble One, Weeping for What He Loves and Shrouding the Body."[15]

It will be remembered from descriptions given in earlier chapters that the Kosmic Mind principle (like the Greek Ouranos) aurically surrounded the Demiurge (Gaea) in its mental embrace. Correspondingly then we here find the deity of the eighth pylon gate being given the graphic title "Blazing Fire, Unquenchable Flame, Whose Flames Reach Far, Slaughtering without Warning, Whom None May Pass Because of the Pain She Causes."*[16] This then is the state of those kosmic *akhu* whose polarization is outward from the demiurgic soul-body, extending toward the concentrically enfolding, higher kosmic planes of Being. Consequently, the ninth pylon seems to have represented the second kosmic plane of consciousness; here, somewhat by way of confirmation, the associated deity was called "He Who Makes Himself."[17]

The Seven and Nine Initiations

It seems very likely from this same progression that the Egyptians (and the Ancients in general) regarded there as being not just seven but rather nine initiations in all, related to the self-reconstituting "spark" of the Kosmic Mind principle. Thus a notional tenth initiation or progression would have resulted, in their view, in the "divine spark" being reassimilated back into its own originating causal essence, within the Kosmic Mind. In practical terms, however, the final two initiations (the eighth and ninth) were of a pan-solar nature and—probably along with the sixth and seventh—would almost certainly have been taken at the pyramid complex at Saqqara, rather than at Giza.

The Seven Halls

By way of correspondence with the pylon name associations, the Egyptian tradition also had Ani progressing through a series of halls (i.e., representing the states of consciousness between the symbolic pylons).[18] These halls, however, relate to the seven purely solar world states. Thus Ani starts in the first hall in the physical state and before attempting to enter the second he invokes the powers of the god Tehuti to sublimate (in his own nature) the mutually antagonistic energies of Set and Horus, which are characteristic of the astral,

---

*The phrase "Whom None May Pass" here appears synonymous with the phrase "Ring-Pass-Not" found in both ancient Hindu and also twentieth-century theosophical writings.

self-centered personality state. In approaching the third hall, he associates himself with the god Geb, who is himself the final adjudicator of the conflict between Set and Horus and who thus makes the Horus nature (in Ani) dominant. Thus the Higher Mind is now shown as having absolute dominance over the personality.

As he enters the fourth hall and its associated state of consciousness, Ani identifies himself as a mighty bull,[19] thereby asserting his newly found power as a self-conscious Spiritual Ego. In the fifth (as the raised master adept) he is depicted as finally conquering the serpent demon Apep (Apophis) as well as bringing back together all the various hitherto scattered parts of Osiris' body and thus reconstituting the backbone (spine) of his father Osiris. This brings about the resurrection of the fully awakened and semidivine Osiris nature in himself, leading in the sixth hall to his becoming Heru-Behutet (the winged solar disk and avenger of his parent). Finally, in the seventh hall he becomes an omniscient divine being, perpetually in the presence of Ra himself.[20]

Underground Initiations

In the ancient traditions, the higher Mysteries were always performed underground, either in caves or in artificially (i.e., architecturally) prepared sepulchers such as those found in the pyramids at Giza. There appear to have been two primary reasons for this practice. The first was one of sympathetic association; the cave or underground chamber was seen as symbolically representative of the cave of the soul—that is, the Underworld state into which the "spark" fell and within which it had to achieve self-engendered enlightenment before being able to reemerge into the open air and natural light of day. Second—and perhaps more obviously—there was the need for *absolute* secrecy in relation to the rituals performed, plus constant security of the thereby magically conditioned environment.

One might also add a third, however, that is to the effect that neither stellar nor solar nor lunar influences could be directly (or perhaps even indirectly) picked up underground. Thus the various influences brought to bear would have been regarded as much purer. Additionally, it would have been relatively simple to accumulate and maintain the high quality of the atmospheric presence by its own psychomagnetic isolation, thereby increasing its sacredness to a very potent degree, which would itself act as an automatic trigger for all future rituals held there.

It is for such reasons that architecturally designed temples—always affiliated to a particular god or goddess in every religion—were (and are) quite different in nature. They were oriented toward a greater or lesser degree of public ceremonial—inevitably involving a variety of rituals, intended to invoke and bring the god's nature in Nature down to earth. By thus grounding it, society as whole was believed to benefit from the cyclically re-creative or regenerative influences of the demiurgic hierarchies thereby summoned, while also ensuring that the work of those same hierarchies was constantly oriented toward Man and thus not allowed to follow their natural tendency toward the chaotic. The initiatory cave or chamber, however, put man in isolation from such influences and thereby either forced him into a state of supreme critical subjectivity or otherwise enabled him to reorient himself (progressively) to the fact that he was indeed a "spark" of the great and Unknowable Mind, which itself lay beyond the very consciousness of even the highest of the demiurgic hierarchies.

As previously indicated, it was this, and the sympathetic association of the tumulus or sacred mound with the awakening Eye (or phallus) of the Deity, that caused ancient humankind always to maintain its most sacred rituals belowground. Even the pyramid can be seen as an extension of the same concept—although taken into a somewhat higher metaphysical dimension. For the pyramid shape itself represents a star—or, rather, the mundane aspect of its overall nature, within the greater soul-sphere that aurically enfolds it. But even at Giza the main pyramids had to be clothed in gleaming white limestone in order to reflect all solar influence in its totality, so that no faint influence of the Aten— the fallen aspect of the solar Demiurge—could in any way penetrate its inner initiatory chambers. It is otherwise interesting to note, in this connection, that the only external entrances into the three main pyramids face due north—*toward the circumpolar stars*, the focus of the incoming extra-kosmic influences entering our local home universe. That in itself would appear to confirm that the subterranean chamber in each of the Giza pyramids was an initiatory cave for the initiate of the associated degree facing the immediately next stage of his evolutionary progress. That then brings us very logically to the next stage of our considerations on this topic.

The Formal Places of Initiation

In order to understand the underlying symbolism of Giza—the Egyptian Ra-stau—we have first of all to bear in mind its geographical location relative to Heliopolis—the latter being the location where the progressive imparting of the esoteric relationships between mundane and higher sacred knowledge took place. As previously suggested, the east side of the River Nile was symbolically associated with the solar gods and their combined fall through the higher solar states into semi-objective existence within the fourth solar state. Here they became the seven groups of Horus beings, aspects of which (lesser "divine sparks" of a human nature) were to be projected even further into the lowest three solar states, which together comprised twenty-one substates. As we also saw elsewhere, Heliopolis was the capital of the nineteenth nome district, whereas Memphis was capital of the twentieth and twenty-first nomes, the former of these two extending northward toward and almost certainly incorporating the Giza district.*

*The geographical size and extent of the various nome districts varied enormously.

In metaphysical terms, the twenty-first solar substate (counting upward) represented the expression of the Higher Mind, the luminously radiant emanation of the fallen higher Horus "sparks" on the fourth solar plane. Correspondingly, the nineteenth solar substate symbolically represented the highest state attainable by the mere intellect of man, while the twentieth substate was a sort of psychospiritual synapse, or no-man's land, through which all upward- and downward-flowing influences had to pass.

The west side of the River Nile was symbolically associated with the individualizing god nature in man. Consequently, it was entirely logical that the candidate for initiatory testing—having learned as much as he could in purely theoretical terms at Heliopolis—had to cross the river (itself symbolic of the Milky Way) in order to separate himself from the mass. Thus he passed on to the mount of Manu, over on the west bank of the river, on which stood the sacred plateau of Giza. Here, as we have otherwise suggested, the five purely human initiations were undergone. However, the subsequent initiations required a sympathetic change of location, southward to Saqqara, which had a psychospiritual association with the fourth of the seven solar states and the seven groups of fallen Horus "sparks." Thus it would appear that at least one aspect of these higher initiations had to do with the specific assignment of the candidate to one or other of these seven groups—and thus with one or other of the seven pyramids found in this general area, between Memphis and the Faiyum. But let us return to Giza.

The Esoteric Significance of the Constellation of Orion

In terms of the symbolic association of earth and sky, we are already familiar with Robert Bauval's intuitive perception that the three main pyramids at Giza are representative of the three stars of Orion's Belt, the latter lying astride the line of the celestial equator, which thereby divides the whole figure of the gigantic constellation into a great duality. That which lies on one side represents the divine; the other side represents the material. Thus the three central stars represent the transitional pathway of the soul between the spiritual and material nature of the demiurgic Deity, with the attendant Sphinx playing a crucial mediating role.

The whole point of the association of Osiris (and thus Orion) with the human condition—and the process of initiation that led to liberation from it—was that Orion (and thus Osiris) symbolically represented the sevenfold kosmic *physical* body of a gigantic kosmic Intelligence. It has seven stars, thereby equating it with the seven states of solar being *comprising* the kosmic physical plane, these latter states being those that the divine Man overshadows, as we have already seen. Of the seven stars, the lower two were symbolically concerned with purely astral and terrestrial life. The two highest correspondingly had an entirely subjective association. It is thus the central three that were of crucial importance in the process of evolutionary transition from the astral soul state to that of the

Divine Soul. These three—the equivalent of *atma-buddhi-manas* in the Hindu system—thus expressed the three emanations of the higher "divine spark"—that is, Spirit, Soul, and Mind. In alchemical tradition, these were aether, fire, and air.

As we have also elsewhere seen, the fourteen scattered parts of the body of Osiris in the Egyptian tradition actually represented the fourteen substates of the *kosmic* astral and mental planes, which had to be reintegrated to make the superior god nature whole again. But because Man was seen as the microcosm of this macrocosmic Being, he too was involved in the very same process of reintegration—although within the seven *solar* planes constituting the kosmic physical plane. His problem therefore was to discover the nature of the fourteen elemental substates comprising the corresponding *solar* astral and mental planes of his being and, by bringing them together fully under his control, so likewise to subjectively reconstitute himself. However, he could only do this by using his intuition (the higher instinctive spiritual reflex) to bring to bear the nature of the higher "divine spark" via his evocation and implementation of the powers of the *atma-buddhi-manas* triad within his own nature. That then served to bring about an inevitable transmutation of his consciousness from a material to a spiritual orientation.

The Symbolic Influence of the Three Pyramids

Now it follows quite logically from all this that the three Giza pyramids were symbolic of the influences of these three same aspects, which had progressively to be brought to bear upon the widening and deepening consciousness of the initiate. Thus the Men-kau-ra pyramid imparted the coordinating influence of the Higher Mind upon the lower mind and emotional reflexes of the novice; the Khepren pyramid imparted the coordinating influence and knowledge of the spiritual soul upon the more advanced initiate facing the third degree; and the Khufu pyramid (The Great Pyramid) did the same for the highly advanced initiate who was becoming directly responsive to the Spirit itself—the pure Breath of the parent "divine spark."

It needs to be carefully borne in mind, however, that these main pyramids would have been places of testing *only*. The knowledge that flowed or was imparted in relation to each initiation would have come to the successful initiate only later, once he had, so to speak, opened the door of further sacred knowledge himself by passing the initiatory test. With that in mind, let us now take a closer look at the practical sequence of initiatory testing.

The Actual Sequence of Initiation at Giza

As otherwise described in *Land of the Fallen Star Gods,* the fact that there are ten pyramids in all at Giza is highly symbolic, as is also their orientation generally to the rising Sun and to each other. But the seven subsidiary pyramidlets give the distinct impression of being merely preparatory in a somewhat more personal sense than the main ones. There are two possible ways of looking at the sequence of initiations in relation to the three main pyramids at Giza. One could assume quite simply that each of the pyramidlets was related to an initiation and that the first three were thus intended to be related to the Men-kau-ra pyramid, the transitional fourth to the Khepren pyramid, and the fifth, sixth, and seventh to the Great Pyramid. There are, one might think, reasonable grounds for supporting this case. However, the other alternative takes into consideration subsidiary issues and, it is suggested, is thus perhaps the more likely to be accurate.

The alternative view might start at the other end (see fig. 12.4), with the King's Chamber in the Great Pyramid—so strongly related by tradition to the raising of the master (at the fifth degree—the last of the purely human initiations). Here we have the two ventilation shafts, so-called, already formed and unimpededly aimed directly at

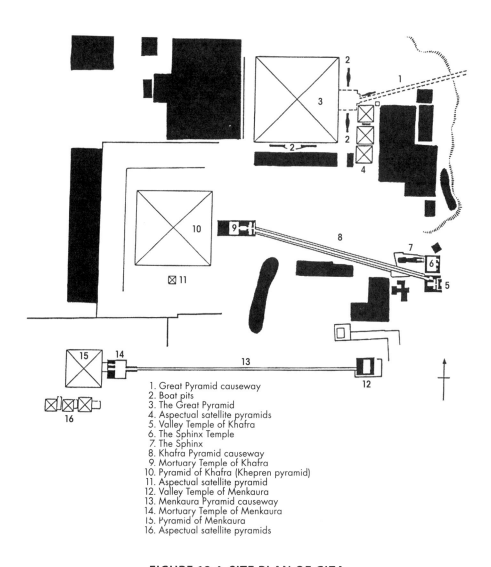

1. Great Pyramid causeway
2. Boat pits
3. The Great Pyramid
4. Aspectual satellite pyramids
5. Valley Temple of Khafra
6. The Sphinx Temple
7. The Sphinx
8. Khafra Pyramid causeway
9. Mortuary Temple of Khafra
10. Pyramid of Khafra (Khepren pyramid)
11. Aspectual satellite pyramid
12. Valley Temple of Menkaura
13. Menkaura Pyramid causeway
14. Mortuary Temple of Menkaura
15. Pyramid of Menkaura
16. Aspectual satellite pyramids

FIGURE 12.4. SITE PLAN OF GIZA

Orion's Belt on the south flank and Thuban (within the constellation of Draco) to the north while proceeding directly from the chamber itself to the outer casing of the pyramid. When we look at the Queen's Chamber, however, the "ventilation shafts" do not quite reach the outer casing, although aimed at Sirius (symbolizing the lesser kosmic cycle) and Polaris in Ursa Minor (the polar star at the celestial summer solstice).

The implied symbolism, one might suggest, is that the initiate at this stage (that of facing the fourth degree)—although possessing the instinctively sensed spiritual orientation—has not yet quite managed to penetrate the outer barrier to fully liberated spiritual existence. The fact that the initiates of the degrees associated with these two chambers both seemingly enter the interior of the pyramid from the Grand Entrance via the Grand Gallery appears to signify that both have attained the spiritual dimension of consciousness, although only one has so far attained the associated faculty of spiritual vision. It is instructive that the access to the Queen's Chamber is on the same level as the Grand Entrance while that to the King's Chamber involves yet another upward climb. Yet more symbolism here for sure!

When we look at the only other known chamber in the pyramid—the Great Subterranean Chamber—we find that its shaft is also directly aimed at the circumpolar stars. However, although the initiate of this degree enters the pyramid via the Grand Entrance too, he proceeds *downward* (at the very same angle as the Grand Gallery proceeds upward), the chamber itself being well below ground level. This raises the rather interesting issue of why the initiate of the third degree should have been permitted to use the same access—unless he were actually facing the fourth degree. However, that would imply that he had already taken the third degree in the Khepren pyramid. But, in addition, why would the initiate of the fourth degree be allowed to see the Grand Gallery, related to the fifth degree?—unless of course it was only on his way out *after* the fourth degree had already taken place and was perhaps intended merely to show him that the job was not yet finished.

In *Land of the Fallen Star Gods* the suggestion was made that the candidate for initiation in the Queen's Chamber had to make his own way there by finding and then climbing up the narrow "umbilical" passage, which early Egyptologists dubbed the "tomb robbers tunnel" (now known as the Well Tunnel).[21] This winds upward from the base of the Great Subterranean Passage to the base of the Grand Gallery, next to the passageway leading directly to the Queen's Chamber. Although such a climb might strike the reader—particularly if he has been inside the Great Pyramid—as particularly horrendous and requiring incredible bravery, it seems entirely logical from the viewpoint of ancient Egyptian metaphysical thought. After all, the candidate had to be tested for an act of supreme courage (of his convictions) and be made to feel that he was embarking upon a potential "path of no return" if he were really intent upon achieving his spiritual goal. Is this not, after all, what the whole process of initiation was fundamentally all about?

The Khepren Pyramid and the Sphinx

Turning next to the Khepren pyramid, there are, one might suggest, a number of ancillary esoteric pointers to the associated degree of initiation to be undergone within it. First of all, whereas the Great Pyramid's causeway points toward the rising Sun at the winter solstice, the Khepren pyramid's causeway points toward the rising Sun at the summer solstice. At that time the Sun is at its greatest height during the year—surely a metaphor for the initiate who had already achieved in his humanly ambitious nature all that mere man was physically, emotionally, and mentally capable of! The second very obvious metaphor is the Sphinx itself, with its human head on a lion's body, facing due east across the River Nile.

Now the Egyptian word for sphinx was Aker, and as we saw in chapter 6, Aker was a creature associated with the fifth of the seven solar dimensions of consciousness—that of the Mind. Consequently, we can suggest with some sound reasoning that the Sphinx represents the Higher Mind and lower mind aspects of man—his abstract imagination and his merely aggressive and acquisitive intellect.

On the damaged stela between the paws of the Sphinx we read of its dedication to the individual—one Prince Djehutymes (who supposedly became the pharaoh Khepren)—who fell asleep and had a dream (while sitting in the shade of the Sphinx after a day's exhausting hunting in the vicinity) that the Sphinx appeared to him and promised that he would become king of Egypt if he removed all the desert sand surrounding the great statue and then restored the temple dedicated to the god.[22] As usual, Egyptologists have taken what is written quite literally as a historical tract. However, if read *esoterically*, the meaning is quite different. It is actually aimed, we suggest, at the candidate for initiation to the third degree, whose task is to clear away all the constantly shifting emotional and psychological debris *in his own subjective nature* before he can take command of the "Egypt" of his own being. In confirmation of that, the name Djehutymes appears to be derived from Tehuti-mes(k)—Tehuti being the god of Mind-knowledge and *mes(k)* being an Egyptian word (which has come down in English as *mesh*) meaning "coordination."

Greek-oriented scholars have somehow managed, however, to turn Djehutymes into Tuthmosis IV—an apparently real dynastic king! However, the idea that even a prince of Egypt would actually dare to indulge himself in hunting in the immediate area of a highly sacred precinct and then subsequently loll around in the middle of it is near farcical—*unless treated as an allegory.* Interestingly, the name Khepren (Khep-ren), supposedly adopted by the successful initiate, is clearly related to the Sphinx itself, whose Egyptian god-name was Ra-Temu-Khepera-Heru-khuti.* This triply compound name itself has a definitely significant meaning for the candidate:

- Ra-Temu signifies the arising solar deity (in Man)
- Khepera signifies his godlike ability to re-create a new persona for himself, at will
- Heru-khuti (Horus-of-the-Horizon) is the latent *semidivine* consciousness in Man

The associated pyramidlet is on the south side—representing material existence— but it is incredibly small by correspondence with even the Men-kau-ra pyramidlets. The implied symbolism here, one might suggest, is that the purely personal ego of the candidate facing this initiation has to become hugely diminished if he is to succeed. To some extent this view is augmented by the position of the passages and single internal chamber in the Khepren pyramid.† The chamber is dead center and crucially balanced exactly at external ground level, while the access passage is below ground level and the egress passage above it. The implied symbolism here seems to be that the initiate emerges from the experience on a higher plane from which he can look down at the mundane plane.

That then leaves the Men-kau-ra pyramid—the smallest of the three main ones—to play host to the first two initiations and the stage of basic probation that preceded them in all the various world traditions. The causeway to the Men-kau-ra pyramid faces due east, to the position of the rising Sun at the spring equinox—thereby symbolizing the early, rising spiritual nature in the candidate for these preliminary initiations. Of the three pyramidlets, we can suggest that the first (the smallest) was symbolically related to absolute control over the physical senses and the appetites. The second related to control of the emotions and also to the autonomic (lower) psychic nature, and the third to the lower mind principle.

---

*Heru-khuti was Lord of the Two Horizons, by virtue of the fact that, as the metaphorical embodiment of the Spiritual Ego in Man, it was he who initiated the cycle of incarnation and he to whom the lesser "divine spark" returned at the end of it. This same cycle was paralleled by the solar orb rising and setting daily in the horizon, and so Heru-khuti played an indispensable part in the daily cycle of the Sun god Ra, himself the metaphorical embodiment of the vital individuality in man. In some pictures (e.g., see fig. 5.9) he is depicted as having a fivefold crown of solar jugs resting upon the cataract horns of Khnemu. But note that only three of the jugs have solar orbs above and below them; the other two (in the background—representing the lowest two solar planes) do not. He is also carrying a hand scythe (like Kronos) to symbolize his role as the harvester of human experience. Heru-khuti is elsewhere depicted with a double-faced hawk head with an *utchat* above it. All these symbolisms, however, point in exactly the same direction.

†The second pyramid was otherwise known to the Egyptians as that of Ra-kha-f, or Kha-f-Ra—that is, the Spirit of Ra (Budge, *Gods of the Egyptians,* vol. 1, 470 et seq).

Astral Travel and the Initiate

We turn next to the issue of the actual subjective progressions made by the initiate as he (according to his degree) moved between the various planes of consciousness. But first of all we have to consider which aspect of him was actually involved in those moments and in the capacity to register experience and knowledge related to them. These days we tend to think rather blithely of "ascending through states of consciousness" without actually considering the mechanics and dynamics involved in that process. The Ancients were *most* concerned about such things, however, because the whole point—as they saw it—was to be able to remain self-consciously aware of what was going on at all times, rather than return to waking consciousness wondering whether it had all been a dream or not.* This principle is to be found precisely the same in the Hindu system and also that expressed by the Bardo Thodol, the Tibetan equivalent of the Egyptian Book of the Dead.†

Quite clearly, the physical body stayed precisely where it had been left prior to the individual's departure, as did also the *ka,* or double, which was itself attached to it. The astral soul, or *ba,* however, withdrew its infusing *kha*—the spirit nature that actually animates the body—and then departed toward its own natural home within the World Soul of our planet. This, as previously described, was known to the Ancients and to medieval philosophers as the sphere of the Moon; it was within this unified (but lesser) heaven world that the *ba* became temporarily reunited with the educational influence of the *sah,* or spiritual soul, which normally descended no lower into the sphere of material existence.‡

It followed that the individual capable of maintaining his focus of consciousness was able to astrally travel wherever on the planet he wished (or was permitted) to go. However, as the *ba* transited through the astral and mental states of being en route to the *sah,* it lost contact with the objective Earth state and became involved in a literal sea of elemental existence. If unaware of this within the *ba,* the *kha* nature would rise automatically to the *sah.* But if it became conscious of its external environment, it ran the risk of fascination, or fear, or disorientation, thereby making it very much more difficult for the higher nature to haul it in. Severe disorientation under such circumstances could then lead to elemental possession. Thus it became vitally important for the initiate of the earlier degrees to know the "geography" of this volatile elemental environment and also to have within his

---

*Hence the Zen story of the man who—appearing very anxious over his breakfast and asked by his wife exactly what was wrong—replied that he had had a dream during the night that he was a butterfly. When asked what was wrong with that, he further replied that he was now not sure whether he was actually a butterfly dreaming that he was a man!

†Which clearly indicates that the occult tradition within the Mystery Schools throughout the Middle East, and probably generally throughout the ancient world, was universal in its aims, its principles, and its methodology.

‡The link of consciousness between the *sah* and *ba*—being non-locational—was, however, maintained at all times during the life incarnation, until the natural process of permanent withdrawal that precedes physical death.

immediate (subjective) armory various pre-memorized rituals by the use of which he could repel "boarders" and steer his way clear to his destination. In so doing, his confidence and his spiritual individuality developed in tandem.

For the more highly qualified initiate (of the third degree and above), the problem evidently no longer applied, because he had already conquered all sympathetic elemental response within his own nature—by his own ethically and ascetically based self-disciplines. Consequently, the sheer power of his presence passing through these astral and psychological shoals would have been seen as having the same effect as in the case of a whale or shark passing through shoals of fish in the ocean, even though the *ba* itself was not of a predatory nature. By virtue of this peaceful travel, the senior initiate was undoubtedly also able the more effectively to retain the higher teachings he absorbed through his constant cyclical contact with the *sah*,* thus to return to Earth in full waking consciousness with them intact.

A further experience seems to have been accorded to both the senior initiate and also on rare occasions to certain lesser individuals either apparently selected for spiritual missions on Earth or who otherwise had somehow managed to invoke the spiritual individuality within the *sah* in relation to a quest for specific higher knowledge. In the latter case we come across the occasional description (in Hermetic circles) of the individual (like the early eighteenth-century mystic Swedenborg) having broken through the bounding sphere of the Moon and being able to travel (obviously in the *sah*) among the planets, as well as consciously coming into contact with the spiritual beings who populate this sidereal plane of existence in their bodies of light.†

Death and Continuity of Consciousness

It would appear from the various Mystery Traditions that the developed contact between the *ba* and *sah* among the initiates of higher degree was so strong that they were able to link the two consciously, at any time, by a mere act of will. Not surprisingly—bearing in

---

*It would appear, by virtue of the vastly superior power of the *sah,* that the *ba* was able to remain in its presence only for a relatively short period before becoming spiritually reassimilated into it. However, sustained meditation at this level has sometimes been recorded as resulting in the head and features of the awoken initiate being so radiant that it was impossible for bystanders actually to look directly at him. This is undoubtedly the basis for the artistic medieval aureole around the head of the saint.

†This concept of conscious astral travel has long been recognized in the Far East as one of the primary faculties of the highly developed initiate of the Raj Yoga tradition. Very rationally believable stories of it abound in relation to the experiences of Western travelers in Tibet and Nepal over the last two centuries. But it is found in various shamanistic traditions around the world too—only, in these cases, the individual shaman (whether male or female) is *very* rarely found to be in conscious control of what is going on and has to use drugs or other stimuli to achieve what the initiated Tibetans, for example, manage purely by an act of will. Shamans also tend to use the direct aid of elemental forces. This the Mysteries forbade.

mind that the *sah* contained an individualized semidivinity—the most advanced individuals were regarded as literal demigods, capable of transcending death itself.

It is in relation to these various concepts that we find in the Egyptian occult tradition direct reference to the stages of death involved in the initiatory process. For example: "My father has not died the second death for my father (Osiris the king) possesses a spirit in the horizon."*[23] As previously indicated, "the horizon" referred to is the World Soul within which the *sah* has its semipermanent abode. The equivalent solar horizon, however, is that solar body (the great *ashet*) enfolding the whole solar system, from which the *sah* itself is emanated via the *ashem,* in accordance with far greater *sidereal* cycles. In other parts of the Pyramid Texts of Unas we also find the advanced initiate saying of himself very directly, "I possess a spirit in the horizon."[24]

The second death just mentioned is clarified in Plutarch's brief treatise entitled "On the Face Which Appears in the Orb of the Moon," in which he, in the person of one Sylla, notes that man is a being existing in multiple states simultaneously, these consisting of body, soul, and *dianoia,* correlating to Earth, Moon, and Sun. The first death, said Sylla, "is that of the body in which it dissolves into earth again; the second death occurs . . . when the soul (*ba*) is resolved into the Sphere of the Moon and the Spirit passes into celestiality, freeing the most divine aspect of Man, the image of which is 'in the Sun.'"[25] It is toward this divine image in the Sun, says Sylla, that all Nature yearns in different ways. However, what is not made clear is that what is actually meant by "the Sun" is the crystal sphere of the solar firmament, not the Sun in the sky.

In further reference to the two thresholds of soul existence we otherwise find: "The double doors of heaven are open for you"[26] and also "He [the initiate] shall come forth by day and he shall not be repulsed at any gate of the Tuat, either coming or going. He shall perform all the transmutations which his heart bears within it and he shall not die."[27] Then in confirmation of the same: "I shall not be turned back at the gates of the Duat. . . . I am one who collects for himself his efflux in front of Rastau."[28] We also find "I have entered the world as a man of no understanding and I shall come forth in the form of a strong Khu [spirit] and I shall look upon my [astral soul] form which shall be that of men and women forever."[29]

Initiation as Liberation

As previously suggested, then, the aim of the initiate was ultimately to transcend the limitations of existence within the kosmic physical plane as a whole and thereby rise to the greater sevenfold sphere of kosmic Being as a literal god. But in order to do that, he had to move far beyond the degree of achievement attained even by the Risen Master Mason,

---

*The first death involved separation of the *ba* from the *ka*; the second death resulted from the reabsorption of the *ba* into the *sah*.

The Mystery
Tradition and the
Process of Initiation

by progressing through the sixth and seventh degrees to a qualitative state of celestial existence of which we can have no conception. Whether such achievements were possible in truly ancient Egyptian times we cannot say, although the traditions appear at least to suggest it. But such later initiations and direct god-associations would not have taken place at Giza. It seems far more likely that they took place in the pyramids farther south and between Memphis and the Faiyum—that is, at Abusir and Saqqara, where there seems to have existed a direct association with the Pleiades.

In the final analysis, therefore, the whole process of initiation in the ancient Mysteries was seen as leading to the state of Everlasting Life as an individualized god-being, with a yet further evolving *kosmic* consciousness. And bearing in mind the very clear statement in the *Hermetica*—"But Life is the union of body and soul. Death then is not the destruction of things, but [merely] the dissolution of their union"[30]—the whole structure of modern Egyptological thought on ancient Egyptian mysticism as being unilaterally based upon a morbid fascination with and fear of death finally falls to the ground in pieces.

The Silence of the Initiate

To conclude on a rather more contemporary note, one might observe that the modern equivalent of initiation in the Mysteries has become decidedly tarnished through widespread and usually unrepresentative publicity (frequently involving self-publicity). The Ancients made a great point of keeping such matters behind a veil of silence and *apparent* secrecy. The reason for this is, however, generally not appreciated in our brash democratic age, where anything discreet seems to be increasingly regarded with almost instant suspicion. The same sort of unthinkingly reactive attitude has regrettably led many archaeological scholars in the field of ancient culture into falsely believing that such lack of openness was itself merely indicative of either a superstitious attitude or a technique of hierarchical control over subordinates, for political reasons.

In fact, silence—hence apparent secrecy—was ever regarded as a proof of self-discipline and control over one's own ego. Additionally, because the Mystery School training led (quite naturally, through self-discipline) to the individual developing an ever-increasing power in his subtler perceptual faculties, overt display was regarded as both unnecessary and unwelcome. The neophyte or initiate used his powers only for the benefit of others. He also maintained his sense of spiritual individuality and equilibrium by an ever-wakeful respect for others, in conjunction with an increasingly ascetic or abnegatory attitude toward his own needs and feelings. However, this involved no sort of egregious humility.

Modern Misunderstanding Regarding the Principle and Practice of Initiation

Whereas the popular modern Western attitude to the subject of initiation is that it involves access to secrets concerning occult powers over Nature, the true initiatory tradition took a very different view. While the unfolding development of such powers by the individual derived entirely from his own efforts, it was generally recognized that most of such powers were of a purely psychic nature and thus related to the lower orders of existence. As the Mystery Schools were involved in training the individual to free himself from the thrall of the lower world orders, as already described earlier in this book, it would have been illogical for them to encourage the individual toward their use. Consequently, while the existence of such powers was clearly recognized, their actual use would have been naturally very restrained. This same approach is still found to be axiomatic among, for example, true Zen and Sufi orders today.

Bearing in mind how much public interest has been focused in the direction of ancient Egypt arising out of fascination with occult phenomena, one cannot help but wonder what the general reaction would have been if this perhaps more prosaic reality were better known and understood. But that in no way detracts from the extraordinary and magnificent nature of ancient Egyptian civilization and culture in the round—even if we still do not know for sure when it first appeared and what its true origins were.

The Future of the Sacred Mystery Tradition

We live in an age that appears to be dominated by either a spectrum of materialistic creeds or a creed of general materialism, all associated with scientifically based and consumer-oriented technological development. In addition, the modern science of physics tries to assure us that its research confirms that Deity is an unnecessary concept. Yet, perhaps paradoxically, this same age has seen a hugely increasing desire for things that appeal to our subjective nature, much of which presents itself under the blanket heading of spirituality. However, the vast proportion of what we interpret as spiritual would have been seen by the Ancients as nothing of the sort—in fact, no more than pertaining to the worlds of merely psychic or psychological phenomena. The Ancients would also have pointed out that science only deals with process and has no capacity to answer the most fundamentally important questions about existence.

Because our age has otherwise become seduced and infected by the feeling that everything should be simplified and packaged for easier and quicker consumption and assimilation, Western society at least tends to balk at the idea that true association with the spiritual side of life might require much more personal effort, of an altogether deeper kind than that involving a mere change of lifestyle. But that is largely because Western society in general has managed to confuse the words *simplicity* (i.e., naturalness) and *simplification* (i.e., un-naturalness due to human reductionism). This development has gone hand in glove with the general (and highly unfortunate) trend toward overspecialization in society, a phenomenon that has led to undue importance being given to the separative independent application of the Mind function, rather than keeping it tethered to the naturally intuitive, correlative function of the Intelligence. That, in turn, has led to an often fragmented perception of natural reality, with consequently widespread social and cultural disorientation—plus misunderstanding and aggressively antisocial behavior.

A large part of this problem has come about not only through the failure to apply simple common sense, but also through forms of prejudice induced by disillusionment with the corruption of society, plus an associated lack of historical perspective. This led, centuries ago, to religion becoming divorced from its natural association with philosophy and science, through the overintellectualization of later Greek philosophers. This schism was then curiously perpetuated in reverse by Christian theologians who appropriated philosophy for their own use and cast out science. Nascent (Western) intellectual science then made the gross mistake of detaching itself completely from both philosophy and religion, while using a distorted form of metaphysics to justify its subjective speculations. Thereafter, once the supposed understanding of the structure of the atom became the basis of all orthodoxy, it was a short and immediate step to religion and philosophy being considered altogether unnecessary and for metaphysics to be cast out as well with the bathwater. However, this has led to the development of a widely self-oriented but otherwise perspectiveless view of what humanity and Nature itself might actually be about.

The Separation of Philosophy, Religion, and Science

To the Ancients, the separation of philosophy, religion, and science would have been unthinkable, because they represented the three fundamental aspects of Universal Nature itself, fused in man's intelligence—the sense of unitary self-existence, the sense of the sacred, and the sense of the multiple Mind function. These three—like the Hindu *atma-buddhi-manas* or the Christian Father, Son, and Holy Spirit—were considered inseparable except in their application within the field of knowledge or understanding. The ancient Mystery Traditions of the world regale us with plenty of allegorical stories of what disastrously happens when such schisms as this occur in man's nature. Yet, as academically oriented science currently holds sway on the world scene, with philosophy largely ignored and religion either disoriented or in the hands of ignorant zealots, what could possibly be done to redress the situation? Well, in the short term, the answer would appear to be "very little." Yet there are brighter signs on the horizon that give some degree of encouragement—at least to those who study the evolution of human ideas and culture.

It is coming to be generally accepted in the field of science that the current greatest and most challenging frontier with which it has yet to come fully to grips—let alone cross—is that of *consciousness* itself. But here lies the nub of the problem as regards a proper understanding of the ancient Mysteries on their own terms. While many (perhaps most?) of the world's leading scientists and thinkers see (and often openly say) that brain, mind, and intuition are all quite different—a view clearly supported by the non-locality aspect of quantum theory—the associated rationale of their relationship has not yet been developed. Or perhaps it would be more accurate to say that, while its various parts may already be

The Future of the Sacred Mystery Tradition

367

available, they have not yet been scientifically coordinated in a manner (i.e., according to formulated laws) that might achieve general acceptance.

But here lies another problem. Because mainstream science has dispensed with both metaphysical philosophy and the concept of Deity, it has no answer to the simple query as to how and why the universe functions in harmonic balance within very narrow parameters and in line with strict laws. The Ancients, of course, took the view that Universal Order existed because of the existence of Universal Mind, applied by hierarchies of Universal Intelligence in deference to a commonly shared sense of Universal Purpose. But, as mainstream science refuses to even countenance the possible usefulness of that metaphysical approach adopted by the Ancients, how can it see beyond its own self-induced myopia?

Fear on the Part of Science Itself

Perhaps the greatest obstacle faced by science is its own obstinately self-engineered but wholly artificial independence from philosophy and religion—an independence largely based upon fear that, with their potential regeneration, it would lose its current social primacy of status and once again become a merely junior partner. But that itself is based upon a more general misunderstanding involving the idea that philosophy, religion, and science are completely separate disciplines in the first place. They are not. They commonly interface and interweave with each other in all sorts of very practical ways, each however having primary, secondary, and tertiary aspects, which are constantly involved in an eternally shifting, blending, and counterbalancing dance. However, it is the metaphysical rationale of this same constantly transitional movement that is currently missing.

Because of this, notwithstanding the increasingly accepted view that there is such a thing as the "spectrum of consciousness," our modern idea of the interplay between subjective and objective existence remains fuzzy and undiscriminating. We sometimes have a sort of hazy perception that philosophy, religion, and science are all merely aspectual expressions or different means of accessing the one overall field of a Universal Consciousness, but our focal length remains, as yet, limited and inconstant.

The Problem of the Nature of Material Existence

One of the other major obstacles to further progress is the commonly held view that there is such a thing as inert or inorganic matter, notwithstanding the fact that science still currently adopts the wholly unsupportable position that organic life emerges from it. Once modern scientific theory openly accepts that the omniverse must be fundamentally organic in its essential nature, with both dormant and active potentials inherent in all states of Matter, all sorts of other forward conceptual steps will become possible. One of these will inevitably involve the automatic association of the spectrum of Universal Matter with the spectrum of Universal Consciousness. Thereafter, the next progression would naturally involve an examination of the dynamics and mechanics of how forms actually arise in nature, before emerging into physical objectivity. That itself would naturally lead to an understanding of the (metaphysically definable) nature of planes of being and consciousness at the base of the spectrum of subjective and objective existence.

Now all this might perhaps be envisaged as taking place purely within the field of our own planetary environment, on Earth. However, this did not satisfy the Ancients, who translated it into a universal context. Yet their further conceptions were clearly not based entirely upon mere scientific or even metaphysical theory. Some of their ideas were so radically specific (even if couched in metaphor and allegory) that they must have had an experiential base. In other words, they understood that the field of even subjective consciousness had to have some sort of material existence attached to it and that this could therefore be accessed (and progressively traversed) at first hand by the trained and self-disciplined (and thoroughly self-aware) intelligence. The Tibetan Book of the Dead is quite unambiguously categorical about this, as are also certain of the Vedic texts. One is therefore drawn inevitably to the probability that such a view was held universally throughout the ancient world—at least, among the initiated priesthoods of the time.

Yet Again, the Soul Principle

Nevertheless, the inevitable question that arises out of all this is, "But how did they do it?" Well, one might as well ask how someone rides a bicycle. One just does, through learning at first hand how to coordinate physical effort, forward and lateral motion, balance, visual discrimination, and overall control. Without all of this in simultaneous function, under the mastery of the individual's own intelligence, nothing would happen. There would be no experience. But the Ancients took the view that the very same principles applied within the world of what *we* regard as purely subjective experience. However, the nature of the subjective "bicycle" had first to be perceived and its general principles understood; this is where the Sacred Mysteries came in.

The subjective bicycle is of course the soul vehicle, which the Ancients saw as being able to traverse its own limited field of conscious being. Thus the *ba* or astroterrestrial soul—being an emanation of the planetary World Soul of our Earth—had relative freedom of movement and function throughout the auric field of the latter. Correspondingly, the *sah* or spiritual soul had relative freedom of movement, knowledge, and function throughout the solar system. Yet it had to be realized by the individual that the soul was merely the vehicle of his own Higher Intelligence, the overall observer and controller.

Now, to us, this suggestion might seem altogether extraordinary on the grounds that the existence of the soul cannot be proved under (artificial) laboratory conditions, using scientifically approved technology. But that is only because modern (Middle Eastern and Western) mankind has become psychospiritually paraplegic and cannot even recognize soul and spirit as possibly having an experientially factual existence. How then could it develop a modern metaphysical rationale (based upon firsthand perception) of the seamless way in which Mother Nature works behind the scenes?* Science on its own constantly runs out of steam when faced with such issues and has yet to answer the simple question as to why it is that—as shown by quantum theory—Order always emerges from Chaos and returns to it. But the Mystery Traditions passed down to us show again and again that the Ancients fully understood the question and that they also had the answer.

This then is surely where the ancient wisdom tradition is of such radical (as well as palliative) value in a modern context. If we make the effort to dig past the superficially exciting gloss of associated psychic phenomena to the metaphysical dynamic that provides Universal Nature with its ethereal "chassis," it rapidly becomes obvious that Existence itself is actually an eternally extant process within the field of Universal Being. What we call Consciousness can then be seen to involve the actual experience of sequentially parallel states of sub-Being within that field, an experience the Ancients likened to a current passing through a river or ocean. Hence Man the "divine spark"—as the higher expression of Divine Purpose—merely passed through the river/ocean of material existence (Nu-Nun) within the kosmic Life wave (the barque of Ra).

According to the Ancients, then, the *meta*-physical reality was the true and eternally permanent reality. The ephemeral local effects experienced by the "divine spark" as it passed through the Underworld of planetary existence, with all its intriguing but transient phenomena, were thus to be objectively noted and their rationale understood. But Man himself, like the Vedic Krisna, had to remain apart, or suffer the consequences of an aspect of his intrinsic god-self being dragged down through the vortex of self-association into the long cycle of spiritual ignorance and constant rebirth, until he managed (in the Egyptian style) to "gather all his members together" and find his way out again. This is the central lesson that the ancient Egyptian, Vedic, Tibetan, and other traditions impart to us, and it is one we forget or trivialize surely at our own short-term psychological inconvenience and our long-term spiritual peril.

---

*Science insists upon artificial definitions that psychologically divorce different aspects of Nature from one another, even where directly or indirectly related in their essential natures. Hence, for example, attraction, surface tension, magnetism, and gravity are all unnaturally separated instead of being seen as but different aspects and applications within the spectrum of one single principle.

APPENDIX A

THE GEOMETRICAL CORRESPONDENCE TO THE CYCLE OF INVOLUTION AND EVOLUTION

The nature of the Pythagorean right-angled 3-4-5 triangle as a metaphor for the Divine Trinity of Father-Mother-Son has long been understood by students of Hermeticism. However, the direct association with the seven planes or divisions of solar existence and the cycle of incarnation of the (solar) Logos is not very well known. A brief explanation is given here as follows.

The diagram in fig. A.1 represents the sphere of solar existence encapsulated by the kosmic consciousness of the solar Demiurge. The spherical line or arc symbolizes the principle of Consciousness, while the straight lines connote the form-building instinct in Nature. As we can see, this sphere has two poles of inward emanation, which themselves give rise to a fundamental duality within the sphere—hence the latter being called the Divine Father-Mother. As earlier explained, each emanation is itself triple in nature and the two combine yin-yang fashion to contain a proportion of the chaotic matter of space, which thereby becomes sevenfold in nature, in response. The positive point of emanation (that of the Father aspect) generates out of itself a trinity known to Christian theologians as Father–Son–Holy Spirit, these three being respectively associated with the three highest planes or divisions. As we also saw earlier, these were attributed in the Egyptian tradition to Kheper-Ra, Amen-Ra, and Mntw-Ra.

The demiurgic consciousness and the form-building instinct, which were primordially separated at the positive pole, temporarily reunite at that point where the form-building instinct has generated out of itself the first three solar planes or states of being. This temporary union generates a semidivine hierarchy of beings (as One Being initially) with an associated consciousness—the *atman* of Hindu tradition, which is synonymous with

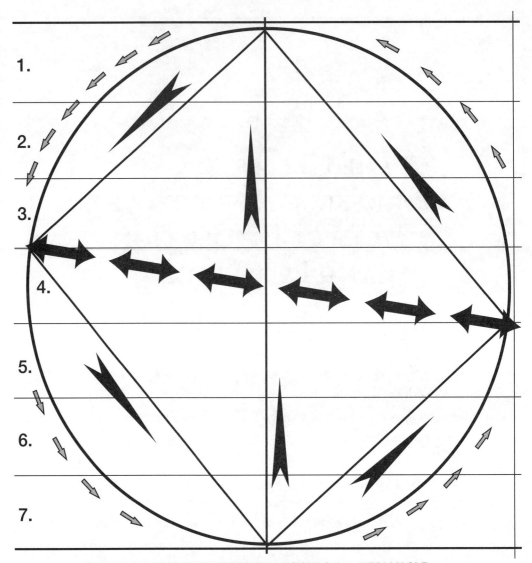

FIGURE A.1. THE EVOLUTIONARY KOSMIC 3-4-5 TRIANGLE

Osiris in the Egyptian. These are the "divine sparks" drawn out of the demiurgic horizon or firmament and thus made to fall from Grace. The nature of Creation being fundamentally dualistic, however, this emanation itself divides into two separate hierarchies, one of which remains within the fourth solar state—as it were, shuttling backward and forward cyclically between the third and fifth solar divisions. The other, however—a hierarchy of *lesser* "divine sparks"—heads downward into the depths of Matter, progressing through four solar divisions until it reaches the negative demiurgic pole.

At this latter point, this hierarchy of "descending sparks" temporarily reunites with the lowest aspect of demiurgic consciousness (a point referred to in the Egyptian tradition as "when Ra was old and tired"), the product of this union being the human being and its form of intelligence. As we can see from the diagram, this point brings about a subtle form of reunion between the two demiurgic poles, involving the completion of the Pythagorean 3-4-5 triangle. However, this juncture involves only one half of the overall solar cycle.

The hierarchy of human "divine sparks" now detaches itself from the demiurgic consciousness and strikes out independently, upward through the three lowest solar divisions or planes—toward the lowest point of influence of the Osirian *atman*. The eventual (but again only temporary) union of their consciousness with it then takes place at the junction of the third and fourth planes. This is the "gate" of the god Seker. Upon crossing this latter threshold, a further natural division occurs, for as the sacred Egyptian texts confirm, there are two ways back to the home heaven, one directly by land and the other less directly by sea—esoteric metaphors for either respective progress individually within a form (of spiritual matter—the individualized *atman*) or progress en masse within the barque of Ra itself. Once returned to the positive demiurgic pole, the rectangular cycle is completed.

Now, quite apart from helping to explain the natural sequence of evolutionary progression faced by Man, this 3-4-5 configuration and the rectangle produced by doubling it up* give rise to an astronomical association. Referring back to fig. 2.11, we can see that the vertical line symbolizing the 5 is representative of the plane of the Milky Way. The diagonal line that runs between the junction of the third–fourth and the fourth–fifth solar divisions is then representative of the plane of the ecliptic path. As this is clearly associated with the (25,920-year) cycle of the circulation of the Osirian *atman,* we can perhaps understand why the Ancients regarded it as having such a special spiritual significance. For at the lower end of this cycle there would appear to be an opportunity for ordinary humankind to unite their consciousness with that of spiritual intelligences and thus progress more easily and quickly back toward the higher divine pole of celestial Origin, while at the higher end, new infusions of higher beings would join the Great Year cycle—in other words, the gods and demigods would return. Geometry, astronomy, and metaphysics would thus appear—as one might perhaps expect—to have been in complete concord in the minds of the Ancients.

---

*It is worth noting in connection with this matter that the standard size of enclosure of the Egyptian temple—as defined in the Edfu Texts—comprised a rectangle of 300 x 400 cubits, "contained by the Ogdoad," in other words, the demiurgic sphere that aurically enfolds and also informs the sevenfold system with its Life-force.

The Geometrical
Correspondence to
the Cycle of
Involution and
Evolution

373

APPENDIX B

POLAR MISCONCEPTIONS

Some of the suggestions put forward in this appendix would undoubtedly be regarded as thoroughly heretical by mainstream science. However, without putting them to the fore, it would be generally impossible to demonstrate the practical effects of the Ancients' own conceptual way of thinking, which allied metaphysics with what we would regard as modern physics. As we shall see, the Ancients appear to have been aware of some things our modern astronomers and astrophysicists have not yet even begun remotely to consider. The example to be dealt with here involves the principle of concentricity—as applied specifically to our solar system in general and to the Earth in particular.

On the subjects of poles and polarity, it has for some time been known by scientists that the Sun's upper and lower hemispheres rotate in opposite directions. This is itself directly comparable with the fact that the equatorial winds and currents on either side of the Earth's equator also flow in opposite directions. But that phenomenon is a clear indication of vertical electromagnetic/barometric pressure being applied from both above and below, thereby producing the coriolis effect. The other effect is necessarily that of producing a piezoelectric discharge at the core (of either the Sun or planet Earth), thereby affecting both magnetism and gravity. Now the reason for mentioning these issues in a book of this nature is that such phenomena have to do with the fundamental nature of Duality, which the Ancients clearly saw as having terrestrial and celestial counterparts to the metaphysical one.

Contrary to popular belief—as the Earth's crust itself is not magnetic—our planet's true North and South Poles must actually be found many miles *above* its surface, within the vortices of highly charged particles descending from the ionosphere. However, one might conclude that the energies emanating from (and retreating to) the Earth's core must themselves create sympathetic *gravitational* poles close to the Earth's crustal surface, and it is suggested that it is the shifting location of these that paleomagnetic scientists have ever confused with the (ionospheric) North and South Poles.

Now the Earth's core relative to (a) its outer crust and (b) the ionosphere bears a direct

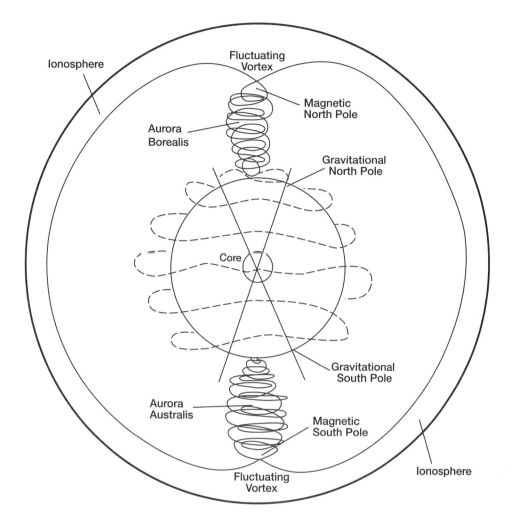

Ionosphere

Fluctuating
Vortex

Magnetic
North Pole

Aurora
Borealis

Gravitational
North Pole

Core

Gravitational
South Pole

Aurora
Australis

Magnetic
South Pole

Ionosphere

Fluctuating
Vortex

Not to scale or detail

FIGURE B.1. EARTH'S MAGNETIC VS. GRAVITATIONAL NORTH AND SOUTH POLES

parallel to the center of the galaxy relative to the galactic halo and the galactic corona (as shown in fig. 1.1) respectively. From the ancient viewpoint, the solar system would logically be arranged in the selfsame way according to the Hermetic principle "As above, so below." Thus the Earth's core would have to be seen (like the nucleus of the scientist's atom) as a reservoir of potential energy that fluctuates according to the electromagnetic pressure brought to bear upon it by the ionosphere.* Relative to its ionosphere, the Earth's core would thus be electrically positive—as is the Sun to the auric field enfolding the solar system as a whole.

---

*Perhaps paradoxically, as ionospheric influence diminishes, so the gravitational pull toward the Earth's core would *increase*.

As outlined in the early chapters of the book, the Ancients took the view that the principles of direction and evolutionary motivation in Nature originate in the auric "firmament" or "horizon" that surrounds each celestial body, be it a solar system or a planet. Here, according to their way of thinking, were to be found the directing Intelligences behind each such scheme of Creation, all of them involved in a dynamically meditative state, their directed attention itself being the "motor" behind all energetic phenomena in our part of the universe. The centrifugally operative energies at the central core of each such system would quite logically fluctuate in sympathetic response to these hierarchies of Intelligence being (meditatively) focused inward or outward. The associated reasoning derives from the simple idea that when the kosmic deities within the auric firmament of the solar system turn their attention inward, their literal concentration must cause the solar aura to contract, thereby increasing the pressure within the solar system. As a direct result, the amount of energy emanated by the Sun (the Egyptian Aten) would increase dramatically—hence the cyclical sunspots that appear at each end of the twenty-two-year solar cycle of "inbreathing" and "outbreathing."

This variability of solar energies must, in turn, have an effect upon the auric firmament of the Earth and the consciousness of the directing Intelligences that were considered to inhabit it. For, in response to the discharge of solar energy at either end of the twenty-two-year solar cycle (akin to the thunderbolts of Zeus), the Earth's electrically charged auric envelope (the ionosphere) would itself logically expand in order to contain it. This is the male/female creative principle in action.

Now, as a direct consequence of the ionosphere expanding, the centrifugal energies from the Earth's core—the essence of which may be said to constitute what we call gravity—would diminish. When the ionosphere contracts, however, it would increase dramatically, with the electrical sympathy between the two resulting in those polar phenomena known to us as the Aurora Borealis and the Aurora Australis. The interactive electrical activity that then takes place is almost certainly what is directly responsible for cyclically revitalizing the Earth's own *ka* or double, which itself extends from some way below the crust, upward into the lower atmosphere, thereby providing the finely balanced environment in which various forms of organic life (including the human) are able to exist and thrive.

It is not difficult to see the logic of each and every celestial field cyclically encountering points in its own orbital passage resulting in highly increased electrical or electromagnetic activity and of its own response affecting all other celestial bodies within the immediate vicinity of its home field. The whole of existence is, in this way, to be regarded as electrically self-stimulating and self-balancing—a concept that was fundamental to ancient metaphysical thought. The only question that remains—in the face of this wonderfully symmetrical order—is whether one believes it to be the result of pure chance or of intelligently directed control.

As we can see from fig. 2.2, while the Earth rotates on an oblique axis (always set at 90 degrees to its plane of orbital rotation around the Sun), its magnetic North and South Poles remain vertical to the plane of the interplanetary magnetic field—which lies in the same plane as the zodiacal constellations. But the very same principle appears to apply to the orbit of our solar system as a whole around its own parent star. Hence it is that the magnetic poles of both the Sun and the Earth remain invariably set at the same angle. Notwithstanding this, it does seem that the Earth's gravitational or geomagnetic pole does tend to wander, rather than eternally staying in exactly the same place. But why should this be so? Well, bearing in mind that the whole organism is electromagnetically operated and that there is a variable electrical charge involved, there seems to be little doubt that the strength of the interplanetary magnetic field would itself vary according to the electrical energies being emanated by the Sun*—as solar scientists are just beginning to realize. Quite apart from affecting the Earth's own climate (and undoubtedly the size of the ozone holes), our planet's geomagnetic poles would otherwise tend to wander slightly according to the relative strength or weakness of the interplanetary magnetic field.

These issues—while interesting in their own right—appear at somewhat of a tangent to the mystic metaphor and allegory of the Ancients. What the latter appear to have been primarily concerned with involved the psychospiritual opportunities involved in crossing the river of consciousness and remaining upright in line with the principle of Ma'at. Yet their approach to knowledge of the world of environmental phenomena was all-embracing and it seems unlikely that these polar considerations would have escaped their interest or the detection of its underlying principles.

As we saw in chapter 2, the celestial polar orientation of the Earth moves with the changing circumpolar stars during the 25,920-year Great Year. However, because our solar system is orbiting around its own parent star, the orientation of the celestial pole changes by 180 degrees at different ends of this great cycle. Hence it was that the Egyptian priests were able to say to Herodotus that, within the time span of their own astronomical records, they knew of the Sun "rising twice where he now sets and setting twice where he now rises." In other words, their records went back considerably more than fifty-two thousand years. Modern astronomy does not believe this because modern astronomy has not yet taken into serious consideration the possibility that our solar system revolves around a parent star—with all the consequences arising out of such a relationship. As a result, one of the major misconceptions arising among catastrophe theorists in recent years has been regarding the Earth's supposedly turning turtle through cyclical polar reversal. Following the rationale of the Ancients, it can be very simply seen why this is not the case after all.

---

*In response to the cyclical expansion and contraction of the auric field of the solar system.

APPENDIX C

THE FUNERAL POSITIONS OF ORION-OSIRIS

As described in *Land of the Fallen Star Gods* (fig. 9.8), the ancient Egyptians rather curiously pictured the body of Osiris (in the temple of Dendera) moving around in no less than twenty-three funeral positions. Now twenty-three is a rather curious prime number, which seemingly has no clear relationship with anything else in the Egyptian tradition—except for the headdress of Hathor shown in fig. C.1. However, it is otherwise shared by the Hindu god Siva Nataraja, depicted in C.2.* As fig. C.1 shows, the crown emanating from Hathor's head has twenty-three flowers projecting from it, while she herself holds a twenty-fourth in her right hand in the form of a scepter. Is there a common significance?

Well, to begin with, some sort of cycle is clearly being symbolically intimated. And, bearing in mind how the gods were regarded as descending from the seventh and highest (divine) plane of the solar sphere of Being, we might reasonably speculate that 23 = 3 x 7 + 2. Alternatively, we might observe that a cyclical movement downward or upward through twelve states (7 + 5) and then back to the point of commencement would take twenty-three phases. The curious thing is that both of these, in relation to the sevenfold system of planes of being, each with seven substates, produces a movement to the same point. If we count downward from the cusp of the kosmic divine and semidivine states in the greater septenary system, we arrive at the cusp of the second and third subplanes within the fifth kosmic plane. Correspondingly, if we count upward twelve subplanes from the upper cusp of the solar Underworld and the second kosmic plane and then

---

*Siva Nataraja is shown with varying numbers of flames surrounding him; each such distinction appears to signify a particular celestial soul-sphere, the cycle of which is denoted by the number of flames. In this particular image, there are twenty-two—the twenty-second being in his left hand, which also points to the seventh—suggesting that it is symbolic of *pi* and the soul-sphere surrounding our own Sun, with its twenty-two-year sunspot cycle.

FIGURE C.1. THE CROWN EMANATING FROM HATHOR'S HEAD HAS TWENTY-THREE FLOWERS PROJECTING FROM IT, WHILE SHE HOLDS A TWENTY-FOURTH IN HER RIGHT HAND IN THE FORM OF A SCEPTER.

describe a circle returning to the same cusp, we also pass through twenty-three phases, the uppermost point of which is the cusp of the second and third subplanes in the fifth kosmic plane. Well, so what?

The underlying essence of the idea—bearing in mind the direct association between Osiris and the constellation of Orion and the spiritual soul principle—is that both the latter are involved in a twenty-threefold cycle of astronomical influence or activity.

FIGURE C.2. SIVA NATARAJA

We perhaps otherwise need to take into account the fact (already mentioned) that the traditionally seven Pleiades and five Hyades together add up to a twelvefold round. Consequently, "surrounding their father Atlas-Orion in their grief," a kosmic influence passing down through them and back to its point of origin would also take twenty-three phases to complete.

THE PRIMARY CELTIC FESTIVALS

The four main Celtic festivals of Imbolc, Beltane, Lughnasadh, and Samhain were celebrated in Alba (the ancient name for Britain) in our modern months of February, May, August, and November respectively. None of these even nearly coincide with the annual solstices and equinoxes; consequently, the particular reasons for holding them at these times—although believed to have been astronomically or astrologically derived—have never been discovered or confirmed beyond doubt. In fact, they appear to be very much more closely associated with the *celestial* equinoxes and solstices associated with the Great Year and the zodiacal signs of Aquarius, Taurus, Leo, and Scorpio respectively. The confirmation of this appears to be supported by the associated rituals attached to each of the festivals, as follows.

The Festival of Imbolc

This festival took place in February during the cycle of influence of Aquarius and was regarded as marking the commencement of spring. It was referred to as "the Making of the Bride's Bed."

The Festival of Beltane

This, taking place during the month cycle of Taurus, became known as May Day; the celebrations revolved around maypole dancing and "jumping the fire" or running between two fires.

The Festival of Lughnasadh

Taking place during the month attributed to the zodiacal sign of Leo, this festival involved the ritual of the first cutting or harvest of the corn, the sacrifice of a sacred bull, and its replacement with a younger one. An additional ritual involved the placing of a symbolic head on top of a hill and then having it trampled over by somebody dressed up as Lugh, the Celtic god of light.

The Festival of Samhain

This festival, in November, under the aegis of the zodiacal sign of Scorpio, seemingly marked the ending and beginning of the Celtic year. With the advent of Christianity it became known as All Souls' Day, when the whole community relit their home fires from the sacred fire, produced by the rays of the Sun. At this festival there also took place the ritual of rolling a flaming hoop down a local hill.

APPENDIX E

THE SLAUGHTER OF MANKIND

There are several known myths associated with the great god Ra, and this one is of particular interest because its underlying allegory actually has to do with the foundation of the solar world scheme, even though it is presented in the sense of a preceding destruction. The story is set against the metaphorical background of Ra "having grown old"—meaning that the great kosmic Life cycle he represents has become encrusted in material existence, of the seventh and lowest *kosmic* order. He is then depicted as becoming aware that Mankind is complaining about him behind his back, notwithstanding the fact that they owe their very existence to the creative power of the Eye of Ra. The implied meaning here, however, is that (divine) Mankind has been given nothing creatively useful to do because Ra's own creative instincts—on which they are wholly reliant—are (temporarily) at a standstill. Hence the implication is of a certain downward point having been reached in the unfolding sequence of the greater kosmic cycle.

Ra calls to his side Nu, the eternal god of the great waters (his father *and* son), and asks what he should do about Mankind, which by now has fled en masse into the mountain (i.e., the mound of kosmic physical existence), supposedly in order to escape his wrath. The other assembled gods then advise sending down the goddess Hathor to deal with them. She duly descends to the mountain and "slays" Mankind, while the goddess Sekhmet (an alter ego of Hathor) wades about during the night in Mankind's "blood"—that is, the Life principle. Ra then orders the production of a highly potent form of "beer" (although "spirits" would surely be more appropriate in this context), which is then poured over the regions of the four heavens, thereby flooding them. The next morning (i.e., the beginning of the next kosmic subcycle) Sekhmet arrives and drinks up large quantities of the "beer" and "blood," thereby assimilating Man himself—and thereby becoming "drunk"—and she makes no further attempt to continue on with the slaughter.

The essence of the myth is that a proportion of divine Mankind is being assimilated into a lower form of kosmic existence. Sekhmet is the wife of the god Ptah, who is jointly responsible with Khnemu for creating the sphere of the seventh and lowest kosmic state.

The "blood" of divine mankind represents Man's semidivine essence, which Sekhmet assimilates, thereby bringing about its cellular segregation as the *sek-hem* within the *sek-het*. This same segregation brings about the generation of a form of perceptive spiritual consciousness known by the root word *her*, which in turn gives rise to an even greater degree of individualization in the form of seven *groups* of spiritual soul-bodies—that is, *het-heru*, each otherwise known as a *hat-hor* (Hathor). This is why there were seven Hathors.

The mythic story ends with Ra getting tired of being around mankind. The god Nu then commands the god Shu (the principle of light) to take over. The goddess Nut (symbolizing the celestial vault) is then made to mutate (metaphorically) into a cow, with Ra seating himself on her back. In other words, the Ra principle retires to his celestial mansion (the demiurgic heaven world), while Mankind, now remorsefully waking up to its lèse-majesté, arms itself with weapons and sets off to do battle with the enemies of Ra— that is, the elemental forces in the lower dominions of terrestrial or planetary Nature, through incarnation.

Ra, upon approvingly noting this, forgives Mankind all its past sins, then raises himself yet further up into the celestial heaven world, where he creates a kingdom (i.e., a definite state) in which all mankind is eventually to be assembled. He then creates below this "the Field of Peace (Sekhet-hetep) in which green herbs are planted," thereby immediately generating the secondary field of Sekhet-Aaru, in which are to be positioned the stars themselves. These fields (i.e., states of Being) are made to exist within the body of Nut, and, so as to support the additional weight, Ra orders Shu to place himself directly beneath her.

The essence of what is being allegorically said in this last paragraph is that Ra, the Life wave that descends from the highest kosmic plane to the lowest—which incorporates the future solar-terrestrial world scheme—contains the latter within a heaven world (the biblical firmament). Within this he generates the divine and semidivine states, the latter being that in which the stars themselves are to exist. Finally, the principle of light—evidently in both stellar and solar—is activated and our *local* universe is then complete and ready for action.

Interestingly, the story otherwise ends with Ra calling the god Geb (god of the earth, i.e., the seven solar planes in toto) into his presence and scolding him for the fact that the strife with mankind has arisen because of the activity of the serpents in Geb's kingdom. Geb is told in the future to keep proper control over them, but in addition, Ra says that he too will maintain a permanent observation over things from his high heaven world and that he will give "to those of mankind 'who have knowledge of Words of Power,' dominion over them [the serpents]."[1] This then is yet another confirmation that it is the serpent-soul principle in Nature that distracts Man from awareness of his own natural divine state and that the adept (or spiritual Magus) is one who regains his divinity by learning how to bring the soul principle under the control of his Higher Self.

APPENDIX F

CORRELATIONS BETWEEN THE ANCIENT EGYPTIAN AND TIBETAN MYSTIC SYSTEMS

As already described, there appears to be a phonetically immediate correlation between the ancient Egyptian god Ptah and the (Dhyani) Buddha of the Tibetan system. However, there are a great many other synchronicities between the two systems. One major one involves the fact that both possessed a Book of the Dead, the Tibetan version being called the Bardo Thodol. As W. Y. Evans-Wentz, probably the best-known translator of the latter, makes clear, "Although the Bardo Thodol is at the present time used in Tibet as a breviary and read or recited on the occasion of death . . . one should not forget that it was originally conceived to serve as a guide not only for the dying and the dead, but for the living as well."[1] In other words, it was intended for the occult education of trainee initiates, or neophytes, in relation to their nightly passing (consciously) through the subtle states of Being between the astral and spiritual souls. Thus, if approached in the same vein, the Egyptian Book of the Dead would be translated and interpreted in a very different manner than the stiff and unimaginative one pursued by orthodox Egyptological scholars such as W. O. Faulkner, notwithstanding their erudition.

In the Tibetan Bardo tradition we otherwise find that the Buddha figure is shown as possessing four Herukas—Vajra, Ratna, Padma, and Karma—each with its own Shakti, or female magical power.[2] However, if taken as Heru-ka, the word rapidly becomes synonymous with the Egyptian idea of a consciousness double—that is, an ethereal vehicle for different qualities or types of consciousness.

The Bardo Thodol text is itself based upon the number forty-nine,[3] which is of course the square of seven. This also accords with the ancient Egyptian concentric metaphysical system, described earlier as comprising seven kosmic planes, each made up of seven subplanes. The lowest of these septenary subsystems then became the objective kosmic world—that of the solar universe. We find this same forty-ninefold system in the Hindu metaphysical tradition as well.

In the Buddhist tradition of Tibet, we find the priesthood divided into a duality, one group wearing red hats and the other yellow hats. This looks remarkably like the red and white crowns of Lower and Upper Egypt, which symbolized psychic and spiritual consciousness respectively.

Akin to the Egyptian practice of mummification, the Tibetans practiced embalming of dead bodies too—but only those of high lamas or saints. Evans-Wentz describes the Tibetan process as involving the body first being packed in a box of marsh salt for about three months, then "after the corpse is well cured, it is coated with a cement-like substance made of clay, pulverized sandalwood, spices, and drugs. This adheres and hardens and all the sunken or shriveled parts of the body, such as the eyes, cheeks and stomach having been rounded out by it to their natural proportions, a very Egyptian-like mummy is produced."[4]

The Tibetans also had a Chamber of Judgment in their scheme, again very similar to the Egyptian. In both versions there is a symbolic weighing of the good and bad aspects of the individual's character. In the Egyptian version it is the baboon ally of Tehuti who supervises the actual weighing. In the Tibetan tradition it is a monkey-headed god.[5] In the Egyptian system the monster Amemet stands ready to devour all the residual matter left after the good is separated from the bad, while in the Tibetan tradition a group of elemental creatures likewise wait to carry off the individual's psychic dross to the place of Underworld Chaos, by way of natural restitution.

The supreme heaven world of our local universe, according to the Tibetans, is Og-min[6]—the transitional state leading from the solar world system to the greater kosmic system of which it forms part.[7] If treated phonetically, Og-min becomes *akh-min*,* which would quickly equate with the Egyptian *akh-het*. One might also draw a straight phonetic comparison with the Celtic heaven world of Tir-nan-Oc.

Finally, in the same way that the Egyptian *neteru* and *akheru* fell from the fourth kosmic state of Being, so in the Tibetan system the *lha-ma-yin* (i.e., the *asuras*) were expelled from the fourth kosmic state because of their pride.[8]

Min has the same root meaning in both the Tibetan and Egyptian as *Man* does in the Sanskrit—that is, the Mind principle. Hence the Og-min or *akh-min* is the primordial state in which the hierarchies of higher "divine sparks" exist *before* they fall from Grace into the lower, purely solar field of existence, from the Kosmic Mind.

NOTES

Introduction

1. Broglie, *New Perspectives in Physics.*
2. Squire, *Celtic Myth and Legend,* 229.
3. Ibid., 230.

Chapter One: The Spheres of Creation

1. Plato, *Timaeus,* ch. xiv, 342.
2. Ibid.
3. Scott, *Hermetica,* 413.
4. Gosse, *The Civilization of the Ancient Egyptians,* 118.
5. Scott, *Hermetica,* 247.
6. McLeish, *Children of the Gods,* 2.
7. Ibid., 3.
8. Ibid., 8–11.
9. Ibid., 17–18.
10. Temple, *The Crystal Sun,* 268 (quoting *Aristarchus of Samos* by Sir Thomas Heath).
11. Sejourne, *Burning Water.*
12. Allen, *Star Names,* 380.
13. Ibid., 400.
14. Budge, *The Egyptian Book of the Dead,* cxxii.
15. Allen, *Star Names,* 381.

Chapter Two: The Astronomical and Astrological Dimensions of Creation

1. Allen, *Star Names,* 393.
2. de Santillana and von Dechend, *Hamlet's Mill,* 292.
3. Allen, *Star Names,* 431.
4. McLeish, *Children of the Gods,* 2, 25, et seq.

5. Temple, *The Crystal Sun,* 103 (referring to Macrobius's *Commentary on the Dream of Scipio,* ch. xii, 1–5).

6. Scott, *Hermetica,* 205.

Chapter Three: The Multi-Sevenfold Mill of the Gods

1. Allen, *Star Names,* 450.

2. Ibid., 204.

3. Stoyanov, *The Other God,* 46.

4. Allen, *Star Names,* 205.

5. Ibid., 206.

6. Ibid., 456.

7. Ibid., 58.

8. Budge, *A Hieroglyphic Vocabulary,* 111 and 439.

9. Hutton, *The Stations of the Sun,* ch. 8.

10. Allen, *Star Names,* 307–9.

11. McLeish, *Children of the Gods,* 34.

12. Murray, *The Splendour That Was Egypt,* 188.

13. Graves, *The Greek Myths,* 56; McLeish, *Children of the Gods,* 9.

14. Allen, *Star Names,* 386.

15. Graves, *The Greek Myths,* 194; McLeish, *Children of the Gods,* 133.

16. Allen, *Star Names,* 387.

17. Ibid., 389.

18. Ibid., 393.

19. Allen, *Star Names,* 399–400.

20. Ibid., 400.

21. Ibid., 402.

22. Ibid., 393.

23. Ibid.

24. Graves, *The Greek Myths,* 73 et seq.

25. Ibid., 74.

26. de Santillana and von Dechend, *Hamlet's Mill,* 386 (quoting from Sir James Frazer's *Folklore of the Old Testament*).

Chapter Four: Kosmic Genesis— The Origin and Nature of the Gods

1. Scott, *Hermetica,* 233.

2. Ibid., 209.

3. Herodotus, *The Histories* II, 73.

4. Rees, *Just Six Numbers,* 51.

5. Budge, *The Gods of the Egyptians,* vol. 1, 294 and 300 (quoting from Br. Mus. papyrus no. 10,188).

6. Ibid., 89.

7. Ibid., 298 et seq.

8. Ibid., 458 (quoting from Plutarch's *De Iside et Osir,* ix).

9. Ibid., 463.

10. Ibid., 465.

11. Ibid., 454 and 458. Text of Unas, line 626.

12. Budge, *The Gods of the Egyptians,* vol. 2, 356.

13. Budge, *The Gods of the Egyptians,* vol. 1, 501.

14. Ibid., 502 (quoting from the Book of the Dead, ch. lxiv, line 8).

15. Ibid., 502.

16. Budge, *The Gods of the Egyptians,* vol. 2, 356.

17. Ibid., 61 (quoting from the Book of the Dead, ch. xvii).

18. Budge, *The Gods of the Egyptians,* vol. 1, 430.

19. Ibid., 407.

20. Ibid., 403.

21. Ibid., 406 and 412.

22. Ibid., 412.

23. Ibid.

24. Budge, *The Gods of the Egyptians,* vol. 2, 90–92.

25. Budge, *The Gods of the Egyptians,* vol. 1, 417.

26. Ibid.

27. Ibid., 420.

28. Murray, *The Splendour That Was Egypt,* 179.

29. Budge, *The Gods of the Egyptians,* vol. 1, 425 (quoting from the Book of the Dead, lvii, 6).

30. Ibid., 424.

Chapter Five: Sidereal Genesis— The Origin and Nature of Man

1. Budge, *Egyptian Religion,* 46 (quoting from the papyrus of Nesi Amsu).

2. Pyramid Texts, para. 458, utterance 302.

3. Budge, *The Dwellers on the Nile,* 99.

4. Budge, *The Gods of the Egyptians,* vol. 1, 159.

5. Ibid., 38, quoting from the Pyramid Texts of Unas).

6. Budge, *Legends of the Egyptian Gods,* 43–45.

7. Budge, *The Gods of the Egyptians,* vol. 2, 47.

8. Ibid., 33–34.

9. Budge, *The Gods of the Egyptians,* vol. 1, 38–39.

10. Budge, *The Gods of the Egyptians,* vol. 2, 61 and 104.

11. Ibid., vol. 2, 125–27.

12. Ibid., 264. See also *Egyptian Religion,* 67.

13. Book of the Dead, ch. clxxxiii.

14. Budge, *The Gods of the Egyptians,* vol. 2, 126.

15. Budge, *The Gods of the Egyptians,* vol. 1, 468.

16. Ibid., 469.

17. Ibid., 470.

18. Ibid.

19. Ibid., 469.

20. Ibid., 470.

21. Ibid., 470 et seq.

22. Ibid., 472.

23. Ibid., 473.

24. Ibid.

25. Ibid., 475.

Chapter Six: Man, the Multiple Being

1. Scott, *Hermetica,* 215.

2. Ibid., 199–201.

3. Ibid., 183.

4. Budge, *Egyptian Religion,* 191.

5. Budge, *The Gods of the Egyptians,* vol. 1, 360 et seq.

6. Ibid., 42.

7. Budge, *The Gods of the Egyptians,* vol. 2, 145.

8. Ibid., 144.

9. Ibid.

10. Budge, *The Gods of the Egyptians,* vol. 1, 6.

11. Ibid., 5.

12. Ibid.

13. Pyramid Texts, para. 1256, utterance 532.

14. Budge, *The Gods of the Egyptians,* vol. 1, 505.

15. Faulkner, *The Ancient Egyptian Coffin Texts,* vol. 3, 134.

16. Erman, *A Handbook of Egyptian Religion,* 15.

17. Faulkner, *The Ancient Egyptian Coffin Texts,* vol. 3, 132.

18. Ibid., 185.

19. Murray, *The Splendour That Was Egypt,* 172.

20. Budge, *The Egyptian Book of the Dead,* lxxiii.

21. Budge, *The Gods of the Egyptians,* vol. 1, 297.

22. Budge, *The Gods of the Egyptians,* vol. 2, 120.

23. Budge, *The Gods of the Egyptians,* vol. 1, 160

Chapter Seven: The River Nile and Its Symbolism

1. Gordon, *Land of the Fallen Star Gods,* 46 et seq.

2. Budge, *The Nile,* 351.

3. Ibid., 171.

4. Ibid., 157.

5. Ibid., 132.

6. Ibid., 100.

7. Ibid., 152.

8. Herodotus, *The Histories,* 104.

9. Budge, *The Nile,* 803.

10. Ibid., 786.

11. Gordon, *Land of the Fallen Star Gods,* 57.

12. Temple, *The Crystal Sun,* ch. 9.

13. Gordon, *Land of the Fallen Star Gods,* ch. 8.

14. Budge, *The Gods of the Egyptians,* vol. 1, 175; vol. 2, 148.

15. Budge, *The Gods of the Egyptians,* vol. 2, 43.

16. Ibid.

17. Ibid., 117–18.

18. Budge, *The Gods of the Egyptians,* vol. 1, 332.

19. Budge, *The Gods of the Egyptians,* vol. 2, 61.

20. Ibid., 58.

21. Ibid., 62.

22. Ibid., 60.

23. Ibid., 59.

24. Budge, *The Gods of the Egyptians,* vol. 1, 365.

25. Ibid., 472.

26. Allen, *Star Names,* 403.

27. Herodotus, *The Histories,* 129.

28. Gordon, *Land of the Fallen Star Gods,* 123 et seq.

29. Budge, *The Gods of the Egyptians,* vol. 2, 157.

30. Ibid., 61.

31. Ibid., 95–96.

32. Ibid., 96.

33. Ibid., 97.

Chapter Eight: The Ancient Colonization of Egypt

1. Berlitz, *The Mystery of Atlantis,* 135 (quoting Diodorus Siculus).

2. Budge, *The Nile,* 141.

3. Proclus, *Commentary on the Timaeus,* book 1.

4. Scott, *Hermetica,* 397.

5. Blavatsky, *The Secret Doctrine,* vol. 2.

6. Gordon, *Land of the Fallen Star Gods,* ch. 3.

7. Herodotus, *The Histories.* See also Versluis, *The Egyptian Mysteries,* 4.

8. Cremo and Thompson, *Forbidden Archeology,* 11, 13, 97, 99, 111, 115, and 117.

9. Gordon, *Land of the Fallen Star Gods,* 52 and 217 (quoting Schwaller de Lubicz).

10. Ibid., 53 et seq.

11. Blavatsky, *The Secret Doctrine,* vol. 2, 351 et seq.

12. Plato, *Timaeus and Critias,* 33 et seq.

13. Budge, *The Nile,* 750.

14. Ibid., 141.

15. Murray, *The Splendour That Was Egypt,* 14 and 319.

Chapter Nine: The Spread and Decline of Ancient Mystic Culture

1. Herodotus, *The Histories,* 116–18.

2. Berlitz, *The Mystery of Atlantis,* 157.

3. Knappert, *The Aquarian Guide to African Mythology,* 186.

4. Ibid., 32.

5. Ibid., 188.

6. Ibid., 54.

7. Ibid., 81.

8. Ibid., 29.

9. Ibid., 186.

10. Sykes, *Who's Who in Non-Classical Mythology,* 164.

11. Ibid., 196.

12. Ibid., 163.

13. Ibid., 166.

14. Hancock and Faiia, *Heaven's Mirror,* see chs. 10 and 11.

15. Gordon, *Land of the Fallen Star Gods,* 53.

16. Wilford, "On Egypt," 298 et seq.

17. Herodotus, *The Histories,* 150 and 345.

18. Ibid., 149.

19. Budge, *The Dwellers on the Nile,* 174.

20. Gordon, *Land of the Fallen Star Gods,* 60.

21. Graves and Patai, *Hebrew Myths,* 130 et seq.

22. Ibid., 163.

23. Ibid., 156.

24. Ibid., 226.

25. Ibid., 254 et seq.

26. Curl, *The Art and Architecture of Freemasonry,* 24.

27. Ibid., 204.

28. Ibid., 54.

29. Ibid., 32.

30. Herodotus, *The Histories.* See also Mackey, *The Mythological Astronomy of the Ancients.*

31. Gordon, *Land of the Fallen Star Gods,* ch. 4.

32. Scott, *Hermetica*, 137.

33. Stoyanov, *The Other God*, 124.

34. Ibid., 125 (referring to works by Ethel S. Drower and Kurt Rudolph).

35. de Santillana and von Dechend, *Hamlet's Mill*, 309.

36. Stoyanov, *The Other God*, 179 and 180.

Chapter Ten: Egypt's Sacred Art, Architecture, and Statuary

1. Gordon, *Land of the Fallen Star Gods*, ch. 8.

2. Pyramid Texts, para. 1278, 202.

3. Gordon, *Land of the Fallen Star Gods*, 8.

4. West, *The Traveler's Key to Ancient Egypt*, 252.

5. Proclus, *Commentary on the Timaeus*, vol. 1, 228.

6. Murray, *Egyptian Temples*, 132.

7. Murray, *The Splendour That Was Egypt*, 239.

Chapter Eleven: The Ritualized Magic of Egypt

1. Scott, *Hermetica*, 359.

2. Mead, *Apollonius of Tyana*, 110 et seq.

3. Budge, *The Gods of the Egyptians*, vol. 2, 214.

4. Versluis, *The Egyptian Mysteries*, 14–15.

5. Blavatsky, *Isis Unveiled*, vol. 1, 495 et seq.

6. Budge, *The Dwellers on the Nile*, 169.

7. Murray, *Egyptian Temples*, 50.

8. Herodotus, *The Histories*, 117.

9. Pyramid Texts, para. 2291.

10. Pyramid Texts, paras. 586–92.

11. Pyramid Texts, paras. 316–19.

12. Budge, *Book of What Is in the Underworld*, div. 7.

13. Murray, *The Splendour That Was Egypt*, 179.

14. Budge, *The Gods of the Egyptians*, vol. 2, 8 (quoting from the Hymn to Amen-Ra).

15. Ibid.

Chapter Twelve: The Mystery Tradition and the Process of Initiation

1. Herodotus, *The Histories*, 114 and 116.

2. Graves, *The Greek Myths*, 44.

3. Gosse, *The Civilization of the Ancient Egyptians*, 15.

4. Budge, *The Dwellers on the Nile*, 169 et seq.

5. Gosse, *The Civilization of the Ancient Egyptians*, 18–19.

6. Ibid., 19–20.

7. Mead, *Thrice Greatest Hermes,* vol. 3, 286.

8. Scott, *Hermetica,* 205.

9. Budge, *The Gods of the Egyptians,* vol. 1, 162.

10. Blavatsky, *Isis Unveiled,* vol. 2, 364 et seq.

11. Stoyanov, *The Other God,* 80.

12. Hall, *Freemasonry of the Ancient Egyptians,* 106 et seq.

13. Curl, *The Art and Architecture of Freemasonry,* 44.

14. Budge, *The Egyptian Book of the Dead* (Papyrus of Ani).

15. Ibid.

16. Ibid.

17. Ibid.

18. Ibid., 259–60.

19. Ibid.

20. Ibid.

21. Gordon, *Land of the Fallen Star Gods,* 194.

22. Budge, *The Gods of the Egyptians,* vol. 1, 472.

23. Pyramid Texts, para. 1585.

24. Ibid., para. 350.

25. Versluis, *The Egyptian Mysteries,* 51 (quoting from and commenting on Plutarch).

26. Pyramid Texts, para. 251.

27. Ibid.

28. Coffin Texts, 236.

29. Papyrus of Nu, Br. Museum, 10477-13.

30. Scott, *Hermetica,* 217.

Appendix E: The Slaughter of Mankind

1. Budge, *The Gods of the Egyptians,* vol. 1, 363 et seq.

Appendix F: Correlations between the Ancient Egyptian and Tibetan Mystic Systems

1. Evans-Wentz, *The Tibetan Book of the Dead,* lix.

2. Ibid., xxvii.

3. Ibid., 6.

4. Ibid., 26.

5. Ibid., 36.

6. Ibid., 62.

7. Ibid.

8. Ibid., 63.

BIBLIOGRAPHY

Allen, Richard Hinckley. *Star Names: Their Lore and Meaning*. 1899. Reprint, New York: Dover, 1963.

Baikie, James. *Egyptian Papyri and Papyrus-Hunting*. London: Religious Tract Society, 1925.

Bauval, Robert, and Adrian Gilbert. *The Orion Mystery: Unlocking the Secrets of the Pyramids*. London: Heinemann, 1994.

Bauval, Robert, and Graham Hancock. *Keeper of Genesis: A Quest for the Hidden Legacy of Mankind*. London: Heinemann, 1996.

Berlitz, Charles. *The Mystery of Atlantis*. London: Souvenir Press, 1976.

Besant, Annie, and Bhagavan Das, trans. *The Bhagavad Gita*. Adyar, India: Theosophical Publishing House, 1926.

Blavatsky, Helena Petrovna. *Isis Unveiled*. 2 vols. 1877. Reprint, Los Angeles: The Theosophy Co., 1980.

———. *The Secret Doctrine*. 2 vols. 1888. Reprint, Adyar, India: Theosophical Publishing House, 1979.

———. *The Voice of the Silence*. 1889. Reprint, Los Angeles: The Theosophy Co., 1987.

Broglie, Louis de. *New Perspectives in Physics*. New York: Basic Books, 1962.

Budge, E. A. Wallis. *The Dwellers on the Nile*. 1885. Reprint, London: Religious Tract Society, 1926.

———. *The Egyptian Book of the Dead: The Papyrus of Ani in the British Museum*. 1895. Reprint, New York: Dover, 1967.

———. *Egyptian Religion*. 1899. Reprint, New York: Gramercy, 1975.

———. *The Gods of the Egyptians*. 2 vols. 1904. Reprint, New York: Dover, 1969.

———. *A Hieroglyphic Vocabulary to the Theban Recension of the Book of the Dead*. London: Kegan Paul, 1911.

———. *Legends of the Egyptian Gods*. 1912. Reprint, New York: Dover, 1994.

———. *The Nile: Notes for Travellers in Egypt*. London: Thos. Cook and Son, 1910.

———. "Translation of the *Papyrus of Nesi Amsu*" *Archeologia* 52 (1891).

Clark, R. T. Rundle. *Myth and Symbol in Ancient Egypt*. London: Thames and Hudson, 1960.

Cremo, Michael, and Richard Thompson. *Forbidden Archeology: The Hidden History of the Human Race*. Los Angeles: Bhaktivedanta, 1998.

Curl, James Stevens. *The Art and Architecture of Freemasonry*. London: Batsford, 1991.

Darwin, Charles. *On the Origin of the Species*. London: John Murray, 1859.

de Santillana, Giorgio, and Hertha von Dechend. *Hamlet's Mill*. London: Macmillan, 1970.

Dionysius the Areopagite. *The Celestial Hierarchy*. Facsimile. Whitefish, Mont.: Kessinger, 2004.

Dowson, John. *A Classical Dictionary of Hindu Mythology and Religion, Geography, History, and Literature*. 1879. 8th edition. London: Routledge and K. Paul, 1953.

Erman, Adolf. *A Handbook of Egyptian Religion*. London: Archibald Constable, 1907.

Evans-Wentz, W. Y., ed. *The Tibetan Book of the Dead*. 1960. Reprint, New York: Oxford University Press, 2000.

Faulkner, Raymond O. *The Ancient Egyptian Coffin Texts*. 3 vols. London: Warminster, 1973–78.

———. *The Ancient Egyptian Pyramid Texts*. 1969. Reprint, Oxford: Oxford University Press, 1998.

French, Peter. *John Dee: The World of an Elizabethan Magus*. 1972. Reprint, New York: Routledge, 1987.

Gordon, J. S. *Land of the Fallen Star Gods: The Celestial Origins of Ancient Egypt*. Rochester, Vt.: Bear & Co., 2013.

Gordon, Stuart. *The Encyclopedia of Myths and Legends*. London: Headline, 1994.

Gosse, A. Bothwell. *The Civilization of the Ancient Egyptians*. London: T. C. & E. C. Jack, 1915.

Graves, Robert. *The Greek Myths*. 1955. Reprint, London: Book Club Associates, 1985.

Graves, Robert, and Raphael Patai. *Hebrew Myths: The Book of Genesis*. London: Cassell & Co., 1964.

Griffiths, John Gwyn. *The Conflict of Horus and Seth from Egyptian and Classical Sources*. Liverpool, UK: Liverpool University Press, 1960.

Hall, Manly P. *Freemasonry of the Ancient Egyptians*. 1937. Reprint, Los Angeles: Philosophical Research Society, 1999.

———. *The Secret Teachings of All Ages*. 1928. Reprint, Los Angeles: Philosophical Research Society, 1975.

Hancock, Graham, and Santha Faiia. *Heaven's Mirror: Quest for the Lost Civilization*. London: Michael Joseph, 1998.

Herodotus. *The Histories*. Translated by A. Selincourt. London: Penguin Classics, 1983.

Hutton, Ronald. *The Stations of the Sun: A History of the Ritual Year in Britain*. New York: Oxford University Press, 1996.

Iamblichus. *Theurgia, or The Egyptian Mysteries*. Translated by Alexander Wilder. New York: The Metaphysical Publishing Co., 1911.

Knappert, Jan. *The Aquarian Guide to African Mythology*. London: Aquarian Press, 1990.

Lapp, Gunther. *The Papyrus of Nu*. Catalogue of Books of the Dead in the British Museum, vol. 1. London: British Museum Press, 1997.

Lemesurier, Peter. *The Great Pyramid Decoded*. Revised edition. Rockport, Mass.: Element Books, 1996.

MacCulloch, J. A. *The Religion of the Ancient Celts*. London: Constable, 1991.

Mackey, Sampson Arnold. *The Mythological Astronomy of the Ancients*. Mecosta, Mich.: Wizards Bookshelf, 1973.

MacNeill, Máire. *The Festival of Lughnasa*. 1962. Reprint, Oxford: Oxford University Press, 2008.

Macrobius. *Commentary on the Dream of Scipio*. Translated by W. H. Stahl. New York: Columbia University Press, 1952.

———. *Conviviorum Saturnaliorum Septem Libri*. Paris: Classiques Garnier, n.d.

Mau, August. *Pompeii: Its Life and Art*. 1899. Reprint, Whitefish, Mont.: Kessinger, 2007.

McLeish, Kenneth. *Children of the Gods*. Harlow, Essex, England: Longman, 1983.

Mead, G. R. S. *Apollonius of Tyana*. London: Theosophical Publishing Society, 1901.

———. *Thrice Greatest Hermes*. 1906. Reprint, Boston: Weiser Books, 2001.

Murray, Margaret. *Egyptian Temples*. 1931. Reprint, London: Sampson, Low, Marston, 1939.

———. *The Splendour That Was Egypt*. 1949. Reprint, London: Sidgwick and Jackson, 1962.

Naydler, Jeremy. *Temple of the Cosmos: The Ancient Egyptian Experience of the Sacred*. Rochester, Vt.: Inner Traditions, 1996.

Oldfather, C. H., trans. *Diodorus Siculus*. Cambridge: Harvard University Press, Loeb Classical Library, 1969.

Plato. *Timaeus and Critias*. Translated by D. Lee. London: Penguin Classics, 1977.

Pococke, Edward. *India in Greece*. London: John J. Griffin and Co., 1852.

Proclus. *Commentary on the Timaeus*. Translated by T. Taylor. London, 1820.

Rees, Martin. *Just Six Numbers: The Deep Forces That Shape the Universe*. London: Weidenfeld & Nicolson, 1999.

Reymond, Eve A. E. *The Mythological Origin of the Egyptian Temple*. Manchester, England: Manchester University Press, 1969.

Scott, Sir Walter, trans. *Hermetica*. Bath, England: Solos Press, 1993.

Sejourne, Laurette. *Burning Water: Thought and Religion in Ancient Mexico*. Boston: Shambhala, 1976.

Sheldrake, Rupert. *A New Science of Life: The Hypothesis of Morphic Resonance*. Rochester, Vt.: Park Street Press, 1995.

Squire, Charles. *Celtic Myth and Legend*. 1910. Reprint, New York: Dover, 2003.

Stoyanov, Yuri. *The Other God: Dualist Religions from Antiquity to the Cathar Heresy*. New Haven: Yale University Press, 2000.

Stutley, Margaret, and James Stutley. *A Dictionary of Hinduism*. London: Routledge and Kegan Paul, 1977.

Sykes, Egerton. *Who's Who in Non-Classical Mythology*. London: J. M. Dent, 1952.

Temple, Robert. *The Crystal Sun*. London: Century, 2000.

Versluis, Arthur. *The Egyptian Mysteries*. London; New York: Arkana, 1988.

West, John Anthony. *The Traveler's Key to Ancient Egypt*. Wheaton, Ill.: Quest Books, 1996.

Wilford, Francis. "On Egypt and Other Countries Adjacent to the Ca'li' River, or Nile of Ethiopia. From the Ancient Books of the Hindus." *Asiatic Researches; or, Transactions of the Society, Instituted in Bengal, for Inquiring into the History and Antiquities, the Arts, Sciences, and Literature of Asia* 3 (1799): 295–468.

Index

Aah with *menat*, 334
aakhu-t, 280. *See also*
    pyramids
Aaru (divine world), 184
ab, 162, 170–71
Abraham allegory, 256–57
Abu Simbel temples, 298–304
    dual trinity of gods at
        entrance, 274
    external giant god figures at,
        302–3
    first intermediate chamber
        of male temple, 300
    holy-of-holies at, 299,
        300–301
    metaphysical
        correspondences of statues
        at, 301
    middle chamber of male
        temple, 299
    supposed involvement of
        Rameses II, 298, 303–4
    symbolic location of, 300
Acropolis, 245
adytum, 290–91
aeonic serpent, 98
Aeons, defined, 98
age of Egyptian monuments, 2
Ak(e)r, 164, 178–80
akh
    as the divine spirit, 160, 162
    as the expression of Divine
        Purpose, 136–37
    function of fallen sparks,
        140–41

local home of, 138
sekhem of, 160, 162–63
self-willed expression
    reignited by, 138–39
Akhenaten, 27n, 210, 211
al-biruni canal, 207
Alkyoneus, 50
Amemet, 166, 181, 183
Amen-Ra, 106, 109–11
Amenti, 98–99
Americas
    early European knowledge
        of, 249
    mound builders of, 255–56
amulets, 311
angels
    Islamic tradition and, 173,
        174
    Khnemu-Ra and, 118–19
Ani (candidate for initiation),
    351–52
ankh, ritual involving, 313
Ankhor Wat, Egyptian
    influence on, 248, 254
anu (soul principle), 99–100,
    306–7, 369–70
Anubis, 82, 150
Apep, vanquishing of, 326–28
apron, ceremonial, 334–35
Apuat, 137, 138, 182
apuat tool, 72, 201, 214
archaeoastronomy
    defective attitudes in, 8–9
    ignored by Egyptologists,
        51

architecture. *See* art and
    architecture
Aries, 54–55
Aristotelian thought, 8
art and architecture
    architectural angles, 277–78
    association with the sacred,
        273
    of Atlanto-Caucasian type,
        235
    culture visible in, 272–73
    defined, 273
    differences of Egyptian from
        Indian, 243
    Egyptian exactitude in, 275
    Egyptian influence on
        Ankhor Wat, 248, 254
    Egyptian influence on
        Greek, 259
    foundations of classical
        architecture, 276–78
    geometric metaphor in, 276
    mathematical proportions
        in, 276–77
    modern vs. ancient, 275
    of mound builders, 255–56
    Nile temple generalities,
        278–79
    obelisk or stele, 292–93
    pyramids, 253–55, 277,
        279–83
    sidereal influences grounded
        by temples, 280
    temple itself, 288–92
    temple pylon, 283–88

truth conveyed by, 275
visual archetypes in, 273–75
ziggurats, 253–55
See also statuary; temples
"As below, so above" principle, 67
ashemu, 139–40
As'r, 164. *See also* Osiris
As't. *See* Isis
astral soul-body, 131–32, 310
astral travel and the initiate, 361–62
astrological influences
    destiny of Man and, 18
    holographic nature of, 17
    of local system, 43
    of Ra, 29
    reality of, 18
    of the spring equinox, 41n, 42
    Taurus and, 58
astrology, true nature of ancient, 30
asuras vs. *suras*, 136
Atlantean Root Race, 228
Atlantis, 233–38
    Atlanto-Caucasian type, 234–35, 236–37
    cataclysms in, 233, 237
    Egyptian cultural separation from, 251
    flight from, 233–34, 237–38
    hieroglyphic tradition origins in, 251
    mind state of Atlanteans, 235–36
    of Plato, 237–38, 250
    religious culture in, 235, 305–6
Atlanto-Caucasian type
    appearance of, 234–35
    links maintained with origins of, 238
    rise and fall of, 236–37
Atlas, divine light and, 83
Atum-Ra, 106, 119–20, 146–47

Aurva or Aur-Ba, 48
Awareness, Consciousness and, 59

ba, 162, 164–66, 309, 361–62, 363
Bailey, A. A., 13–14
Bel, 51n
Beltane festival, 42–43, 381
benben bird. *See* phoenix
benben stone, 216, 217, 280
big bang theory, 17n
Blavatsky, H. P., 13–14, 226, 228, 234–35
Blue Nile, 192
brain, mind and, 9
Budge, E. Wallace, 13, 218
Bull deity
    Heavenly Bull, 73–74
    misunderstandings about, 35
    Mithras and, 75, 76
    in Pyramid Texts, 78
    Taurus and, 35, 36
bullfight tradition, 58

Cancer constellation, 53
Canis Major and Canis Minor, 80
carbon-based biosphere, 104–5
Casaubon, Isaac, 13
cataclysms and cataclysmic cycles, 232–33, 233n, 237
cataracts of the Nile
    circumpolar star associations, 201–2
    illustrated, 195
    major temples north of the First Cataract, 203–4
    mixed esoteric metaphors, 202–3
    nome districts of Egypt and, 198
    sacred land of Meroe/Merawi, 199, 200–201
    sacred places with foreign associations, 199

sevenfold divisions of, 194–96
    view toward the second, 191
Caucasian Root Race, 228
Celtic Myths and Legends, 8
Celts
    euhemerism toward myths of, 8
    May Beltane festival of, 42–43
    primary festivals of, 381–82
    three-legged cross of, 49–50
ceremonial dress and accoutrements, 328–36
ceremonials, 315–16, 320–22, 341–43
chakras, 169
Chamber of Judgment
    Ani tableau, 180, 181, 182–84
    differences of symbolism for, 181–82
    illustrated, 181
    Pepi tableau, 180–82
    sequence of antechambers in, 182–84
Chaos prior to Creation, 95, 97
Christianity
    divorce of religion from science and, 367
    Egyptian Coptic sources of, 268
    Egyptian influence on, 268–69
    magical rituals in, 320–21
circumpolar constellations, 47–48
Clark, R. T. R., 94
Commentary on the Timaeus, 293
consciousness
    Ancients' view of, 59
    Awareness and, 59
    celestial vs. local, 225
    death and continuity of, 362–64

in Man, sequence of
evolving, 141–44
modern vs. ancient, 158
sequential unfoldment of
mankind's, 227
sevenfold system of planes
of, 63–69
constellations
circumpolar, 47–48
intelligent purpose of, 17
roles in great fall and return,
55–56, 58
sevenfold, 88–90
southern and northern sky,
214
See also specific constellations
Coptos ceremonial, 321–22
Coptos temple, 203
corridor of ancient civilization,
219
cosmic vs. kosmic, 14
cows, seven celestial, 105
Creation (involution)
Ancients' view of, 94–95
geometrical correspondence
to the cycle of, 371–73
Hermetica on immortality
of, 16
kosmic, lower triad of,
116–20
man as the alpha and omega
of, 18
Mayan legend of, 28
objective, sequence of, 101
Ouranos myth of, 23–26
privation principle of, 20
root state of, 95
sequence of unfoldment
of soul-body qualities,
228–29
sevenfold principle in, 103–4
soul principle and, 99–100
Creator. *See* Demiurge
Cremo, Michael, 6, 231
crocodile god (Sebek or
Sebek-Ra), 47, 69, 106,
116–18

crook and flail, 335–36
crowns, red and white, 328–
30, 332
Crystal Sun, The, 5, 27
cultural degeneracy, principle
of, 230–31
curriculum of Egyptian
Mysteries, 346–47
Cush or Kesh, 242–43
cycles in Nature, law of, 224
Cyclopes, 23, 25

Darwin, Charles, 6
death, continuity of
consciousness and, 362–64
de Broglie, Louis, 3
decans
ancient Egyptian system of,
21
gearing function of, 40, 68
Hermetica on, 20
saros cycles of, 21–22
degeneracy, principle of,
230–31
Delta of the River Nile, 217
Demeter, 53
Demiurge (Creator-Deity)
duality and triplicity
emanating from, 63–64
seven planes of being in, 65
three aspects of, 100–101,
103
triple essence of, 63
Demiurgos
Logos vs., 95
in primordial state, 97
Dendera temple, 203, 289
Dendera zodiac, 47, 48, 69–70
Dionysian Mysteries, 337,
338–39
Dionysius the Areopagite, 272
Diospolos Parva temple, 203–4
Divine Law, omniverse
expressing, 63
divine sparks
egohood and, 171
emergence as man, 31

as expressions of the Will of
God, 31
fallen, 31–32, 226
fifth hour journey of, 179
function of fallen sparks,
140–41
groups of, 31
Man as, 133–35
Djed (or Tet) Pillar, 32–34
Draco
as circumpolar deity, 69
esoteric implications of,
70–71
great fall and return and, 52
Man eaten by, 71n
in Persian tradition, 71
and the seventh kosmic
state, 88–90
Ursa Major and Ursa Minor
enfolded by, 71
in Zoroastrian tradition, 71
duality principle, 66, 109
Duat, 45
duration vs. time, 28
dynastic succession, Egyptian,
264–65

Earth
orbital cycle of solar year,
38–39, 41
sevenfold sequence of
spheres containing, 40
time cycles affecting, 30–31
true vs. magnetic North pole
of, 39
ecliptic pole, wobble in, 46
education and Egyptian
Mysteries, 343–47
curriculum, 346–47
forms and centers of,
343–44
Heliopolis Academy,
344–47
efflux, 177
Egyptian Earth year, 46
Egyptian history and ancient
culture, 218–43

advanced culture without industrialization, 5

architectural comparisons with other cultures, 253–56

belief in hierarchy of divine Intelligences, 222–23

commerce with Asia, 249

corridor of ancient civilization, 219

corruption and decline of, 262–67

dating of, generally, 2, 220–22, 230

devotion to absolute accuracy in, 250–52

differences from Indian art and culture, 243

dynastic succession in, 264–65

First Intermediate Period, 266–67

four and seven in, 239–42

Greek culture vs., 244, 245

Kabbalah correlations with, 257–58

length of history, 2, 220–22, 230–33

Masonic tradition and, 260–62

mummification, 170, 263–64

Old Testament and, 2

orientation of scripts, 252–53

orphans of the mystic tradition, 267–69

other cultures' language related to, 246–48

pan-African fertilizations and, 246–47

populist approach to, 4–5

Ra in other cultures, 247–48

separation from Atlantean culture, 251

Southeast Asian correspondences, 248

spiritual bias of imagery in, 10–11

symbolic temple art in, 10, 11n

transoceanic and transcontinental spread of, 248–50

understanding on its own terms, 11

See also art and architecture; statuary

Egyptian Mysteries, 340–46
basis of, 343

ceremonials vs. rituals in, 341–43

education and, 343–47

Greek Mysteries identical with, 337–38, 340–41

rites in, 340–41

Tibetan correlations with, 385–86

triple sequence of, 157

See also initiation

Egyptologists
allegory and metaphor ignored by, 51

archaeoastronomy ignored by, 51

astrology not understood by, 30

limited understanding of, 1

Egypt seasons, threefold, 46n

Elephantine island, 203

Eleusynian Mysteries, 337, 338

energy follows thought, 17, 309

Ethiopians, 200–201

ethnology
Atlanto-Caucasian type, 234–35, 236–37, 238

correlations of the Fourth and Fifth Races, 239–41

Indo-Caucasian type, 235

principles of differentiation, 229–30

Root Races, 226, 228, 234–35

sequence of unfoldment of soul-body qualities, 228–29

seven primary soul types, 225–26

as taboo subject, 225

euhemerism toward Celtic myths, 8

evolution
Darwinian vs. Egyptian theory, 32, 222

geometrical correspondence to the cycle of, 371–73

liberation and, 60–61

sequence of evolving consciousness, 141–44

simplistic nature of Darwinian, 6

Eyes of Ra and Horus, 261, 322–26

fall from Grace. *See* great fall and return

Festival of Lights, 322

flail and crook, 335–36

Forbidden Archeology, 6, 231

freemasonry, 259–62, 322

funeral positions of Orion-Osiris, 378–80

galactic corona, 40

galactic halo, 40

Geb, 145, 147

gender confusion, 340

Genesis, biblical book of, 20

geographical correlations of the Fourth and Fifth Races, 239–41

geography, spiritual, 239

geometry
cycle of involution and evolution and, 371–73

evolutionary kosmic 3-4-5 triangle, 371, 372, 373

of free-standing temples, 291–92

metaphor in architecture, 276

non-physical, of temple pylon, 284–86

Giants, 23, 25

Giza

angles of the Great Pyramid, 277

"homeward trail" at, 282

initiation sequence at, 356–59

main arguments centered on, 1

Orion and, 76–78

overfascination with, 1

site plan of, 357

Sphinx and Great Pyramid, 281

symbolism of, 354–55, 356

Teotihuacan layout copying, 254

three pyramids at, 283

gods

Egyptian, Man vs., 11n

as ethereal heads, 95n

genesis of the lesser gods, 145–47

Hermetica on making, 307

Man vs., 136

mill of the, 64, 69

Titan, 23, 25–26

See also specific gods

great fall and return, 52–58

astrological Underworld and, 57

critical points in, 52

decans' gearing function and, 68

downward sequence of, 52–53

Orion constellation and, 56, 58

role of Aries in, 55

role of sphere of Taurus in, 55–56

soul-spheres of fallen sparks, 62–63

Great Pyramid

angles of, 277

Great Subterranean Chamber, 358

illustrated, 281

initiation sequence and, 357–59

King's Chamber, 357–58

Queen's Chamber, 358–59

symbolism of, 356

Great Year

Ancients' understanding of, 41

celestial months in, 45

importance of, 37–38

Orion's rise and fall during, 77

scientific misunderstandings about, 40–41

southern and northern skies and, 214

Greek culture

Egyptian culture vs., 244, 245

Egyptian influence on, 259

priestesses in, 316–17

Greek Mysteries, 337–39, 340–41

Hall of Judgment, *ab* in, 170–71

Hall of Records, 1

halls of initiation, seven, 352–53

Hancock, Graham, 4

Hathor (cosmic cow goddess), 120–23

headdresses, 330–33

heart chakra, 170–71

heaven worlds, 184–87

heka (practical magic), 307–8

Heliopolis, 215–17

Heliopolis Academy, 344–47

Henen-su, 212–13

Herakleopolis Magna, 210–11

Hermetica

Aeons defined in, 98

on destiny and necessity, 37

on the divine nature of man, 60

on the fall of Man, 130

on the immortality of creation, 16, 158

on immortal vs. mortal bodies, 223

on instinctive intelligence, 160

on making gods, 307

on Mind and body, 159–60

on order, 306n

organization of the spheres in, 20

translation used in this book, 13

on the universality of life, 97

on the work of the Decans, 62

Herodotus, 190, 196–97, 244

Her-shef, 212

Heru-behutet, 156–57

Heru-hekennu, 156

Heru-khenti-an-maati, 153

Heru-khenti-khat, 153

Heru-khuti, 153–54

Heru-merti, 153

Heru-neb, 153

Heru-pkhart, 152

Heru-sma-taui, 155–56

Heru-ur, 147, 148, 151

Hesperides, esotericism of, 83–84

Hidden History of the Human Race, The, 6

hieroglyphics, 251, 252–53

Hindu tradition, 247–48, 249. *See also* Indian culture

Homo sapiens, age of, 6

Horus

Eye of, 322–26

multiple nature of, 150–57

pole symbolism of, 51–52

Horus-Set, 154–55

Horus the Elder, 151, 183

Hp(i) (Nile god), 193–94

Hyades
    atma-buddhi principles and,
        90–91
    esoteric implications of,
        84–85
    as rain bringers, 90
    and the seventh kosmic
        state, 88–90
hydro-engineering by
    Egyptians, 196
hylozoism, 94n

Imbolc festival, 381
Indian culture
    Atlantic islands known early
        in, 249
    differences from Egyptian,
        243
    magicians and fakirs in,
        314–15
    priestesses in, 317
    Ra in the Hindu tradition,
        247–48
    view of the Pleiades, 85
individuality, complexity of,
    31–32
Indo-Caucasian type, 235
Indo-European languages, 253
initiation
    astral travel and the initiate,
        361–62
    Battle of Kadesh metaphor
        and, 286
    at Dendera, 289
    formal places of, 354–60
    hazardousness of, 348,
        358–59
    as liberation, 363–64
    Masonic tradition, 350–51
    modern misunderstanding
        of, 365
    Nile crossover at Thebes,
        204–6
    non-physical geometry of
        temple pylon and, 284–86
    Osiris-Ani experiences of,
        351–52

    in the pyramid, 281–82
    raison d'etre of, 347–48
    sequence at Giza, 356–59
    sequence in Greek tradition,
        338–39
    seven and nine initiations,
        352
    seven grades of, 348–50
    seven halls of, 352–53
    silence of the initiate, 364
    statuary symbolizing
        degrees of, 293–97
    third degree, 296–97
    three aspects of, 347
    underground, 353–54
intelligence
    ancient approach to, 10–11
    instinctive, 160
    mind vs., 9, 126
    ordering principle of, 9
involution. *See* Creation
Ishtar, 53
Isis (As't)
    ba principle and, 164–65
    function of, 164
    principle of, 147
    As'r and, 164
    subtle vehicle of, 148
    worship of, 337
Islamic tradition, 173–74

jackal, metaphor of, 80–81
Judaic mystic tradition,
    256–58
Jupiter, 25

ka, 167–69
    dark matter as, 34n
    defined, 162
    double principle of, 65,
        167–68
    as the fourth state, 66, 168
    Pleiades and, 91
    seventh or lowest state and,
        65n
    symbol of, 65–66
    tomb offerings for, 168

Kabbalah, 257–58
Kalevala, 64n
Karnak temple, 204, 206, 286,
    287, 289–90, 296–97
Kesh-mir, 242–43
Kesh or Cush, 242–43
kha, 162, 167, 361
khaibit, 162, 167
khat, 162, 169–70
Kheper-Ra, 106, 107–9
Khephron pyramid, 356, 357,
    359–60
Khnemu-Ra, 106, 118–19
Khonsu, triad with Amen-Ra,
    Mut and, 109–11
Khufu pyramid. *See* Great
    Pyramid
kilt, 333–34
kneph, winged disk of, 161
Knights Templar, 260
knowledge, soul principle as
    source of, 306–7
Kom El Ahmer temple, 210
Kom Ombos temple, 203
kosmic spheres
    auric sheaths of the Milky
        Way, 19–20
    innermost as fourth in
        series, 22
    relative power of, 22
    saros cycles of the decans,
        21–22
    septenary principle of,
        20–22
    sevenfold, solar scheme
        within, 96
kosmic systems, seven planes
    of being in, 65
kosmic vs. cosmic, 14
kouros statue, 278, 293–95
Kronos, 23, 25, 26

Lake Moeris, 197
Land of the Fallen Star Gods
    aims of, 2
    al-biruni canal in, 207
    on cataclysms, 233

Chamber of Judgment in, 180

on commerce between Egypt and Asia, 249

criticisms about sweep of, 7

on the Egyptian handover, 262

on Giza pyramids, 356

on the "homeward trail" at Giza, 282

on initiation and courage, 358–59

Nile valley discussed in, 191

nome districts of Egypt in, 207, 215

on Seker, 174

on star movements and myths, 37

on Teotihuacan, 254

this book as sequel to, 1

languages

hieroglyphics, 251, 252–53

historic similarities in, 246

Indo-European, 253

Nagri script, 251–52

orientation of Egyptian scripts, 252–53

words for teachers and priests, 262

"Left Hand Path" of magic, 308

Lemurian Root Race, 228

liberation

Ancients' view of, 61

evolution and, 60–61

initiation as, 363–64

renunciation needed for, 34

life

Mntw-Ra as conveyor of, 111

universality of, 97

Life wave cycle, 67

light

astral, magic and, 307

carbon synonymous with, 105n

divine, Atlas or Shu and, 83

kha as, 167

for temples, 288, 290

linear-rational thought, limitations of, 8

literary references in this book, 12–14

Logos

defined, 16n

Demiurgos vs., 95

originating, of sidereal systems, 27

lotus metaphor, 142–44

Lower Egypt, 207, 208, 215

Lughnasadh festival, 381–82

Luxor obelisk and pylon, 292

Luxor temple, 204, 206

Ma'at, 126–28

magic, 305–36

astral light and, 307

Atlantean, 235, 305–6

ceremonials and rituals, 315–16, 320–22

degenerate form of, 305

development of physical spirituality, 310–11

dress and accoutrements, 328–36

Eyes of Ra and Horus, 322–26

Indian magicians and fakirs, 314–15

as power to cause change in Nature, 308

practical (*heka*), 307–8

priesthood and priesstesshood, 316–20

problems facing the neophyte, 309–10

refusal to use for oneself, 308–9

spells and mantras, 326

statuary and sympathetic magic, 293

theurgy and thaumaturgy, 320

vanquishing of Apep, 326–28

wonder workers, 314–16

Words of Power, curses, and charms, 311–14

Man

as the alpha and omega of Creation, 18

astrological influences and destiny of, 18

complexity of individuality in, 32

divine nature of, 60, 130n

dual or triple souls of, 43–44

eaten by Draco, 71n

Egyptian gods vs., 11n

ethnology of, 225–26

as fallen divine spark, 32, 133–35

gods vs., 136

Hermetica on the fall of, 130

Islamic tradition and, 173

man vs., 14n, 131

primordial nature of, 137–39

sequence of evolving consciousness in, 141–44

seven planes of being, 135–36

subtle organism of, 159, 160, 162–72

the Underworld as below, 26

man

age of *Homo sapiens*, 6

baptism of the unknown god-man, 132

Man vs., 14n, 131

sequential unfoldment of consciousness of, 227

the slaughter of mankind, 383–84

soul-bodies surrounding, 131

Mandaean culture, 267–68

mantras, 326

Mariette, Alphonse, 272

Masonic tradition, 259–62, 322, 350–51

material existence, the problem of, 368–69

Mau, August, 337

Mayan creation legend, 28

May festival, 42–43

measurement unit, Egyptian, 276–77

media, 1, 10

Memphis, 214–15

menat, 333, 334

Men-Kau-Ra (Menkaura) statue, 293, 294, 295

Men-kau-ra pyramid, 356, 357

Meroe/Merawi, 199, 200–201

Merope, 86–88

Middle Egypt, 207, 208, 209–10

Milky Way
  auric sheaths of, 19–20
  fields of influence as souls, 19–20
  kosmic sphere enclosing, 16
  time cycles in, 30–31

mill of the gods, 64, 69

mind
  ancient approach to, 10–11
  body and, 159–60
  brain and, 9
  dual heads of Aker representing, 179–80
  intelligence vs., 9, 126

Mithras, 75, 76

Mntw-Ra, 106, 111–12

Moeris lake, 197

Moon
  left Eye of Horus and, 325
  sphere of, 131–32

mound builders, 255–56

mummification, 170, 263–64

Mut, triad with Amen-Ra, Khonsu and, 109–11

Mystery of Atlantis, The, 246

Mystery Schools
  focus of, 59–60
  freemasonry, 259–62

the future of the tradition, 366–70

Greek, 337–39

See also Egyptian Mysteries

Nagri script, 251–52

name, death and, 171–72

Naydler, Jeremy, 158, 305

Neb-er-tcher, 107–8

nefer, 142, 143–44

Nefer-Temu, 142–43

Neheb-kau, 212

Nephthys, 147, 148

neter, 143–44

Net/Neith goddess, 106, 112–14

New Age
  conspiracy theories and, 7n
  Establishment view of, 4
  lack of discrimination in, 4
  orthodoxy questioned by, 3
  sources of theories of, 269

Nile, the. *See* River Nile

nome districts of Egypt, 198, 207, 209–10, 215

nonlocality, Ancients' understanding of, 62n

North pole, true vs. magnetic, 39

Nut, 145, 147

Oannes, 134

obelisk or stele, 292–93

obliquity of the ecliptic, 46, 49, 50

Old Testament
  Abraham allegory, 256–57
  Egyptian history and, 2
  Masonic tradition flavored by, 260
  misunderstandings about, 8

Origen, 272

Orion
  bullfight tradition and, 58
  cyclical inversion of, 78–80
  esoteric implications of, 76, 355–56

funeral positions of, 378–80

Giza connection and, 76–78

great fall and return and, 56, 58

relationship with Taurus and Aries, 54–55

rise and fall during the Great Year, 77

seven stars of, 76–78

and the seventh kosmic state, 88–90

Orphic Mysteries, 337, 338, 339, 341n

Osirian hierarchy, 147–48

Osiris
  allegorical myth of, 148–50
  in Chamber of Judgment, 183
  Christian theology and, 268
  function as As'r, 164
  funeral positions of, 378–80
  initiatory experiences of, 351–52
  missing phallus of, 150
  Orion and, 355–56
  principle of, 147
  Seker and, 174
  Sirius and rebirth of, 82
  spiritual soul of Man and, 163–64
  subtle vehicle of, 148

Ouranos creation myth, 23, 25–26

Oversoul, galactic corona as, 40

pan-African fertilizations, 246–47

Pandora myth, 26

Pantheism, 94n

Persephone, 53

pharaohs, vainglory of, 265–66

Philolaus, 27–28

philosophy, separation from religion and science, 367–68

phoenix (benben bird)
  dead-parent metaphor,
    102–3
  as divine messenger, 94
  Heliopolis and, 215
  illustrated, 102
physical bodies
  khat, 162, 169–70
  soul-spheres and existence
    of, 43
planetary systems, seven
  planes of being in, 65
Plato
  Atlantis of, 237–38, 250
  on the privation principle of
    Creation, 20
  on the stars as Beings, 17
Pleiades
  atma-buddhi principles and,
    90–91
  Chinese view of, 85–86
  esoteric implications of,
    85–88
  fourth solar state and, 91
  Great Year of, 37–38
  importance of, 85
  Indian view of, 85
  lost Pleiad of, 86–87, 91–92
  orbit of, 82–83
  and the seventh kosmic
    state, 88–90
  Sisyphus/Merope myth and,
    86–88
  solar system as part of, 35
  sphere of, 40
Pleione, 83
poles
  apparent wobble in ecliptic,
    46
  Egyptian symbolism of,
    51–52
  great fall and return via,
    52–58
  misconceptions about,
    374–77
  Nile associations with,
    201–2

true vs. magnetic North, 39
Pole Stars, celestial, 43
populist approach to Egyptian
  history, 4–5
precession of the equinoxes, 41
priesthood and priesthood,
  316–20
  gender and roles of, 339–40
  priestesses, 316–18, 339
  priesthood in Egypt, 319–20
  theurgy and thaumaturgy,
    320, 321–22
  training in, 318–19
Proclus, 293
Prometheus, Pandora and, 26
psychology, irrationality
  affirmed by, 9
Ptah, 114–16, 267–68
Pun(t), 243
pyramids, 279–83
  as *aakhu-t*, 280
  angles of the Great Pyramid,
    277
  benben stone and, 280
  as celestial vehicles, 280–81
  initiation in, 281–82
  stars represented by, 279–80
  stepped (ziggurats), 253–55
  symbolism of Giza
    pyramids, 356

quantum science, irrationality
  affirmed by, 9

Ra
  Amen-Ra, 106, 109–11
  astrological influence of, 29
  Atum-Ra, 106, 119–20
  barques of, 29, 67, 145, 342
  derivation and use of the
    name, 107
  Eye of, 261, 322
  in Hindu tradition, 247–48
  Kheper-Ra, 106, 107–9
  Khnemu-Ra, 106, 118–19
  Man as, 328
  Mntw-Ra, 106, 111–12

Neb-er-tcher and, 107–8
Net/Neith goddess, 106,
  112–14
Sebek-Ra, 106, 116–18
seven aspects of, 106–12
as ubiquitous Pacific god,
  247
Ra-Mau, 146–47, 211
Rameses II, 298, 303–4
Ramesseum ruins, 205, 297
Rastau, 176–77
Red Crown, 328–30, 332
redemption. *See* great fall and
  return
reincarnation
  ancient belief in, 340
  ba purged before, 166
  Seker and, 174–75
religion, separation from
  philosophy and science,
  367–68
ren, 141–42, 162, 171–72
Rennenet, 171
Ring-Pass-Not heaven worlds,
  100
ritual dress and accoutrements,
  328–36
rituals, 316, 341–42
River Nile
  al-biruni canal, 207
  Blue Nile, 192
  cataracts of, 194–96, 198–
    204
  circumpolar star
    associations, 201–2
  Delta of, 217
  east side of, 204
  functional mouths of,
    196–97
  geological sources of,
    191–92
  Heliopolis on, 215–17
  Hp(i) as the god of,
    193–94
  importance of, 190
  initiatory crossover at
    Thebes, 204–6

major temples north of the
First Cataract, 203–4
Memphis on, 214–15
Meroe/Merawi on, 199,
200–201
nome districts of Egypt and,
198, 207, 209–10, 215
of the North, 206–7
sevenfold divisions of, 195
of the South, 206
Thebes on, 204–6
Ursa Minor shape in bend
of, 201–2
view toward the second
cataract, 191
west side of, 204, 355
White Nile, 192
Root Races, 226, 228

sah, 162, 163–64, 361, 362–63
Samhain festival, 382
scarab, 108–9, 311
scepters, 336
scholasticism, 2, 3–4
science
author's stance toward, 2
dark matter not understood
by, 34n
dependence on
technological support,
2, 3
dogmatism in, 3
fear on the part of, 368
quantum, irrationality
affirmed by, 9
separation of philosophy
and religion from, 367–68
Scott, Sir Walter, 13
Sebek or Sebek-Ra, 47, 69,
106, 116–18
Secret Doctrine, The, 226, 234
Seker, 174–76
Seker boat, 175–76, 177
sekhem, meaning of, 160,
162–63
Sekhet Aaru (heavenly fields),
185, 186

Sekhet-Hetep, 185
Sekhet-Hetepet, 185
Sekhet-Hetepu, 185–87
Sekhet-Sanehemu, 187
semidivine (*akas-ic*) state, 139,
140
serpentine circles, 98
Seshat/Seshata, 128–29
Set, 147, 148
set-akh or Setek, 137
seven celestial maidens, 72
sevenfold kosmic world, 24
sevenfold principle, universal,
103–5
shadow energy, 167
Shu, 83, 125–26, 145
Shu-Khan, 223
sidereal systems
leaning Djed Pillar
metaphor for, 33–34
originating Logos of, 27
ring of cold fire
surrounding, 27n
seven planes of being in, 65
soul-spheres and revolution
of, 43
silence of the initiate, 364
simplicity vs. simplification,
366
Sirius
beliefs about Beings from,
135
cycle of rebirth and, 81–82
orbital cycle of, 81
Pleiades' orbit around,
82–83
Sisyphus, 86–88
Siva Nataraja, 20
slaughter of mankind, 383–84
sleep, *ba* travels during, 165–
66, 309, 361–62
snakes and ladders, 54
solar system
as part of Pleiades, 35
sevenfold scheme of, within
the kosmic scheme, 96
sphere of, 40

soul principle (anu), 99–100,
306–7, 369–70
soul-spheres
of fallen sparks, 62–63
of our local universe,
44–45
physical bodies owing
existence to, 43
revolution of sidereal bodies
and, 43
soul types, seven primary, 226
Southeast Asia/Egyptian
correspondences, 248
spells, magic, 326
Sphinx, the, 281, 359
spiritual geography, 239
spring equinox, astrological
significance of, 41n, 42
Squire, Charles, 8
stars
fixity of, 68–69
intelligent purpose of, 17
pyramids representing,
279–80
statuary, 293–304
at Abu Simbel, 298–304
Colossi of Memnon, 297–98
kouros, 278, 293–95
Ramesseum ruins, 205, 297
symbolizing degrees of
initiation, 293–97
sympathetic magic and, 293
use as oracles, 293
visual archetypes in, 273–75
See also art and architecture;
specific statues
stele or obelisk, 292–93
Sun
Akhenaten's worship of, 27n
orbital movement of, 38
porous surface of, 28
right Eye of Horus and, 325
scholars' misunderstanding
of, 27
as triple, 27
true vs. physical, 27, 29
suras vs. *asuras*, 136

talismans, 311, 312, 314

Ta'Urt
  as circumpolar deity, 69–70
  as concubine of Set, 47, 69
  in the Dendera zodiac,
    69–70
  Heavenly Bull attached to,
    73
  holding Ursa Minor, 47, 48
  Sebek on the back of, 47
  as undertaker, 74

Taurus
  astrological influences and,
    58
  Bull deity and, 35, 36
  bullfight tradition and, 58
  celestial Pole Stars in sphere
    enfolding, 43
  relationship with Orion and
    Aries, 54–55
  role in great fall and return,
    55–56
  sphere of, 40

Tefnut, 83, 126

Tehuti (Thoth), 123–24, 181,
    183, 210

Tell-el Amarna, 210

Tem or Temu, 120, 142

Temple, Robert, 5, 27

temple pylon, 283–88
  as barrier to casual entrance,
    283
  for Battle of Kadesh,
    286–87
  mistaken for triumphal
    arches, 283
  non-physical geometry of,
    284–86
  statues beside, 287–88

temples
  adytum of, 290–91
  free-standing, geometry of,
    291–92
  great forecourt of, 288
  inauguration of, 321

lighting for, 288, 290
pillars of, 288–91
roof of, 288
stellar and solar alignments
    of, 290
See also art and architecture;
    statuary; specific ones

thaumaturgy, 320

Thebes, 204–6

thesu, 162, 169

theurgy, 320, 321–22

Thina temple, 210

Thompson, Richard, 6, 231

Thoth (Tehuti), 123–24, 181,
    183, 210

three-legged cross, 49–50

Tibetan correlations with
    Egyptian Mysteries,
    385–86

time
  cycles affecting Earth,
    30–31
  duration vs., 28
  nonexistence of, 28

Titan gods, birth of, 23,
    25–26

triangle, kosmic 3-4-5, 371,
    372, 373

twelve hours of the night, the
    Duat and, 45

twenty-three, 50n

Unas (god-man), 133–34, 144

underground initiation,
    353–54

Underworld
  access provided by Rastau,
    177
  astrological, 57
  initiatory Nile crossover at
    Thebes, 204–6
  nature of, 26–27
  as septenary entity, 66

unit of measurement,
    Egyptian, 276–77

Upper Egypt, 207, 209

uraeus, 330, 331, 332

Ursa Major
  esoteric implications of,
    73–74
  hearse of, 74
  mutual revolution with Ursa
    Minor, 74–75
  Nasoreans and, 70n
  Orion enfolding, 71
  and the seventh kosmic
    state, 88–90

Ursa Minor
  apuat shape of, 214
  esoteric implications of,
    71–73
  mutual revolution with Ursa
    Major, 74–75
  Nile bend echoing shape of,
    201–2
  Orion enfolding, 71
  and the seventh kosmic
    state, 88–90
  Ta'Urt holding, 47, 48

Ur-Shu, 223

Versluis, Arthur, 244

visual archetypes, 273–75

vulture cap or headdress,
    330–32

wands, 336

White Crown, 328, 329, 332

White Nile, 192

winged disk of kneph, 161

wonder workers, 314–16

Words of Power, 311–14

Zep Tepi, 53

Zeus, 25

ziggurats or stepped pyramids,
    253–55

zodiac
  Dendera, 47, 48
  sphere of rotation of, 40